Advance praise for **Brand Society**

'This is a stupendous piece of work. It's both academic and pragmatic. It ranges from forbidding high theory to easy-reading case studies. It's great. Without question, it'll go down as a landmark study of brands and branding.'
Stephen Brown, Professor of Marketing Research, University of Ulster

'Max Weber argued that modernity was a process of disenchantment; on the contrary, argues Kornberger, in this evocative and important study: modernity is a realm of continuous re-enchantment. At the centre of the enchanted webs spun in modernity is the brand – and the *Brand Society* – explored through a rich collage of philosophy and social science, a virtual anthropology of the organized seduction of our being, as Jonathan Richman said, in love with the modern world.'
Stewart Clegg, Professor and Research Director of CMOS, Faculty of Business, University of Technology, Sydney

'Rethinking brands means rethinking marketing, reconsidering the implications of organizational culture and organizational identity, displacing the usual assumptions about the relationship between production and consumption – in short, turning many of your major preconceptions about economic life and society inside out. Kornberger offers a glorious, thought-provoking ride – from branding a city in Scotland to quotations from esoteric philosophers to Cubism and Google's CEO Eric Schmidt. Buckle up and enjoy the ride.'
Joanne Martin, Fred H. Merrill Professor of Organizational Behavior, Emerita, Graduate School of Business, Stanford University

'This book provides fascinating insight in the tremendous value of well-managed brand transformation programs. It leaves no stone unturned and covers in a very balanced way the diversity of both the internal cultural aspects and the external brand community building. Great food for innovative brand thinking and for concrete brand activation!'
Ruud Polet, Global Brand Marketing Manager, ING

'In *Brand Society* Martin Kornberger takes you on a compelling ride through the new landscape of branding. From the clothes we wear, to the companies we work for and the society we live in – this exciting books argues the importance of branding and why we should care. From evocative cases and bold conceptual arguments, Kornberger makes the point that consumption and production of brands are intertwined and shows how this transforms the way brands are being consumed and produced. This book leaves food for thought for both brand aficionados and those with a stake in creating or analyzing brands.'

Majken Schultz, Professor, Copenhagen Business School, and co-author of *Taking Brand Initiative*

Brand Society

Brands are a *fait accompli*: they represent a mountain range of evidence in search of a theory. They are much exploited, but little explored. In this book, Martin Kornberger sets out to rectify the ratio between exploiting and exploring through sketching out a theory of the *Brand Society*. Most attempts to explain the role of brands focus on brands either as marketing and management tools (business perspective) or as symptoms of consumerism (sociological perspective). *Brand Society* combines these perspectives to show how brands have the power to transform both the organizations that develop them and the lifestyles of the individuals who consume them. This holistic approach shows how brands function as a medium between producers and consumers in a way that is rapidly transforming our economy and society. That's the bottom line of the *Brand Society*: brands are a new way of organizing production *and* managing consumption. Using an array of practical case studies from a diverse set of organizations, this book provides a fascinating account of the way in which brands influence the lives of individuals and the organizations they work in.

Martin Kornberger received his PhD in Philosophy from the University of Vienna. Currently he holds a joint appointment as Associate Professor in the School of Management and the School of Design at the University of Technology, Sydney. He is also a visiting professor at Copenhagen Business School and co-founder of the leading branding agency PLAY, where he was co-director from 2003 until 2008.

Brand Society

How Brands Transform Management
and Lifestyle

Martin Kornberger

CAMBRIDGE
UNIVERSITY PRESS

CAMBRIDGE UNIVERSITY PRESS
Cambridge, New York, Melbourne, Madrid, Cape Town,
Singapore, São Paulo, Delhi, Tokyo, Mexico City

Cambridge University Press
The Edinburgh Building, Cambridge CB2 8RU, UK

Published in the United States of America by Cambridge University Press, New York

www.cambridge.org
Information on this title: www.cambridge.org/9780521898263

First published 2010
Reprinted 2010

A catalogue record for this publication is available from the British Library

Library of Congress Cataloguing in Publication Data

Kornberger, Martin, 1974 –
    Brand society : how brands transform management and lifestyle / Martin Kornberger.
       p. cm.
    ISBN 978-0-521-72690-0 (pbk.)
    1. Brand name products.   2. Brand name products–Management.
    3. Popular culture.   I. Title.
    HD69.B7K66 2010
    658.8′27–dc22
    2009036646

ISBN 978-0-521-89826-3 Hardback
ISBN 978-0-521-72690-0 Paperback

For Jessica

Contents

Figures

Preface

Proposition

Brands are a *fait accompli*. They are much exploited, but little explored. This book is about rectifying the ratio between exploiting and exploring through sketching out a theory of the brand society.

Why the brand society? On the most basic level, brands are a phenomenon that links and reorganizes the two fundamental spheres of production and consumption, which have been separated since the Industrial Revolution. Brands fundamentally transform how we manage an organization's identity, how we think of its culture and how we organize innovation. Simultaneously, brands transform the politics, the ethics and the aesthetics of consumption. Brands traverse society on the diagonal: following them means moving sideways, from production to consumption, from management to lifestyle, and back. Following this movement, the book turns into a treasure-hunt map rather than a surveyor's chart that measures a well-known, established territory.

Where to start? The good thing is that everybody experiences brands as part of their lives. That's also the problem: the things that are closest to us are often the most mysterious and unknown. When I started thinking about brands, I thought of products. Then, I tried to see them as images, as packaging, as a way of dressing things up that is certainly costly, maybe manipulative, but ultimately inconsequential because it's superficial. It was a thought by Mary Douglas and Baron Isherwood that, for me, suddenly turned brands into something else, something more: 'Forget that commodities are good for eating, clothing, and shelter; forget their usefulness and try instead the idea that commodities are good for thinking; treat them as a non-verbal medium for the human creative faculty.'[1]

How can we understand brands as a non-verbal medium for thinking? How does a brand's combination of magic and logic work? It can be expressed

[1] Douglas and Isherwood, 1979/2005: 40–41.

as a formula: brand = functionality + meaning. 3M is innovation (not Scotch tape); Disney is entertainment (not just movies); Lexus is luxury (not just a means of transportation); Nike is performance (not just shoes); and so on. How right Marx was when he said that a commodity appears at first sight to be a trivial thing, but looked at again, 'it is a very strange thing, abounding in metaphysical subtleties and theological niceties'.[2]

But brands are more than a means to fight our 'status anxiety' with an ever-increasing number of status symbols.[3] They are props and scripts that help us to perform our identities. In fact, brands are ready-made identities. They are so mashed up with our social world that they have become a powerful life-shaping force. Here's our suspicion: with the concept of lifestyle, brands have become the dominant blueprint that fundamentally shapes the way we live our lives. Lifestyles are patterns that shape our taste, behaviours, action, preferences and beliefs; they are like a mosaic made up of individual brands.

But brands don't just transform society into lifestyle tribes. We shape brands as much as they shape us. In fact, without us as their silent partners in crime, they would not exist at all. When *Time Magazine* announced its Person of the Year in 2006, it was *You* – *You* because you started to generate content, watched each other's movies on YouTube, viewed each other's photos on Flickr, programmed your own personality in Second Life, became an instant expert on Wikipedia and ran your own retail shop on eBay.

What was *Time Magazine's* excitement about? For the first time, technology enabled people to effectively challenge and circumvent the privileges of organizations as producers of content. Passive consumers turned into co-producer-activists. In this new world where everybody can up- and download their fifteen minutes of fame, social organization centres around interaction between individuals and businesses: markets are conversations in which interaction drives transaction.

Brands are the interface for this rapidly expanding conversation between consumers and producers. The result is a radical new configuration of production and consumption: the monopoly of organization is being subverted by the creativity of the networked community.

But an interface is not simply a mechanism for connecting two separate entities. Rather, it changes the way both sides operate. So do brands; they have a fundamental impact on the way organizations are managed. Brands

---

[2] Marx, 1867/1976: 163; of course, Marx saw the reason for the fetishism of the commodity as result of the social character of labour, not consumption.
[3] De Botton, 2004.

function as the new organizing principle for business; they enable the conceptualization and design of business from the outside in. Rather than following the old model of closed, inward-looking and technology-centred companies, brand-driven organizations maximize their surface area in order to have maximum contact with their environments. That might make them superficial, but it definitely makes them more engaging (and entertaining).

In short, brands become an organization's lifeline to the external environment. As such, they fundamentally challenge how we think about the identity of organizations, their culture and their capacity to innovate. Branding becomes a new management framework that turns old wisdoms upside down by conceptualizing the organization from the outside in.

That's the bottom line of the brand society: brands are a new way of organizing production *and* managing consumption. As the dominant story goes, we moved from a society of producers to a consumer society (roughly beginning in the 1920s and 1930s). The shift, so we're told, occurred when society changed from a focus on production towards a focus on consumption. This thesis divides the world into production and consumption.

What we suspect, however is that the transformation of the past from producer to consumer society has fundamentally changed the nature of both production and consumption. Our key point is that brands turn consumption into lifestyles that can invent and subvert the order of things. At the same time, brands become a mechanism for managing organizations. In this scenario, the brand becomes the central axis for organizing production and managing meaning. The brand is the interface between production and consumption that transforms the economy and society.

Design

Brands are a fact looking for a theory. The phenomenon has been ignored by management (which has been too focused on the organization of production), marketing (which has been too focused on serving the powerful and institutionalizing itself as part of the brand society), economics (theoretically, in a perfect market, brands should not happen, period) and sociology (which has been too absorbed with the consumer society thesis).

This book is designed like three overlapping concentric circles that feed off these disciplines. Part I introduces the topic (Chapter 1), makes sense of the concept of brands (Chapter 2) and offers some glimpses into the black box of brand-making (Chapter 3).

Part II explores brands' impact on how we manage and organize. We argue that organizational identity, one of the key concepts in current management theory, is managed and enacted through brands (Chapter 4). We suggest that brands reframe organizational culture as a linking mechanism between internal cultures and external brand communities, engaging both in the co-creation of value (Chapter 5). Finally, we take a look at how innovation that is organized around brand communities moves from closed to open (Chapter 6). Branding fundamentally changes how we think and manage identity, culture and innovation. Put simply, branding is the catalyst for these seismic shifts in the organization of production.

The third part of the book explores how brands transform consumption. The central concept is that of lifestyle. Through lifestyles, brands become hegemonic engines of plurality. Brands thrive on difference and diversity, not on conformity and control. This paradox delineates the space in which we will discuss the politics (Chapter 7), ethics (Chapter 8) and aesthetics (Chapter 9) of brands.

Depending on which side of the fence you stand on, you will see in brands a symptom of the ongoing colonization of our lives, an extension of Empire or the subsuming of human creativity under capital (that is, exploitation). On the other side, you can see brands as the avant-garde of a participatory democracy in which people vote with their dollars. Brands span both sides. As such, brands need to be analysed as a new set of practices, as a new technique of managing, as a new form of what Foucault has described as 'governmentality'. Such new forms are neither good nor evil *per se*, but they may well be dangerous. What is needed is not a value judgement about brands but an analytical apparatus, a theoretical language that enables us to understand the magnitude and the intensity of the transformation brands bring about.

Modus operandi

Theories make bad brands: they're abstract; they lack real-world relevance and hence are of little use. No wonder most books fulfil the ironic function that Daniel Dennett ascribes to them – of being just a library's tool for creating another library.[4] The *zeitgeist* asks for practical theories and real-world solutions.

[4] Quoted in Taleb, 2007: 290.

I can't help but imagine the ideal book as resembling a plumber's van, filled with tools and instructions and with checklists on the passenger seat. But could a checklist drawn up in Sydney be relevant for a problem experienced in Stockholm? Could a solution to a problem in Las Vegas do the same trick in London? And is a good idea in Rio still a good idea in Rome?

In this book, I'd like to propose the opposite. I'd like to advocate abstract thinking, and to make the claim that abstract thinking helps us to understand much better what is happening. And I would assert that this understanding is a better springboard for action than ostensibly practical tips and tricks.

Ironically, it was Hegel who set out to demonstrate that abstract thinking might be more practical than the advocates of the 'real world' want us to believe. In his thought-provoking short essay 'Who Thinks Abstractly?', he gives the example of the execution of a murderer. The 'uneducated', practical mob sees nothing but the murderer in the person being executed. But the educated few try to trace the criminal's mind and the reason for his deeds in his biography, education or bad family relationships that made him 'embittered against the social order – a first reaction to this that in effect expelled him and henceforth did not make it possible for him to preserve himself except through crime'.[5]

It is refreshing to see that abstract thinking was as much *en vogue* in 1808 as now, some 200 years later. Hegel turns the relation between abstract and practical on its head: for him, abstract thinking is what common people do when they describe a thing or person with one word – the murderer is a murderer and nothing else. Doing so means abstracting all the qualities of the murderer and forgetting them. The theorist, on the other hand, is interested in those qualities and wants to know more about them; the theorist does not take the label murderer as an explanation but rather as something that needs explaining. Their thinking is more empirical – more practical. Abstract thinking means 'to see nothing in the murderer except the abstract fact that he is a murderer, and to annul all other human essence in him with this simple quality'.[6] So who thinks abstract? Probably those managers who do MBAs and uncritically believe they have discovered 'the one best way to manage', as preached by some management guru; those managers who manage by benchmarks and best practice derived from others; those managers who want to become good leaders by being followers of some idealized management hero.

[5] Hegel, 1808/1966: 113.
[6] Hegel, 1808/1966: 113.

The ethnographer who shadows a manager, the anthropologist who is a fly on the wall in business meetings, the sociologist who looks at cultural influences and the psychologist who studies personal relations are trying to find the peculiar, the special, the different in what they study. They turn over things and acknowledge that truth is a function of one's perspectival. What's called practical and relevant is often ill-equipped to see that what we can know is a function on the perspective we take. It prefers the certainty of the abstract over the probability of the concrete.

To put it another way the difference is not that researchers get fired up about theories and ideas and managers don't. Managers are exposed to bad theories and ideas all the time – think Total Quality Management (TQM), Business Process Reengineering (BPR) or the Balanced Scorecard. These are all abstract ideas in Hegel's sense, and research has shown that they are far less useful than their originators claim.[7] The manager who reads these books and takes their 'tools' seriously is like Don Quixote reading all those novels about knights until he started to read the world as a subtext to his books. How many managers read Jack Welch's chivalry stories and then attack some kind of windmill? What Edward Said said of *Don Quixote* might well be true for most business books: 'It seems a common human failing to prefer the schematic authority of a text to the disorientations of direct encounters with the human.'[8]

In this book, we will explore the human, the grey and the messy. We cannot offer advice on what you should do – such advice would be misguided. What we will do is help you to understand better what is going on in our brand society, and what its consequences are. We will not focus on the spectacle that brands offer but on the underlying structures that make them powerful in the first place. Cocteau once said: 'I look at the scaffold for the king from the carpenter's perspective: The structure of the scaffold is of more interest than the actual execution.'[9] Similarly, we will not chase the sensational but will work our way through the empirical.

---

[7] A good example is David Cooper's and Mahmoud Ezzamel's work on the Balanced Scorecard (2008).
[8] Said, 1978/2003: 93.
[9] Cocteau, 1958/1988: 99 (my translation).

Acknowledgements

Every book is a *mixtum compositum* of many voices. Writing means cultivating those voices and civilizing their relations to each other. There are three ongoing conversations in my life that I'd like to hold responsible for this book.

First, and most important, is the branding agency PLAY, which I co-founded in 2003 and co-directed until 2008 with two partners, Johannes Weissenbaeck and Simon Horauf. The company name expressed the idea that we wanted to play *with* the rules of the game, not *within* them. To launch our company and build networks, we created Sydney Esquisse, Australia's first and finest festival for art and design. The festival was an adrenalin shot into the veins of Sydney's creative body. It put me in touch with all sorts of creatives, from publishing to graphic, product, fashion and web design. As our first commercial job, we took on the editorship of *(inside) Australian Design Review*. To make money, we registered the domain name PLAY Consulting and positioned ourselves as a brand consultancy. To reflect our diverse backgrounds in management, marketing, strategic planning and design, we adopted Majken Schultz and Mary Jo Hatch's definition of branding as alignment of an organization's identity, culture and communication.

But we learnt quickly that markets don't work like academic models, so we were pretty unsuccessful in selling our complex message. To give credit to the model, we were also inexperienced, and the suits we wore wore us. Through a form of trial and error that would not do justice to the finesse of strategy models in textbooks, we evolved into one of the first brand experience agencies.

For one of our first major clients, Adobe, we developed a user-generated design competition that communicated the brand behind the products rather than the technology in the products. We were comfortable in this new niche, and added clients such as ISS, MINI, Jaguar, Subaru, GlaxoSmithKline, Vodafone, Kellogg's, the Sydney Opera House and others to our portfolio. We also focused on the field of professional-services firms, working with

PricewaterhouseCoopers and Australia's leading law firm, Freehills, among others.

During those five years, PLAY grew from the part-time hobby of three recent arrivals into one of Australia's most acclaimed brand experience agencies. In fact, in 2008, PLAY was named Australia's Brand Experience Agency of the Year. When I sold my third of the company in mid 2008, I had spent hours on end with (potential) clients trying to understand their concerns about their brand and how we could help them; writing proposals and putting together presentations for pitches; and thinking about how a particular brand could communicate its meaning. This apprenticeship has provided me with an intimate understanding of both sides of the fence: whereas a company such as MINI was pushing for consumer-oriented and experience-based branding, professional services firms such as PricewaterhouseCoopers used branding internally to re-think and manage their organizations. I started to experience the brand as a central axis that connected the two spheres of production and consumption. My hunch was that this would transform society at large, too – *et voilà*, the basic idea of this book was born.

The second influence that is to blame for what follows is my academic background. I did my undergraduate degree and my PhD in Philosophy at the University of Vienna. The university was founded in 1365, which makes it the oldest university in the German-speaking world. While it might be a pretty decent place to study philosophy, this kind of education does not set anyone up to run a branding agency (just ask Simon or Johannes). It does sharpen your sensibility, though, and trains you to question what is being taken for granted (something clients don't spend much money on). It helped me to see meetings as focus groups, proposals as survey instruments, pitch presentations as participant observation, and PLAY as a whole as an action research project. It also taught me that most of the work of an agency is focused on managing its *performance* – not in the sense of revenue or profits, but in the sense of acting out a script that convinces clients and employees alike that things are progressing according to plan. More of that later.

Finally, I have used my contacts and the friends I made on the way to collect stories and conduct interviews. I've spoken with large global advertising agencies, such as DDB, and small yet globally celebrated creative niche players, such as the Dutch collective Kesselskramer. I've discussed brands with corporates such as Deloitte and ING, who spend hundreds of millions of dollars annually to build their brands, and I have interviewed public organizations such as the City of Edinburgh about how they use the brand to manage their identity. I quote these practitioners extensively not because I think they know more or know better, but because they are like native theorists, with their own explanations for what is happening.

I have to thank the following people for their time, their patience, their support and curiosity: first of all, Simon and Johannes for sharing a company and their friendship; Majken Schultz and Mary Jo Hatch for sparking my academic interest in brands; Paula Parish, my publisher at Cambridge University Press, for believing in my project; my interviewees, including Ailsa Falconer, Christine Shewry, Cindy Carpenter, Danielle Bond, David Redhill, Gary Hardwick, Lesley Martin, Matt Eastwood, Matthijs de Jongh, Paul Hugh-Jones and Ruud Polet, for taking time out of their busy schedules to talk to me about their ideas on brands; Deirdre Livolsi for making initial sense of my manuscript; Cindy Carpenter, Chris Carter and Stewart Clegg for a torturous line-by-line reading of it; Joanne Martin for detailed comments on Chapter 5; and Julien Cayla and Nick Ellis for getting halfway through it.

The following people (in no order other than that dictated by their parent's choice of first name) have provided motivational messages, chatty conversations and/or insightful information – all equally welcome distractions from the solitude of writing: Alan McKinlay, Albert Muniz, Alfons van Marrewijk, Barbara Czarniawska, Charlotte Krenk, David Bevan, Douglas Holt, Edward Wray-Bliss, Emmanuel Josserand, Eric Von Hippel, Gavin Jack, Giuseppe Delmestri, Haldor Byrkjeflot, Ian Clarke, Janne Ryan, Joanne Jakovich, Jochen Schweitzer, Johann Fueller, Jonathan Schroeder, Martin Piber, Matthias Kornberger, Mia Nyegaard, Miriam Greenberg, Marianne Stang Våland, Nancy Chau, Paul du Gay, Rana Fakhoury, Richard Badham, Sabine Gilhuijs , Søren Askegaard, Stephen Brown, Tyrone Pitsis, and Yun Mi Antorini. Last but not least, I want to express my gratitude to the three institutions that provided me with the support and freedom to pursue my project: the University of Technology, Sydney, my home since 2002; and my two homes away from home, the University of St Andrews, Scotland, and Copenhagen Business School.

Then there are many people to whom I could not talk but whose ideas I absorbed through their books. Branding is a new and therefore fragmented field in which the marketing talk of consultants and more serious academic-speak can co-exist on the same shelf – an amazing mix of highly critical books and others that quote Plato on Pepsi and Nietzsche on Nike.[10]

So where does all this leave us? Like any text, this book is a cross-section, a frozen moment in those conversations, a 'tissue of citations, resulting from

---

[10] Braun, 2004.

the thousand sources of culture', as Roland Barthes said. 'If he [the author] wants to express himself, at least he should know that the internal "thing" he claims to "translate" is itself only a ready-made dictionary whose words can be explained.'[11]

I'd happily subscribe to this idea. After all, a ready-made thing is not produced nor created but chosen off the shelf, and what metaphor could be more apposite for a book on branding?

[11] Barthes, 1967.

Part I

Brands and branding

1   Introduction: the brand society

Brand cosmogony

The problem with theories is their inherent lack of evidence. In more than 100 years of social science research, the list of laws discovered is embarrassingly short, and that's a polite way of putting it. More critically minded spirits would claim that not a single law has been revealed. Brands pose the opposite problem: there is an indisputable amount of evidence without theory.[1] Think ING. Think iPod. Think Virgin. Think Coke. Think Google.

The problem is, to paraphrase Nassim Taleb, that the minds of the gods cannot be read by witnessing their deeds.[2] The generator of reality is different from this reality itself. What we see on shelves in supermarkets as brands is not what went into the making of them. Similarly, truth does not reside somehow *inside* things but in knowledge we harbour *about* those things. This begs some questions: How do we know about brands? How do we think of brands? What does our cosmogony of brands look like?

The story of Menocchio sheds some light, albeit a strobe light, on these questions. Menocchio was born in the small hill town of Montereale, located in the

---

[1] We have taken Rem Koolhaas' Manifesto for Manhattan as inspiration for our argument. He suggests that the fatal weakness of manifestos is their lack of evidence: 'Manhattan's problem is the opposite: it is a mountain range of evidence without a manifesto' (Koolhaas, 1978/1994: 9).

[2] Taleb, 2007: 8.

Friuli region of north-eastern Italy. On 28 September 1583, when Menocchio was 52 years old, he was accused by the Holy Office of heresy. At the heart of the allegation was Menocchio's strange cosmogony. It went like this:

[I]n my opinion, all was chaos … and out of that bulk a mass formed – just as cheese is made out of milk – and worms appeared in it, and these were the angels. The most holy majesty decreed that these should be God and the angels, and among that number of angels, there was also God, he too having been created out of that mass at the same time.[3]

Of course, this was heretical: God being created out of chaos, angels characterized as worms in cheese – this did not align with the strict dogma that the Catholic Church had formulated to counter the Protestant movement spreading across Europe.

It would be easy to dismiss Menocchio's cosmogony as madness, but if we leave the question of its truth aside for one moment, we see a miller from Friuli thinking about the world; he tries to explain things. As he put it to the inquisitor, 'I have an artful mind, and I have wanted to seek out higher things about which I did not know.'[4] Where did Menocchio get his ideas from? How did he construct his map of the world?

Besides some translated chronicles and legends, he read the Bible in the vernacular, possibly the Koran and a travel book by Sir John Mandeville written in the fourteenth century telling fantastical tales about travels to India and China. Through reading, Menocchio's mind was no longer limited by the bounds of geography. With Mandeville, he visited the Orient and learnt about pygmies, men with heads of dogs and sheep growing on trees. Menocchio used this fantasyland as an ideal point from which to distance himself from the present and criticize it. He speculated that different races have 'different laws', where people live 'one way and some the other' and 'some believe in one way, some in another'.[5]

During the interrogations, Menocchio's relativism turned into fatal criticism: 'Yes Sir,' he answered the Inquisitor, 'I do believe that every person considers his faith to be right, and we do not know which is the right one: but because my grandfather, my father, and my people have been Christians, I want to remain Christian, and believe that this is the right one.'

Although there are more than 400 years between Menocchio and us, he is much closer to us and our thinking than we might want to believe (or

[3] Ginzburg, 1976/1992: 53.
[4] Ginzburg, 1976/1992: 12.
[5] Ginzburg, 1976/1992: 45.

admit). He 'learnt' – but not in the sense of adaptation; rather, his learning was a process of appropriation of foreign things, a translation of the
unknown into the known and familiar. Halfway between Menocchio's mind
and the pages his eyes scanned curiously, a weird and wonderful new world
appeared that was more seductive, more powerful and more consequential
than its origins.

When we write, when we think, when we try to imagine, we are in the
same world as Menocchio: Mandeville-style fable books around us and websites in front of us 'inspire' our imagination and 'spark' our creativity in a
quite similar way as Menocchio's books inspired him. We might be led on the
same critical adventure as was Menocchio. The *status quo*, the way things are
done, may become stretched and distorted, obscured and amplified. When
we read a book, study an article, interview a branding expert or surf the web,
there is a filter that turns some of the data into valuable information and
stories while other bits remain white noise. This filter tells us more about us
than about the subject at hand. What we know is a consequence of our time,
a function of our culture – not its source.

Brands are the corollary of a particular way of conceptualizing, practising
and institutionalizing a theory that has not been articulated yet. We grab
what we can find and assemble explanations for what we call, for want of a
better term, 'brands'. Indeed, brands are things, they are tools, they are processes; they explain, they seduce, they corrupt; they are used by corporations
and those who fight them. Brand knowledge itself comes from sources as
colourful as Menocchio's readings: as Douglas Holt put it, branding derives
from 'a cultural historian's understanding of ideology as it waxes and wanes,
a sociologist's charting of the topography of contradictions the ideology produces, and a literary critic's expedition into the culture that engages these
contradictions.'[6]

As a young, fledgling field, it is still in the making, on the move, influenced
by agencies and consultancies as much as by scholarship and research. The
boundary between truth, half-knowledge, common sense and sales talk is
often hard to draw.

Things, including brands, have a weird status in this world – a status that
Günther Anders described in his analysis of TV as 'ontological ambiguity'.
A TV image is neither real nor imaginary; it defies the definition of either
an event or a representation of an event. Anders regards these particulari-
ties of the media-world as giving rise to 'ontological ambiguity' because the

---

[6] Holt, 2003: 49.

transmitted events are present and absent at the same time, real as well as fictitious – they are phantoms.[7]

Brands resemble these phantom-realities: they are beyond true and false, just as fashion is beyond beauty and ugliness. So what we know about them is precarious: just as Menocchio made his cosmos, we make our world by learning from foreign countries, reading foreign case studies and listening to foreign voices. Our cosmology is not all that different from Menocchio's, where god, worms and angels mingled in cheese; we talk equally confidently about consumer segments, brand values and the four Ps (product, price, place, promotion) that mingle in markets. Menocchio's story is a salutary reminder to take our own knowledge with a pinch of salt, a healthy dose of criticism and an injection of some irony and satire.

Menocchio serves as an important signpost at the beginning of our journey. Brands are phantoms, distinguished by an ontological ambiguity that renders it impossible to measure them like a sack of wet sand sitting on the ground. Rather, our way of thinking, with all its in-built mythologies, convictions and rationalities – in short, our epistemology – is what renders brands visible and knowable in the first place.

Equally importantly, this does not mean that the journey is an egocentric trip through our collective mind. A signpost directs us on a journey but it does not take the journey itself. Similarly, Menocchio makes us aware of what it means to know and theorize, but this does not relieve us of the need to produce our own explanations to allow us to make sense of our world and orient us in our thinking.

'The century of the self': a short genealogy of the past

Branding is at once one of the most artificial and yet most real forces in our society. A look at the past explains its current power. *The Century of the Self*, a BBC 4 documentary made by Adam Curtis and broadcast in 2002, tells the story of the twentieth century and how powerful politicians and corporate leaders used Freud's theory of the unconscious to control the masses. At the centre of the story is Edward Bernays, Freud's nephew. He was the first to link mass-produced goods to the subconscious, arguing that people are driven subconsciously by irrational and emotional forces that can be satisfied with products. Simultaneously, this would render individuals both happy and

---

[7] Anders, 1956.

docile. It would give rise to an all-consuming self that seeks development and expression through acts of consumption.

Edward Bernays had worked for the US's propaganda machine during World War I and successfully recast President Woodrow Wilson as a liberator of the world. When Bernays joined Wilson in Versailles for the peace negotiations, he was stunned by the emotional attachment the masses had to the president. From then on, his question would be: How can we use the propaganda of war in peacetime? Because the word 'propaganda' had a dubious reputation, he invented a new term and called his peacetime propaganda 'public relations'. In his famous book from 1928, *Propaganda*, he wrote: 'The conscious and intelligent manipulation of the organized habits and opinions of the masses is an important element in democratic society. Those who manipulate this unseen mechanism of society constitute an invisible government which is the true ruling power of our country.'[8] Reading his uncle's work, Bernays was convinced that hidden inner forces were the true motivators of human decision-making. Of course, this was dangerous since the dark side was lurking under a thin veneer of civilization, ready to break out and wreak havoc. For him, it was clear that democracy was an unsuitable mechanism for governing society. So the masses needed to be controlled through the manipulation of their irrational impulses. People could not be convinced with rational information; rather, they had to be seduced and manipulated into doing what was best for them. Corporate America liked that message.[9]

One of Bernays' first assignments was to get women to smoke cigarettes. After World War I, smoking was still a male prerogative and it was taboo for women to smoke in public. The cigarette manufacturer Hill asked Bernays to come up with a way to get women to smoke cigarettes. After being paid a handsome fee and consulting a leading psychiatrist, Bernays had the solution: the cigarette was a male symbol, representing the phallus. The only way to make women smoke, therefore, was to change the symbolic meaning of the cigarette. And this is exactly what he did. He organized for a group of women at the New York City Easter Day Parade to have cigarettes strapped to their legs; at a signal, they would all light up during the parade as a sign of resistance against a male-dominated society. The cigarette would become

---

[8] Bernays, quoted in Danser, 2005: 71.

[9] Back in Vienna, Uncle Sigmund was less pleased with his nephew's entrepreneurial, one-sided application of his *oeuvre*. Freud's notion of the subconscious was far more complex than Bernays' reading admitted. His simplistic idea that organized communication in the form of propaganda could rectify the most tragic yet fundamental fact of mankind must have ranked between naïve and dumb in Freud's mind.

synonymous with an act of rebellion – it would be seen as a 'torch of freedom'. Smoking would be redefined as a powerful, independent and individual act.

Bernays informed the press about the event. By pretending to leak the news to the media, he created the first guerilla campaign in marketing history. The *New York Times* headline of 1 April 1928 thundered: 'Group of Girls Puff at Cigarettes as a Gesture of "Freedom"'. But Bernays did more than that: he redefined a product without changing its functionality or ingredients. He linked the product to emotion and changed the way people related emotionally to it. The object itself had become irrelevant; what counted was the symbolic dimension of the object and the way people related to it emotionally.

In the 1920s, most products were sold on their function, appealing to the need of the buyer. Advertising was information-heavy, hoping to convince potential buyers of the merits of products. Edward Bernays changed this world: it was no longer about the product and its functionality but about the way the product related to people's subconscious desires. A shift occurred, from a focus on needs to the stimulation of desires: while needs can be satisfied through the functionality of a product or service, desire creates and produces an appetite for goods and services that are no longer directly linked to a need. Needs can be fulfilled, desire cannot: as Slavoj Žižek puts it, desire's raison d'être is not to realise its goal or to find full satisfaction, but to reproduce itself endlessly as desire.[10] Whereas products are designed to match needs, brands are created to produce desire.[11] This desire becomes the most powerful force in our society – that is why people relate to society no longer as owners, producers or citizens, but as consumers of brands. Thus brands are the very stuff that dreams (and nightmares) are made of.

But let's return to Bernays. The Freudian philosophy behind his ideas was simple: people are guided by unconscious, deeply irrational forces. They can only be controlled through the enlightened despotism of an invisible government. Social control needs to be built on these emotions. As Bernays put it, 'the engineering of consent' was only possible through manipulation, with the goal of creating 'happiness machines', as President Herbert Hoover put it in a speech he gave to a group of advertising executives. 'You have transformed people into constantly moving happiness machines that have become the key to economic progress,' he said. In this vision, people were not in control of

---

[10] Žižek, 1997: 39.

[11] It is important to note that this is confined to the affluent Western world – in their introductory essay, 'The Politics of Necessity', Morgan and Trentmann (2006) draw the distinction between the desire and the political struggle over the provision of basic goods and services such as electricity and water. See also Slater's excellent essay on 'Consumer Culture and the Politics of Need' (1997).

their lives – it was their desires that led them. Big business positioned itself as being able to channel and control this desire for the good of society.

Ernest Dichter, who had an office in Vienna nearby Sigmund Freud's, was in many ways Bernays' successor. He applied the idea of therapy to groups of people talking freely about products. Rather than using relatively arid surveys or questionnaires, it was about understanding the inner self and its barriers to certain actions. The focus group – now a commonplace feature of modern marketing – was born. Dichter's big breakthrough came with a study of Betty Crocker cake mixture. Women were not buying the product, and Dichter's focus groups showed that they felt guilty about using a ready-made cake mix; it was too easy and made them feel as if they were not doing their jobs. Dichter's solution was simple: on the package instructions, tell the woman to add an egg. This worked on two levels. First, it gave the woman the feeling she was actually baking a cake rather than simply buying one ready-made. Second, and more psychoanalytically, Dichter argued, adding an egg was a highly symbolic action, equivalent to a woman giving her eggs to her husband. Sales of Betty Crocker cake mix soared.[12]

What Dichter did was link a mundane product to a hidden desire or fear and use this emotion to sell the product. The product was a mere symbol that could overcome hidden barriers. It became a therapeutic tool – something that made people feel better, more secure, more confident or independent. Shopping became 'retail therapy'. With that, companies stopped looking at action and behaviour and instead focused on values, symbols and culture. They started to produce things that fitted into what was summarized as 'life-style' – a way of thinking and being. Maslow's hierarchy of needs was the intellectual justification for this new movement, with self-actualization as the highest goal of human endeavour.

In this world, brands become a prosthesis, or an extension of the self. They represent value, and value is a statement to others as well as an expression of the inner, true self. To buy a brand means to buy a value. This also creates an unlimited-demand side of the market, an ever-growing inner self that expresses itself with ever-new brands.

This was good news for business – people who self-actualized were the best possible consumers. Brands were the tools used to detach 'things' from the limited functionality of products and make them the engine of an endless desire for self-actualization and lifestyle. With the rise of brands, business

---

[12] See Packard, 1957: 70.

stopped serving individual needs and began to create, manage and control desire.

ING: a short theory of the present

The concept of branding had an impressive career since its inception. Bernays, and later Dichter, focused on the external effects of the brand. For them, the brand was a mechanism to engineer the relation between organization and its environments. Today, branding is management's weapon of choice to structure the *internal* functioning of organizations. We want to write a theory of that present: understanding what happens while the paint is still fresh, the gun still smoking, the engine still warm. So let us fast forward to the finance giant International Netherlands Group, better known as ING.

'ING Leads the Way in Nationwide Brand Experience and Loyalty Study' announces the headline of a recent study by a US market research firm.[13] ING outperformed other well-known brands – such as Toyota, Volkswagen, Southwest Airlines, Radisson, GM, Hyatt, Google, Wonderful World of Disney and Oprah – in creating a superb customer experience and a sense of community. How does ING, almost a century after Bernays' early experiments, create and use its brand?

ING is not only a well-known brand but also a massive business: its 120,000 employees look after 85 million clients in more than 50 countries. In 2008, it was rated as the seventh largest company in the world.

Reason enough to visit ING's headquarters, an iconic building in Amsterdam's high-growth corridor designed by Roberto Meyer and Jeroen van Schooten. The design already tells you that you're not just approaching any kind of company: the shoe-shaped building floats on 9- to 12-metre high columns so people can actually see through the building when they stand in front of it. Inside, it has not only a large number of offices with a view, but it also has interior gardens and patios. Powerfully, the building tells a story about ING and communicates its brand: openness, transparency and easy access, ideals that are at the core of ING.

Ruud Polet, Global Head of Brand Marketing, meets me in the lobby. In many respects, the story of how I got in touch with Ruud reflects the bank's brand: I simply sent an email to info@ing.com and asked whether anybody would have time for an interview about ING's brand. A couple of days later

---

[13] See www.highbeam.com/doc/1G1-169123803.html (accessed 2 August 2008).

I received an email from Ruud's office suggesting I meet up with him. I was truly impressed with ING's directness and openness.

ING is a young company. The brand came into existence in 1991 as the result of a merger of a bank and an insurance company. 'ING grew by acquisitions, buying more than 40 or 50 different brands,' Ruud says.

We did not re-brand them, we just let them be what they were. They just used an endorsement – at the bottom it would say 'Member of ING'. We had a house of brands. In 2000, we started the journey to rationalise them and create one brand – ING. In 2004, the then new CEO, Michel Tilmant, redefined ING as being guided by three simple values: being easy to deal with, treats me fairly, and delivers on promises. What keeps him sleepless is reputation – this is the key asset in our business. It is the trust that people have in your brand. As they say, 'reputation comes on foot but goes on horse' – it takes a long time to build but can vanish quickly. We decided to build one brand to build our reputation worldwide. We might merge with someone – but whatever happens to us, I want to be the leading brand in that partnership. That's as close as you will get to a survival guarantee for ING these days!

Now, four years later, ING is taking it to the next level and positions itself around one single value – 'easier':

Based on a lot of research, 'easier' turned out to be a kind of complex concept: what people meant by easier was easy to contact; be able to give a clear overview of what you're doing for me; if you are transparent; if you are fast and efficient; and if you can provide me advice when I need it – then people would regard ING as 'easier'.

Research found that 'easier' was appealing and relevant for most people, as Ruud explains: '40 per cent of potential prospects were willing to switch to ING if ING was easier than its competitors. That was the business case for our board to redesign the brand around one single, simple position: "easier".'

'Easier' is an overarching concept; it communicates clearly what ING stands for. HSBC's 'The World's Local Bank' is a nice concept, but it does not really help a customer to see value. 'Easier' communicates a clear advantage, a clear value for the consumer. 'In five years there will be only three global finance brands – and ING will be one of them,' Ruud says confidently. The brand is the key asset towards achieving this objective.

The brand is not externally focused, however. 'Before we can announce that, we have to become easier inside the company,' says Ruud.

So we are going through a total change programme that turns the business upside down. We're not thinking about communicating 'easier' at the moment – maybe we never will. We have to *do* it – rather than talk about it. This is what I am working on every day – to make 'easier' stick to the business, not as a buzzword but as something that changes the business. Toyota called it *Kaizen* – we simply focus on 'easier' and use it to change the business.

Research showed Ruud and his team that there are two topics that are barriers to becoming 'easier'. One is a people topic, the other a business topic: implementing change and decision-making, and IT and processes. 'To become "easier" we need to help all our businesses eliminate those barriers,' he says.

That's what my job as brand manager is. So it is not a branding topic but a business topic. It's a change programme, not a marketing initiative. The brand becomes an integrative platform – change people, HR people, marketing people, IT people, executives. The brand is the common territory for discussing issues and aligning solutions. For instance, our CEO banks on the brand – he is now Chief *Easier* Officer, with his key responsibility being to drive the concept of 'easier'.

In summary, the brand becomes the internal organizing principle of ING. The brand aligns the different functional areas and redefines the task of the leadership. Of course, you might say to promote this way of thinking is the job of a brand manager – but does this prove that ING is really structured around its brand? Might it not be just wishful thinking on the part of the brand department, imposing itself on everybody else and creating a fantasy in the liminal (and inconsequential) space of an interview with an outsider?

Borrowing the description by Peter Miller and Ted O'Leary of management as a congenitally failing operation, we have to understand branding as a new, powerful and contagious management concept.[14] Brand managers do control extensive budgets, they do have significant resources at their disposal and their discourse represents a powerful and hard-to-dismiss logic. That does not mean that their vision will be realized: rather, they represent an important and innovative force that shapes organizations – but sometimes in ways that have been neither anticipated nor desired by management.

The brand axis: organizing consumption and production

Branding is not simply a collection of new business tools or a mere reflection of cultural change in society at large. Rather, as our two examples of Bernays and ING have shown, it is a new kind of thinking that has deeply infiltrated the way we manage organization and markets, production and consumption. Brands are a new axis that connects production and consumption with each

---

[14] Miller and O'Leary, 1987.

other. With Bernays, commodities turned into brands that convey meaning. At ING, the brand entirely transforms the internal operations of the organization. The ING brand re-structures how the organization engages with its environments and how it manages, organizes and strategizes internally.

How did branding evolve into such a powerful organizing principle? In the story of *The Century of the Self*, we witnessed the birth of something important: a product was not defined by its functionality anymore but by its symbolic powers and associations. In fact, changing a product did not require changing its functionality. Rather, it meant changing people's perceptions and interpretations of the product – which is an entirely different matter. Something started to happen, to emerge between people and products, that could not be attributed to people nor to the product. The brand emerged as interface between the emotional world of consumption and the rational world of production. The brand was that powerful yet hard to define interface where supply met demand that persuaded and seduced.

In fact, the brand turned faceless commodities into personal and emotional goods. Goods became social objects, or, as Zaltman put it, '[b]rands are units of social consumption'.[15] A whole new mythology of consumption was born: people ascribed stories and powers to everyday objects. And those objects functioned as social and cultural markers, depicting one's place in society in relation to others.

Of course, anthropologists always argued that objects had magical powers. Think of the cross in Catholicism, or bird feathers, tiger teeth and various animal parts in other religions. But in these cases the object receives its powers through an ideology that spans the lifeworld of its inhabitants. With brands, there is no overarching ideology: the objects themselves start speaking, and they refer to nothing else than their own reality. Brands do not transcend their own horizon. The second big difference is that those brands and their 'aura' were miraculously and meticulously produced in order to make profits.

Bernays' branding of cigarettes was the blueprint for the injection of meaning into products. The simple algebra of branding (functionality + meaning = brand) travelled far and wide. It was copied in literally every industry and soon became the twentieth century's dominant mode of producing and consuming. The subject was organized around that formula: its highest value, self-actualization, could only be achieved through accessing the meaning in the products surrounding the consumer that for short intervals satisfied the burning desire inside. In reality, talk about supply as being driven by demand

---

[15] Zaltman, 2003: 227.

and consumer needs as the first – and most important – 'fact' was little more than a convenient fable that helped to legitimate business. The desire to self-actualize, which by definition could not be satisfied, created ever-new opportunities for business. It culminated in the concept of lifestyle, where goods form the patterns of a life that is styled around brands.

But this is only half the story. The other half is that brands started to challenge and rearrange the way production was organized inside corporations. It was not enough that a company would produce brands while remaining anonymously in the background. Nor was it enough that a firm attached meaning to its output as a mere afterthought. Increasingly, companies realized that they needed to brand their businesses and inject them with meaning as a whole. Big businesses run by what Reich has called 'corporate statesmen',[16] such as Ford in the US or Siemens in Germany, were always concerned about their reputation. Their proprietors saw themselves as patriarchs of society, with a moral obligation to influence its fate. It was their often idiosyncratic personalities that determined the values of the company.

ING's brand is organized differently. Its current CEO, or brand manager, is hardly in a position to instil his personal values into the 120,000-employee business. The brand is becoming the organizing principle inside ING: rather than being simply a marketing tool, the brand becomes the integrating platform whereby different teams from HR, IT, operations etc. discuss the future vision of ING.[17] To 'be easier' is in fact as much a vision as a brand. To 'be easier' is the key strategic insight because it aligns the internal operations with the external environment's expectations. If this is done well, it comes as close to a survival guarantee as you can get in the now so-volatile banking sector: a strong brand that is anchored in the minds and hearts of people around the globe is hard to buy and then scratch. A strong brand produces trust and legitimizes an organization, which are key to survival. Hence the brand is not just the mythology of a product but also the tool companies use to manage their internal organization.

Managing consumption

As so often in life, it might be easier to agree on what brands are *not* than what they might be. First, they are not mere packaging or sugar-coating.

[16] Reich, 2008.
[17] This argument is at the core of Majken Schultz and Mary Jo Hatch's work on corporate branding – see Hatch and Schultz, 2008.

At ING, the brand has very real effects on the structure and strategy of the organisation; while the brand might be seductive, it would resemble gross negligence to put it aside as mere rhetoric. Second, it is not one of marketing's special functions: rather, the brand works across the organisation and affects everything, from communication to identity and culture. Third, brands are not about propaganda or PR; although power and control are key elements of branding, brands always bring about points of openness, difference and resistance. The brand is not owned by the business – it relies on interpretation and sense-making by both insiders and outsiders, and that's a dangerous business. Fourth, branding does not only work on a product level: whereas brands emerged first in the FMCG (fast-moving consumer goods) market, they cannot be restricted to soap and chocolate bars. Today, some of the biggest and most interesting brands – such as ING and IBM – are service businesses. Importantly, they don't have to be for-profit either. Greenpeace, The Red Cross and Oxfam are all brands that compete for the hearts and then the hip pockets of people.

While we could add more to the list of what brands are not, trying to zoom in on them is tricky. One source of confusion is industry itself, which constantly churns out new terms around the topic with rather limited shelf-lives, including 'brand equity', 'brand identity', 'brand strategy', 'brand image', 'brand reputation', 'brand promise', 'brand culture', 'brand experience', 'brand positioning', 'brand architecture' and 'brand awareness'. The word 'brand' seems to sell as soon as it is put in front of a more or less complex second word. The resulting conceptual inflation does not help the clarity of the term. The brand of branding is, shall we say, a little confused.

In the beginning, things were a bit simpler. Let's think of one of the first brands: Ivory Soap, from Procter & Gamble. It was invented in 1879, and because it was hard to differentiate from other soap products, it was, from the beginning, branded as pure white soap. Seven years after its launch, the first Ivory Soap baby appeared on the packaging. In 1886, the first colour print ads promoted the brand in *Cosmopolitan*. In 1924, promotional events started to take place, including the first Ivory Soap Sculpture Contest. In 1952, just five months into the launch of television in the US, Ivory Soap travelled via airwaves into the homes of Americans.

The promotion of Ivory Soap did not focus on the functionality of the product, however. From its earliest days it focused on the *values* of the soap. A focus on functionality would have made it impossible to differentiate the more expensive Ivory Soap from other, cheaper products. Hence Ivory Soap was built upon the fine difference between cleanliness and purity. Ivory Soap turned from a commodity into a brand: what people bought was not a bar of soap but the idea(l) of purity.

For competitors, this positioning was hard to undermine or copy. The brand differentiates the product from other competing products. Ivory Soap had meaning – it meant something more than just a soap bar, something people could identify with.

Ivory Soap wasn't an exception. At the dawn of the nineteenth century, when Nietzsche wrote apocalyptically about the Death of God, the advertising industry praised the Rise of Goods, spending $50 million in 1864 and more than $500 million in 1900.[18]

Branding turns a commodity into a cultural entity. In that sense, the brand is the meaning of a commodity. A bar of soap remains a commodity unless a symbolic or cultural dimension (purity) is added – *et voilà*, the slippery mix becomes a brand.

What's true for soap might not be true for other endeavours, you might argue. Let's take another slippery example: politics and the election of the president of the United States. In his book *The Selling of the President 1968*, Joe McGinness describes the total makeover of Richard Nixon during his campaign, comparing soap and US presidents: Why don't we turn the president into a brand with a few simple yet distinctive messages and sell our candidate like Madison Avenue sells soap on TV?[19] What caused a moral outcry when the book was published is today accepted practice in politics. Differences between candidates are carefully created and measured through opinion polls and focus groups daily.

Let's look at another example: the world's most iconic brand, Coca Cola. It seems brands can even change our taste preferences. A blind-tasting test between Diet Coke and Diet Pepsi shows a 51% to 44% preference for Diet Pepsi – as long as the testers are kept in the dark. Once they are told about the brands, the preferences change, from 65% for Diet Coke to 23% for Diet Pepsi. How annoying if you happen to work for Pepsi: obviously people do not buy what they like better, but what they think they like better. It's a subtle difference, but one worth millions of dollars in annual sales. How do brands manage to rearrange the taste buds on our tongues? The answer is that brands are not functional commodities but social and cultural icons. Coke represents an

---

[18] Fox, 1984; Lears, 1994; Marchand, 1985.
[19] Rutherford, 2000: 41.

American ideal, and this is why (many) people love it and drink it. The actual functionality of the product is secondary.[20]

This is true for almost every business. In the *Financial Times* of 4 August 1999, an executive from probably the most iconic manufacturing business in the US, Ford, stated: 'The manufacture of cars will be a declining part of Ford's business. They will concentrate in the future on design, branding, marketing, sales and service operations.'[21] Ford, that powerful US manufacturing icon that pioneered the moving assembly line, sees manufacturing as a declining part of its business and will focus more on branding. You can guess why: cars become increasingly similar and for customers it becomes increasingly difficult to differentiate between them. Hence the brand of the product becomes more important. If you buy an Audi, VW, Skoda or Seat, chances are they were built in the same factories, have the same engines and were built on the same platforms because they all belong to Volkswagen. What's different, however, is their brand – the meaning that they evoke in the customer's mind.

In some cases, organizations go as far as seeing their product solely as a manifestation of the brand. Take the example of Nike. As Phil Knight says, for years Nike saw itself as a production-focused company, 'but now we understand that the most important thing we do is market the product. We've come round to saying that Nike is a marketing company, and the product is our most important marketing tool. What I mean is that marketing knits the whole organization together.'[22] Nike had to learn that lesson. In the early days, it produced shoes for athletes. As its popularity grew, Nike realized that most customers did not need the functionality of high-tech athletic shoes. Thinking functionally, Nike concluded that its shoes were completely over-engineered for everyday use and stripped the design out of them. The result was that customers were upset and stopped buying the shoes. Not that they missed the functionality; what they missed was the Nike spirit. Customers wanted to wear shoes like their idols. Learning that normal customers loved over-engineered sports shoes, because such shoes communicated something that customers could not get anywhere else, fundamentally changed Nike's understanding of what it is. While the brand is the core of Nike, its products are but tools to communicate the brand.

---

[20] Holt, 2004; a plethora of experiments in the tradition of psychologists Kahneman and Tversky have been undertaken, showing that our decision-making processes are little influenced by the actual functionality of a product. Walker's book, *Buying In* (2008), offers an excellent summary of many of those experiments (including several variations of the Coke vs Pepsi experiment).

[21] Quoted in Olins, 2002: 51.

[22] Knight, quoted in Lury, 2004: 59.

Think Swatch. When Nicolas Hayek turned the Swiss watch industry around and the global market on its head, he did so by redefining the very idea of a watch. What he did was make a watch a fashion accessory that allows the wearer to express their individual identity. It's no longer (just) about functional time-measuring devices. Swatch's design principles, such as colour, shape and theme, were inspired by the fashion industry, including the idea of several new model launches per year in line with the seasonal calendar of *haute couture*. The meaning of the product is transferred – almost magically – onto the owner and provides him or her with a ready-made identity-building device. Brands become extensions of who we are: they are the atoms that make up our lifestyles. That's how they become part of life itself. As Diesel's Renzo Rosso said, '[w]e started selling jeans, and now we are selling a way of life'.[23]

The product is not simply a commodity defined through its function, nor does it simply have an added symbolic dimension. Rather, conceptualizing the product as brand, as ING, Ivory Soap, Ford, Nike, Swatch, Diesel and others do, turns the product into but one dimension of the brand. In fact, the product turns out to be nothing but the material extension of the brand.[24]

The increasing complexity of products and services puts more and more emphasis on the brand as facilitator of decision-making. Think of a computer, a car or any other high-tech product. Most of us have hardly the time nor the expertise to evaluate all the different products and choose the optimal one. Very few of us will pore over past issues of periodicals such as *Which Magazine* to discover the inside story on products. But as consumers, we make satisficing choices. More often than not, these choices are facilitated by the brand.

For instance, Intel was hugely successful at branding a highly complex product. Rather than trying to explain why its micro-processors were better than the competitors' product (something most people would not have understood anyway), Intel agreed to contribute to the advertising costs of its clients if the 'Intel Inside' logo was featured on their products. The consequence was that end-users assumed that Intel must be something special, otherwise well-known companies such as IBM or Compaq would not advertise that they have Intel inside.[25] Rather than branding its different micro-chips (e.g. '386 inside'), Intel focused on strengthening its corporate identity. In 2001, ten years after

---

[23] Wipperfürth, 2005: 106.
[24] Askegaard, 2006: 100.
[25] The story is taken from Aaker, 1996: 12–13.

the launch of the campaign, Intel had spent $5.5 billion on it, pushing its brand with almost 2,000 partners on 90 per cent of all PC advertising.[26]

That works for quite simple commodities like micro-chips. It's amplified considerably when we move towards a sophisticated service and experience economy where intangibles are bought and sold. Think of ING: whereas you might say you think Coke tastes better than Pepsi, it's very hard to compare services. Is ING better than HSBC? Can I compare the services the two different firms offer? Probably not, since they are hardly identical. As a brand manager of a financial services firm lamented, '[l]ife would be much easier if we were a Kit Kat'.[27] Whereas goods can be touched, looked at and compared, services are intangible. The hallmark of good or bad quality is the perception of the service. Like beauty, performance and value lies in the eyes of the beholder. Hence the creation and management of perceptions becomes crucial. The brand acts as a 'relationship fulcrum' linking the internal culture with the external promise.[28] We'll return to this important point.

In summary, what people consume are not products or services, but brands. Simply put, consumption cannot be understood as the rational buying decisions of individuals – it is a far more complex phenomenon than that. As Mary Douglas and Baron Isherwood state in their book *The World of Goods*, '[c]onsumption is the very arena in which culture is fought over and licked into shape'.[29] As anthropologists, Douglas and Isherwood assumed that every object carries social meaning and is used as a communicator. Goods are markers of social roles, flags at the 'visible bit of the iceberg which is the whole social process'.[30] They are signs that communicate: the utilitarian part of objects – providing shelter, keeping warm etc. – is in fact only a small part of their function. 'Being fit for consumption', they write, 'means an object being fit to circulate as a marker for particular sets of social roles.'[31] A cheapish digital watch does a better job at showing the time than an expensive self-winding Rolex; a Hyundai moves you at the same speed through the city traffic jam as a Rolls Royce. The difference between branded and unbranded goods lies in their ability to act as markers of social identity.

[26] Miller and Muir, 2004: 26; Hatch and Schultz, 2008: 52.
[27] Devlin and Azhar, 2004.
[28] Riley and de Chernatony, 2000.
[29] Douglas and Isherwood, 1979/2005: 37.
[30] Douglas and Isherwood, 1979/2005: 50.
[31] Douglas and Isherwood, 1979/2005: xxiii; see also Csikszentmihalyi and Rochberg-Halton, 1981.

No wonder Ford, Nike, ING and others focus more and more on the production of brands rather than goods. After all, what people want is a brand; the product is but one manifestation of it. Products and brands relate to each other like gynaecology and sex: one fulfils a purpose, the other mesmerizes indefinitely. They are the stuff our dreams (and we) are made off.

Managing production

Traditionally, organizations have been studied through the lenses of different disciplines. This paradigmatic promiscuity afforded researchers more freedom (and fun) than the monotony one perspective provides. Psychologists studied the behaviour of leaders and followers and the dynamics between them; sociologists studied the industries and structures in which organizations were embedded; anthropologists researched the cultures, practices and myths of everyday organizational life; and economists looked at organizations as mechanisms to optimize transaction costs. Who's right? Probably none of them, and probably all of them.

We argue that organizations are constituted through those different perspectives. This means that these perspectives are performative: they create what they purport to describe, which is a fancy way of saying that organizations do not exist 'outside' the way we talk about them and think about them. Like Menocchio's world, our ideas about branding are the result of a highly complex filtering exercise. But the result of this exercise is powerful: our theories frame our ways of making sense of the world, and they form the launch pad for our actions to change it. Menocchio's world was frighteningly real (and not 'abstract' in Hegel's sense).

The different disciplines that study organizations constitute a rather interesting geography of knowledge. Organizations emerge in the midst of a series of conflicts between transaction and interaction, between the individual and structure and between practice and rules. Organization is at the translation point between society and its institutions on the one hand, and the individual and its psyche on the other. It is a *relais*, a transmission mechanism.

Looking at the number of organizations and their enormous impact on our lives, it is a fairly safe hypothesis to claim that we live in a 'society of organizations'.[32] But organizations are in trouble. Organization is a way of reducing complexity and creating order; it is based on routines, and they are

---

[32]   Perrow, 1991; Drucker, 1993.

based on recurring events, and they are based on the idea of a stable society. This stability is vanishing quickly. Instability becomes the norm. Hence organizations try new mechanisms to cope with uncertainty and be more closely linked to their environments.

Management and organization theory have focused on internal rationality (or the lack thereof) in situations of 'muddling through', and organized anarchies that resemble 'garbage cans'.[33] At least, this is how organization theorists over the past decades have described the changing image of organizations from rational machines to chaotic, irrational and political networks.[34] Institutional theory has highlighted isomorphism (copying and mimicking) as a key learning mechanism, and culture studies have shown that enshrined practices and routines are often stronger than formal policies.

While these theories are valuable in their own right, they all suffer from focusing *inside* the organization. Most theories are obsessed with unscrewing the black box that is an organization, and peering into it to discover the organization's inner workings. Quite often, researchers are more surprised about their findings than those whom they study. Theories that postulate organizations as rational have been developed by scholars – not by managers – after all.

In this search for enlightenment, the concept of brands emerges as one of the most promising frameworks for an alternative understanding. As I mentioned in the introduction, brands expand the surface level of the organization as they attempt to put every internal function in touch with the external environment. Traditional organizations are characterized by deep hierarchies, strict boundaries that close and protect them from the outside, and they store immense knowledge internally (often more then they know themselves). Brand-driven organizations are flat, maximizing their surface level to provide maximum interaction with the environment. Organizational knowledge necessary for the production of goods and services can be outsourced as integrated global supply chains offer everything on sale – everything but the brand. The brand becomes the face (or better: the mask?) that gives production character and consumption something to fall in love with and remember. Through this brand surface, external ripples are translated directly into internal impulses, and internal rumblings are amplified and made sensible to the outside.

---

[33] Lindblom, 1959; Cohen *et al.*, 1972.
[34] See the books by German organization theorists Günther Ortmann (2003a and 2003b).

The concept of branding is a promising evolution of our thinking about organizations because it allows us to think from the outside in. Take the example of ING again: it uses the brand to structure its internal operations; at the same time, the brand engages ING with the world and frames it as being part of its community. The brand has the power – both organizationally as well as conceptually – to bring together strategy (what is ING's competitive positioning in the marketplace?); people (what is ING's culture that can deliver the brand?); operations (how should we structure our IT systems so it supports our brand promise?); and marketing (how do we engage with [potential] customers?).

Hence brands are increasingly becoming the internal organizing principle of business. Brands provide an outside-in perspective that enables organizations to think innovatively about how they can engage with their environment. The old logic of technology-driven organizations focused first and foremost on internal capabilities. The new logic of branding puts markets and mindsets first and ensures that internal operations follow their demands. Brands become an organization's lifeline to the world. Of course, what kind of 'life' is admitted through the brand-lifeline is a different matter (see, especially, Part III).

The brand as interface

Brands are interfaces: they mediate between production and consumption; between the planned system of organization and market forces; between control and desire. Brands form a new axis that connects inside and outside and traverses society on the diagonal.

Every connection also marks a difference. Brands represent a system that Baudrillard described as 'industrial production of differences': every little aberration, alteration and anomaly is consumed by brand strategists in their conquest for unique and attention-catching brands.[35] In the words of Askegaard, brands are a hegemonic vehicle for endless diversity.[36]

This marks a major shift in the social and cultural politics of our times: while traditional power regimes were based on sameness and homogeneity, branding is preoccupied with differences and heterogeneity. Brands are the cultural engine rooms in which every difference that might make a difference is exploited.

[35] Baudrillard, 1970/2003.
[36] Askegaard, 2006.

A philosophy of difference, as Deleuze suggests, is based on intensity. In fact, difference in itself is intensity.[37] Brands create a world of differences and, by extension, intensities. Of course, those differences are partly borrowed, partly engineered, and the intensities might be created and sustained by large sums of advertising money – but that does not disqualify them. Rather, brands might well be the most ubiquitous and pervasive cultural form in our society.

It is precisely this ubiquitousness and pervasiveness that gave rise to the title of this book: *Brand Society*. Put simply, brands transform the way we organize production and the way we consume; brands also put these two spheres in touch with each other, acting as an institutionalized window or medium between them. If we're right, brands are rapidly becoming one of the most powerful of the phenomena transforming the way we manage organizations and live our lives.

Pervasiveness and ubiquitousness pose an analytical challenge. Branding is not just a new heading for shelves in the library: it is a symptom and symbol of what Said has called our modern political-intellectual culture, and as such it has less to do with markets and business than with us. Branding is our *zeitgeist*: *Google Zeitgeist* puts Apple's iPhone as the fastest-rising item on the 2007 *zeitgeist* index.[38] *Zeitgeist* is the master of our times. Nietzsche speaks of the 'digestive power' of the *zeitgeist*, which is 'more like a stomach than anything else'.[39] It absorbs and assimilates, weaving the new and the old into one blanket that heavily covers the contours of our mindmaps.

Branding as cultural form is our *zeitgeist*. It digests what's foreign to it and turns it into itself. The anti-brand manifesto *No Logo* is a brand, just as much as the anti-advertisers and sub-vertisers from *Adbusters* are a brand. Thus we need to unravel the abstract thinking that's manifest in the *zeitgeist* and develop a more refined concept of the brand.

In order to do so, we will discuss four major schools of thought in the next section, and analyze how existing theories might be useful for our own endeavour.

---

[37] Deleuze, 1968/1994.

[38] See www.google.com/intl/en/press/zeitgeist2007 (accessed 2 August 2008).

[39] Nietzsche, 1886/2002: 158: 'That commanding something which the people call "spirit" [*Geist*] wants to be master within itself and around itself and to feel itself master: out of multiplicity it has the will to simplicity, a will which binds together and tames, which is imperious and domineering ... The power of the spirit to appropriate what is foreign to it is revealed in a strong inclination to assimilate the new to the old, to simplify the complex, to overlook or repel what is wholly contradictory.'

2 Making sense of brands

The Deloitte brand

Usually, when I meet David Redhill over breakfast at Bondi Beach, he is just coming back from an early-morning surf. I am not sure how many senior partners of global accounting firms surf, but David seems to be an exception in many ways. It starts with his rather eclectic background: he was born in Singapore, has Russian ancestors, worked in London, Barcelona, San Francisco and New York, and now lives in Sydney, near the beach. His career is no less colourful: he was Global Head of Marketing for Landor before joining Deloitte. Landor is one of the leading global brand strategy and design consultancies. Its client list reads like a who's who of the business world, and includes Accenture, BP, Procter & Gamble, FedEx, Microsoft, Pfizer, HP among many others.

David is Chief Marketing Officer at Deloitte and a key member of a multinational team developing the Deloitte brand on a global level. For him, the move from FMCG to knowledge-intensive firms is the best thing that ever happened. 'It is more exciting to sell ideas than dog food,' he says. Knowledge-intensive firms such as Deloitte increasingly engage in branding, which makes it a very dynamic and challenging field: as David puts it, auditors are designed to take things apart, and being creatures of habit, this is what they do with brands and branding practices too. To make branding work in a firm where every senior executive is hardwired to facts and figures requires a very clear idea of why branding is important – or in business speak, how it adds value. That's why David is ideal to talk to – if he can convince his partners, I should be able to convince you, my dear reader, too.

The structure of Deloitte adds to the complexity of its brand. Following the passage of the Sarbanes-Oxley Act in response to the collapse of Enron, the company separated into national firms. If one national group were to go down, the fallout would be limited to one market, and the deadly domino effect of the Anderson disaster would be avoided. Deloitte is thus a member firm headed by a Swiss *Verein*. The different national firms are loosely coupled by a cooperative agreement. 'Whatever we suggest doing,' David explains, 'we need their agreement, otherwise members can opt out. They need to see value in branding. You need to come up with a strategy that works for each and every one of the 140 national member firms.'

According to David, branding is not a nice-to-have gadget but an absolute necessity for survival: 'Let's face it: technical competence becomes a commodity. It's simply not enough to be an expert to stand out and differentiate yourself strategically. Market research shows that very clearly – ask CEOs what they consider to be different between the Big Four accounting firms and they reply "I could not get a cigarette paper between the Big Four." '[1]

How can Deloitte differentiate itself strategically? How can it create a unique identity? How can it engage with its environment? And what does it mean for (potential) employees to work for Deloitte? As we shall see, the brand provides a coherent set of answers to these issues.

David explains the function of the brand: 'Today brands are no longer understood as trademarks; they are not asking you to keep your hands off. Rather, they're an invitation to participate, to actively construct meaning.' This is a key point – brands need interaction and engagement, otherwise they remain empty vessels. David continues: 'The brand is a platform for a common identity and consistent expectation. But the key issue is how companies engage and interact with society. At Deloitte we understand our brand as an open platform. Through blogs, internal fora, Facebook applications and so on we not only allow but actively encourage our people to create, shape and run with our brand.'

For instance, the website Greendotlife.com is an open forum about working at Deloitte. People can put comments online – as you would expect, some

---

[1] The Big Four accounting firms that operate globally are Ernst & Young, PricewaterhouseCoopers, KPMG and Deloitte.

are quite critical, others are fun. 'Greendotlife is very much a case of control by the people,' David explains. 'And it's out of our control. We're not even sure who set it up, but it is amusing and very edgy. That's an important departure from the old regime: a brand is not imposed, it is not controlled top-down. Every organization is a micro-society with its own culture, and it is this culture that forms and shapes and drives the brand.'

Of course, running the $27-billion-in-revenue Deloitte network as an open platform carries its own risks. If people tinker with the brand too much, and if they cross the fine line between creative use and abuse, the reputation of an institution can be jeopardized. In Deloitte's case, that reputation has been nurtured since 1845, when the then 27-year-old William Welch Deloitte opened his own accountancy office opposite the Bankruptcy Court on Basinghall Street, London. David seems to be relaxed about the risk: for him, the alternative is to try to control the meaning of the brand – and this is a course he regards as being condemned to failure. So taking the calculated risk of an open platform is better than choosing the guaranteed-to-fail course of closing the brand's meaning and stopping people from interpreting the brand.

'The old model of branding', David explains, 'was centred around the idea of determining what a brand is unilaterally. This doesn't work anymore: if you try to prescribe meaning, you lose all credibility and legitimacy in an instant. This way of thinking is far too rigid, inflexible and hegemonic.'

Opposed to that monolithic approach are more flexible ways of managing brands. 'Modality' is a word David uses a lot: the brand becomes a kit of parts that people can use and appropriate locally like a resource-box. The prefabricated tools ensure some homogeneity while the local *bricolages* allow for alignment with a local context.[2] For instance, Disney's golden rule is 'Don't Mess With The Mouse' while other elements of its identity can – and indeed have to – change. Where does the fiddling and changing stop with Deloitte?

At the beginning of 2002, when David started his work, Deloitte faced what he describes as 'visual anarchy'. There was no global identity for Deloitte but literally hundreds of inconsistent dialects that resembled a Tower of Babel. The way people presented the firm on brochures and presentations, the way it communicated with staff and future employees and its client interaction were far from promising a consistent quality experience. 'The collapse of Enron and Anderson was in many respects the "perfect storm",' David

---

[2] The French word '*bricolage*' describes the creative and resourceful use of a diverse set of materials that are put together to form a whole – regardless of the original purpose of the elements (see de Certeau, 1980/1984).

recollects. 'It forced people at the top to think about their future in different ways, and acknowledge that, if we want things to stay the same, we have to change everything.'

For Deloitte, a key question was how to differentiate between itself and the other three big accounting firms. Of course, staying too close to the others would make it tricky to build the firm's profile. Paradoxically, too much differentiation might place the firm off the cognitive map of clients. Positioning thus has to solve the identity paradox of being similar enough to be seen as a competitor and simultaneously being different enough to be seen as unique.

For Deloitte, the solution became to position itself as 'human brand'. To be a human brand means being approachable and down to earth. A symbol for that new identity was the change of name from DTT (Deloitte Touche Tomahatsi) to Deloitte. David tells a story from his days at Landor:

Fedex came and said they had a branding problem because people called them Fedex and not Federal Express. I found that very odd – what better thing can happen to a brand than that people give you a nickname and start using you as a verb by saying "I've fedexed it"? The same was true for our firm: clients called it Deloitte, so we asked our executive team why we should play around with the acronym of DTT if people call us Deloitte? As a people brand we can differentiate ourselves from the likes of PwC, KPMG and EY, whose acronyms do not really convey human values. So our idea – which was successful in the end – was to call ourselves Deloitte, full stop.

Today, Deloitte's logo is its name followed by a green dot. Period.

'The brand is not the logo or the name; it does not matter what you call something', David adds. 'Imagine you are in the high-tech industry in 1983, all your competitors are called Microsoft, Cisco, Sunsystems etc. – surely a name like Apple sounds odd and wrong!' So if it is not the visual identity, what lies at the heart of the Deloitte brand globally? What is its identity across the 153 countries in which it operates?

The key question, according to David, is 'What are the one or the two things you remember – how do people file us in the filing system in their mind?' For him, one of the core ideas that positions Deloitte is 'symbiosis': as the 'human brand' among the Big Four, Deloitte believes in collaboration and partnership. The philosophy behind this is simple: nothing great has ever been achieved by one person alone. 'Everybody has someone – who do you have? Clients have goals and we can partner to help them getting there', David explains. This simple idea has big implications.

Says David, 'It forces you to step into the shoes of your client. Clients don't wake up and say "I need a consultant and a tax guy"; they wake up and say to themselves "Maybe I have a performance issue" or "Are we managing risk responsibly?"' This is where the positioning as partner becomes powerful: it forces the business to rethink and restructure itself. David goes on:

We are structured around functional areas such as audit, tax and consulting. But taken that we promise to be partners of our clients, this internal structuring is of very little interest to them. We need to gear our firm towards solving the problems as our clients experience them. Unfortunately, their problems don't come packaged in departments. So we had to rethink the very core of what we do and who we are. Auditors? Tax advisors? Consultants? Or something else?

This is where David gets really excited – what follows is, according to him, the best idea he ever had:

The whole firm has to help in solving problems – across teams and divisions. Hence I redefined our identity in Australia around five new key areas: compliance (how to play by the rules), transaction (how to manage business), risk (make sure things are on track), governance (are we behaving ethically?) and performance (how can we drive growth?). Instead of asking the market 'where can we apply our expertise in audit, tax and consulting', we began telling them about the five ways we could help them – which covered just about every major challenge or opportunity a business faces.

Following from this, the brand has important internal implications for Deloitte: the brand reorganizes internal structures. Teams are composed differently. Training and development is remodelled. Routines, practices and internal cultures are questioned. For instance, Deloitte Australia's 7 Signals is a programme of continual cultural reinforcement that is aligned with the brand values. As David explains, 'Our 7 Signals remind us of the behaviours that set us apart: we recruit and retain the best, talk straight, play to win and think globally, grow and improve, aim to be famous, empower and trust and have fun and celebrate. Our Signals are, in the end, an expression of who we are.' Put simply, the brand has a fundamental impact on the organization. The brand becomes a strategic driver, a new and powerful means of managing meaning within the organization.

In addition to life inside Deloitte, branding has powerful external ramifications. The brand changes the way Deloitte interacts and engages with clients and what David calls, more generally, society. The brand positioning as 'partner' who believes in symbiosis to create better results leaves ample space to localize the message.

David shows me one of the series of Deloitte ads that are ubiquitous across Australia's major airports. The image shows a slice of buttered white bread topped with coloured sugar granules. The copy reads: 'On our own we are good, together we are great.' I say that I don't get it. David laughs and reassures me by adding that his South-African CEO did not get it either because the ad is quintessentially Australian: 'What you see is "fairy bread" – something you have at every children's birthday party in Australia. It's buttered white bread with coloured sugar granules. Everybody in Australia has an emotional connection to it. On their own they're good, together they're brilliant.' This shows how a global brand can localize its expression while communicating the same key idea – the value of symbiosis.

A follow-up campaign focused on communicating that Deloitte understands the challenges of modern business problems. A series of billboards and ads showed the eye of a person with different copy lines reading 'CEO – leader and listener', 'CFO – steward and strategist', 'Board member – monitor and mentor', and so on. The brand carefully choreographs the way people see and think of Deloitte. It's highly localized and engages parts of our society publicly about issues Deloitte deems important. Recognizing the different, sometimes contradictory, facets of roles in business, Deloitte shows that it thinks holistically and not in functional silos.

Of course, the brand is an aspiration and 'you will never arrive there', as David never gets tired of reminding me. But on the journey, the brand leaves nothing untouched: through the brand, David manages the corporate differentiation strategy, cultural change, integration of service lines and engagement of clients and non-clients to maintain credibility and keep an eye on the competitors' moves.

David convinced his accounting colleagues that branding is a serious business challenge or opportunity (depending on how you look at it). Brands become an integral part of what managers do when they manage their businesses. When even hard-nosed accountants engage in branding, it has moved far beyond a fancy word for promoting washing powder or other FMCGs.

Part of the success of branding lies in its reach: it touches upon every aspect of the business. One half of its success is due to its internal impact: the brand becomes important in the management of strategy, structure, culture and identity. The other half is down to its external effect: the brand manages a business' engagement with its environment.

Branding is also a challenge for the control-obsessed business-as-usual approach: a brand is not simply what management wants it to be; it cannot be defined in a monolithic way. As Marty Neumeier put it, a brand is not what you say it is, it is what *they* say it is.[3] A brand is a sign that has power only through other people's interpretations of it. While interpretations can be channelled and corrected, control is never rendered perfect. Hence the brand is a (more or less) open platform, an arena in which different people with different interests negotiate the meaning of the organization.

Finally, as a field of practice, branding is young; like youth it is frisky yet often bemused and bewildered. For David, the lines between the brand, culture, identity, communication, strategy and marketing are blurred. Just as in surfing, he's riding a wave that does away with old categories.

'Make things as simple as possible, but no simpler': the brand box[4]

How do writers make sense of branding? What are their different perspectives? Not surprisingly, there is no single definition of the notion 'brand' that researchers and practitioners would agree on. Our discussion of different perspectives is driven by Einstein's dictum and a rather pragmatic analysis of the literature.[5] We have developed a simple two-by-two matrix that explains not everything, but a fair bit.

Figure 2.1 is a conceptual map of the territory that we will explore in the following chapters. Maps don't simply represent a territory. The famous London subway map designed by Harry Beck in 1931 is useful precisely because it is not precise: all you need to know when you're underground is the relation to places and lines – hence the diagrammatic map works very well. So what kind of brand map do we draw? Clearly, no one could do justice to the metres and metres of shelf space packed with books on branding. Our map is not the result of the quantity surveyor's work; rather, we drew up a kind of treasure map that sacrifices accuracy for plausibility and detail for direction.

The first quadrant of our map welcomes branding as an additional implement in management's toolbox. Management is the driver of branding, and the focus is squarely on the level of the individual organization and (most often) on its products and services. One of the key advocates of this take on branding is David Aaker, esteemed E. T. Grether Professor of Marketing and Public Policy at Berkeley and author of over 100 articles and 14 books.

---

[3] Neumeier, 2005.
[4] The quote is attributed to Albert Einstein.
[5] See Schultz' insightful discussion of different disciplines that have contributed to branding (2005); whereas her story is narrated from a disciplinary perspective, we have chosen a more problem-oriented approach.

	Focus on agency	Focus on structure
Organization and production as level of analysis	*Thesis*: Brands as management tool *Question*: How can we use the brand as a management tool next to other functions? *Exemplary theorist*: David Aaker (e.g. 1996)	*Thesis*: Brands as corporate catalyst *Question*: How can we use the brand as new paradigm to manage corporations? *Exemplary theorists*: Mary Jo Hatch and Majken Schultz (e.g. 2008)
Society and consumption as level of analysis	*Thesis*: Brands as sign *Question*: How do brands perform as signs, symbols and icons in society? *Exemplary theorist*: Marcel Danesi (e.g. 2006)	*Thesis*: Brands as media *Question*: How do brands as new interface re-structure interaction between stakeholders? *Exemplary theorist*: Celia Lury (e.g. 2004)

Figure 2.1   The brand box.

Quadrant two – brands as corporate catalysts – challenges this view: in this interpretation, the brand becomes the central, integrative function that manages the entire corporation. Products are only one by-product of successful branding practice. What both perspectives have in common is a focus on top management, which is still the locus of action. Majken Schultz and Mary Jo Hatch, both at Copenhagen Business School, are the two theorists who have pushed this school of thought furthest.

As we move into the second half of our map, the spotlight moves from top management onto the consumer. Quadrant three – brands as signs – is a perspective that gives agency to brands: as symbols they create meaning that structures our world. Importantly, the context in which brands are analysed is not the individual organization but society. Rather than writing about the production and organization of brands, this view looks at brands from the outside in, taking on the consumer's perspective. An exemplary scholar in this tradition is Marcel Danesi, who works as Professor of Semiotics and Linguistic Anthropology at the University of Toronto, Canada.

Finally, the fourth quadrant identifies a school of thought that conceptualizes brands as media. Adherents of this line also think of brands from the vantage point of a consumer society. But rather than analysing brands as individual signs, they argue that brands are institutionalized structures. Their focus is on brands as a media that links society, organizations and individuals. Celia Lury, a Professor at the Department of Sociology, Goldsmiths, University of London, has developed this perspective most profoundly.

Brands as managerial tool

'Corporate Brand Reputation Outranks Financial Performance as Most Important Measure of Success' concluded the survey of CEOs and leaders from the World Economic Forum in Davos in 2004. According to this research, reputation is a more important measure of success than stock market performance, profitability and return on investment.[6] Thus brands become a property that is carefully built, managed and controlled: the brand value of the FTSE top 100 companies amounts to a third of their total value. One third of all wealth in the world consists of intangible brands. For instance, the estimated brand value of Coca Cola and Microsoft is $134 billion, which is roughly the gross domestic product of Singapore.[7]

Branding might solve several management problems at once. As such, it follows in the tradition of management ideas that are valued because they promise to solve the problems organizations face regardless of global context and local peculiarities. Managerialism is the label that has been used to describe the ideas and practices that promise to increase performance, effectiveness and efficiency through the application of universal management principles. These days, managerialism itself has a bit of a branding issue. Launched as the rise of a new managerial class, refined (or some would say ossified) through countless MBA programmes and promoted by armies of consultants, managerialism is the belief that basic principles of management can be applied to any organization for the improvement of its performance. Managerialists are quite serious about this 'any' – it includes hospitals, prisons, high-tech companies, governments, rice fields, schools, you name it. Managerialism is functional because it accepts certain ideas and practices based on their usefulness for management.[8]

Of course, branding represents a fabulous new opportunity for the functionalist mind to add yet another tool to the management toolbox. The promises of branding are enormous: increased market share, control of market boundaries (e.g. barriers to entry for competitors, or entry into new

---

[6] See www2.weforum.org/site/homepublic.nsf/Content/Corporate+Brand+Reputation+Outranks+ Financial+Performance+as+Most+Important+Measure+of+Success+.html (accessed on 2 June 2008).
[7] Clifton, 2003.
[8] Functionalists explain institutions, organizations and practices as serving a particular need that they manage to satisfy. In this view, brands exist because they serve the important function to differentiate and protect an organization in a more and more complex environment. Functionalism presupposes that things are linked through means-end relationships that can be traced back by an independent observer – as we shall see, a highly problematic assumption.

markets for their own brands), lower price elasticity, premium prices, internal cultural alignment, the attracting of talented staff and gaining trust from stakeholders, to name but the most important ones.[9]

The creation of entry barriers through branding is a particularly interesting example. To introduce a new soap powder brand in the UK market, you have to invest approximately £10 million for the launch campaign alone.[10] Of course, these costs are prohibitive for a newcomer and will stop potential competitors from entering the market in the first place. On the other hand, strong brands can help you enter new markets: think of Virgin, which enters any market in which its brand resonates. Or think of the soccer club Manchester United, which makes the most out of its 50 million fans worldwide by selling them everything from MU TV to MU Mobile and MU Finance.[11]

Companies also simply buy brands in order to gain instant access to markets. When Ford bought Jaguar, it was not that interested in Jaguar's factories and the somewhat ambiguous capabilities of British car manufacturing: what Ford was after was, of course, the brand Jaguar. The same is true for BMW's takeover of Rolls Royce or MINI. In these examples, brands are a weapon of conquest or defence of market share.

Not surprisingly, brand theorists such as Aaker define brands as 'battleships':

A brand can be likened to a ship in a fleet facing an upcoming battle … The brand manager is the captain of the ship, who must know where his or her ship is going and keep it on course. The other brands in the firm, like other ships in the fleet, need to be coordinated to achieve the maximum effectiveness. Competitors correspond to enemy ships; knowing their location, direction and strength is critical to achieving strategic and tactical success. The perceptions and motivations of customers are like the winds: it is important to know their direction, their strength and possible changes.[12]

The metaphor of the brand is obviously inspired by the strategic management canon, which, in turn, is inspired by warfare.[13] The captain of the ship is no longer the MBA-educated strategist but the trendy brand manager. Everything else stays the same: coordination, effectiveness and competition are key to success, and the organization itself is depicted as a passive ship on stormy seas, in need of firm direction from its leader.

---

[9] See Clifton and Simmons, 2003; Miller and Muir, 2004.
[10] Miller and Muir, 2004: 30.
[11] Miller and Muir, 2004: 35.
[12] Aaker, 1996: 21.
[13] See Carter *et al.*, 2008, for a more detailed critique of the strategy discourse.

Taking branding seriously has far reaching implications for a business itself; branding will seek to refashion the organization to ensure that its brand hierarchy (sometimes referred to as brand architecture) maps onto the corporate hierarchy. Take the brand Volkswagen: it is hierarchically split into brands that include VW, Porsche, Audi, Skoda, Seat etc. These sub-brands are differentiated again: VW is split into Lupo, Polo, Golf, Eon, Passat, Touareg etc. The difference between the old and new hierarchy is that brands restructure the business to represent consumer preferences inside the organization. For instance, the Marriott brand is divided up into more than twenty different brands, including Marriott Hotels and Resorts (the flagship brand of quality-tier, full-service hotels and resorts), the JW Marriott Hotels and Resorts (the most elegant and luxurious Marriott brand), the Courtyard by Marriott (a moderately priced lodging brand for business travellers), the Residence Inn by Marriott (designed as a 'home away from home' for travellers staying several nights), and so on.[14] The brand creates a new hierarchy, a new order among parts of the business. Rather than following internal lines of authority or functional divisions, this order is derived from the external environment. The imagined logic of consumer desires, collected and expressed as brands and sub-brands, has the capacity to restructure the internal business operations.

Aaker and Joachimsthaler have developed this approach further by introducing their brand leadership model. In this model, the brand takes on the function of the strategic tool for the organization. Whereas the classical brand management model was reactive, tactical, short-term oriented and local, the brand leadership model is proactive, visionary, long-term oriented and global.[15] While the old model had an exclusively external focus, the new leadership model focuses on the external as well as the internal environment; rather than focusing on sales, it focuses on the brand identity as driver of strategy. Put simply, branding claims the leadership role in organizations. Far from being a function of the marketing department, branding commands an influence across all organizational units. Not surprisingly, Aaker and Joachimsthaler subsume organizational structure and processes under the brand leader's responsibility – in fact, the 'first challenge' of a successful brand manager is organizational: 'the organization must establish a brand-nurturing structure and culture'.[16]

---

[14] See www.marriott.com/corporateinfo/glance.mi#brand0 (accessed 3 June 2008).
[15] Aaker and Joachimsthaler, 2002: 8.
[16] Aaker and Joachimsthaler, 2002: 25 and 26.

The goal of this approach is to establish brand equity, which is defined as 'a set of assets (and liabilities) linked to a brand's name and symbol that adds to (or subtracts from) the value provided by a product or service to a firm and/or that firm's customer'.[17] The four main asset categories include brand awareness (e.g. is the brand on the cognitive radar of people?), loyalty (e.g. does the brand have followers?), perceived quality (e.g. do people perceive the value of the brand?) and, finally, brand associations (e.g. to which socio-cultural landscape do people relate the brand?). Interestingly, all four dimensions talk about relationships between the brand and the consumer. In fact, none of the four assets lies within the product – they surface as a result of interaction between producers and consumers.

For Aaker and other representatives of the managerial approach, the brand is owned and controlled by the corporation. Hence interaction between producers and consumers is dangerous as it potentially dilutes the brand. Relationships between both parties have to be either controlled or cut off. The issue of control is one of the weak points of the managerial approach. Remember David Redhill, Deloitte's brand manager? Ironically, although he is a manager, his approach is much more critical and less functionalistic than Aaker's. David is actually aware of the limited controllability of the brand. Greedotlife.com is but one example (see beginning of this chapter).

The second key issue is that the managerial approach does not focus on the social, cultural and political aspects of branding. Its functionalist assumptions make it blind to the social construction and consumption of brands.[18]

The leadership of Coca Cola can tell a story about the cultural meaning of brands. In the 1980s, as the centenary of Coke approached, Coca-Cola executives were engaged in some soul searching. Something was not right. The perennial runner-up Pepsi was edging closer and closer each year, which provided the impetus for the Coke leadership team to try something radical: they decided to change the Coke formula. After ninety-nine years of continuity, it is difficult to understate the dramatic nature of this change. It was headline news – which of course illustrates the iconic qualities Coke enjoyed. The change was designed to refresh the brand that did not quite refresh its consumers as it used to. After one of the biggest market testing programmes ever, involving some 200,000 consumers, the new formula was confidently unveiled.

---

[17] Aaker, 1996: 7–8.
[18] See Kärreman and Rylander, 2008.

What Coke did not take into its managerial account was the cultural significance of Coke for its US consumers. After a couple of days, all over the country people started to get together and complain about the new taste. They felt betrayed, as if someone had stolen their identity. After only eleven weeks, and in the face of hundreds of thousands of angry citizens, Coke brought the old formula back as Coke Classic and let the new one slowly disappear. Asked whether this was the biggest marketing stunt in history or whether they made the worst mistake ever, their chairman answered: 'We're not that dumb, and we're not that smart.'[19]

That's the problem with managerialism, and Aaker's translation of it into branding: brands are much more complex, social entities. At the same time, the complexity that Aaker *et al.*'s tools suggest is out of place and misleading. Part of what they sell as practical tools is often either common-sense or nonsense. For instance, Miller and Muir argue that '[b]rands with high market share are often more popular precisely because they're more popular'.[20]

I think we're ready to move on from this, aren't we?

Brands as corporate catalyst

Mary Jo Hatch and Majken Schultz described the shift towards corporate branding as the second wave of branding. Schultz and her colleagues have argued that the corporate brand represents 'the idea that the organization and everything it stands for is mobilised to interact with the stakeholders the organization wants to reach and engage them in dialogue'.[21]

According to this perspective, the corporate brand is made up of four distinct elements: first, the strategic vision that expresses top management's aspiration for the organization; second, organizational culture, which expresses how employees enact values, beliefs and basic assumptions; third, stakeholder images developed by outsiders, including customers, media and others; and finally, at the juncture of these three perspectives, the brand identity emerges as a reflection of how the organization perceives itself.[22]

It is important to understand the symbolic nature of the corporate brand. As Hatch and Schultz argue, the brand is 'symbolically created through acts

---

[19] The story is based on the BBC documentary *Coke vs People*; see also www.thecoca-colacompany. com/heritage/cokelore_newcoke.html (accessed 15 June 2008).
[20] Miller and Muir, 2004: 27; other mistakes include the claim that IBM bought PwC in 2002 (page 183) – of course, IBM bought PwC's consulting business, not PwC!
[21] Schultz *et al.*, 2005: 12.
[22] Hatch and Schultz, 2001; Schultz, 2005.

of interpretation that occur throughout the population of stakeholders who keep it alive by producing, reproducing and sometimes changing its social and cultural meanings'.[23]

Because of its interdisciplinary nature, corporate branding is understood as one of the few concepts that allow the integration of strategy, organization and marketing.[24] Its focus is on the core identity of an organization that brings these different functions together. Yun Mi Antorini and Majken Schultz explicitly argue that it is grounded in 'all functions and business areas in the organization'.[25]

Mary Jo Hatch and Majken Schultz understand the brand as the key strategic principle that organizes the corporation. They argue that brands have evolved from a focus on products to a focus on the corporation. Examples of this shift are the case studies of Deloitte and ING that we have discussed above. In both cases, branding is not about a particular product but about the internal structuring of the organization. The brand becomes the focal point to manage an organization's culture and identity, and align them with other corporate functions such as IT.

Brands become a mechanism to manage the organization from the outside in. Corporate branding is cross-disciplinary, it is driven by the CEO and top management, it has a long organizational life-cycle and 'managerial and organizational processes align the company behind brand identity'.[26] While the symbolic dimension of organization and leadership has been recognized as an important area for the 'management of meaning',[27] the brand offers a new practice for the management of meaning.

In organization theory, there is a growing focus on branding and its impact on internal audiences. Recently, for instance, Kärreman and Rylander have argued that 'branding practice may be usefully understood as management of meaning, i.e. systematic efforts from top management to influence and shape frames of references, norms and values among organizational members'.[28]

The shift from branding as product-focused practice towards branding as managing the corporation is dramatic. Take, for example, Richard Branson's Virgin empire: 'Virgin is perhaps the most high-profile early 21st-century example of this. It is not what Virgin does that defines it, it is how

---

[23] Hatch and Schultz, 2008: 29.
[24] Schultz *et al.*, 2005; Hatch and Schultz, 2008.
[25] Antorini and Schultz, 2005: 221.
[26] Schultz, 2005: 27; Hatch and Schultz, 2008: 9.
[27] Smircich and Morgan, 1982; Pondy, 1978.
[28] Kärreman and Rylander, 2008: 108.

it does it. Virgin is hardly a corporation at all. It is really a brand that holds together a series of more or less otherwise completely unrelated products and services.'[29] It is not in *what* Branson does that defines his brand but in *how* he does things. As the corporate provocateur himself puts it, 'Virgin loves to, we all love to, take industries and shake them up and make sure they're never the same again.'[30]

There are two key aspects of the corporate approach. The first is the relevance and importance of branding on a corporate level (as opposed to an organizational or mere product level). Virgin, for instance, runs dozens of different companies turning over some $25 billion per year; what they have in common is nothing but the Virgin brand – a certain attitude towards how things should be done. Interestingly, many of these businesses are joint ventures with other firms – whereby Virgin lends its powerful brand to another product. Or think of the easyEmpire that now spans easyJet, easyCar, easy-Value, easyMoney, easyCruises, and so on: all those businesses are held together by a set of values and an attitude that's 'easy'. Second, the corporate approach to branding includes a strong focus on the internal effect of branding (as opposed to an exclusive focus on the external environment). Because Virgin is defined through the 'how' it does things (not the 'what'), people who determine how things are done are crucial to creating the brand.

The corporate perspective on brands is important because it puts the brand on the agenda of CEOs and boards. It's no longer a marketing function that tries to add meaning to a bar of soap: it's more fundamentally about the meaning of an organization. However, we are not sure whether this approach comes in the form of a second or third new wave that suggests a certain chronological order of events. One could argue that corporate brands are as old as the corporations themselves. As Marchand has so minutely shown, at the beginning of the twentieth century the American corporation was in trouble.[31] Rapid growth, mergers and increasing market domination resulted in a legitimacy crisis. Although corporations were treated as persona as a consequence of the *Santa Clara County* v. *Southern Pacific Railroad* case in 1886, the persona was without a soul. Corporate empires run by J. P. Morgan or Rockefeller controlled large parts of people' lives without having any kind of personality. The problem also spread inside those large corporates: with what should employees identify? The solution was in the creation of a corporate

---

[29] Olins, 2002: 61.
[30] Quoted in Hatch and Schultz, 2008: 85.
[31] Marchand, 1998.

soul – or a brand, as we would say. The corporate quest for social and moral legitimacy was played out in massive public-relations initiatives.

Take the example of AT&T:[32] In 1894, its monopoly patent expired. Facing competition, AT&T pulled all registers to undermine its much smaller, local rivals. Hence AT&T was seen as the foreign, big and heavy contender that tried to destroy outright the local players. However, its bullying strategy was not successful. As a result, its market share reduced from 100% in 1893 to 51% in 1907. Additionally, it had to face public suspicion and antagonism.[33]

Because AT&T could not win this war, it started to work on its brand and launched one of the first brand-building campaigns more than a century ago, in 1908. The first ads appeared in June and July 1908, re-casting the image of AT&T as a company that was committed to 'One Policy, One System, Universal Service'. Although ads were long, information-heavy and clumsy ('we work *with* you and *for* the public'; 'agitation against legitimate telephone business … must disappear'[34]), they heralded a new era: building a corporate soul that would give the corporation meaning and personality. In this respect, corporate branding was always on the agenda of leaders. The quest for reputation and legitimacy was thus recognized very early on as central to organizational survival.[35] The brand offered itself as the ideal relationship fulcrum to the external world.

What the corporate branding perspective does not take into account is how consumers of the 'corporate soul' make sense of the brand. Rather, the brand is imagined as something that can be created and manipulated by top management. We would argue that this approach is too top-down and too much focused on the corporate level. As Umberto Eco has remarked, the author has very little control over the text she produces, and the reader has power over her interpretations.[36] Similarly, the internal and external consumers of the brand interpret the brand in their own, often idiosyncratic, ways. Their interpretation will be framed by their cultural, social and political context. Hence the meaning of brands becomes embedded in power relations and interests. Emphasizing this interplay between the authors and readers of brands opens up new ways of understanding the brand as a medium. Intellectually, this is challenging, as it forces us to think more dialectically about brands; practically, it promises to reveal more of the

---

[32] Our summary follows Marchand, 1998: Chapter 2.
[33] Marchand, 1998: 49.
[34] Marchand, 1998: 52 and 53.
[35] Pfeffer and Salancik, 1978.
[36] Eco, 1979.

complexity characterizing the practices through which brands are consumed. The next two approaches take this critique as a starting point and develop a more critical view of branding.

Brands as sign

Influenced by the disparate fields of linguistics, philosophy and anthropology, there is an insightful stream of branding research that analyses brands as signs. Søren Askegaard declares the 'notion of branding to be a strategically produced and disseminated commercial sign (or a set of signs) that is referring to the value universe of a commodity'.[37] What does this mean?

Take a product like the shoe brand Dr Martens.[38] Originally, they were developed in the mid 1940s by a German doctor, Klaus Maertens, after he had a skiing accident. The bouncing soles he developed proved to be a hit, and he went on and sold his shoes to elderly women who had foot problems. In the 1960s, The Griggs Company bought the licensing rights for the shoe and started to produce it in the UK, giving rise to one of the most iconic post-war brands.

Initially, blue collar workers bought the shoes as working shoes. As a first sub-culture, skinheads started to wear the boots as a sign of belonging to the working class. The skinheads would wear different coloured laces – often a signifier of which right wing faction they belonged to. In the seventies, the punk movement made Doc Martens their trademark of rebellion. By the eighties the shoes had become mainstream and the British gay scene adopted them, along some other elements of the skinhead culture. By the nineties, the shoes had made it across the Atlantic and were worn by the leaders and followers of the grunge and indie music scene.

As Wipperfürth put it, Doc Martens, originally developed as a medically superior product, transformed themselves into an unlikely canvas for self-expression among sub-cultures. It worked so well because there was a whole code of communication that the shoes (unintentionally) provided, including which ones one would wear and, most importantly, how one would lace up one's boots. One could use up to twenty eyelet holes on each side and different colours for the laces. This provided a simple yet highly visible grammar that different sub-cultures could use to express their identity. This flexibility

---

[37] Askegaard, 2006: 91.
[38] We follow Wipperfürth's account (2005: 17–18).

made it possible for the shoe to become a symbol for both the extreme right and the extreme left, and pretty much everyone in between.[39]

Another interesting case is that of Burberry – a luxury clothing brand in the UK. The traditional market for Burberry was privately educated English Sloanes and the country set. The brand also appealed to those outside the UK who were interested in consuming classic English fare. About a decade ago, something happened: the brand – certainly for reasons out of its control – became the favoured garment of British youths closely associated with football hooliganism and gang violence. Sales boomed and Burberry now had two core markets – one of which it was not entirely comfortable with. It became common in British cities for pubs to have signs up outside making it clear that those wearing Burberry would not be served. Of course, Burberry's brand managers did not craft the brand for hooligans; rather, the brand was hijacked and re-appropriated by an audience that was never targeted by the corporate meaning-makers.[40]

Of course, brands do not wait until consumers start to read them differently. Meaning is often induced. Danesi argues that when 'a product-commodity becomes a brand, its use value is supplemented by a number of further associations'.[41]

Let's take a mature industry like the car industry. Coming up with names in this industry is a true science that takes up considerable resources. Danesi explains the art of naming and differentiates between several categories of car names, including animals (e.g. Jaguar, Beetle etc.), persons (Escort, Cavalier, Kadet, Edsel – after Ford's younger son, which famously flopped), places indicative of lifestyle (e.g. Corsica, Outback etc.), music indicative of artistry (Cortina, Capri, Allegro, Prelude etc.) and foreign associations (e.g. Fiesta, Ka etc.).[42] Of course, this also works the other way round: Chevrolet's Nova sold poorly in Spanish speaking country as it means 'no go' in Spanish.

Here, a brand is something that emerges from a commodity by adding associations. Danesi uses the example of Brillo: it is more than a detergent; in order to understand Brillo, one needs to understand the associations around Brillo and their effects: 'A product has no identity; a brand does. It garners an identity through its name, its association with cultural meanings, its

---

[39] Wipperfürth, 2005: 20; Appadurai, 1986; see also Hebdige's entertaining account on *Subculture: The Meaning of Style* (1979), where he analyses how 'humble objects' like safety pins got hijacked by the punk movement and took on new, subversive meanings. Finally, Walker's brilliant book *Buying In* (2008) offers many more examples, including the celebrity brand Timberland and hip hop's appetite for brand de- and reconstruction.

[40] Chris Carter has brought this excellent example to my attention – thanks!

[41] Danesi, 2006: 3 and 21.

[42] Danesi, 2006: 49.

dissemination through mass-manufacturing and advertising campaigns, and other strategies designed to give it what can be called "cultural relevance".[43]

The movement from product-commodity to brand is a semiotic transformation. Through advertising, packaging, design etc., the product-commodity transforms into a brand. This has two important implications: first, brands become mental constructs that evoke different meanings; second, brands are powerful because they influence the social and cultural fabric of our world. Think of fashion brands that function as identity-lenses for sub-cultures. For someone who is able to read them, these fashion brands communicate who is included and who is excluded from a community. Wearing the wrong scarf in the wrong section of a soccer stadium can be a rather troublesome experience. In short, brands are cultural expressions and not just corporate enterprises.

Brands as signs do not operate independently from each other. Rather, one has to think of brands like letters in an alphabet that have to be combined according to grammar to produce meaning. Brand meaning can emerge out of the interplay of different signs. Saussure, and after him a whole range of predominately French theorists, have stressed the same point in relation to language: signs only make sense in relation to each other, while, studied individually, they are meaningless. Brands follow this structural logic. Take the example of Helly Hansen, the Norwegian sports brand, which was 'hip' for a short while in progressive popular music circles. It was the association of an otherwise not very spectacular Norwegian sports brand with African-American street culture in New York that made it spectacular. Helly Hansen became an indicator for 'cool'.

Hip hop culture in particular appropriated brands and hijacked their meaning. Chuck D, front man of Public Enemy, tells 'It was *you* that was important, and everything else would define you *after* you defined yourself. It wasn't like a brand defined you, *you* defined the brand.' When Chuck D wore a Philadelphia Phillies baseball cap on MTV, the P simply stood for Public Enemy. Hip hoppers used upper-class brands such as Louis Vuitton, Gucci and Mercedes Benz and plastered them all over their tracksuit pants.[44]

American Brandstand tracked the number of brand mentions in the lyrics of the Billboard Top 20 singles chart. In 2004, 40 per cent of all Billboard Top 20 songs mentioned at least one brand. As Lucian James, mastermind behind

[43] Danesi, 2006: 25.
[44] Walker, 2008; the Chuck D quote can be found on pages 85–86; see also the *Black Style Now* exhibition that explores how hip hop transformed pop culture: www.mcny.org/exhibitions/past/black-style-now-hip-hop-fashion-in-new-york-city.html (accessed 15 June 2008).

the study and founder of brand consultancy Agenda, explains, 'If 50 Cent mentions Gucci, you know it's a global metaphor for success. When he talks about taking women back to the Holiday Inn, you know that's a different kind of night than if he took a woman to the Four Seasons. He uses brands as metaphors to convey an idea very quickly.'[45]

Ironically, brands become social signifiers that communicated the rebellion against the status quo that produced and consumed these very brands in the first place.

Sometimes, brands start a collaboration to manage the semiotic mix. Take Shell and Ferrari in Formula 1, Gore Tex and Adidas in sports wear, Sony and Ericsson in mobile phones or the iPod and the Irish rock band U2 in music. The examples are endless but the goal remains the same: to 'potentialise and actualise meanings between signs'.[46]

The sum total of semiotic meaning culminates in objects that are no longer commodities but 'concepts: the brand as experience, as lifestyle'.[47] Signs take on a social life and become markers of identity.[48]

Importantly, the brand meaning cannot be determined by any one agent, be it a manager or a consumer. Rather, cultural codes constrain and enable the production of meaning.[49]

The brand as sign perspective understands society as something that needs to be read and interpreted, like a text: the fall of the Berlin Wall is a sign for democracy, the destruction of the Twin Towers is sign of terrorism, and so on. The crucial thing is that what we experience is more often the sign – and not the object that is signified. The fall of the Berlin Wall is much more than the collapse of some bricks and mortar. Equally, 9/11 was not only about the Twin Towers but, more significantly, it changed the face of war and the world forever. In an image-driven, media-saturated environment, the sign eventually becomes more important then the signified. Jean Baudrillard has described this new reality as hyperreality. What he means by this is that the sign or image becomes more real than the actual reality of a situation. Think about terror: between the late 1960s and 2005, about the same number of Americans were killed by terrorists as died through lightning or allergic reactions to peanuts. More people drown in bathtubs in the US than were killed by terrorists worldwide since 9/11.[50] Notwithstanding that the loss of

[45] See Scanlon, 2005.

[46] Uggla, 2006: 86.

[47] Klein, 2000: 24.

[48] Eco, 1973.

[49] Schroeder and Salzer-Mörling, 2006: 1.

[50] Bobbitt, 2008: 7.

life is equally tragic, unsafe bathtubs and bathing practices are less discussed than terrorism. Why? Because terrorism is composed of not just killings but images, texts, speeches, videos of beheadings, and so on.

But that is not all that new. Already, Feuerbach lamented that the sign becomes more important than the object it signifies. In the preface to the second edition of *The Essence of Christianity*, he writes:

> But certainly for the present age, which prefers the sign to the thing signified, the copy to the original, representation to reality, the appearance to the essence ... illusion only is sacred, truth profane. Nay, sacredness is held to be enhanced in proportion as truth decreases and illusion increases, so that the highest degree of illusion comes to be the highest degree of sacredness.[51]

Society itself becomes a spectacle, a collage of images, a mere representation that mediates 'social relationship between people'.[52] In such a society of consumerism and spectacle, appearance becomes reality and truth an illusion. In his 1962 book *The Image*, Daniel Boorstin wrote that '[t]he American citizen ... lives in a world where fantasy is more real than reality, where the image has more dignity than its original'.[53] The difference between appearance and reality, between truth and illusion, vanishes. All that is left is a sea of empty signifiers that endlessly refer to themselves. Take Nike's 'Just Do It' campaign, which conjures up some kind of nervous hyperactivity without specifying what it is one should 'just do' – except that whatever it is, one should just do it while wearing a pair of Nike trainers.

Sociologists such as Jean Baudrillard and Pierre Bourdieu have argued that our consumer society values differentiation more than identification and solidarity.[54] Consuming brands means introducing a difference into one's life. And to be different is the key to building one's identity. Modern consumption has turned Maslow's hierarchy of needs into an endlessly self-recreating spiral. What consumers look for in objects is not the satisfaction of a need but the chance to actualise their selves and be different. Since difference is defined in relation to other elements, the semiotics of brands that creates differences is more seductive than the monotony of products.

In the semiotic discourse around brands, there is a strong and critical focus on the consumer society that has taken over planet Earth. The basic premise

[51] Feuerbach, quoted in Debord, 1967/2006: 11.
[52] Debord, 1967/2006: 12; there is an interesting tension between Debord and Foucault: the former argued for a society of the spectacle whereas the latter rejected that, arguing for a society of surveillance by saying we are much less Greeks than we believe – that we are not in an amphitheatre but in a panoptic machine.
[53] Boorstin, here quoted in Rutherford, 2000: 232.
[54] Baudrillard, 1970/2003; Bourdieu, 1979/2007.

is that we are less defined by what we do than by what we consume. You are what you consume, not what you produce. In the consumer society, the consumer experiences a rhetoric of empowerment. Companies bend backwards to please the new customer-kings and worship them for their loyalty. The spectacle of consumption becomes the chief product; or as Debord pithily noted, '[it resembles] the material reconstruction of the religious illusion'.[55] Thus in the theatre that is the consumer society, brands are the props and scripts for staging ever-new theatrical spectacles.

Brands as media

For Celia Lury, a brand is not a commodity but 'a set of relationships between products or services' in time.[56] This definition adds a dynamic component to branding as it makes a brand a relational concept. First, things are not simple objects but it is the relation between them that constitutes what we call object.

Take the example of a car: a car consists of lots of parts that form together what we call car. It is also the interaction with the environment that makes a car a car: the other traffic, the road signs, the street conditions, the weather, and so on. These things change and evolve over time, and hence the relationships are inherently dynamic.

The brand emerges out of this network of relationships. Ford the car company is a brand that manages the relation between its consumer, producer, dealer, products, finance deals (leasing etc.), and so on. In this new constellation, the brand plays the role of a new kind of *logos* – it organizes exchange in markets. In this context, *logos* refers back to its Greek origin, meaning speech, account and logic. As opposed to *mythos*, *logos* represents the torchlight of rational knowledge. For Lury, brands represent a different kind of rationality that organizes the economy.[57] Bear with me – this sounds more complicated than it is.

Lury uses Simmel's philosophy of money to illustrate the step-change.[58] For Simmel, money is such a powerful medium because it is able to quantify qualities. Money introduces what Simmel described vividly as 'merciless objectivity' through which every quality is dissolved into a relative variable

[55] Debord, 1967/2006: 18.
[56] Lury, 2004: 1.
[57] Lury, 2004: 5.
[58] See Simmel, 1907/1978.

that can be compared.[59] That time is money shows the link between quantifiable time and money as its linear measure. Simmel did little to conceal his contempt for this: 'Money, with all its colourlessness and indifference, becomes the common denominator of all values; irreparably it hollows out the core of things, their individuality, their specific value, and their incomparability.'[60]

For Lury, the central feature of a brand is its capacity to reintroduce a sense of quality and meaning into exchange; it brings values back into the equation; it becomes a 'social currency' and 'a way in which people bring meaning to various exchanges'.[61] While the traditional focus was on price, in marketing this is expressed through a focus on three other 'Ps', including product qualities, place of distribution, promotion tools and, occasionally, a fifth 'P': people. Brands focus on value, not on price. They manage these relationships, and by doing so they manage the *controlled re-introduction of quality into the means of exchange*.[62]

This makes brands a new medium that connects consumers and producers, and demand and supply. Brands are a medium with which markets are organized through values and meaning.[63] Rather than brands being signs, they are elevated to institutional phenomena. Brands provide emotional connection between people and commodities. They are on the crossroads between commerce and creativity, the roundabout link that brings the logic of capital and the magic of creativity together. As Lury suggests, brands can be seen as the interface, the frame that allows consumers and producers to interact. Since there is a premium on interactivity, brands fulfil an important role by creating a symbolic exchange between society, organization and individuals. From this perspective, brands play an institutional role. That's why brands are a medium.

The Danish scholar Adam Arvidsson suggests understanding brands as the 'institutional embodiment of a new form of informational capital – much like the factory embodied the logic of industrial capital'.[64] He analyses the brand not as simple cultural phenomenon but as institution. He understands the brand as a managerial device that subsumes and appropriates what consumers do with it in their minds and how this can be turned into surplus value and profit. Brands are the extension of the logic of capitalism and

---

[59] Simmel, quoted in Lury, 2004: 5.
[60] Simmel, 1902/1950: 414.
[61] Lury, 2004: 10.
[62] Lury, 2004: 5.
[63] We use the term *relais* to describe a brand's capacity to relate two or more things as well as act as a catalyst that changes the elements which are linked.
[64] Arvidsson, 2006: i.

subsume consumption to the logic of surplus value generation. Brands play an important role since they pre-structure action and create a 'frame' between action and semiosis, or between doing and interpretation.[65] In fact, a brand can be seen as a 'frame of action' as defined by Goffman. It is not so much the actual product or event that is being consumed; rather, the real value lies in the experience that is provided through the context – and this context is created through the brand. In doing so, brands structure a possible field of action for consumers. Brands manage consumers' lives through prescribing lifestyles, something we will return to later. Arvidsson's point is that the as yet unproductive part of capitalism (consumption) becomes subsumed under and exploited by capital as well. Creative consumption 'allows the subsumption of these kinds of practices as a source of surplus value'.[66] For Arvidsson, '[b]rand management exploits the productivity of the consumer'.[67]

While this institutional view is innovative, it is important to be suspicious of the somewhat crude exploitation claim. Again, Arvidsson: 'In this sense the brand as propertied frame of action is but one aspect of a general movement towards the commodification and capitalist appropriation of the bio-political framework in which life unfolds.'[68] We think that this view is too one-dimensional. What Arvidsson – and to a lesser degree, Lury – present is a grand narrative about never-ending capitalist exploitation that moves on and on relentlessly, colonizing ever-more parts of daily life.

This view is problematic as it paints an overly deterministic picture: brands seem to exercise an almost absolute power. But consumption is not just about manipulation but also about use and abuse in de Certeau's sense. Subcultures that used Doc Martens were creative *bricoleurs* – and not remote-controlled dummies led astray by a brand manager. Most critically, the brand as media perspective seems to suggest that brands colonize parts of life that at least until now have been spared from capitalism's greed. However, the idea that one aggressor invades life and occupies it, is simply naïve. If one force colonizes another one, both parts change. Change happens through co-evolution and not through a process of coercion.[69] When brands become cultural forms, they do change culture; but culture also changes how brands (and by extension, business) operate: while pop stars become more and more like brands, brands themselves become increasingly entertaining.

[65] Arvidsson, 2006: 7–8, with reference to Lury, 2004.
[66] Arvidsson, 2006: 42.
[67] Arvidsson, 2006: 70.
[68] Arvidsson, 2006: 13.
[69] Deleuze and Guattari, 1980/1987.

Instead of a definition

Definitions put boundaries around mental objects. Brands traverse those boundaries and redraw our mental map of the world. Hence it might be more appropriate to think about the 'brand' of the term 'brand' rather than try to define it.

Brands are not one thing but many. The truth is a function of the perspective one chooses to take. Brands are tools with which we manage organizations: think of Deloitte's 7 Signals, which is a brand-driven internal change programme. Brands function as corporate catalysts: for instance, Deloitte's business structure that articulates its traditional functions in ways that are defined by clients' needs is a major shift. Brands are also signs: for example, Deloitte's ad campaign aimed at adding meaning to the otherwise hard to differentiate service offer. Finally, the brand is a medium: Deloitte's brand is its interface to its internal and external environment, as sites such as Greendotlife.com illustrate.

The brand is the institutionalized yet contested space in which producing and consuming takes shape. As such, branding describes a field rather than a single phenomenon or object. Instead of thinking of a brand as an object, we can also conceptualize it as the result of a set of practices. In the next chapter, we will scrutinize the practices that create brands. Rather than understanding the brand as a thing (brand as noun), we will analyse what goes into the making of a brand (branding as verb).

Following our explorative take (remember: treasure hunter vs quantity surveyor), we will take samples of the field at different parts of our journey. Like the four points of the compass, the four concepts will give us a sense of direction.

Of course, other directions and perspectives are possible too. Like any 2x2 table, ours simplifies to the point of it being almost unjustifiable. But only almost.

3 The making of brands

Market economy

Before we analyse the way brands are manufactured, it might be helpful to briefly describe the economic context in which they circulate. The next two sections will take the scenic route past the economic backdrop against which brands take shape. We will use Michel Callon's notion of economy of qualities to set the scene. Of course, if you're in a hurry (or if you're Michel Callon), feel free to jump straight to the section on advertising practice.

How are brands brought into existence and how are they institutionalized? What roles to they play in the contemporary market economy? If brands are about interaction between individuals, organizations and society, how do they relate to our economy, which is based on transactions?

In many respects, Thomas Hobbes' theory of social and political order sets the scene for our argument. He paints a picture of a bi-polar world in which either order, civility, sovereignty and rule flourish, or a state of chaos prevails in which *homo homini lupus est* 'and the life of man is solitary, poor, nasty, brutish and short'.[1]

Hobbes atomizes society into individual actors, who are nothing but calculating machines driven solely by self-interest. This reckless pursuit of individual interests creates, on a societal level, total disorder. According to this logic, salvation can only be achieved if everybody cedes their individual powers to a Leviathan, a kind of benevolent dictator-state. As the American sociologist Mark Granovetter put it neatly, Hobbes' citizens 'lurch directly from an undersocialised to an oversocialised state'.[2] Current proponents of a neoliberal market economy follow a Hobbesian logic: they argue for a strong law and order state as the only means of guaranteeing maximum individual freedom.

In order to realize their freedom, individuals rely on the market as a neutral mechanism where demand and supply meet. In the neoliberal vision, the market state eventually replaces the nation state. The objective of the market state is to maximize the opportunity of individuals. Its constitutional order will 'resemble that of the twenty-first century multinational corporation or NGO rather than the twentieth century state in that it will outsource many functions, rely less on law and regulation and more on market incentives, and respond to ever-changing and constantly monitored consumer demand rather than voter preferences expressed in relatively rare elections'.[3]

Put simply, the market and its transaction mechanisms ensure that individuals can realize their opportunities, while a strong law and order state ensures that people play by the rules. This model treats transaction as the basic form of social interaction: in fact, interaction follows transaction.

Of course, this view has been widely criticized. One of its most prominent critics is Granovetter. He argues that 'the behaviour and institutions to be analysed are so constrained by ongoing social relations that to construe them as independent is a grievous misunderstanding'.[4] His argument stresses the role of 'concrete personal relations and structures (or "networks") of such relations in generating trust and discouraging malfeasance'.[5]

In Granovetter's account, transaction follows interaction: trust precedes exchange, and reputation makes repeat exchange possible in the first place. Especially in a risk society where environmental disasters and corporate

---

[1] Hobbes, 1651/1962: 143.
[2] Granovetter, 1985: 485.
[3] Bobbitt, 2008: 87.
[4] Granovetter, 1985: 482.
[5] Granovetter, 1985: 490.

wrongdoing cannot be pushed aside as 'transaction costs', 'latent side effects' or 'externalised costs', reputation and trust become the key resource for a functioning society.[6]

Granovetter uses the concept of reputation to make his point. Reputation is a concept that is intricately linked to branding. As reputation researchers Fombrun and van Riel argue, reputation can be understood as the general estimation in which one is held by the public.[7] In other words, reputation is determined by the brand image that stakeholders have. In an increasingly global economy, reputation is less instilled through personal relations because we hardly know the people we deal with. Instead, brands take the place of personal relations.

Think of eBay: the $60 billion that were traded in 2007 among its 280 million customers rely on a simple ranking mechanism that turns individual sellers into micro-brands that are concerned about their reputation.[8] Whether you look at eBay, choose a business school at which to do an MBA or think of a charity to which to donate your money, brands are the characters you trust and buy, and concern about their brand reputation might be the only motivation that stops firms from behaving unethically.

The 'networks of relations' are responsible for the production of reputation.[9] What circulates in these networks and what is created in the conversations taking place within them are not products but brands. Brands become a new form of media through which people see and make sense of the world. It is not about the transaction logic of market states but about the interactions and qualities of brands within networked societies. Increasingly, brands will play an important part in keeping our interaction-based, new economy – which is based on global connectivity – going because they are the medium in which connections and exchange occur.

Economy of qualities

Michel Callon and his collaborators developed the concept of 'economy of qualities' to understand this new form of organization of markets.[10] How does a product turn into a good that we can exchange?

---

[6] Power, 2007; Beck, 1986/2007.
[7] Fombrun and van Riel, 1997.
[8] See presentation at the 2008 Annual Meeting of Stockholders, available at http://investor.ebay.com/index.cfm (accessed 25 August 2008).
[9] Granovetter, 1985: 491.
[10] Callon et al., 2002; Callon, 1998.

The transformations that create a good have to strike a balance between two contradictory poles: the good has to be different in relation to other products – otherwise there would be no incentive to buy it – but it also has to be similar to other, already existing goods – otherwise it would be tricky for consumers to understand which need it promises to satisfy. Callon and his colleagues describe this process as a 'qualification-requalification' process. Within this process, a good is defined as a 'combination of characteristics that establish its singularities. This singularity, because it stems from a combination, is relational … Defining a good means positioning it in a space of goods, in a system of differences and similarities, of distinct yet connected categories.'[11]

Branding is the practice that strikes the balance between qualification and requalification.[12] Brands allow a complex double movement that needs to be accomplished for markets to function. This singularizes goods, positions them uniquely and differentiates them from others. On the other hand, 'it makes the good comparable to other existing goods so that new markets are constructed through the extension and renewal of existing ones. Different and similar, singular and comparable, such is the paradoxical nature of the economic goods constituting the dynamics of markets.'[13]

Two of my colleagues and I researched the emerging business-coaching industry in Australia and found a similar paradox existed at an organizational level.[14] Business coaches use a series of discursive moves to make themselves different from consultants but stay within a certain client need area at the same time. For instance, business coaches claim to be facilitators, not experts; process-focused, not answer-driven; emotional, not just rational; flexible, not rigid, and so on. In order to establish their identity in the market, they have to accomplish the impossible: to be familiar enough to fit into a clients' expectations and be different enough to provide clients with a tempting reason to try out something new.

This positioning exercise makes it possible to address the paradox of supply and demand: being similar enough to fit into existing categories and connected to the list of qualities in consumers' minds that is attached to a good. Simultaneously, it allows a good or service to be different enough to be seen as unique in the combination of values it offers to the potential consumer. This

---

[11] Callon *et al.*, 2002: 198.

[12] Callon *et al.* argue that the balance is achieved through tests or trials that include 'specific metrological work and heavy investment in measuring equipment' (Callon *et al.*, 2002: 198). We would argue that testing is part of a larger branding process that is better able to square the circle of sameness and difference.

[13] Callon *et al.*, 2002: 201.

[14] Clegg *et al.*, 2007.

adjustment is fragile, as it 'is temporary and constantly threatened because it operates against a background of substitutability and comparability'.[15]

Markets are therefore not stable structures. Rather, they come about through branding practices that relate the new to the old: markets are *performed*.[16] In this context, brands can be seen as basic elements of that performance. Brands are institutions, as they provide the interface between producer and consumer that allows for the complex interplay and qualification of goods. They generate the trust that is the basis of all market exchanges. Brands mediate the relationship between people. They represent value (quality), not price (quantity). As such, brands play an important institutional role.

This is Lury's argument: brands mediate between supply and demand.[17] Brands represent the controlled reintroduction of quality into products. They inject values and culture into products. They create trust. They are the basis of reputation. Thus brands organize markets. As Howard Schultz, CEO and founder of Starbucks said,

I think the brand equity of the name Starbucks has supplied a level of trust and confidence, not only in the product, the trademark, but in the experience of what Starbucks is about. At a time when there are very few things that people have faith in. It's a fragile thing. You can't take it for granted. It's something that has to be respected and continually built upon.[18]

Brands are fragile things – they give faith and supply trust. But how are these fragile things built? The way brands are produced is fascinating: agencies carefully inject meaning into products and organizations, turning them eventually into brands. How does this process work? How is meaning produced?

Advertising

At the beginning of the twentieth century, the hopes for advertising were high: 'Whenever one of us goes to the theatre or picks a necktie, we are responding to definite laws. For every type of decision – for every sale in retail stores – basic laws govern the actions of people in great masses.'[19]

---

[15] Callon *et al.*, 2002: 201.
[16] Callon, 2006.
[17] Lury, 2004.
[18] Quoted in Lury, 2004: 30.
[19] Resor, quoted in Kreshel, 1990b: 83. We draw extensively on Kreshel's research at the archives of JWT from 1915–1925 that shows how JWT's advertising business came into existence. See also the excellent book by de Grazia (2005).

This quote is from Stanley B. Resor, who ran J. Walter Thompson (JWT) for almost half a century. JWT was (and remains) one of the world's largest ad agencies. At JWT, Resor pursued two related objectives. The first was to discover the laws of human behaviour and, building on these laws, to position advertising so that it could be used as an effective marketing tool. The first task brought a strong focus on science with it. In the time of scientific management, the notion of science had a strong appeal in the business community. Whereas scientific management focused on the control of the internal organization of production, advertising promised to control the human element outside the production process through managing consumption.[20] Indeed, as the capacity to produce increased, 'the business community adjusted its focus to the consumption side of the economic equation'.[21] Advertising was conceptualized as the 'engineering of demand' and its practitioners were 'consumption engineers'.[22] Resor argued that mass-production machines such as Ford would 'fall of their own weight without the mass marketing machinery which advertising supplies'.[23]

Resor's second task was to professionalize the advertising business itself. The scientific approach that JWT embraced had the power to legitimize advertising as practice. JWT invested in science – it had its own 'University of Advertising' where one could go through a two-and-a-half-year training programme: 'The training programme instilled "professionalism" via rigorous preparation, and at the same time served as a visible symbol of Thompson's dedication to effective advertising.'[24]

Against this backdrop, an unlikely alliance between John B. Watson, the founding father of behaviourism, and JWT was forged. After an extra-marital affair made his life and work difficult at Johns Hopkins University, Watson was hired by Resor in 1920. He enjoyed a meteoric rise and became Vice President in 1924. His billings were more than $10 million and included clients such as Johnson & Johnson Baby Powder and Pebeco Toothpaste. Watson's objective was not only to understand human behaviour but to be able to predict and control it. For him, the selling process was a form of control of human behaviour. In order to exercise this control, he linked emotion

---

[20] There are two excellent books that discuss the control of the production process through mechanization: see Beniger, *The Control Revolution* (1986) and Gideon, *Mechanization Takes Command: A Contribution to Anonymous History* (1948).

[21] Kreshel, 1990b: 82.

[22] Krehsel, 1990a: 50.

[23] Kreshel, 1990a: 51.

[24] Kreshel, 1990b: 84.

to consumption: 'After all, it is the emotional factor in our lives that touches off and activates our social behaviour, whether it is buying a cannon, a sword or a plowshare – and love, fear and rage are the same in Italy, Abyssinia and Canada.'[25] For Watson, the difference between an advertising agency and a psychology lab was not that great: 'it can be just as thrilling to watch the growth of a sales curve of a new product as to watch the learning curve of animals and men'.[26]

The strategy behind Resor's move was clear: scientific knowledge should add legitimacy to the young professionals who claimed to be able to control consumption. Ironically, Watson did not discover the laws that make you buy toothpaste, but he did function as a living ad for JWT, embodying the new spirit of advertising in its scientific quest for prediction and control over human behaviour. Besides that, Watson demonstrated that behaviourism could make a psychology student a lot of money.[27]

Despite its efforts, advertising never managed to establish itself as a profession to the extent architects, lawyers or accountants did. In 1955, Gardner and Levy lamented that advertising 'has been subject to pressures ... that well-established professions refuse to tolerate'.[28] For them, there are several explanations for the low level of professionalization and power of the industry. First, advertising is a profession of creativity and individuality, which are hard to professionalize; second, the effects of advertising are hard to measure; third, large, single-client accounts can mean life and death for an agency, as dangerous dependencies on a couple of big clients form; and finally, everyone thinks they know what a good ad should be like. After fifty years, advertising had established itself – but it was still in search of its own soul.

This search would come to a temporary rest, as advertising strove less to mimic the rational professions of law, medicine and accounting and commenced to search for its identity in the creativity of the artist. From the sixties on, the fate of the profession was linked to that elusive notion of creativity and started to become inextricably meshed up in the cultural context of society.[29]

---

[25] Kreshel, 1990a: 53.

[26] Kreshel, 1990a: 52.

[27] Kreshel, 1990a: 55, quoting Winkler and Bromberg.

[28] Gardner and Levy, 1955: 38.

[29] For excellent and detailed historic accounts, see Lears, 1994; Marchand, 1998; Frank, 1997; and de Grazia, 2005.

Economists of quality

The Swinging Sixties changed everything. The sixties were a busy time for revolutionaries: counter-culture, anti-war movements, social movements, drugs, music … and as if this was not enough, the advertising industry staged its own upheaval, dubbed the creative revolution. The creative revolution describes the move from scientific promotion and sales techniques based on laws to highly artistic and creative brand expressions. The aim was no longer to discover those laws and apply them mechanically; rather, ads had to translate commodities into brands with a unique aesthetic value, just like a work of art.

Resor and Watson were clearly proponents of a scientific ideology of advertising. The famous 1923 book *Scientific Advertising* by Claude Hopkins outlined the approach:

The time has come when advertising has in some hands reached the status of a science. It is based on fixed principles and is reasonably exact. The causes and effects have been analysed until they are well understood. The correct methods of procedure have been proved and established. We know what is most effective, and we act on basic laws.[30]

Ads were based on research, polls, statistics and scientific rules for layout and design. Creativity was seen as an un-organized, non-rational and eccentric form of expressiveness that would result in purely subjective brand communication. In his 1958 book *Madison Avenue, U.S.A.*, Martin Mayer defends this position and models advertising along the lines of the scientific rationality that supposedly governed clients' organizations. Brand communication was rule-based, process-driven and based on proven methods that led to predictable results.

In reality, the ads that were engineered by this scientific machinery were boring, repetitive, predictable and had little effect. Its aesthetic was compared to Soviet Realism: cars from the big three Detroit manufacturers were put next to jet fighter planes and radar dishes; Buick built a 'B 58' model, Oldsmobile offered an 'F 85'; Buick promised bluntly to satisfy the 'Joneses' in one ad: 'What a wonderful sense of well-being just being seen behind its wheel. No showing off. Just that Clean Look of Action which unmistakably tells your success.'[31] The ads 'were always populated with idealised white

[30] Quoted in Frank, 1997: 40.
[31] Quoted in Frank, 1997: 61.

nuclear families, manly husbands, fawning wives, and playful children'.[32] Above all advertising's dogmatism clashed with the mundane realities of American life and the actual experience of Americans.

In the 1960s, the 'creative revolution' turned this order upside down. Adman Bill Bernbach was the chief insurgent. According to Frank, '[h]e invented what we might call anti-advertising: a style which harnessed public mistrust of consumerism – perhaps the most powerful cultural tendency of the age – to consumerism itself'.[33] Bill Bernbach became synonymous with the creative revolution. Before he started his own agency, he wrote a letter to his boss at advertising giant Grey, warning that they might fall into the 'trap of big business': 'I'm worried that we're going to worship techniques instead of substance … Advertising is fundamentally persuasion and persuasion happens to be not a science, but an art … Let us blaze new trails. Let us prove to the world that good taste, good art, good writing can be good selling.'[34]

Of course, his boss did not listen, so Bill had to blaze new trails with two friends, forming his own agency, DDB. For Bernbach, rules were set by the establishment and had to be bent – if possible, broken – by advertising. Intuition, imagination, creativity and spontaneity trumped the safety of pseudo-scientific rules.

DDB rose to fame with a series of ads for the Volkswagen Beetle. One showed a gleaming new Beetle with the heading 'Lemon'. The copy read: 'This Volkswagen missed the boat. The chrome strip on the glove compartment is blemished and must be replaced. We plug the lemons; you get the plums.' This was a new kind of language – rather than saying 'Our cars must pass an inspection test', it was attention-grabbing, intelligent and ironic.[35] It was not derived from market testing or some kind of scientific law; rather, it had its origins in a Big Idea that advertisers would chase from now on.

In order to succeed, a new creative team was established: the duo of copy-writer and art director as creative engine. Before DDB, these figures were sitting in different departments, one coming up with some visual ideas while the other tried to squeeze in their copy. From now on, they were working in tandem, manufacturing that Big Idea. Soon, the creative team became the engine room of agencies all over the world.[36]

---

[32] Frank, 1997: 61.
[33] Frank, 1997: 55.
[34] Quoted in Tungate, 2007: 52–53.
[35] Tungate, 2007: 56.
[36] Nixon, 2003.

The industry had changed forever. Ad agencies followed the new DDB model and bought into the creative revolution. The boring car ads quite literally changed overnight: Dodge invited people to 'Join the Dodge Rebellion' (1965) by breaking away from their everyday lives and attacking everything that's dull; Oldsmobile campaigned as 'Youngmobiles' (1967), which was about individualism and being different; and Buick took the populist route with one of its campaigns, accompanying the claim 'we're talking your language' with realistic imagery of an average couple.[37]

In the UK, Collett Dickenson Pearce (CDP) modelled itself after DDB and was to revolutionize advertising from the late sixties onwards. Others such as Saatchi and Saatchi followed and went on to create some of the most striking campaigns of the twentieth century, such as the HEC ad in which a guy rests his hands on his baby bump, the copy reading: 'Would you be more careful if it was you who got pregnant?' Or think of the introduction of Apple's Macintosh computer with a thirty-second ad that was aired during the Superbowl in 1984. The TV ad, obviously influenced by George Orwell's novel, was called *1984*. Its core message was that with Macintosh, 1984 won't be like Orwell's *1984*. The *Blade Runner*-style ad showed a woman running from an army of robots who were chasing her, until she enters a control room and smashes Big Brother's gigantic eye, which was watching and controlling everyone. The subtext was that Apple was different, and that Big Brother – presumably IBM – would be challenged by a new, more feminized way of doing things.[38]

The new-found brand expressionism was here to stay. Rather than dwelling on utopian Soviet Realism, style, irony, humour, individuality and difference became the master concept of brand communication. Ad agencies discovered popular culture and counter-culture as idea mines for their own creative quest. To exploit this counter-culture, agencies had to dive into the intimate depths of society and learn about what moved people. As the famous ad woman Mary Wells put it in 1966, 'we are completely geared to our time. We are terribly aware of the current sounds and fears and smells and attitudes. We are the agency of today.'[39] Ad agencies became lifestyle experts, obsessed with how people lived their lives. Broad demographic data was deemed as useless; psycho-graphic and socio-graphic knowledge, spiced up with qualitative insights, provided a much more powerful launch pad for brand campaigns.

---

[37] See Frank, 1997.

[38] See Apple's 1984 Macintosh ad on Youtube at www.youtube.com/ watch?v=OYecfV3ubP8 (accessed 17 June 2009).

[39] Quoted in Frank, 1997: 124.

A good ad was not based on science, nor on communication describing the functionality of the product. Think of the Absolut Vodka ads, which single-handedly built a brand though iconic communication. Think of BMW's series of short films entitled *The Hire*, featuring acclaimed Hollywood directors and stars like Madonna. Think of Toscani's Benetton ads showing kissing nuns or the blood-stained uniform of a soldier. As Toscani put it, 'the product is more or less the same. The difference is the communications.'[40] Advertising reinvented itself – from the scientific approach inspired by Watson and others, to a profession in pursuit of Big Ideas for not always so big products, such as shampoo, cereal or toilet paper. The Big Idea was intertwined with subjectivity and irrationality. In a pro-logo book published by *The Economist* (not exactly known as an avantgarde pop-culture publisher), we read: 'Unlike pure science, [brand] identity is a triumph of opinion backed up by assertion. Its subjectivity is the very property that allows you to be bold and get away with it. The world's greatest identities are irrational, just like brands.'[41]

Like art, advertising was creative expression that had to resonate with the creative context and lifestyle of the wider culture. It had to reflect but also shape the *zeitgeist*. As such, ads were linked to the 'intertextual universe of media culture'.[42]

In search for ever-more edgy, creative and provocative ads, agencies became inextricably meshed with pop culture, especially movements at the vanguard of youth culture. Advertisers started to see their work as genuine cultural production. For instance, a typical creative knowledge worker attests in an interview: 'Being fascinated by everything is really important. Like tuning into something that's already there. Being receivers for that, being interested in everything – culture, aeroplanes, books, films, everything. And then eventually, if you let yourself, it can come out of you in the work.'[43]

Culture speaks through the advertiser: he is like a medium that connects the commercial objective of the client with the cultural lifestyle of the consumer. In order to do so, advertising has become an integral part of our culture: 'advertising attempts to sell goods, by appealing to consumers through gender identity, celebrity endorsement, romantic imagery, notions of achieving happiness or contentment, and other cultural dimensions not tangibly related to the advertised products or service'.[44]

---

[40] Quoted in Tungate, 2007: 148.
[41] Allen and Simmons, 2003: 126.
[42] Arvidsson, 2006: 54.
[43] Nixon, 2003: 81.
[44] Malefyt and Moeran, 2003: 2.

Two people exemplify the transition from a scientific-rational approach to a more creative professional identity. The scientist Watson moved into advertising to discover laws of behaviour, but his approach had little appeal for consumers and was of limited success. Some fifty years later, the ad industry produced another iconic and soon-to-be very wealthy character that embodied the changing profession like no one else: Andy Warhol. He glided effortlessly from the commercial world into the art world, claiming that there is no difference between exhibiting in a shop window or a gallery. Advertising, and brands as its products, became a cultural form that was inextricably meshed up with society.

In summary, advertising embeds products, services and organizations in cultural contexts that are meaningful for consumers. It creates brands by linking culture and commerce. This marriage has fuelled the growth of the ad industry: it now extends to the creation of content for TV shows, sponsorship of events, product placement in films, and so on. Advertising has become inextricably meshed with culture and, in turn, culture feeds on the resources of corporates. Ad agencies become the 'black box of cultural continuity and change'.[45]

In the next section we will unscrew one very successful black box, the Dutch advertising agency Kesselskramer, hoping to understand how continuity and change are enacted simultaneously in the production of brands.

Inside the black box

Kesselskramer is one of the most awarded and prestigious ad agencies in the world. Now in its eleventh year, it is based in Amsterdam but has been looking after global clients, including Diesel, Nike and MTV. The agency's office space is an old church in the centre of Amsterdam. On the elevated altar, the two creative directors share a desk. They are surrounded by glittering seventies furniture, a disco ball and an umbrella, which adds to the surreal mix. The virtual Kesselskramer is not less out there. The website changes every couple of weeks into a seemingly unrelated clone of the ad agency. Depending on when you visit, you will find Kesselskramer as plumber, dentist or Texan-hat manufacturer, including a whole collection of cowboy hats. The website doesn't tell you about the agency's services, clients or portfolio. All it offers is to send an email to church@kesselskramer.com.[46]

---

[45] Malefyt and Moeran, 2003: 4.
[46] See www.kesselskramer.com (accessed 25 September 2009).

I was intrigued by Kesseslkramer, and on a visit to Amsterdam I decided to drop by. A couple of emails later I was shaking Matthijs de Jongh's hand. Matthijs is the strategic planner at Kesselskramer and one of its five owners. He's been there from the outset eleven years ago.

'We're independent so we can do stupid things and reject clients if we want to,' says Matthijs at the start of our conversation. He makes it very clear that Kesselskramer is not like any other business:

We like to grow – but mentally. We like to be challenged with different kinds of tasks. So what are we about? If I had to summarise it in one word, it would be 'diversity'. We are almost obsessed with doing many kinds of jobs in different countries with different people and in different contexts – we work for MTV Japan, we work for a small budget hotel in Amsterdam, we work for NGOs, we work for Diesel, and we do our own projects.

What makes Kesselskramer so sought after as an agency? Matthijs runs me through the work his agency has done for the Dutch mobile phone provider Ben. Kesselskramer created the brand from scratch and then developed brand experience and communication strategies to bring the brand alive. The first challenge was timing: Ben was the fifth firm to enter the Dutch mobile phone market, and most people thought that it was already saturated with four companies. All four competitors were about bigness and technology, and had brand names such as KPN, Libertel, Telfort and Dutchtone that stressed their technophile heritage.

Matthijs explained the brand strategy. What the agency decided to do was avoid presenting the client as a high-tech institution. Instead it sought to make the brand personable, likeable and desirable. Says Matthijs,

So we called the mobile phone company Ben, which means 'to be' in Dutch. We followed up with clever brand communication: the poster campaign featured real people; a sticker campaign educated people about mobile phone etiquette; when Ben sponsored the Dutch Olympic Team in Salt Lake City, we decided to have a big Ben Party in Salt Lake City. We invited all the people called Ben from Salt Lake City, filmed the party and cut the footage into fifteen commercials that were aired on TV. The idea behind it was to connect people with people – not stars with TV viewers.

Ben became a runaway success. After the German giant T-Mobile bought the company in 2002, it scrapped the name and introduced T-Mobile. Five years later, T-Mobile decided to reintroduce Ben because the brand name still registered 60 per cent awareness among the Dutch population.[47]

[47] See www.cellular-news.com/story/29383.php (accessed 19 August 2008).

But Kesselskramer's approach – using popular culture to pursue commercial objectives – is not applauded everywhere. Matthijs gave a talk about the Ben brand at one of the universities in Berlin in front of some thousand people. One of the other speakers was creative guru Brian Eno. Matthijs recollects that the talk went well – until Brian Eno raised his hand and then his voice during question time. 'He said he hated it', tells Matthijs.

It was one of the most hypocritical stories he ever heard. You are trying to sell mobile phones, and you use emotion to make money. I answered: thank you very much; this is true. We use this commercial space, playing on people's emotion, but at the end of the line it is a commercial operation, yes. You should never underestimate the audience, it understands this purpose.

At the heart of Kesselskramer is the desire to explore and exploit culture. If it was just about commercial objectives, the agency would not need to work in a church. Rather, Kesselskramer is about making money and culture at the same time. As Matthijs tells, Kesselskramer spends up to a third of its time on its own projects. One of those projects was *The Other Final*. Fed up with the commercial and competitive nature of the soccer world championship, Kesselkramer organized its own final, to be played on the same day as the real final. The teams were Bhutan and Montserrat, the two lowest ranked teams in the FIFA World Ranking. The game was played in Bhutan, and Bhutan won 4–0. The documentary of the competition won a couple of awards and was aired on TV. People loved the spirit of the event: it was about love of the sport, and not the money.

Another self-generated project is the photo exhibition *In Almost Every Picture*. Creative Director Erik Kessels found a box of photos of an unknown woman while strolling through a flea-market in Barcelona. The photos were taken by the woman's husband and showed her travelling, in front of monuments and engaged in a number of other innocent little pleasure-seeking tourist activities. Erik dubbed the images 'vernacular photography' because they were testimony of people's everyday lives. *In Almost Every Picture* became a massive success and Erik left Kesselskramer to exhibit his work in galleries around the world as photographer-artist.

Whether it is creating the mobile phone brand Ben or organizing *The Other Final*, Kesselskramer is a cultural engine that applies its talents to the commercial and cultural worlds alike. The agency's passion, together with its skills, allow it to play in both worlds. That also tells us about the relationship between the two worlds: advertising is embedding brands in culture, and culture is advertising consumable ideas to an attention-poor audience.

Advertisers are Callonian economists of quality: they search for cultural differences in Bhutan or Barcelona, and these cultural differences shape commercial brands into singularities.

A series of agencies that came into existence in the 1990s embody this new cultural consciousness. Creative hothouses such as Naked, Mother, Anomaly, Denuo and StrawberryFrog, rather than being made up of the acronyms of founding fathers (no mothers – sorry), present themselves as radicals that understand pop- and counter-culture. If you go to Mother's website, you'll see videos featuring skateboarders jumping through the office. This stands for pure presence: as Mary Wells Lawrence, founding partner of creative hothouse Wells Rich Greene, put it in 1966, we are completely geared to our times, and we are terribly aware of everything. The currency of the agency is being hip, cool and trendy. They celebrate the image of creative renegades and commercial avant-gardists who could have been artists, writers of film producers – it just so happened that they ended up in advertising. What sells them is that they are radical, free and authentically entrenched in popular culture. And they're for sale.

Frédéric Beigbeder's novel *99 Francs* (2000) (the title being simultaneously the price of the book – very clever) is the anti-manifesto of this world of advertising. The autobiographical novel tells the story of Octave Parango, creative director in a Parisian agency, who makes a career in advertising – up to the point where he cannot deal any longer with clients he hates and their banal products. Using any drug he can get his hands on to get on with life, Octave literally goes mad in a meeting where they discuss the communication of a zero-calorie yogurt. The book is as much a symptom as a symbol of advertising culture: smart, creative, arrogant and simultaneously deeply frustrated, self-destructive and haunted by inauthenticity.

The cause of this ambivalence is the schizophrenic nature of the advertising profession: it is trapped between the more rational approach, a legacy of its early days, on the one hand, and the creative revolution that celebrates the Big Idea on the other.[48] Agencies mirror this conflict internally by employing account managers as well as creatives. The account team is responsible for meeting the business objectives of the client; positioning the product in relation to its target audience; developing strategy and the overall brand; research; and developing the creative brief. The creative team has to come up with the Big Ideas and bring the vision alive through campaign execution,

---

[48] In his book *Fables of Abundance*, Jackson Lears (1994) follows this contradiction through the history of advertising and identifies it as nothing less than the source of American culture.

which includes art directing, photography, copy writing, design, and so on. Conflicts between client and agency about brand strategy, consumer preferences and communication are reintroduced into the agency itself through conflicts between planners and creatives. Account planning develops 'marketing strategies that at least appear to be based on objective, *scientific* criteria derived from in-depth qualitative and quantitative data', whereas creatives 'work according to intuitive, *artistic* ideas that may have little actual relationship to the expressed marketing aims'.[49] Because of these structural conflicts, advertisers need to tolerate a high level of ambivalence and ambiguity.

The structure of the industry itself adds to the ambivalence. Advertising is a truly globalized and highly concentrated industry. Although clients have an apparently bewildering amount of choice, most agencies are owned by one of the five big global networks (Omnicom, WPP, Interpublic, Publicis and Havas). The Big Five consolidate accounts and serve clients globally, not unlike the Big Four accounting firms. These massive global conglomerates host many different, specialized and often competing agencies. Because the global players include competing portfolios in their network, they can work for clients that compete in the marketplace. Also, they are sheltered from economic cycles. The downside is that the big-business nature of the industry and the creative identity of the industry players are not a good fit. Not surprisingly, the mix is a constant source of tension. The practices of advertising are ways of dealing with this tension.

Practice of advertising

Advertising is a mediator between supply and demand, between the desire of consumers and the capability of producers. As such, it deals with a complex series of translations in order to reconcile the two:

The product is really like a topological monster whose metric changes as it goes from hand to hand: it is effectively a thing when it comes out of the workshop, but it is plans and models before its construction, a market study for the marketing manager, a beautiful form in the sketchbook of the artistic director, a simple, easily memorisable name for the writer, a mixture of magazine titles and television audiences for the media planner, sales figures for the enterprise[50]

---

[49] Malefyt and Moeran, 2003: 5.
[50] Hennion and Méadel, 1989: 202.

Advertising deals with this polyphony not by reducing the many voices but by reproducing them in the brand – it includes all the differences that might make a difference, thus turning a mere commodity into a desirable brand. Through a series of translations, it combines them and reconciles them. Advertising can credibly claim to do so because it is situated at the interstices of commerce and culture. The magic of creativity is the black box in which the actual translation happens. It is a process of negotiation in which the confrontation between supply and demand, between producer and consumer, is repeated and localized until the 'big opposition has not disappeared into a great big melting pot' but has been translated into 'an unlimited series of small local oppositions'.[51] Both supply and demand are remodelled in the brand (i.e. the brand functions as an interface) so that the object already contains its market, and the market already accommodates the product in a particular niche.

In the words of Hennion and Méadel, what makes an object desirable is

to have in front of us not a strange object, but an object that already contains us since we have been incorporated in it by a thousand techniques from the moment of its production ... The product traces out the consumers, the consumers the products: the familiarity of the couple has replaced the otherness of the confrontation between the reality of things and the illusions of desire.[52]

We have to imagine this translation process as an act of a high-wire performer. Just as a high-wire performer constantly makes little moves to gain overall stability, ad agencies celebrate instability and creative chaos. For instance, the *Harvard Business Review* dubbed the London-based ad agency St Luke's 'the most frightening company on earth'. The unique structure of the company enables it to master the paradox of combining culture and commerce. It is entirely owned by its employees and, as the founder, Andy Law, says, they are Star Trekkers, routinely asked to

go where they have never been. Our employees must take nothing for granted; they must peel away all the levels of their personalities to become who they really are. That's frightening. It's terrifying to have no pretences about yourself, yet that's what gives you the psychological resources to question all the rules ... what accounts for our creativity is that we constantly go deeper into ourselves than other people do.[53]

The search for the inner self, the peeling away of one's personality so one can question all the rules, this is how ad agencies represent themselves in

51 Hennion and Méadel, 1989: 208.
52 Hennion and Méadel, 1989: 208.
53 Coutu, 2000: 145.

order to claim credibly and legitimately that they can reconcile creativity and commerce.

As Bourdieu has argued, 'habitus' and 'fitting in' – having a feel for the game – can often be more important than formal education. Hence recruitment is done 'on the basis of "connections" and affinities of habitus, rather than formal qualifications'.[54] In most agencies, and surely at St Luke's, attitude is as closely monitored as actual performance. Part of the rhetoric is about constantly being on the move. For instance, St Luke's opened an office in Stockholm:

Why Stockholm? We didn't analyse the market to see whether there was an opportunity there. But we analysed ourselves and saw that we needed a bigger canvas for people to experiment on, and we needed a more diverse group of employees to produce more creative work. So we are going to Stockholm to set the creative process on fire by doing some intercultural experimentation. We are going to learn from people who were taught to think differently than we were and whose culture requires them to communicate in a different way. We are mixing the creative gene pool.[55]

In their work practice, people at St Luke's do unusual things. They intentionally de-stabilize the workplace in order to keep habit at arm's length. If you were an employee, on commencing working in the morning you would not know where you would be sitting in the office, and your contract and actual job might change without any notice. At St Luke's, everything is in constant flux. This is one way of dealing with the paradox of institutionalizing creativity. But, or course, it only works for a limited time before a new company will come along and be more frightening.

Today, no one is frightened of St Luke's anymore.

Performing brands

Because of the tensions within their industry and their organizations, and the ambiguities of their practices, advertisers have to engage in what Goffman, described as impression management. According to Goffman, when people offer a service, there will be precious little time available 'for eating the pudding that the proof can be found in'.[56] Hence the audience will be forced to

---

[54] Bourdieu, 1979/2007: 151.
[55] Coutu, 2000: 146.
[56] Goffman, 1959: 2.

accept certain symptoms and signs as indicators of the quality of the service and the seriousness of the provider. The provider will have to express these qualities and the audience will need to be impressed. This impression management is enacted in what Goffman has called 'setting'. The setting of an agency includes many things: agency staff are following an elaborate dress code that is somewhere between creative, smart, casual and professional. Whereas the expectation is for account managers to be more formal, creatives can wear ripped jeans to client meetings. It is key that the two balance each other out.

The actual office is another opportunity to set the scene for a convincing performance. Offices – preferably called studios – are usually located in edgy areas of the city. In most cases, this has little to do with the cost of rent, which would be the same elsewhere – at least in Sydney. It is more about signalling that the agency is where the next big thing will happen. While corporate clients prefer the prestige and convenience of the central business district (CBD), they rely on the buzz of the fringe to build their identity.

The importance of place is matched by studios' interior design, many of which are a veritable extravaganza. Take the Sydney office of Kastner & Partner, the global agency for Red Bull. Once you exit the lift, you are lost in a kind of mirror cabinet where you see nothing but reflections of yourself. On a small table you will find a little plastic toy that serves as doorbell. Once you squeeze it, one of the mirrors turns out to be a door, which opens, thereby inviting you into the agency. Inside, a fancy assemblage of furniture – including seventies chairs suspended from the ceiling and a fireplace that turns out to be a TV – makes you feel like you are in a twenty-first-century creative's *Alice in Wonderland*. Nothing is left to chance and everything, however prosaic, communicates. This extends to the mineral water that clients are served: preferably a fancy yet not generally well-known French brand.

These symbols of creativity are quite stereotypical and are shared by most agencies. Because of the limited repertoire that agencies use to perform their identity, clients can reasonably quickly understand a new agency in case of a change of accounts. For instance, agencies signal that they are passionate about their work with names such as Naked, Love, Mother or PLAY. Although some people might be truly passionate, the value of being passionate has been institutionalized in the industry and serves now as proxy for being creative. In fact, in order to perform certain tasks (such as making a presentation to clients), one has to display passion. As Goffman pointed out, the vocabularies that agencies use to create a certain impression are neither created by the agency nor by individuals. They are not invented but selected, learned and copied.

For Goffman, performance means sustaining a particular definition of the situation, and by extension, of what reality is.[57] Consequently, everything a performer does has to cement the framing that creates a certain reality. Thus in order to combat uncertainties, the performances of advertising agencies are highly ritualized and routinized.[58] What, then, are the rituals and routines of advertising agencies?

The process usually starts with a brief from the client. It covers objectives, audience profile, brand positioning, communication strategy, competitive intelligence and so on. The first hurdle for the agency is answering the brief in the form of a presentation. Often, this is a competitive process, and the presentations are, in fact, a pitch for the work. In this case, a significant amount of time, financial resources and intellectual property will be invested into the presentation; after all, the presentation has to outline a strategy and a detailed work programme to enable the client to make a decision. In a pitch presentation, an agency would usually avoid the risk of presenting highly subjective creative work. Rather, the approach taken is more likely to be rationalized through a methodology, process maps, strategy, scientific models, past experience and market intelligence. Of course, intimate knowledge about the consumer is key: it is the planner's role to 'unlock the rich inner world [of consumers] and discover consumers' hidden emotional connections to products and brands'.[59]

The success or otherwise of a pitch might be only loosely connected to its capacity to answer the brief. As Kristian Kreiner has shown, decisions in pitch situations are highly ambiguous: the reason for winning can be simultaneously the reason for losing.[60] The decision-making process is messy, as Kafka described so well:

When an affair has been weighed for a very long time, it may happen, even before the matter has been fully considered, that suddenly, in a flash the decision comes in some unforeseen place, that, moreover, can't be found any longer later on, a decision that settles the matter, if in most cases justly, yet all the same arbitrarily. It's as if the administrative apparatus were unable any longer to bear the tension, the year-long irritation caused by the same affair – probably trivial in itself – and hit upon the decision by itself, without the assistance of the officials.[61]

[57] Goffman, 1959: 85.
[58] Moeran, 2003; Malefyt, 2003. From an institutional perspective, see also Meyer and Rowan, 1977.
[59] Malefyt, 2003: 143.
[60] Kreiner, 2008.
[61] Kafka, 1922/1998: 70.

Once the agency has been appointed, workshops are an important vehicle for getting the project off the ground. They are especially important for the agency as they allow it to perform and demonstrate competency. Because most creative work is invisible to the client, workshops are important arenas for dramatizing the agency's performance. A process that might have taken several weeks' work is condensed to an hour or less of presentation time. Dozens of creative ideas that have been developed and dismissed don't make it into the final presentation. All the ideas that have fallen by the wayside cost time and money, though the clients do not see them and thus are reluctant to pay for them. Hence workshops provide some front-stage space where the ideas that count and the ones that were discounted can be performed. Lateral thinking, market insights, creative capacity and experience can be demonstrated in workshops much more effectively, as the client can witness how her brand is evolving in front of her eyes.

Malefyt describes how this is achieved through setting aside special off-site space; using a prepared agenda (including breakfast, in which everything is planned); and conducting several rounds of planned activities and brainstorming sessions (pairing client and agency employees for bonding, using role plays to create ambiguity and irony). All these carefully choreographed elements – even down to the language that is used and the models that are employed – result in an impression of the agency as being a highly competent organization.

The models that agencies employ are of special interest. Models or 'theories' such as Maslow's hierarchy of needs, are easy to understand while they simultaneously lend proceedings a scientific aura. They create credibility while breaking complex behaviours down into simple categories. Such maps of human needs and competitor products bring together strategy and marketing. For both the agency and the client, reality exists as an objective truth that has to be revealed – consumer preferences have to be discovered: 'From a marketing standpoint, people are supposed to be driven by needs, wants, and desires that can be fulfilled by buying and using a particular product. The task of marketers, then, is to seek out, appropriate, and then match the particular consumer need with the correct product or brand benefit.'[62]

By categorizing and boxing reality into a 2 × 2 matrix, one does not reveal any kind of truth. Rather, an ideal consumer is constructed through theorizing and abstracting. But something more important happens. What the agency defines through workshops is a frame of reference for future collaboration

---

[62] Malefyt and Moeran, 2003: 24.

with the client.[63] The map creates the territory it supposedly describes. Ideas about reality are jointly created and will be jointly defended. What has been established is a common sense-making mechanism – from now on, the world is read by both the client and the agency with the same new map.

Hence the real value of establishing consumer profiles, brand values and communication strategies

is not realised through the accuracy of representing the consumer or brand in any 'real' way, but rather, through the act of presenting and managing those representations toward some 'real' end with the client … It is the dynamic of finding and shaping information with the client that is essential to relationship building, rather than the actual content of what is being discovered.[64]

Once consumer behaviour and values have been categorized and hence simplified, both the client and the agency can imagine the consumer as a manageable entity. The unpredictable consumer has been transformed into a set of intelligible characters that are likely to respond in certain, predetermined paths.[65]

Those who produce value and creative output in agencies are not those who are best at dramatizing the performance. Most agencies are split into people who perform and people who do, because the activity and the representation of the activity require very different skills. Clients pay for the former, but they consume the latter. It is not about doing the job but making sure that it looks as if the job was done. Managing the impression is more important than managing the actual outcomes.

Integral to a convincing performance by an ad agency is the ability to conceal things from a client. A common example is the way in which agencies underplay the fact that they work for a profit, preferring instead for everyone to believe that it is a labour of love. Or they hide the fact that most of the pitch presentation promises far more than the agency is actually planning to deliver once the job is won. It is a common wisdom in agencies that, on the very day you win a client, you start losing the client. The performances also fall silent on the fact that uncertainty, ambiguity, risk and mistakes are an almost ineluctable part of any creative endeavour; strategic planning, backed up by research, is used to tell a consistent, coherent and logical story that makes the proposed solution seem the only possible one.

Performances conceal the fragility and arbitrariness of the actual process. That is not to say that advertisers do not talk about the creative journey as

---

[63] Malefyt, 2003: 151.
[64] Malefyt, 2003: 158.
[65] Malefyt, 2003: 152, with a reference to Stewart, 1993.

an adventure that was passionately lived through during late nights of working and brainstorming. But these are calculated risks – like cracks in the veneer that should distract from the real abyss. The performance highlights certain values that are hard to fake at the expense of others that are more easily 'negotiated': for instance, if service is about speed and quality, speed will be taken more seriously because a delay is hard to conceal, whereas quality problems can be hidden or attributed to other sources.[66] The ideal that will be adhered to is not the most important one or the one that determines success but the one that is most visible and legitimate.

Finally, the performance hides the fact that the agency is performing a routine process that has been done many times before. Clients want unique solutions and relationships, the story goes. The fact that this uniqueness is carefully cheorographed, and that the agency performs the same theatre with any other client, is written out of the picture.

In summary, the processes that are used in most agencies are highly routinized. We treat these processes not as explanation for how branding works but as symptoms of how the impossible task of matching supply and demand is (thought to be) accomplished. Branding experts resemble what Taleb has called 'non-experts': to manage brands would require managing uncertainties and complexities that are beyond the actual power of a brand manager. Hence they engage in all sorts of games to attribute failure to external events beyond their control and attribute success to skills.[67]

Myth of creativity

The creative revolution made creativity the key resource in agencies. How can we understand creativity? There are several clues that help us answer this question. First, advertising is a genre – a loose set of rules that provides a guiding framework for its enactment. As such, the genre puts limitations on possible ads. For example, the thirty-second TV commercial, a trade show or product sampling are all pre-scripted events that offer very limited flexibility. As the Vice Chairman and Creative Director of DDB, Matt Eastwood, explains in relation to TV ads:

There are clear conventions in marketing beer. First, there are lots of legalities, such as no one under twenty-five years can be shown in an ad, or alcohol cannot

---

[66] Goffman, 1959: 45.
[67] For useful strategies to avoid being blamed, see Taleb, 2007: 151–153.

be related to some kind of sexual conquest. These are the rules – but then there are conventions. Normally a beer ad shows four men drinking beer together. Why four? You don't show one guy drinking on his own because that means he is an alcoholic. Two is, to use a euphemism, gay. Three is an odd number for some reason. Four is a group of friends having a good time together. So it's always four. Being creative means playing within the conventions and coming up with a surprise – but that is a challenge. That's why 90 per cent of ads are simply boring!

Besides the constraints of the genre, the client's brief and marketing objectives are a serious impediment to being creative. Third, agencies are profit-oriented entities, so they usually try to enforce a tight regime on the amount of time and resources spent on a project. Fourth, the paradoxical internal structure of account manager and creatives working side by side often leads to tensions rather than creative outbursts. As Nixon summarizes:

Thus, despite the grandiose claims often made about the work they did or would like to have done, we might profitably interpret the rhetoric of creativity mobilised by creatives as an extrapolation of quite small differences or degrees of differences. In this sense, their cult of creativity was partly bound up with a 'narcissism of minor differences' [Freud] in which creative teams sought to differentiate themselves from other practitioners in the advertising they produced.[68]

After all, creative work might be more self-referential, where the agency is more concerned with impressing others within the ad community and gaining recognition through winning awards etc., which does not necessarily solve a client's problem but satisfies the 'narcissism of minor differences'. In fact, agencies are in fierce competition with each for awards, which add to an agency's reputational standing. They are the ephemeral measure for the equally ephemeral currency of creativity.[69]

Agencies do not necessarily choose to act according to scripts that depict them as creative. Individual agencies are but the peg with which collective ideals are hung temporarily. As Goffman says, identity is not in the peg: rather, agencies are consequences of a complex set of relations between commerce and culture.[70] They perform according to scripts they have not written, and their audiences are looking for clues that have little or nothing to do with real performance. These scripts legitimize agencies, and reduce complexity and anxiety for clients. Creativity is part of that script – but it is routinely

[68] Nixon, 2003: 77.
[69] The annual Gunn Report is a useful source – it creates a league table based on all major global awards. See www.gunnreport.com (accessed 17 June 2009).
[70] Goffman, 1959: 253.

enacted just like a bookie would engage in pseudo-scientific analysis of the race horses before the start signal.

Performing magic

The brand is the medium in which the representation of the product and the representation of the consumer overlap. The two start mirroring and reflecting each other. What happens is that a commodity like beer starts to take on the values of a certain target group, and the target group, in turn, starts building a relationship with the commodity. Williams quite rightly described this process of transforming a product into a brand as magic.[71]

Malinowski said that we can expect magic to occur when we engage in the pursuit of an important end but we are unsure about its outcomes or its chances of success. In these circumstances, magical practices help us to cope with uncertainty – offering a mental technique to 'bridge over the gap and inadequacies' of what we have not yet mastered.[72] In the face of uncertainty, magic is no longer an obscure practice but a quite rational course of action.

Magic in this context is understood as the private use of public symbols directed at individually chosen ends. According to Marcel Mauss' *General Theory of Magic,* three things need to work together to perform magic: the magician, magical representations and rituals.[73]

The magician herself is clouded in secrecy and mystery, set apart in a different space. This description easily fits our description of creatives; they live and work in different spaces, they are dressed differently and their most important asset is not necessarily their professional background but their habitus.[74]

At first, magical representations appear to be weird and unrelated; they are, in fact, organized through laws that are built on the principle of causality. Magic is akin to science before science happened. It is based on three fundamental laws: the law of contiguity, the law of similarity and the law of

[71] Williams, 1980/2008: 49: Branding is 'a highly organized and professional system of magical inducements and satisfactions, functional very similar to magical systems in simpler societies, but rather strangely coexistent with a highly developed scientific technology'. See also McCreery, 1995.

[72] Malinowksi, 1954.

[73] Mauss, 1902/2001.

[74] As Mauss argued, the magician needs to be confident: 'Behind Moses, who touched the bare rock, stood the whole nation of Israel, and while Moses may have felt some doubts, Israel certainly did not' (1902/2001: 161).

opposition.[75] Advertising has laws too: Maslow's hierarchy of needs is one of the most quoted and used laws; others are embedded in planning, branding and implementation processes, which are all logically related to each other. For instance, brand values supposedly engage the target audience; the target audience develops brand awareness; brand awareness then has an impact on purchase decisions, and so on. It is a long chain of cause-and-effect relations that make brand representations magical.

Finally, rituals are productive – they do what they say, they are performative. Not in the causal relationship between gesture and result though – the relation is more complex and expressed in terms such as brand equity. A magician is always worried about the result. So are advertisers. Thus they engage in evaluation exercises that set out to prove that their magic works real wonders and increases an organization's brand equity over time.

For instance, the brand guru and Marketing Professor David Aaker reports on research that found a correlation between return on investment, stock return and brand equity. For him and his co-author, '[t]he conclusion is clear: Brand equity, on average, drives stock return.'[76] Of course, every undergraduate student knows that a correlation does not explain what is cause and what is effect. Higher stock return could also drive brand equity. *Post hoc, ergo propter hoc* is a fallacy. Aaker seems to be the victim of his own fame; in his early days, he was a bit more critical. In 1980, he and his colleague wrote: 'looking for the relationship between advertising and sales is somewhat worse than looking for a needle in a haystack. Like the needle, advertising's effects, even when significant, are likely to be small.'[77]

Another often quoted example is Young & Rubicam's *Brand Asset Valuator*. It is build on a database of more than 13,000 brands from 33 countries that have been measured on 35 dimensions. The different dimensions in the *Brand Asset Valuator* are differentiation, relevance, brand strength, esteem, knowledge and stature. Besides the challenge of quantifying these subjective and qualitative properties, some characteristics are made up of the combination of two or more others. For instance, brand strength is the multiple of differentiation with relevance; stature is esteem multiplied with knowledge, and so on. Of course, there is very little rationale behind these equations, but since they are performed with great seriousness and accuracy, they are taken as truths.

[75] Mauss, 1902/2001: 79.
[76] Aaker and Joachimsthaler, 2002: 23.
[77] Aaker and Carman, 1980: 67.

Lindemann's evaluation of brand value was published by *The Economist* and offers yet another interesting example.[78] His calculation is quite mysterious: what he defines as brand value is simply the sum of all intangible assets in an organization that contribute to profit. Patents, trademarks, intellectual property, human capital and so on become part of the brand value.

Interbrand's yearly report on the Best Global Brands is slightly more complex, yet little more trustworthy. Interbrand determines the brand value as the sum of future earnings attributable to the brand, an analysis of how brands influence demand, and loyalty. It remains unclear how Interbrand can analytically differentiate between intangible earnings that derive from the brand and other intangible values such as human resources, goodwill, trademarks or patents.[79]

Not surprisingly, Interbrand's hit list of strong brands is not a reliable guide to the future: for instance, the 2007 report 'applaud[ed] the sense of leadership' at the 'blessed' Starbucks.[80] Similarly, Interbrand ranked Merrill Lynch, JP Morgan, Goldman Sachs and Morgan Stanley amongst their Top 40. 'The proven, straightforward and profound formula' to evaluate brands is obviously not as objective as Interbrand wants it to be.[81]

In fact, there seems no hard empirical evidence for or against the value of advertising and branding. Economists have, after almost 100 years of research, concluded that in certain industries there is a link between advertising and profitability, but it is impossible to establish a causal relation.[82] Most likely, companies that do well might advertise to create entry barriers and keep potential new market players out of the game.

So what to make of those evaluations? As Arvidsson puts it, the 'validity of these measurements is not so much guaranteed by their accuracy, as it is secured by their legitimacy'.[83] Evaluations are stories, and stories that are told always have a social function, as Mauss pointed out. The magician is authorized by society to perform certain rituals: 'he is a kind of official vested by society with authority, and it is incumbent upon the society to believe in him … He is serious about [magic] because he is taken seriously, and he

---

[78] Lindemann, 2003: 40–41.

[79] See, for a critical analysis of such evaluation from a tax and accounting perspective, Castedello and Schmusch, 2008.

[80] Interbrand, 2007: 4; see critically, www.economist.com/business/displaystory.cfm?story_id=10490218 (accessed 17 June 2009).

[81] Interbrand, 2007: 44. See also the profound analysis of Micheal Power (1992; 1997: 79–82).

[82] Bagwell, 2001; a second explanation from the economist's perspective is that brands act as market signals that help to overcome information asymmetries between producer and (potential) consumer. Brands increase confidence and lower search costs of users. See Erdem and Swait, 1998.

[83] Arvidsson, 2006: 134.

is taken seriously because people have need of him.'[84] Brand managers and advertisers are taken seriously for a similar reason: clients need them in the complex process of matching consumption and production.

Marketing as a discipline might not agree with our description of advertising as magical performance. Mainstream marketing (still) rationalizes behaviour and is looking for that law that makes you go to the theatre or buy stuff at a supermarket that Watson wanted to find.[85] Marketing has to deliver the discursive resources to continue the performance. As such, it has little interest in calling the game magic but is committed to provide players with arguments. After all, the show must go on.

Consequences

Advertising is about the production of differences. In ever so slightly changing fashion, these differences mediate between supply and demand, between product and desire, and ultimately between producer and consumer. As McCracken has suggested, advertising creates new cultural meanings by appropriating symbolic meanings from a non-advertising context and incorporating them in a commercial sphere.[86] Advertising is the avant-garde of capitalism. It is a machine that looks for differences that make a difference. It is an engine that creates exploitable differences.

The sole reason for producing differences is to move and change people: 'advertising has no reason to exist if it cannot move people towards something new'.[87] Advertising is institutionalized change through cultural production. It is a machine that transforms the excluded and peculiar into the included and normalized. Its searchlight is focused on the little side lanes and dead ends that society has created, in order to find exciting mutations of culture that it could re-introduce into consumption.

Advertising not only changes and influences reality but it actually creates reality. Take, for instance, the practice of segmenting markets. Advertisers would argue that they simply divide what they find out there. That's not

---

[84] Mauss, 1902/2001: 119.

[85] The theory of planned behaviour, for instance, provides a framework for analysing the determinants of behaviour and decision-making; at the heart of the theory is the assumption that people behave rationally. In one application, even shoplifting is understood as consumption, and shoplifters are understood as highly rational decision-makers: they 'calculate the costs and benefits of crime and select the alternative with the highest utility' (Tonglet, 2002: 337).

[86] McCracken, 1986.

[87] Kemper, 2003: 38.

quite true. Segmenting actively creates an audience with certain characteristics: 'to segment a market is to create a market segment, not merely respond to an existing one'.[88] In their book *Was There a Pepsi Generation before Pepsi Discovered It?*, Stanley C. Hollander and Richard Germain come to the same conclusion: advertising constitutes what it ostensibly researches.[89]

Advertising also creates blueprints for lifestyles that ultimately become ours. Kemper has shown in his study of advertising in Sri Lanka that advertisers create a certain image of society. The ad shows locals what it means to be Sri Lankan. This image is then projected and consumed by Sri Lankans, who have to build it into their sense of place and self. Even if they reject it, they have to position themselves vis-à-vis the billboard.

Olsen tells the story of the Intimate Apparel Company and how it started selling Warner Bras to younger customers. Key to its success was a promotion booklet with the promising title 'Fifty Ways to Please Your Lover'. Next to glossy full-colour ads of models, their heads thrown back and revealing their cleavage, the copy says '... you feel more like a woman with Warner's underneath'.[90] Obviously, this creates the image of woman as object whose first duty it is to attract males. To do so, the woman needs the brand that allows her to feel like a woman and live 'the objectified feminine ideal' as defined by a male gaze.[91] The Warner Bra moved from a commodity to a brand that gives people identity. Of course, Warner Bra would say it allows women to be who they are and continues the sexual liberation of women. In any case, the brand starts to actively influence and shape people's identities.

When Bacardi launched its alco-pops, it targeted young teens (above the legal age, of course) and showed them how much fun fun could be with the right drink. The three s-values of sun, sea and sand (and sex as the fourth, unofficial one) taught people how to party and what it means to have a good time.

If advertising is such a powerful instrument, is it advertising agencies that control that power? Do they play a panoptic role in the production of consumer culture? Is advertising only the visible part of a much larger conspiracy to control the world? The story goes like this:

Historically advertising has played a leading role in normalising consumption as symbolic social practice and in legitimising the power of corporations (Marchand 1998). That it has done so is due in considerable part to the techniques of consumer

---

[88] Kemper, 2003: 38.
[89] Hollander and Germain, 1993.
[90] Olsen, 2003: 124.
[91] Olsen, 2003: 129.

surveillance and disciplinary control learned and understood by advertising agency professionals. In this sense, advertising agencies act as a panoptic cultural influence in the service of the corporations.[92]

The logic behind this argument is seductive: as Sandage argues, 'it is a proper and justifiable social goal to help consumers maximise their satisfaction. In rendering such help, advertisers must become knowledgeable about the needs, wants and aspirations of consumers and make certain that the object of their informative and persuasive efforts is capable of giving satisfaction.'[93] Thus advertising agencies employ every type of researcher, from discourse analysts to anthropologists, to study consumers in their local contexts. They interview them, they video them, they go through their rubbish, they record their habits, they test their responses, they observe their behaviour, they study their thoughts and they analyse their relationships. The arsenal of social research methods is unleashed in order to understand 'the entire, complex, full social role involved in being a consumer of a particular product'.[94]

The justification of this detective work is that advertising is a classical liberal institution that enlightens mankind: 'Advertising is a friend of the market because it provides information and fosters competition. We *all* benefit.'[95]

Do we really? Critical theorists argue that advertising builds up a massive library of cultural consumer knowledge – and this, in the words of Hackley, enables advertising to be 'an ideological force': 'creative work in advertising can only be effective or striking to the extend that it taps into the cultural meanings and practices of local consumption communities'.[96] The more it does so, the more effective its campaigns. Because the cultural repositories are hidden from the public, they are especially powerful: 'Consumers can see the puppets but not the strings.'[97] This results in an image of advertising as disciplinary machine where 'consumer identities are formed, fantasies of the self are fulfilled and relations reproduced with each successive engagement with the advertising/marketing complex … Advertising acts as an ideological virus that reaches constitutively into consumers' psychology.'[98]

I think you've got the idea: advertising is a kind of dark machinery that exploits culture and manipulates people's identity. Its basis of power is its

[92] Hackley, 2002: 223.
[93] Sandage, 1972/1990: 7.
[94] Costa, 1995: 218.
[95] Rotzoll *et al.*, 1986/1990: 38.
[96] Hackley, 2002: 214.
[97] Hackley, 2002: 214.
[98] Hackley, 2002: 218 and 222.

immense knowledge repertoire: the more that is known about people, the more ways there are of influencing and manipulating them.

It is true that advertising agencies research the infinitesimal. Unfortunately, de Certeau was wrong when he said that only what is used is measured, not *how* it is used.[99] Agencies collect a tremendous amount of knowledge about *how* consumers do things. But is this knowledge really translated into control mechanisms? We'd argue that knowledge serves other functions *as well* – and these other functions might well compete with each other.

As we have mentioned already, models and maps are the medium that helps advertisers bond with the client. Knowledge creates a shared frame, a shared definition of reality, and as long as it is sustained, both the client and the agency will work together. In this respect, knowledge helps to make sense of the world – but it does not necessarily impact on it as much as its critics fear and advertisers wish for.

A second function of knowledge is strategic. In order to build a distinct market position in competition with other agencies, knowledge is a reasonably tangible point of difference. While creativity is hard to judge, consumer insights can be collected, printed and bound. As such, knowledge will rationalize the consumption and legitimize actions taken by the client to manage it. This also implies that knowledge will be collected and edited with an eye on its ability to be consumed by time-poor executives. In such reports, accuracy will be less important than plausibility, and the sensational will replace the empirical. This kind of knowledge might offer only a poor launch pad for the increased exercise of power.

Finally, and this is a very powerful driver, agencies might collect knowledge not because it is useful for their actual branding work but simply because other agencies do so too.[100] As an important part of their performance, agencies study consumer trends and patterns. Research becomes part of the props used on stage: it makes the play more spectacular but not necessarily more effective.

So does advertising knowledge function like a panopticon? We think this hypothesis is not wrong but is too strong. Advertising might perform magic, but it cannot perform the miracle of controlling society totally.

Advertising is an engine of difference: it is (to use Askegaard's phrase again) a hegemonic form of diversity. This means it is a form of power that is

---

[99] De Certeau, 1980/1984: 34.
[100] This is the argument of isomorphism. See DiMaggio and Powell, 1983.

both hegemonic *and* productive. The concept of the panopticon expresses the former aspect very well because it does not pay enough attention to the latter. We will use the concept of lifestyle to explore both aspects and relate them to the power of branding. (See part III.)

Postscript: media buyers

Advertising has reinvented itself through the creative revolution, chasing that Big Idea. It started to focus on the messages, trying to come up with ever-snappier, happier images and copy. Of course, this is a game that is subject to the law of diminishing returns: while the audience's expectations grow with each round, the agency resources and client budgets remain the same – which makes for an unhappy end. Indeed, what we can observe is the rise of media planning agencies that start to take over the role of advertising agencies as guardians of the brand.[101]

Media planners started off as an unglamorous branch of the industry. They were its ugly child. Their reason for being was that they purchased media space in bulk and could therefore provide cheaper rates for advertising agencies' clients. This was neither strategic nor sexy. But then, towards the millennium, ad agencies experienced increasing competition from media buyers.

One of the reasons for the newfound love between clients and media buyers was the contracting economy. In 1996, only 1.32% of the British gross domestic product was spent on ads; five years earlier it was 1.6%. In 1993, employment in the ad industry reached a thirty-year low. Ad agencies that had led the field found themselves under increasing pressure. Clients pushed for more accountability and clear planning. But ad agencies, with their reliance on creativity, performance and magic, were ill-equipped to play the new (language) game. That was exactly when media buyers entered the scene more assertively.

A second, maybe even more important development was the fragmentation of communication channels. In 1980, there was only one commercial TV channel in the UK, offering 88 minutes of ads per day. In 1993, there were 15 channels, offering more than 1,500 minutes of ad broadcasting per day. Commercial radio stations grew from 26 in 1980 to 125 in 1992.[102] With the advent of the internet and the further development of information and

---

[101] Nixon, 2003, Tungate, 2007.
[102] Nixon, 2003: 45.

communication technology, the fragmentation of the media landscape has exploded. Today, you not only have specialized media but increasingly influential social media, including publication media (Wikipedia), sharing media (Youtube), networking media (Facebook), entertaining media (World of Warcraft), virtual world media (Second Life), and so on.

Ad men need only have read McLuhan's book *Understanding Media* to page 9 to learn that the medium is the message 'because it is the medium that shapes and controls the scale and form of human association and action'.[103] So, whoever controls the medium controls the message. If they had kept reading, they would have found another interesting piece of information in regard to changing media: 'it is the framework itself that changes with new technology, and not just the picture within the frame'.[104]

Context is king: the web or mobile phone screens are not only new media but they also demand the creation of new content. The short thirty-second TV commercial that ad agencies got used to did not work in the new framework. Media buyers stepped in and reached out for the hand of the client to guide them through the new media landscape. They promised the client they would lead them through the jungle of new channels and develop the right content for each one. Understanding the medium was more important than having one Big Idea. In fact, lots of small ideas that worked their way through micro-media were much more effective.

As is so often the case with the topic of branding, practice is ahead of theory. I interviewed Gary Hardwick, founder of Ikon Communications, a media planning business established in 1999. Nine years after its establishment, Ikon employed several hundred people and was regarded as one of the most innovative players in the field. Gary explains how the industry looked when he started out: 'Up until mid to the end of the 1990s, media was traded as a commodity – an afterthought to creative thinking; creative first, media second. The media process was too far down the food chain. The creative process dictates that we should do TV, and media planning simply booked space.'

Of course, for an ambitious media planner such as Gary, this was hardly a satisfying situation. 'We tried to change the industry and how we were positioned in the food chain. We thought of media planning as a consulting service. The key question was: Would it be more important to think of the context

[103] McLuhan, 1964/2006: 9.
[104] McLuhan, 1964/2006: 238.

where the brand is placed, and then think of content?' Put in another way, the media buying industry took McLuhan literally.

How did Gary's firm innovate and change the industry?

First, we introduced a better understanding of consumers. We looked at existing databases about consumer insights and filled the gaps for new channels, such as online, experiential, mobile or sponsorship. We looked at all channels – basically at everything that could be used to communicate a brand, from mobile phone screen to Olympic Games. Second, we wanted to be media neutral. In the old days, media agencies got a percentage – normally 10 per cent – of their media placement as revenue. We did not want to share media commissions because you're likely to recommend channels that make you money. But you would not recommend sponsorship or experiential because you would not get a fat commission – despite the fact that this might be best for the client. So we got rid of the normal commission structure and sold us as fee-for-service business. We agreed on a profit share with clients and benefited when sales or brand awareness levels went up. Clients have a right to audit our books, so it's all 100 per cent transparent: there are no kickbacks from big media networks. Third, we introduce flexible media dealing. Usually media agencies placed all bookings at the beginning of the year. We invented a more dynamic trading system like at the stock market. Of course, because media planners bought millions in advance, they had to push money to that network where they still had space towards the end of the year they dealt with – regardless of changes in the market. Finally, we changed the internal culture of typical media buyers and motivated our team by linking 20 to 25 per cent of their salary directly to outcomes of our clients – so they were really sharp in negotiating.

Not surprisingly, Gary did not make a lot of friends in the industry: 'Other media buyers and networks hated us – but clients loved it! Because we were audited, we could prove that our dynamic trading principle gives you better return on investment.'

In the long run, these new strategies led to change in the industry.

We try to understand the motivation of consumers with Maslow's hierarchy of needs. While this is not new, we think innovatively about the channels through which you can touch consumers and where they might be more receptive. For instance, we did the campaign for Commonwealth Bank [one of Australia's Big Four banks] to promote an optimistic brand image though the message 'Everyday is a New Day'. In this case, we were looking for uplifting media; you don't go for news because you cannot control the context in which your ad will be aired. Rather, you try to put the message in a happy environment.

Indeed, the medium is the message.

Media planners such as Ikon also pioneered new ways of measuring impact. Advertising never really got much further than the old saying '50 per cent of your expenditure will be effective – we just don't know which half'. Media planners thought differently: 'You have to prove that ads are an investment, not cost. Marketing managers become almost paranoid that their status would be dwindling unless they could prove that they contribute to the bottom line. The key is accountability: you need tools and software to measure impact and provide proof.' Media planning, with its background in analysing how many people watch which programme when, has an intrinsic advantage over creatives.

Ad agencies were taken by surprise with this new thinking. They still loved their thirty-second TV commercial. They overlooked the fact that content could be used online, in shopping centres or as mobile soap operas (called mobisoaps). The big ad agencies were not flexible enough to create media-driven communication. A lot of smaller, more specialized agencies popped up to do exactly that. However, they are controlled and orchestrated by the media planning agency that guards the brand. As Gary says, 'the link between business and brand is owned by the media agency'. The Big Idea turns into lots of small ideas that can come from any point in the network and that flow through any channel.

The global ad agency McCann-Erickson has an rather naïve (or cynical) slogan that reads: 'The Truth Well Told'. While this might have been the role of agencies in the past, the future will be different. Multiple conversations, many of them consumer-led, will form the polyphony out of which brands emerge. Rather than 'The Truth Well Told', brands will grow around 'Stories Well Shared'.

Part II

How brands transform management

4 Identity

Trailer I

In the second part of this book, we argue that brands offer new, compelling ways of thinking about managing organizations. We argued in Chapter 2 that brands are often understood as new management tools or corporate catalysts that restructure organizations. While we do not always share the optimism of some of our colleagues that brands will make organizations more effective, we want to explore the implications and unintended consequences for management practice and theory.

This chapter draws on the notion of identity and argues that brands are identities-in-action that allow stability to be maintained while simultaneously enabling change. Chapter 5, 'Culture', takes as its point of departure the idea that brands are enacted in the behaviour of organizational members. The brand becomes the 'way we do things around here'; in short, an organization's culture and its brand become intrinsically related to each other. Finally, Chapter 6 explores the way external, open-source communities crystallize around brands and co-create new ideas, services and products. In this view, the brand becomes the medium that connects internal cultures and external communities.

Identity, culture and innovation are but three concepts that are transformed through branding. Whether these transformations create more effective or fairer organizations I cannot say *a priori* from the comfort of my office chair, but it seems tempting for many writers to understand brands as the latest tool slotting neatly into the manager's repertoire, improving efficiency and effectiveness. Brands could have ambiguous effects on management practice, however. As in Johann Wolfgang von Goethe *Sorcerer's Apprentice*, tools tend to develop a life of their own. In Goethe's poem, the apprentice performs magic and transforms a broom into his servant – who is soon out of control. When the apprentice cuts the broom into two, all he does is create two brooms that are twice as hard to control. The apprentice's famous cry, 'The spirits I summoned, I can't get rid of them!' serves as reminder that what looks like a solution for today might turn into tomorrow's problem. Hence we will keep a critical eye on some of the unintended consequences that brands might bring about.

We will start our journey by looking at city brands in general, and then zooming in on the newly developed Edinburgh City brand as case study. The case study will show how the making of identity can be described as a practice that is framed by the notion of the brand.

City brands

For Balzac, Paris was an organism that could not be exhausted: 'Paris is indeed an ocean. Sound it: you will never touch bottom. Survey it, report on it! However scrupulous your surveys and reports, however numerous and persistent the explorers of this sea may be, there will always remain virgin places, undiscovered caverns, flowers, pearls, monsters – there will always be something extraordinary, missed by the literary diver.'[1]

His description of the Paris of 1834 sees the city not as territory that can be surveyed but as ocean. Nothing could be further from Balzac's view than the dominant logic shared by many contemporary city managers. Those

---

[1] Balzac, 1834/1962: 17.

virgin places, undiscovered caverns, flowers, pearls and monsters need to be captured and talked about. Increasingly, city managers see cities as competing entities on a global battlefield for talent, trade and tourism. In order to succeed in this struggle, cities have to position themselves as attractive and prosperous identities. The most effective tool for doing so is crafting a city brand: in fact, cities re-imagine themselves as brands.[2]

Competition between cities is, of course, not a new phenomenon. From ancient Greece to Machiavelli's Italy, city-states were in competition with each other for power, influence and wealth. What is new is the global scale of the competition, made possible through league tables and city rankings that have been mushrooming in recent years. For instance, the Globalization and World Cities (GaWC) Research Network Leading World Cities Index from 2004 identifies London and New York City as clear leaders, followed by Los Angeles, Paris and San Francisco. Incipient global cities were Amsterdam, Boston, Chicago, Madrid, Milan, Moscow and Toronto, and global niche cities included Hong Kong, Singapore and Tokyo (financial) and Brussels, Geneva and Washington, DC (political and social).

Similarly, the Worldwide Centers of Commerce Index ranks global cities as follows: London, New York, Tokyo, Chicago, Hong Kong, Singapore, Frankfurt, Paris, Seoul and Los Angeles.[3] Anholt's City Brand Index ranks Sydney before London, Paris, Rome, New York, Washington DC, San Francisco, Melbourne, Barcelona and Geneva.[4] These league tables first and foremost create competition. They 'measure' the success of cities, compare them and in doing so create winners, losers and those in between.

The Fortune 500 nirvana for cities is attaining the status of global city. According to Sassen, global cities are centres for management of the global economy; they provide advanced services and telecommunication facilities to support the management of the global economy; and they serve as headquarters for global corporations.[5] Sassen regards global cities as important drivers of globalization. The implication is clear: a city manager is under considerable pressure to move up those league tables and establish the city in question as a regional, if not global, heavyweight. As we shall see, cities such as Edinburgh start to develop brands to deal with these new challenges. It seems that those persistent explorers of which

---

[2] For an overview of city branding, see van Ham, 2001; Patteeuw, 2002; Caldwell and Freire, 2004; Trueman *et al.*, 2004; for a more critical account, see Greenberg, 2008.
[3] Mastercard, 2007.
[4] Anholt City Brands Index, 2006.
[5] Sassen, 1991.

Balzac spoke finally managed to produce 'scrupulous surveys and reports' that crystallize in the city brand: the brand is the medium and the tool for creating that identity.

The Edinburgh 'Inspiring Capital' brand

Ailsa Falconer is Edinburgh's Inspiring Capital City Region brand manager. She is the first brand manager the city has employed in its long and august 1,000-year history. Prior to joining the local administration, Ailsa worked for ten years at branding giant Unilever. Her colleague, Lesley Martin, works as team leader for strategy and economic development of Edinburgh.[6]

'Edinburgh has to keep pushing boundaries and cannot rest on its laurels,' Ailsa explains. 'We cannot afford to stand still – we face an increasingly competitive global marketplace for trade, tourism and talent, and if we want to succeed we have to be innovative and take the lead.' As one strategic document explains, '[w]e have to shout even louder to be heard and do more to ensure that we stand out from the crowd'.[7] In order to attract the '3 Ts' (trade, talent and tourists) Edinburgh must present itself in the 'most powerful and vivid way possible'.[8] Developing Edinburgh as a brand is seen as the vehicle for doing so: 'Key to destination and business success is the building and maintaining of robust brand values. With consumer choice leaning to highly branded destinations, it is the brand strategy that will help to determine who is successful in today's competitive business environment.'[9]

The brand delivers against this promise in several respects. First, the brand makes it possible to compete with other cities. As Lesley tells, the Royal Bank of Scotland has had its headquarters in Edinburgh since 1695. A strong brand that attracts global top talent is key to keeping such an important employer in town. Second, the brand develops a sense of identity that goes beyond council boundaries. While the jurisdiction and the powers of the City Council are clearly limited, the brand does not stop at political boundaries. In fact, the Edinburgh brand includes some 1.2 million people, whereas the City Council itself manages just about half a million. Third, the brand creates an identity beyond those administrative boundaries: the brand becomes the heart of the

[6] The story is based on an interview with Ailsa conducted on 18 April 2008, an interview with Lesley on 2 May 2008 and a detailed analysis of strategy and branding documents of the Edinburgh City administration.
[7] See www.edinburghbrand.com/why_a_brand; (accessed 1 May 2008).
[8] City of Edinburgh, 2007.
[9] See www.edinburghbrand.com/why_a_brand; (accessed 1 May 2008).

shared identity. All communication activities are aligned around the brand – the Council, tourism organizations, the convention bureau, the visitors centre and other organizations use the brand to talk about Edinburgh's identity. The brand defines an identity and a set of values that everybody supports – or at least is urged to support.

What, then, is the brand identity of Edinburgh? The essence of the brand is 'Inspiring Capital'. Inspiration alludes to Edinburgh as 'a dramatic city bursting with ideas and life', Ailsa explains.

There is a drama and magical quality to the city for many people, and it is a place that stimulates the senses and imagination. It is a city of contrasts, with a special atmosphere as a result. Its natural beauty and intellectual tradition have been a springboard for invention and creativity. From the festivals to the telephone and from Dolly the sheep to Harry Potter – Edinburgh clearly inspires. Therefore it is inspiration that is at the heart of the Edinburgh brand.

The second part of Edinburgh's essence – 'Capital' – works through its ambiguity. It promotes Edinburgh as capital of Scotland but also stresses other capitals – social, cultural, political and financial – as being naturally at home in Edinburgh.

Edinburgh's brand identity is characterized by several different values that, taken cumulatively, contribute to a clearly defined brand personality. In the case of Edinburgh, this is particularly complicated as 'it is very hard to put a finger on personality and atmosphere,' as Ailsa recalls.

The key values of the brand are described as follows:

Our research also established a set of values that are distinctively Edinburgh, which reflect past strengths and future ambitions … We hope you will use them to challenge your behaviour and make sure that you've considered each value in turn. The values are an important part of delivering an Edinburgh experience. The values are:

- 'Inventive Visionary' – Edinburgh excels in the arts, science, business and education
- 'Rich Diversity' – Edinburgh has a vibrant and cosmopolitan culture with a great mix of people and skills – all within a setting of inspiring architecture and natural beauty.
- 'Striving For Excellence' – Edinburgh and Scotland share this work ethic, which drives the city's past successes and future ambitions.
- 'Sincere Warmth' – Edinburgh people extend a helpful, genuine welcome to all.
- 'Understated Elegance' – Edinburgh is not boastful or arrogant about its achievements, but quietly confident in everything it does.[10]

---

[10] See www.edinburghbrand.com/why_a_brand; (accessed 1 May 2008).

Ailsa explains:

If we want to strive for excellence, the brand needs an element of stretch. Of course it cannot go as far that the elastic breaks, but it has to stretch. Just claiming 'excellence' would not work because a brand has to inspire and motivate always. You can never arrive at your brand, you always have to develop and morph towards it.

This is an important point – the brand is not simply the essence that reflects what is but is also an idealized image of the identity that one strives to become.

Ailsa stresses that the brand is not merely a logo, a colour or a font – instead it encompasses everything Edinburgh and its people do. Therefore the task of bringing the brand alive extends far beyond printing brochures and airing ads. 'Of course the logo is important,' she concedes.

People interpret it in all sorts of ways. It is supposed to depict lines of influence spreading out from the past, into the present and future. People read it differently, though: they see all sorts of things in it, including fireworks, economic curves, hills, back scratchers, golf driving ranges, the rail bridge … you name it, I've heard it! It is not one dimensional like a castle but means many things. This is a positive thing.

The brand captures, controls and channels everything that expresses the identity of Edinburgh. For instance, the tone of voice of Edinburgh is minutely defined. The following quote attests to the level of detail involved:

Tone of voice means how we say what we say. The words we use send signals about us – they show our audience what we represent as a brand and helps them to understand what we stand for. The way we talk as a brand is as important as the way we look … We are a bright and imaginative city – bursting with talent and creativity. We should use words that reflect this imagination. Bold, striking headlines that grab the imagination, question our assumptions and challenge us to think differently. We use vibrant words that capture people's enthusiasm and create the same impact as seeing the city for the first time. Our headlines should be alive with excitement – we let our passion and enthusiasm shine though. We have a sense of self-belief; we are direct and accurate in what we say but we always display a sense of modesty. If we are talking about an aim or goal, we are direct, matter-of-fact and use correct statistics. We don't need to use excessive exclamations or gushing descriptions. We are straightforward and authentic. We don't use complicated jargon and abbreviations that no one understands. We give clear and decisive directions with what we describe, we are respectful of others – we try not to assume. We use simple and direct words, we try to write in a warm style that is understood and appeals to all.[11]

---

[11] See www.edinburghbrand.com/why_a_brand; (accessed 1 May 2008).

Bringing the brand alive includes everything – from the look of graphics to language, from behaviour to advertising. Thus the brand exercises power by prescribing not only what is said but also how it is said.

The Edinburgh brand is being used beyond the city administration. Ailsa is proud that BAA (which runs Edinburgh Airport), the Edinburgh Chamber of Commerce, VisitScotland and other key organizations have adopted the brand. The unifying objective of the brand is to try and ensure that these different actors talk about Edinburgh consistently. As Ailsa says, '[i]f a key person gives speeches overseas we try to weave all the brand messages in'. This is a powerful intervention that is facilitated and legitimized through the brand.

According to the proponents of the exercise, the outcomes of the branding work are a triptych – the brand is good for people, good for business and good for tourism. It is 'good for the people of Edinburgh', Ailsa explains, because

the brand will help to attract even more employers, giving people improved chances to earn, learn and progress in their careers. The brand will also create renewed pride in the city, and a sense of what it means to belong here. And finally there's the chance to enjoy yourself even more – as a greater variety of sports, cultural and leisure opportunities come to the city.

It is good for tourism, she continues, for a simple reason: 'with everyone saying the same things about the City Region, more tourists will visit Edinburgh and its surrounding areas'.[12]

And it's good for business and investors as it will help to encourage inward investment. Lesley Martin, the city's economic development manager, mentions that Edinburgh already possessed a strong brand as 'Edinburgh – Festival City' that needed to change towards a stronger recognition of the importance of business and science to Edinburgh. With that comes a focus on new sectors of the economy, such as creative industries. The new brand is a clear sign that Edinburgh is moving forward and developing in this direction. As Lesley put it, 'the brand created a sense of confidence in moving forward and giving us a place in the world'.

Looked at from distance, it sounds as if the brand is the answer to all the problems Edinburgh is facing. It also sounds as if it has taken the place of other ways of making sense of the city. Of course, it hasn't. Although, as discourse, branding spreads virally across the globe, individual managers will interpret and use the concept selectively. While there are doubtlessly various

[12] See www.edinburghbrand.com/why_a_brand; (accessed 1 May 2008).

degrees of freedom in the enactment of brands, they represent a new way of talking about cities that will influence managers' mental maps of their world. In turn, these mental maps will inform their actions.

The making of identity

Ailsa and her team are engaged in a process of identity creation for Edinburgh. Of course, this is not to say that Edinburgh did not have an identity *per se* prior to their efforts; it is a more a recognition that Edinburgh City is now engaged in a concerted managerial effort to create and manage its identity. The German philosopher Martin Heidegger has described identity as fundamentally embedded in its context.[13] He coined the rather fancy phrase of 'being-in-the-world' or *Dasein* to express this idea. *Dasein* is not in the world like water is in the bottle; rather, *Dasein* is always concerned about and caught up in its projects and activities. Initially, it is through engagement and involvement that we understand the world. Heidegger argues that we have lost this initial way of engaging with our environment. The division between object and subject, or Descartes' *res cogitas* and *res extensa*, is artificial and separates us from the world. This modern perspective is only one mode of knowing – the scientific – that has disengaged itself from being-in-the-world. When Ailsa defines Edinburgh's brand identity, she first has to transform Edinburgh into an object that becomes a manageable unit. Being-in-the-world – or for our matter, being-in-a-city – always means being entangled in the activities that are occurring. One has a sense of, and is part of, the identity of a place. The discourse of brands changes the way we think of and engage in cities fundamentally.

Edinburgh is looked at from a distance – through league tables, charts, numbers and comparisons. This removed perspective produces a divide between the subject (the brand manager) and the object (Edinburgh). The object can then be analysed and populated with qualities and values. The brand becomes the medium that engages us with the world as it defines who we are in relation to others.

As such, brands can be seen as a mechanism for creating identity. Further, brands can help us think about identity differently. This is the moral of our story of Edinburgh: when managers think about identity, they do not do it in abstract terms. Rather, when they talk about identity, they work on the

[13] Heidegger, 1927/1993.

brand. In fact, as in the case of Edinburgh, the identity and the brand become mutually constitutive concepts. Identity is constructed, negotiated and contested within the framework of the brand. The brand provides the language and the conceptual framework for thinking about identity. In other words, the brand is the tool used to actively manage and model identity.

As such, the brand exercises power: it reduces the myriad of possible values and images that Edinburgh features to four key values. By defining a homogenous brand, events, people and things are written in and out of the city. The 'Inspiring Capital' brand rehearses the city of castles, palaces, smart bars, architecture and the festival. The Edinburgh of *Trainspotting* or *DI Rebus* is written out of the image. The city is, therefore, represented in a particular way. There is no mention of the under-belly and the dark side of drug abuse and illicit crime. The brand casts the city as a consumption hub for the well off. The brand casts Edinburgh's identity in terms that high-income earners would classify as 'good lifestyle'. Branding is thus a unitarist exercise – one that writes out class, diversity, spaces and representations. It writes in cosmopolitanism: where spaces of the city become a work and playground for designers, architects, property developers, financiers, marketers and other global flaneurs. As unitarist exercise, branding needs to be analysed critically.

Identity after Plato

Identity is not just a nice-to-have thing. Identity as conceptualized by the brand strategist lays claim to the strategic leadership of the entire business: 'The strategic imperative concept suggests that the brand identity should drive the business strategy … The strategic imperatives play a key role because they usually introduce some hard choices and lead to the consideration of key options and core issues facing the organization.'[14] The example of the Edinburgh brand illustrates this claim: the brand captures the identity of an organization – or an entire city – and becomes the driver for the overall strategy While the leadership claim of brands is new, their concept of identity isn't.

In his famous story of the cave, Plato argues that all we as humans are capable of seeing are shadows while the truth is in the sun, in eternal ideas. The physical world around us is fickle and ever-changing. Stability is in the world of

---

[14]   Aaker and Jochimsthaler, 2002: 74.

ideas alone. He draws a sharp dividing line between what is visible and what is intelligible. The true identity of things is stable, a never-changing essence. If we experience change, it is because we mistake the shadows for the real things.

Looking at the concept of organizational identity almost 2,500 years later, not much seems to have changed. In their frequently cited paper of 1985, Albert and Whetten argue that identity is central, distinctive and enduring.[15] In a later contribution, Whetten identified the distinguishing attributes of identity as what makes the organization unique: as 'attributes used by an organization to positively distinguish itself from others'.[16] Central and enduring attributes of identity are those that 'are manifested as an organization's core programmes, policies and procedures, and that reflect its highest values. Attributes that have passed the test of time or on some other basis operate as "irreversible" commitments.'[17] Identity is something that has withstood the test of time and is enduring and stable. The true identity is invisible and eternal, while the visible reality is merely a changing reflection of the essence. Like the shadow on the walls of the cave, change is an illusion that does not touch the heart of things. Maybe Plato was right – some things, among them the definition of identity, might never change.

The identity concept in the branding literature parallels the one in organization studies. When brand theorists and practitioners think of brands, they still use a Platonic model.[18] For instance, Aaker suggests: 'Brand identity is a unique set of brand associations that the brand strategist aspires to create or maintain. These associations represent what the brand stands for and imply a promise to customers from organization members.'[19] The core identity is thought of as 'the central, timeless essence of the brand'.[20] For Kapferer, identity is the brand's 'innermost substance'.[21] It is 'the center that remains after you peel away the layers of an onion'.[22] Brands are about the 'truth' and 'authenticity'[23] – they are the soul of the organization, controlled and managed by the brand strategist.

---

[15] Albert and Whetten, 1985; it is important to note that organization theorists including Mary Jo Hatch, Majken Schultz, Andrew Brown, Jane Dutton, Janet Dukerich and others have developed more refined notions of identity that we will discuss shortly (see Corley *et al.*, 2006).

[16] Whetten, 2006: 222.

[17] Whetten, 2006: 222.

[18] As Csaba and Bengtsson (2006) argue, brand management literature fails to engage with the intellectual origins of the identity concept.

[19] Aaker, 1996: 68.

[20] Aaker, 1996: 68.

[21] Kapferer, 1997.

[22] Aaker, 1996: 85.

[23] See, for instance, Nadeau, 2007.

The marketing gurus Al Ries and Jack Trout argued that we live in an 'overcommunicated society'. Hence the brand identity needs to be succinctly summarized in an 'oversimplified' positioning statement. As they put it: 'The only defense a person has in our overcommunicated society is an oversimplified mind.'[24] This idea legitimized treating consumers like infants who had to be presented with clear perceptions of the brand. And to cut through 'the traffic jam in the prospect's mind, you must use Madison Avenue [advertising] techniques'.[25] Of course, one could argue that Madison Avenue was part of the problem and not the solution: surely modern advertising techniques created the overcommunicated society that Ries and Trout lament. Their remedy is to communicate more succinctly by developing unique identity positions for each brand. Again, the fundamental assumption is that identity is the central, distinctive and enduring feature of a product or an organization. In more philosophical terms, identity represents self-sameness.

The identity paradox

In his 1957 lecture *The Principle of Identity*, Heidegger argues that identity is not the self-sameness of A as A. Being cannot be reduced to the identical. The formula $A = A$ expresses only the belonging-togetherness of A with A. To propose that $A = A$ is to already assume that there is a distinction between the first A and the second A. For Heidegger, the principle of identity should be expressed as A with A. Repetition is not possible, hence difference is more fundamental than identity, unity or sameness: in fact, difference is the basis of identity. This is exactly how branding builds identity – from differences.

Difference points at the relation between things. Identity is always relational: it evolves out of the interaction between self and other. As we have seen with the coaching example in Chapter 2, the Other was an important mechanism for developing a sense of one's own identity. It is the ongoing interaction between self and other that creates the dynamic struggle out of which identity emerges. Rather than thinking of self-sameness as a condition for identity, it is the other that is at the heart of identity.[26]

---

[24] Ries and Trout, 1972/2001: 8.
[25] Ries and Trout, 1972/2001: 14.
[26] Said's *Orientalism* (1979) is maybe one of the best examples for this theorem.

Edinburgh the city brand can only articulate its identity of itself as 'Inspiring Capital' by defining a competitive field. Edinburgh's identity is not an essence but a relational construct that is based on the difference between Edinburgh and what it perceives to be its competitors (nationally, Glasgow; for the finance industry, Leeds and London; internationally, Copenhagen and Stockholm etc.).

Branding can be understood as the arena in which these conversations between self and other evolve. A particularly interesting case is if the other is defined as competitor(s) within one industry. The identity of individual organizations can be expected to involve an attempt to establish a unique position within that industry, while at the same time being similar enough to other firms in the industry so as to still be able to define themselves in relation to them. This is a structuralist argument: the nodes are more important than the individual threats; meaning is based on the web, the grammar, the structure of a system, whereas individual identities are mere results of that structure. As Douglas and Isherwood put it, the meaning of objects is in the relation between them, just like music does not reside in a single note but in the interplay of many.[27] The meaning of brands results from the exploration and exploitation of exactly those differences: Coke has meaning as it differentiates itself from Pepsi; Mecca Cola has meaning because it differentiates itself from both Western brands; 7 Up is the Un-cola, and so on. Identity is only meaningful in relation to what it is not: in order to be meaningful, identity relies on its other. Therein lies the identity paradox: to be something, you have to keep one eye on what you are not. Identity presupposes otherness and difference.

The argument of institutional theory is that the more established and mature an industry becomes, the more tightly the network is knit and the more homogeneous firms become. DiMaggio and Powell propose isomorphism – or more colloquially, copying – as a key learning and survival mechanism.[28] But that explains only half of what happens. What institutional theory explains is why firms become more and more similar.

But what we see is that brands are becoming more similar *and* more different *at the same time*. They allow the management of the paradox of sameness and difference: organizations define their identity in reference to others, carefully making sure that they are different enough from them to be seen

[27] Douglas and Isherwood, 1979/2005: 49.
[28] DiMaggio and Powell, 1983.

as different; at the same time, they need to be similar enough to be seen as belonging in the same category, competing with each other by being able to deliver similar solutions to a given problem.[29]

Brands make it possible to manage this paradox. They are based on difference, not identity in a Platonic sense. Brands are relational as they constantly compare ('benchmark') themselves to others. This is what makes brands so successful: they provide identity that is both stable and changing. Brands are in fact organized heresy: they are the search for differences that is tolerated and even supported by the status quo.

Why Plato, identity theorists and brand gurus are wrong

What is the argument against identity as central, distinctive and enduring essence? Ironically, the answer can be found where the problem comes from: in Greek philosophy. Stability is but a temporary illusion: it rests in the assumption that things repeat each other over time. Heraclitus' assertion that you can never step into the same river twice illustrates the point. The argument is that there is no repetition possible without change, or difference, creeping between two experiences. Whatever appears to be a stable identity is only changing beyond our perception. Therefore, in fact, identity is an illusion. As we argued with Heidegger above, difference is more fundamental than identity. A little thought experiment might help us to understand this.

Jorge Luis Borges tells the story of *Pierre Menard, Author of the Quixote*, who attempted to create an identical translation of Cervantes' book. The trick is that Cervantes wrote his 'version' in 1602, while Menard wrote his in 1928. You would expect a translation to be the same – the perfect repetition. Borges asserts otherwise:

'Cervantes' text and Menard's are verbally identical, but the second is almost infinitely richer. (More ambiguous, his detractors will say, but ambiguity is richness.) It is a revelation to compare Menard's Don Quixote with Cervantes'. The latter, for example, wrote (part one, chapter nine):

... truth, whose mother is history, rival of time,
depository of deeds, witness of the past, exemplar and
adviser to the present, and the future's counsellor.

---

[29] This echoes the uniqueness paradox that Joanne Martin and her colleagues (Martin *et al.*, 1983) found in their study of organizational culture. Narratives that employees told about their organizations and that were meant to differentiate them featured by and large the same elements, themes and concerns.

Written in the seventeenth century, written by the 'lay genius' Cervantes, this enumeration is a mere rhetorical praise of history. Menard, on the other hand, writes:

... truth, whose mother is history, rival of time,
depository of deeds, witness of the past, exemplar and
adviser to the present, and the future's counsellor.

History, the mother of truth: the idea is astounding. Menard, a contemporary of William James, does not define history as an inquiry into reality but as its origin. Historical truth, for him, is not what has happened; it is what we judge to have happened. The final phrases – exemplar and adviser to the present, and the future's counsellor – are brazenly pragmatic. The contrast in style is also vivid. The archaic style of Menard – quite foreign, after all – suffers from a certain affectation. Not so that of his forerunner, who handles with ease the current Spanish of his time.[30]

As Menard says fictitiously: 'To compose the Quixote at the beginning of the seventeenth century was a reasonable undertaking, necessary and perhaps even unavoidable; at the beginning of the twentieth, it is almost impossible. It is not in vain that three hundred years have gone by, filled with exceedingly complex events. Amongst them, to mention only one, is the Quixote itself.'[31]

Jorge Luis Borges' short story tells us that repetition is not possible – even if, like Menard, one copies something that happened in the past, it is not the same. Because repetition is not possible, the corollary is that identity as a stable, enduring substance is not possible either.[32] Such a statement seems to fly in the face of practical experience. For instance, do you have a stable identity? Do you have to ask yourself every morning who you are? Do you have to explain every morning to your partner who you are? Probably not. Of course, not everything changes in a substantive sense always. Hence the challenge is: How can we explain identity *and* change? How can things be the same *and* change over time? Plato's solution was to declare the changing part – the visible and physical world – as appearance and restore infinite stability and order in the invisible kingdom of ideas. Heraclitus went the other way, claiming that everything is in constant flux. Who is right?

[30] Borges, 1939/1982: 69.
[31] Borges, 1939/1982: 68.
[32] Another philosopher who worked on repetition is Søren Kierkegaard. He described that problem in his book *Repetition: A Venture in Experimenting Psychology by Constantin Constantius*, where the main protagonist, Constantin Constantius, attempts to find out 'whether or not it is possible, what importance it has, whether something gains or loses in being repeated' (Kierkegaard, 1843/1983: 131). He repeats a visit to Berlin, doing exactly the same as the first time, which culminates in watching the theatre play *Der Talisman*. To his dissatisfaction, repetition is not possible; things have changed and he finds the repetition, despite all effort, undertaken in vain.

Things and words

In order to answer our question, we suggest revisiting a text by the German philosopher Friedrich Nietzsche, which he wrote in 1873, when he was 29 years old, 'On Truth and Lie in an Extra-Moral Sense'. In this remarkable essay, Nietzsche argues that identity is first and foremost created through language. Words stabilize things through inventing 'a regularly valid and obligatory relationship between things ... and this linguistic legislation also furnishes the first laws of truth'.[33] For him, language neither represents nor mirrors reality; the designations and the things do not coincide: 'we believe that we know something about the things themselves when we speak of trees, colours, snow and flowers; and yet we possess nothing but metaphors for things – metaphors which correspond in no way to the original entities'.[34] Language is a metaphor that expresses relation between things and between us and things. Even if we think we know something about the world, in truth we only speak about the world in our words that are far from being reliable proxies for the truth.

'What, then, is truth?' asks Nietzsche, in arguably the most famous passage of his text, to which he answers:

A mobile army of metaphors, metonyms, and anthropomorphisms – in short, a sum of human relations which have been enhanced, transposed, and embellished poetically and rhetorically, and which after long use seem firm, canonical, and obligatory to a people: truths are illusions about which one has forgotten that this is what they are; metaphors which are worn out and without sensuous power; coins which have lost their pictures and now matter only as metal, no longer as coins.[35]

Truths are linguistic devices that hide human relationships we project onto things. Words create truth as people narrate the world: 'As a genius of construction man raises himself far above the bee in the following way: whereas the bee builds with wax that he gathers from nature, man builds with the far more delicate conceptual material which he first has to manufacture from himself.'[36]

What, then, is identity? Identity is accomplished through language, through metaphors, metonyms and anthropomorphisms, and we have forgotten what they are about. What Edinburgh 'is', therefore, is hard to discern.

[33] Nietzsche, 1873/1990: 877.
[34] Nietzsche, 1873/1990: 879.
[35] Nietzsche, 1873/1990: 880.
[36] Nietzsche, 1873/1990: 888.

If we think of substance, we will be lost. But if we think of language, we can see how words create truth, and how words can change what we take for the truth. The identity of Edinburgh is in the language we use, the relation we establish between us, the city and other, competing places. The essence is not 'in' Edinburgh or some kind of essential quality 'attached' to Edinburgh – remember Nietzsche's definition of truth as 'a mobile army of metaphors', the sum of 'human relations, which have been enhanced, transposed, and embellished poetically and rhetorically, and which after long use seem firm, canonical, and obligatory'. Truth is based on relations between people and things, and then cast in language until we think of it as a thing in itself that is firm, canonical and obligatory. Because identity is enacted in language, and not essentially located 'in' things, it can be stable and changing at the same time. In fact, identities are narratives.[37]

Identity and change

There is no identity behind, beyond or underneath language. The only stability we experience is created in and through language. The brand provides a conceptual framework and a set of techniques that managers use to develop an organization's identity. For instance, Edinburgh's identity lies in its discursively constructed brand. If stability is accomplished through language, how does change occur? Again, Nietzsche delivers an important clue:

This has given me the greatest trouble and still does: to realise that what things are called is incomparably more important than what they are. The reputation, name, and appearance, the usual measure and weight of a thing, what it counts for – originally almost always wrong and arbitrary, thrown over things like a dress and altogether foreign to their nature and even to their skin – all this grows from generation unto generation, merely because people believe in it, until it gradually grows to be part of the thing and turns into its very body: what at first was appearance becomes in the end, almost invariably, the essence and is effective as such! How foolish it would be to suppose that one only needs to point out this origin and this misty shroud of delusion in order to destroy the world that counts for real, so-called 'reality'! We can destroy only as creators!– But let us not forget this either: it is enough to create new names and estimations and probabilities in order to create in the long run new 'things'.[38]

[37] Czarniawska, 1997; Christensen and Cheney, 2002.
[38] Nietzsche, 1882/2002: 69–70.

Language does not represent a given reality – in fact, it creates what we take for reality. Language does not merely mirror what happens, but constitutes our world. In a later chapter, we will discuss the Pepsi Generation, which did not simply exist out there but was, quite literally, ushered into being through countless ads that promoted a certain lifestyle. Rather than thinking of identity as 'real' and appearance as 'fake', we argue that appearance becomes, in the end, almost invariably, the essence, and is effective as such. Think of the Edinburgh brand: it becomes the essence, but only because people perform the brand and enact it in every speech, on every website, in every brochure, in every interaction. Quite literally, it is talked into existence. Nowhere is this more obvious than with brands: Edinburgh's identity is an invention, a creation that becomes canonical and obligatory and hence 'real'. Language creates reality – it bestows value onto the world, as Nietzsche says.[39]

As such, language creates, in the long run, new 'things'. The American pragmatist Richard Rorty has described this link between language, change and innovation. He claims that what is interesting and new usually represents 'a contest between an entrenched vocabulary which has become a nuisance and a half-formed new vocabulary which vaguely promises great things'.[40] The method of inventing new things follows language; it derives from re-describing 'lots and lots of things in new ways, until you have created a pattern of linguistic behaviour which will tempt a rising generation to adopt it, thereby causing them to look for appropriate new forms of non-linguistic behaviour'.[41] Once a pattern of usage emerges from the new types of re-description and becomes institutionalized, that which is institutionalized requires no criteria 'common to the old and the new language games. For just insofar as the new language really is new, there will be no such a criterion.'[42] The 'Edinburgh Festival City' brand is as 'true' as the 'Inspiring Capital' brand – according to Rorty, this is not the point. Rather, the new description of Edinburgh will lead to new practices and new behaviours. For instance, thinking of Edinburgh as city region brand with 1.2 million inhabitants rather than as legally defined council (with only some 400,000 people) will instill a new confidence when city managers negotiate with the UK government or the EU about funding.

As Rorty explains, re-descriptions are a tool 'rather than a claim to have discovered essence. It thereby becomes possible to see a new vocabulary not

[39] Nietzsche, 1882/2002: 171.
[40] Rorty, 1989: 9.
[41] Rorty, 1989: 9.
[42] Rorty, 1989: 8 and 9.

as something which was supposed to replace all other vocabularies, something which claimed to represent reality, but simply as one more vocabulary, one more human project, one person's chosen metaphoric.[43] Rorty sees a certain playfulness in this practice, the playfulness being a product of the 'ability to appreciate the power of re-describing, the power of language to make new and different things possible and important.'[44]

For Rorty, there is a tension between a 'final vocabulary' that attempts to stop all future re-descriptions and an open, playful and ironic approach to creating as many new language games as possible. This 'final vocabulary' is made up of words such as 'good', 'truth' etc., to which we revert when we talk about the most important things that we aim to render non-negotiable.[45] This is exactly what Plato (and identity theorists) were aiming at: to call that particular definition of reality that they preferred 'identity' and render it non-negotiable. Identity is constructed out of language and hence it can be deconstructed. Because it emerges from historically grown and shared language games, identity is socially constructed and only temporarily stable. Brands are stories, forged out of a final vocabulary that attempts to define a non-negotiable essence. Brands are identity-in-action, performed through language that presents itself as non-negotiable.

Performing brand identity

Brands are discursively constructed identities that accommodate change and stability. The only way of being able to do so simultaneously is through language. Take the example of Benetton, which charged Oliviero Toscani with the task of developing a new global communication strategy for the brand. On a tour through Paris in 1986, after he passed a street lined with posters of two black children, one covered in a Soviet flag, the other in a US flag, the then leader of the USSR Gorbachev asked 'Who is this Benetton anyway?'[46] The question was spot on: it is not 'what is Benetton selling?' but 'who is this Benetton anyway?' The answer is in the brand.

Benetton's brand identity was built over the years through the careful use of language. At the outset of Toscani's reign, it was about 'all the colours in the world', celebrating diversity. Then it started to move from harmonious

---

[43] Rorty, 1989: 39.
[44] Rorty, 1989: 39.
[45] Rorty, 1989: 73.
[46] Quoted in Rutherford, 2000: 158.

diversity to show the differences between black and white, poor and rich. At the beginning of the nineties, the communication turned more pessimistic: life, disease, illness and death were shown, in an existential gesture, as what ultimately unites mankind. The phantasmagoria of images that followed included a killed soldier's uniform, a dying AIDS patient or an HIV stamp on naked skin. Not surprisingly, these images created controversy. It's important to point out that the actual product did not feature in any of the ads. The brand communication was never focused on fashion; what was created was identity.

This begs the question: Is the Benetton identity 'real' or a mere appearance? There is no substance behind or underneath Benetton; its appearance is its reality, the brand is its identity, built through language and narratives.[47] The brand as such is a 'semiotic engine whose function it is to constantly produce meaning and values'.[48] This is accomplished through language and the ever-new discovery of differences, niches and metaphors. This engine is at the core of identity. It *performs* identity: identities are not revealed or uncovered; they have to be made.

The same is true from a consumer perspective. Brands don't exist like 'things' – what's parked on your driveway is your car; what's in your head is a Mercedes. What is produced in a factory is a product; what is bought by people are brands. Douglas and Isherwood have said that it is the main problem of social life to 'pin down meanings so that they stay still for a little while': 'The choice of goods continuously creates certain patterns of discrimination, overlaying or reinforcing others. Goods, then, are the visible part of culture. They are arranged in vistas and hierarchies that can give play to the full range of discrimination of which the human mind is capable.'[49] In order to be meaningful, goods need to be interpreted. Think of the Doc Martens boots that we discussed in Chapter 2. The brand captures this meaning and makes it possible for both producers and consumers to play with it.

Brands are linguistic representations, images and signs; they do not refer back to 'real' objects.[50] The brand itself is the 'real' object that defies categorization under 'truth' or 'appearance'. The old Platonic logic of where there is smoke there must be fire does not work: because there is a sign, it does not

[47] Borgerson et al., 2006: 183: 'The work, then, remains in the reading of cultural signs, making them as consistent as possible in a way that best communicates the desired image without reference to some mistakenly ontologized referent.'

[48] Heilbrunn, 2006: 103.

[49] Douglas and Isherwood, 1979/2005: 43–44.

[50] See Borgerson et al., 2006: 179, who asks: 'What if we look "behind" the brand and to our amazement there is nothing there? What if there does not exist a *core* or *essential* company behind the brand …?'

mean that there is a signified object. Brands confuse our ontological categories: they are signs that *are* objects.

Power

The reality that language creates is always *socially* constructed. That's the
core of Wittgenstein's argument that there is no such thing as a private language. Language is a social thing, or better: a social activity. He introduces
the notion of language games to explain: 'The term "language-game" is meant
to bring into prominence the fact that the speaking of language is part of an
activity, or a form of life. To imagine a language means to imagine a form of
life.'[51]

Language games are a socially sanctioned form of activity. Wittgenstein
uses the concept of grammar to explain the structuring that works through
language onto our form of life. Grammar is a network of rules that determines
what we can say, which kind of linguistic moves are legitimate. Grammar is
not about using a language that is technically correct but is a set of norms
that prescribes how to use language in a meaningful way. Hence meaning is
socially created, between people who agree on a common language game –
on a form of life.

Think of true aficionados of the Apple brand (whom we will encounter in
more detail in Chapter 6): they speak about Apple as passport to creativity
and freedom that allows them to resist the dark PC world of Microsoft. For
them, the Apple brand gives shape to a peculiar form of life that we call,
for want of a better term, 'lifestyle'. Lifestyles are grammars or patterns that
people use to express their identities and make sense of the world they live
in. Quite literally, lifestyles 'stylise' life as they offer more or less coherent and
socially accepted ways of conducting life. We will pick this topic up in the
third part of the book.

There is an important dimension of power in grammar and lifestyle: since
we cannot change the rules of the game unilaterally, and since we are not
free to invent our own private language, we have to go along with the rules
we find institutionalized in society. Some brands exercise power as they are
highly institutionalized: everybody knows Coke, McDonald's and who wants
you to 'Just Do It'. These brands are probably the language that most people

---

[51] Wittgenstein, 1953/1972: § 23 and § 19, where he wrote: 'To describe a language-game is to describe
a form of life.'

in the developed and parts of the developing world share. Brands are our Esperanto.[52]

Foucault analysed 'truth' as an especially powerful language game: 'In every society the production of discourse is controlled, organized, redistributed, by a certain number of procedures whose role is to ward off its powers and dangers, to gain mastery over its chance events, to evade its materiality.' Truth is a system of exclusion – it 'tends to exert a sort of pressure and something like a power of constraint on other discourses'.[53]

Take the example of Edinburgh: its brand prescribes a discourse, down to the level of detail such as tone of voice, that should represent Edinburgh's identity to tourists, investors and global talent. This identity is but one of many possible stories Edinburgh could tell about itself. Take, for instance, the bestselling book *Trainspotting* by Irvine Welsh, which was made into a movie by Danny Boyle: it represents a significantly different Edinburgh of drugs, prostitution and working class culture that the Edinburgh brand effectively silences. Brands are not just signs: they are markers of identity, which render certain things visible and silence others.[54]

But language is not determined by the speaker or the author. Roland Barthes and others have argued that the true locus of writing is reading.[55] While an author might have certain intentions, it is up to readers to interpret the text. There is not only latitude but also freedom in these interpretations. Reading a brand, consuming a brand, is then a creative act that can spark change. In fact, we will argue that consuming is a creative practice that is almost impossible to differentiate from producing. As such, Edinburgh's identity emerges in a contested discursive space where final vocabularies, new perspectives and subversive interpretations clash.

Brands as stories

We have argued that language is the engine for creating brand identity, not a camera for representing it (to play with the title of Donald MacKenzie's latest

[57] Developed first in 1887, Esperanto is an easy-to-learn language that was supposed to serve as a universal second language. Although no country ever adopted Esperanto officially, by June 2008, Wikipedia featured more than 100,000 articles in Esperanto (see http://en.wikipedia.org/wiki/Esperanto_Wikipedia (accessed 18 June 2009)).
[53] Foucault, 1970/1981: 52.
[54] Greenberg's study on branding New York (2008) provides many more examples of the dominating effects of branding.
[55] Barthes, 1967.

book).[56] It does not capture an essence or eternal stable truth but enacts reality. Brands do not only consist of single signs or words but of complex stories: 'A brand acts as a narrative programme, which must promote a system of material and discursive differences so as to justify and legitimize its existence among other brands and so as to create consumers' preferences.'[57]

Brands are identities built and managed through language. Advertising creates a textuality that aims at stimulating the consumer to experience the brand as opposed to the product. Brands do so by forming the core of network culture that links people, images, text, product and ideas. They create what Arvidsson calls 'cross-mediality'[58] and Marshall refers to as 'intertextual commodity'.[59] Both concepts allude to the seemingly ubiquitous trend in the mass media to re-mediate the same content across different media. Such intertextuality creates space and allows for linking things in unanticipated ways. For instance, Mickey Mouse lives partly in Disneyland but also on TV, in merchandise, at McDonald's, and so on. The value of Mickey Mouse is in its context and cross-references, not in any one product alone. Brands give us intertextual stories that work across different media. They are the only grand narratives that are left.

How is intertextuality achieved? This happens through a multi-channel communication strategy that engages our five senses.[60] In Diesel ads, the image of the carefree lifestyle community is created through a surreal setting not dissimilar to a painting by the fiffteenth- and early sixteenth-century Dutch artist Hieronymus Bosch, in which people engage in social activities that evoke fantasies from a strange and lost paradise. Words are important for creating an image: 'Just Do It' is Nike's strapline, showing professional athletes playing soccer in a threatening *Blade Runner* world; the fashion label FCUK built a brand by playing with that four-letter word; the Subaru Outback captures the adventure of leaving the sealed roads, and with it the everyday, behind. Visual language creates another layer: take the unique look of Benetton ads, which creates reality without any text. Brands turn themselves into art works – Absolut Vodka hired artists such as Andy Warhol, Keith Haring and Ed Ruscha to produce Absolut Art. Another form of creating intertextuality is product placement. For instance, BMW pays the makers

[56] MacKenzie, 2007.
[57] Heilbrunn, 2006: 106.
[58] Arvidsson, 2006: 126.
[59] Marshall, 2002.
[60] Lindstrom, 2005; Danesi, 2006, has analysed this as the synesthetic qualities of an ad.

of James Bond films to put their character in its latest models instead of using the traditional Aston Martin as 007's vehicle of choice.

Intertextuality weaves the language of brands and its context into one narrative until the fine line between 'reality' and 'appearance' blurs: so-called below-the-line brand activities aim at creating experiences that provide a context in which the brand becomes an event in itself. Brands use a 'poetic logic' to create reality, to weave themselves into our culture and make it impossible to differentiate between cultural expressions and brand experiences.[61] Santa Claus was invented by Coca Cola to boost sales over winter; today, Santa is part of children's dreams. Following this logic, Sidney Levy argued that the 'largest activity in marketing is the provision and consumption of stories. This fact is so general and pervasive that it commonly escapes notice ... Stories are bought and sold, they are part of the media of exchange, and they are vehicles for all other goods and services.'[62]

A powerful collection of stories turns brands into the last bastions of powerful myths. According to Levi-Strauss, myths always encapsulate oppositions and work towards their resolution as the story unfolds.[63] Brands draw on strong cultural oppositions and turn them into a shared myth that gives meaning and advice on how we should conduct ourselves. Like language games, brand stories are scripts that we use to enact our lifestyles.

Brands create a new mental and social space in which contradictory identities can be combined into one single story. Heilbrunn shows how McDonald's manages to package competing and contradicting values into the brand:

- practical values: proximity, quality and simplicity of choice
- critical values: value for money (value meal deal), efficiency (McDrive), predictability (standardized offers)
- utopian values: illusion of abundance (soda fountain), scenarios of life (the family restaurant), conviviality (birthday parties), adaptability (McLamb in India, local ingredients etc.), concern for health
- ludic values: fun and surprise (the Happy Meal).[64]

Obviously, there is a contrast between practical and critical values on the one hand and the ludic and utopian values on the other hand. But the brand is able to reconcile these differences and stress different dimensions in different

[61] Danesi, 2006: 116.
[62] Quoted in Zaltman, 2003: 211.
[63] Levi-Strauss, 1958/1963; Holt, 2003.
[64] Heilbrunn, 2006: 110.

contexts. Brands are ambiguous: that's why they are able to re-create a grand narrative around one identity convincingly – although a closer look might reveal that there are many fragmented realities and identities that do not add up to one neat coherent being.

Stories also generate distinct identities. Paul Hugh-Jones, former Marketing Director at Bacardi remembers how Bacardi was looking for an authentic story to position itself against increasingly popular Vodka:

> In the 1990s, Vodka started to grow, playing on its Russian heritage. At Bacardi, we were looking for authenticity in our brand: we needed a story to tell. Authenticity means having a story to tell. Every brand has to have a story. Our story played on the image of Cuba where people live a kind of basic but very happy life. Our story was about sand, sea and sun.

For Paul, authenticity and distinctiveness are more important than traditional differentiation strategies. As he explains,

> In the past, you had a few brands, so you could differentiate yourself from your competitors and create your own unique position. Today, markets are crowded, so the only way to differentiate yourself is to go into a very small niche. But what if you don't want to be in a niche market? Well, then you have to forget about differentiation and look for distinctiveness instead.

Distinct identities such as Cuban Bacardi are built around stories that justify and legitimize the brand.

Brands as grand narratives are not limited to consumer-facing brands. Corporate brands tell their tales about themselves just as well. Think back to the examples of AT&T, ING or Deloitte that we mentioned before. Van Riel provides a step-by-step approach to telling a story that enacts the brand and creates identity.[65] Everything is part of the story – including the culture, the history, the mission and artefacts such as logo and design.

In summary, rather than being product owners, companies will become story owners.[66] The path to true loyalty is through stories: 'It's approaching Marketing as a journalist, an editor, an anthropologist. It's studying the cultural details and taking everything you can to craft a compelling story; then letting that story find its audience and making the final outcome of that story dependent on the audience's (inter-) personal life and experience.'[67] When, as

[65] Van Riel, 2000; Larsen, 2000
[66] Wipperfürth, 2005: 216, quoting Rolf Jensen from *The Dream Society*.
[67] Wipperfürth, 2005: 256.

the *Cluetrain Manifesto* claimed, markets are conversations, brands are the most coherent forms of storytelling.[68]

Image, identity and brand

Dutton and Dukerich argue that identity is dependent on image. For them, identity is what members believe the character of the organization is. Image, on the other hand, is what they believe other people outside think the organization's characteristics are. In their words, 'image describes insiders' assessments of what outsiders think'.[69] One person's image is another person's identity.

This interplay is important for several reasons. First, in an information society, people react to other people's representations of their action. People have access to real-time information on almost anything, almost anytime. Organizational members encounter more images of their organization than before, which convey more fragmented meanings about what the organization is. This also means that self-definitions are not made in isolation but become more often contested and need to be negotiated. Boundaries between inside and outside become more fluid and therefore external stakeholders have more influence and better means to make their voices heard.[70] Finally, the more ambiguity, the more room for interpretation or actions and the more important are images that guide our interpretations.[71]

The interplay between identity and image injects instability into the brand. Clashing descriptions of (ostensibly) the same thing are a trigger for action, including those actions that discredit the other side and refuse to listen to their arguments. This explains why organizations invest heavily in image campaigns: the objective is to achieve congruence between identity and image by closing the gap between the two.

Jane Dutton and Janet Dukerich argue that the interplay between image and identity drives change. Organizations do not wait until the environment or some kind of evolution knocks them out but can observe the 'mirror' and enact change. Dennis Gioia and his colleagues go one step further and argue that, because of the link between image and identity, identity is an inherently unstable and relatively fluid concept. For them, identity is dynamic and a

[68] Levine *et al.*, 2000.
[69] Dutton and Dukerich, 1991: 547.
[70] Hatch and Schultz, 2002.
[71] Alvesson, 1990: 391: 'The more the ambiguity, the greater the material and perceptual space for images.'

'potentially precarious and unstable notion, frequently up for redefinition and revision by organizational members'.[72] Their concept of adaptive instability explains how organizations can somehow stay the same while changing simultaneously: 'Identity and image are dynamically and recursively interrelated; the organization's self-definition is inherently unstable, yet this instability is adaptive for the organization.'[73]

Dennis Gioia *et al.* use the example of Shell trying to sink its Brent Spar platform. The outcry from Greenpeace, consumers and governments (in that order) influenced Shell and forced it to reconsider not only its action but also its identity. Thus the image is likely to de-stabilize and challenge identity.[74] The brand becomes the arena in which those clashes occur and are, at least temporarily, resolved.

Pathologies

Mary Jo Hatch and Majken Schultz have explored two pathologies that result from the dynamic relationship between identity and image.[75] First, if one puts too much emphasis on the external environment, this leads to hyper-adaptation: an organization caught in hyper-adaptation follows every fashion trend head over heels. An example is LEGO in the 1990s, which opened up theme parks, went into LEGO TV, lifestyle, retail, dolls, robotics, software, and so on. In the end, this was a disastrous strategy because LEGO mimicked trends that did not resonate with its legacy.[76]

On the other hand, too much focus on internal affairs results in narcissism. A narcissistic identity is internally focused and equipped with a defence mechanism to block change. Andrew Brown and Ken Starkey have argued that, generally, 'organizations are prone to ego defences, such as denial, rationalisation, idealisation, fantasy, and symbolisation, that maintain collective self-esteem and the continuity of existing identity'.[77] When identity is questioned fundamentally, organizations react with identity-preserving and change-inhibiting actions: 'Information that threatens an organization's collective self-concept is ignored, rejected, reinterpreted,

[72] Gioia *et al.*, 2000: 64.
[73] Gioia *et al.*, 2000: 75.
[74] See also Gioia and Thomas, 1996, where they argue that a desired future image is key to changing current organizational identity.
[75] Hatch and Schultz, 2008: 59.
[76] Hatch and Schultz, 2008: 183.
[77] Brown and Starkey, 2000: 102; see also Brown, 1997; Elsbach and Kramer, 1996.

hidden or lost',[78] whereas information that confirms identity is highlighted and amplified. In this scenario, a narcissistic identity blocks learning and change.

Brands feed off the tension between identity and image. They help to keep the balance between hyper-adaptation and narcissism. Brands are dynamic and involve conversations between 'I' and the image of the 'I' as created by others. The other 'I' can be represented in many ways, including through customer feedback, sales reps, market research, media coverage, surveys, interactions with stakeholders, and so on.[79] The point is that the brand can be understood as platform or arena in which these negotiations about identity take place. The brand is the relation, the interface, between identity and image. This relation can be a catalyst for change as different, sometimes conflicting narratives are, at least temporarily, reconciled in the brand. Brands are the arena in which the comedy of inclusion and the tragedy of exclusion are enacted. As 'form of life', brands subtly shape the way we think about identity of organizations, and by extension, us.

So what?

What have we gained by using brand to understand identity? Branding is a way of managing identity. Opposed to dominant thinking, it does not see identity as essential, Platonistic idea(l). Rather, identity is based on language games. This stresses that identity is a social process. It also makes identity something that can change and embrace conflicting values (remember the McDonald's example). Brand becomes a form of identity management: based on differences between the self and the other, the brand emerges as powerful narrative trying to reconcile conflicts between identity and image. We'd like to think that our perspective has practical and theoretical implications.

First, the concept of branding opens up and links organizations to their external environments. Brands are a way of thinking about engagement between organizations, people and society. If one believes Peter Drucker, organizational survival comes down to the ability to get the organization in touch with its environments. As he concludes with his Viennese charm, results take place outside the organization, while inside, there are only costs.[80] The brand, as interface, is the pivotal link between internal and external. It

[78] Brown and Starkey, 2000: 103.
[79] Hatch and Schultz, 2008: 49.
[80] Drucker, 1995.

allows seeing the organization from the outside in. Rather than perpetuating a narcissistic, navel-gazing and inward-looking perspective, the brand forces the organization to engage with the outside world.

Second, Levitt made the point in his 1960 *Harvard Business Review* article 'Marketing Myopia' that Hollywood went almost broke because it defined itself as in the movie business. In doing so, it overlooked the challenge that TV brought with it – and almost failed. Had it defined itself as in the entertainment industry, it would have seen the changes taking place and could have played a more active role. Put simply, Hollywood's identity was based on a narrow, essential definition based on what it did (making movies), rather than what it meant for people (providing entertainment). To think about one's identity in brand terms puts emphasis on the *raison d'etre*, the meaning of an organization: what you buy is not the drill but the hole in the wall. Brands are about stories, about lifestyles and about context – not narrowly defined product features or incremental technological progress.

Brands conceptualize organizational identity from this perspective. Virgin does not have an industry focus but a focus on challenging 'the fat cats': built around Richard Branson the person, Virgin the brand stands for quality and value for money in boring industries where it can challenge the status quo and do things in a fun way. That's the growth strategy of Virgin – it moves into areas in which it can challenge the status quo. This is important for identity-based strategizing. In this sense, organizations do not simply react to change and mimic others, as institutional theory suggests; rather, through brands, organizations become agents of organized heresy.

5 Culture

Brand = behaviour

Brands, we have argued, are organized heresy: they ensure the continuous importing of differences into the inner sanctum of the organization. There, at the inner sanctum, the brand meets the people who work for the organization. Organizational members are increasingly understood as prime opportunities to express the brand. The idea is simple: the brand experience of consumers is dependent on the way they are treated by organizational members. Hence, so the story goes, the brand equals the behaviour of staff. This chapter analyses how brands write themselves into organizational behaviour and culture. We propose a simple argument: in a service economy, organizations rely on people to make their customers happy. The brand is not built around the product but around the employees who deliver the service and (ideally) create a memorable experience.

Cindy Carpenter heads marketing and HR at Corrs Chambers Westgarth, one of Australia's leading law firms with around 1,000 employees. Before taking on this dual role, she was a brand manager at Unilever, finished her MBA at Wharton and worked for thirteen years as a strategist with the Boston Consulting Group.[1]

Cindy's portfolio heralds the advent of a new era for brand managers. In the context of a professional services firm, the brand is developed and delivered through employees. As Cindy elaborates,

In a professional services firm, the brand is embedded in the people. The brand is really an articulation of your culture. The manufacturing, the delivery, the marketing and the selling of the service are driven by people. To have a powerful brand means to have a high-performing culture and invest in organizational learning that boosts the commerciality and excellence of our advice.

Branding becomes a manifestation of the behaviour of staff. Cindy's dual portfolio reflects the new challenges and opportunities: 'I feel quite privileged to sit across marketing and HR: to implement change and drive strategy you need to focus on people and how their behaviour creates the brand.'

Marketing an intangible service (such as Corr's legal advice) demands a different skill, as brand guru Wally Olins argues: one has to get 'your own staff to love the brand and live it and breathe it so that they can become the personal manifestation of the brand when they deal with customers'.[2] Branding works first internally, and then, as its second target, it focuses on the external market.

Branding claims to be able to do just that – ensure that employees act in accordance with organizational values. In other words, brands are the latest solution to the problem of control. However, this chapter also offers some critical insights: we will argue that it might not be the best use of the concept of brands to fuel the old control fantasies of management. Rather, brands could be a vehicle to open up organizations and span organizational boundaries. Using the brand as the vehicle to link internal cultures and external communities enables what has been dubbed the co-creation of value.

Management, culture and brands

At its most pedestrian, culture is described as the 'way things are done around here'. This comprises all those practices, routines, symbols, myths and stories

[1] Interview conducted on 19 September 2008.
[2] Olins, 2003: 75.

that make up the vernacular of an organization.[3] The culture of an organization is summarized as the taken-for-granted assumptions, beliefs and shared values that underpin employees' behaviour. Culture is a shared pattern of understanding that provides institutions with meaning. And as such, it shapes people's minds: as Schein reasons, it is the underlying assumptions 'which are typically unconscious but which actually determine how group members perceive, think and feel'.[4]

Of course, this represents an irresistible temptation for management. The only reason the love affair between culture and management did not ignite earlier was management's enduring marriage with engineering. It was the emerging threat felt by the US market from more innovative and flexible Japanese competition that made management receptive.

Two McKinsey consultants with links to Stanford's Graduate School of Business, Tom Peters and Robert Waterman, kicked off the frenzy in 1982 when they published the biggest-selling management book ever, *In Search of Excellence*.[5] Its charm is apparent: it is packed with anecdotes, lively stories and checklists. Top management's job was to show leadership through culture-building by making values clear, transmitting them widely, reinforcing them in practice and backing them up. Formal policies, informal stories, rituals as well as rules and constantly walking the talk would ensure a strong culture. These strong cultures were unambiguous, unitary and harmonious. And they were effective. Dissent and conflict were seen as signs of a weak culture and regarded as dysfunctional and unproductive. Top managers embraced these arguments, as did many scholars who produced 'excellence' studies.[6] Improvements in productivity and quality would be the result, they argued, of corporate cultures that systematically align individuals with formal organizational goals. Culture was understood as the glue that should hold organizational objectives and individual needs together.

The insight that culture matters could only come as a surprise to a profession in which Taylorism and Fordism were seen as the technological answer to social problems. Taylor occasionally called his workers 'hands' – he saw them as capability for doing things, not as people who brought values and emotions with them. Elton Mayo and the Hawthorne experiments changed this picture. With expertise in clinical psychology and experience with the

---

[3] For an overview, see Joanne Martin's comprehensive book *Organizational Culture* (2002).
[4] Schein, 1985: 3.
[5] Peters and Waterman, 1982; to be fair, there were others as well that promoted the culture concept from a managerial view, most notably Deal and Kennedy, 1982 and Ouchi, 1981.
[6] Deal and Kennedy, 1982; Kanter, 1984; Pascale and Athos, 1981.

shell-shocked soldiers of World War I, Mayo and his two research assist-
ants, Roethlisberger and Dickinson, learnt in experiments that individuals
followed a 'logic of sentiment' and not only the cold-hearted 'logic of cost
and efficiency' of management.[7]

Taylor's 'hands' had a heart and a mind, too. This brought new possibilities: rather than controlling bodies, management could start disciplining
the mind. Values, practices, beliefs and so on were no longer pathologies that
disturbed the smooth running of the organizational machine. Rather, they
were seen as something that needed to be controlled, channelled and, where
possible, exploited. The concept of culture 'normalizes' what could only be
seen as irrationalities and pathologies in Taylor's scientific system.[8]

Brands emerge as a new force in this transformation. In the beginning,
the brand was a way to control the subconscious of consumers; that was what
Bernays learned from Freud. Now the brand should perform internally what
it did so well externally: create those underlying unconscious patterns that
determine behaviour. Culture is meaning but is largely unconscious and hidden.[9] The brand becomes the tool for accessing and managing meaning.

As mentioned, this idea has proven extremely relevant for service firms, in
which the brand of the company is the behaviour of its employees. The brand
of a law firm, a police service, an airline, a bank – you name it – is formed out
of the interaction between you and the people who deliver the service. Take
Ernst & Young: Danielle Bond, Head of Marketing for the Oceania Region,
says 'our reputation is in our name – and our reputation is in our people. So
we really try to build our brand inside out: our culture is the driver of our
brand.'[10] The behaviour of people at Ernst & Young, Corrs and in literally any
other people business becomes crucial. The service is intangible and cannot be advertised, sampled nor compared like a chocolate bar. Rather, the
delivery process is the actual product. What services companies effectively
sell is a methodology for solving a problem. The journey is therefore pivotal
for the evaluation of the outcome. Often, it is impossible to compare two
services because they are delivered differently and problems shift as they are
solved, which means that the perceived quality of the service is based on a
highly subjective judgement.[11]

Brands are the corollary of the behaviour of organizational employees.
This holds true for service firms, knowledge-intensive firms, organizations in

[7] Mayo, 1933.
[8] Schein, 1992: 4, uses the verb 'normalizing'.
[9] Schein, 1992: 4, describes culture as a 'hidden' aspect of organizations.
[10] Interview conducted on 8 February 2008.
[11] See Alvesson's work on knowledge-intensive firms as 'systems of persuasion' (e.g. Alvesson, 1993).

the experience economy – and this is pretty much everybody today. Think of retail: in her study of the aesthetic labour in fashion retailing, Lynne Pettinger argued that retail is located in the blurred space between production and consumption.[12] The creation of meaning – and hence the creation of the brand – happens in the context of the store, the products on display, the overall experience and ambience and, most importantly, the sales staff. Pettinger shows how the brand determines both the service behaviour of staff as well as their embodiment. For instance, staff in high-end fashion stores are called consultants, they wear suits from their own range, they are styled, wear certain make-up, listen to certain music – in short, they represent a lifestyle that becomes part of the shopper's experience. In other words, behaviour, action, language, dress, mannerisms and habits become brand expressions.

Knowledge workers (in the widest sense of the word) and service staff work in the interstices between the actual product and consumer need. Because they sell something intangible, they have to align the demand and the supply (or what, following Michel Callon, we called the re-qualification process). They are the link that relates the two with each other. People become part and parcel of the brand, which enables the brand to function as the interface between supply and demand. This has strategic importance. As we've seen with the example of Deloitte, technical expertise is no longer the only differentiator between firms; that's a given. What creates a unique and attractive strategic differentiator is the way of doing things – the 'how' rather than the 'what'. ING does what any other of the big banks do, but it does it in an 'easier' way than others. Virgin does what other companies do but with a different 'attitude'. This 'how' is very much based in an organization's culture. And that is why branding starts to overlap with culture. As Danielle Bond succinctly put it, 'the brand really runs the whole show'.

Brand culture

The brand is both the medium through which culture is enacted and the tool through which meaning can be managed. If we look at it via Edgar Schein's simple yet popular culture model, the links between culture and brand become obvious. Schein defines culture as the deep, basic assumptions and beliefs that are shared by organizational members. In his layered model of

---

[12] Pettinger, 2000.

culture, culture is not only displayed on the surface but also has hidden and unconscious elements.

Schein differentiates between three levels of culture.[13] The first level represents artefacts: this includes visible organizational features such as the physical structure of buildings, their architecture, uniforms, interior design, logos, and so on. Such artefacts express brand and culture alike. The second level refers to espoused values. They represent a non-visible facet of culture, as they express the norms and beliefs that employees express when they discuss organizational issues. Take Edinburgh's 'Inspiring Capital' brand: it captures and expresses the values of Edinburgh as a city region and attempts to define the culture of its citizens. The brand becomes the magnifying glass under which cultural values become visible. Once they are visible, they are also open to change – and manipulation.

For Schein, the deep culture is located at the third level, where the basic assumptions are hidden underneath artefacts and espoused values. It includes the basic assumptions shaping the worldviews, beliefs and norms of organizational members, which guide their behaviour without being explicitly expressed. It is the most influential level, since it works surreptitiously and shapes decision-making processes almost invisibly. It is hard to observe, and even harder to change. Brands as tools to manage meaning are (supposedly) a shortcut to those deeply held assumptions. Think of ING's deep-seated change programme, which is driven by the brand, with the purpose to create a new culture around the notion of 'easier'.

Notice the Freudian influence on Schein's conception of culture: the *id*, the third level, is sub-consciousness and hidden in the depths of the mind. Bernays promised almost 100 years ago to access the *id* of the consumer, which should allow control of their behaviour. Now, brand culture promises to access the *id* of employees, and with it the culture of the organization, in the same way.

Managing meaning

Of course, a brand is not the same as these cultural manifestations. There is little to be gained from pulverizing these differences and simply conflating brands with culture. Rather, we'd argue that the brand is a framework with which to manage those cultural manifestations. Joanne Martin differentiates

---

[13] Schein, 1992.

between several types of cultural manifestations, including cultural forms (e.g. rituals and stories), formal and informal practices (e.g. official policies and informal routines) and content themes (e.g. values). Her analytical gaze will help us to understand the relation between the two concepts.

Rituals are important for the cultural life of any organization. Martin defines them as drama that is defined by activities, a choreography and clear roles or scripts.[14] The brand is engaged in rewriting these scripts and provides the props for a successful performance. For example, client interaction in the context of a commercial law firm is a routine event whereby partners and juniors provide professional advice to clients. Rather than following established routines developed by the profession over the years, law firms may start to re-cast the routine in terms of client brand experience: every part of the interaction is audited, checked for consistency with the brand and then re-defined to ensure alignment.

Take the example of Mallesons Stephen Jaques, Australia's biggest law firm and one of the Top 50 worldwide. Paul Hugh-Jones, who is currently Executive Director of Marketing, started out as a food scientist at Mars, then moved into marketing with British Airways and worked as Global Marketing Director for Bacardi before joining Mallesons. When he talks about branding, it is all about the client experience:

It is the same with British Airways or Mallesons: the objective is to make interactions memorable. How to create brand experience? Well, first of all, get the basics right; there is no point in designing a brand experience if the plane is late. The same is true for the legal profession: we analysed all the touch points that our clients have with us. We found that the key value is 'being easy to do business with'. So everything we do is aimed at being easy to do business with.

The whole business is taken apart and re-assembled based on the new value. This includes how lawyers should respond to complicated client requests where the balance between a detailed, and expensive, answer and speed has to be struck.

Stories are another important part of culture. As we have argued in the previous chapter, brands are enacted in stories, and stories are scripts for action. Brands are often created around myths of heroic figures (think Steve Jobs, Richard Branson, Bill Gates etc.) and war stories (e.g. bending and sometimes breaking bureaucratic rules to achieve a desirable outcome). In internal brand communication programmes, these stories are communicated advertising-style to an internal audience. For instance, Deloitte's 7 Signals

[14] Martin, 2002: 66.

programme adorns every wall of the Sydney office, including the bathrooms. Internal newsletters push the stories out, and blogs invite staff to contribute their interpretations.

Humour is another important manifestation of culture. Gadens, one of Australia's Top 10 law firms, decided to use humour as an expression of their culture in their graduate recruitment campaign. Gadens' stand at the 2007 Legal Recruitment Fair in Sydney was dominated by a banner reading 'Individuality is our Creed' above a set of identical looking dark-suited lawyers wearing dark glasses and wigs, some of them chained to their desks. Signs in the background read: 'When you work for us you will never see your family and friends again.' Whereas most firms bombard recruits with the usual gimmicky give-aways such as branded lollies, umbrellas and notepads, Gadens' bag of goodies contained a sample timesheet, a list of after-hours CBD dinner-delivery services and a bus ticket. Asked who among Gadens' lawyers will be attending the fair, Managing Partner Michael Bradley replies: 'A representative selection of some of our finest and most earnest young solicitors may attend, subject to their daily billing targets. If the stall is unattended, it's because we're all doing something more important.' Whereas their competitor firms craft diplomatic statements about the number of recruits they are hiring, Bradley is more open: 'This year we are taking 150 graduates in the hope of there being six or seven of them left standing by February 2008.'

Did Gadens simply lose the plot, or is it responding to the 'war for talent' in a clever and unusual way? We would suggest the latter. The firm might be onto something far more important than a wacky way of communicating. First, and most obviously, Gadens is distancing itself from industry clichés that unify the mass of its competitors in their indistinguishable me-too workplaces. Second, and this is the innovative part, they are engaging with potential recruits in an ironic yet direct way. The firm is poking fun at itself and at institutionalized practices in the industry while still participating in them. It is playing not within but with the rules of its industry. It is being ironic. And it works. According to Bradley, the Gadens campaign is self-selective and ensures that the firm attracts young lawyers who share its sense of humour and, by extension, are comfortable with its culture.[15]

Artefacts are key to the expression and manifestation of culture. Most of them would be developed and produced by the brand manager. Think of the logo, the tone of voice, attributes, design, photography and other artefacts

[15] This story is based on an article that Richard Badham and I wrote for *BRW*, an Australian business magazine. I benefited greatly from Richard's take on irony and humour in organizations.

that the Edinburgh brand has produced as props to narrate a story about it as 'Inspiring Capital'. Or think of contemporary office design: when leading firms such as DEGW strategically transform workspaces into workplaces, the brand-driven design is explicitly thought of as a tool for cultural change.

Besides cultural forms, the culture of an organization manifests itself in its practices. Let's look at one of the 7 Signals of Deloitte, 'Talk Straight', which stands for open, honest and constructive communication between staff and clients. As one of seven core values, 'Talk Straight' drives the Deloitte brand and differentiates it from others. Such a value affects communication practices: when I researched Deloitte over several months, I found that some of the people I talked with were in fact very direct. When asked whether this directness might not be experienced as offensive, people said 'No – we don't beat around the bush, we talk straight!' Obviously, the brand value had an impact on communication patterns. Of course, informal practices might also undermine the formally scripted ones.

As we have argued above, the brand does not equal culture, but as a managerial strategy to manage meaning, it aims to utilize culture as a resource to become effective. It is particularly important in organizations that rely on people to deliver a service; as we said before, if you sell chocolate bars, you don't have to worry about the guy behind the counter. This changes once you move into a more service-driven realm – the behaviour of your waiter is key to a nice dining experience; the behaviour of a call centre operator is key to your banking experience; the behaviour of your lawyer is key to your appreciation of her value. In a service-based economy, people's behaviour becomes part of what the brand promises. Hence the brand expands and tries to manage people through cultural organization. This is nowhere more obvious than in the concept of the employer brand.

Managing the recruitment revolution: the employer brand

Christine Shewry is Global Head of People and Culture at Insurance Australia Group Limited (IAG). IAG is an international general insurance group with operations in Australia, New Zealand, the UK and Asia. It is an umbrella brand with different sub-brands, including Equity Red Star (the UK's fifth-largest motor insurer), CAA (China's largest roadside assistance provider) and the widely known NRMA Insurance in Australia. IAG's businesses underwrite around $7.4 billion's worth of premiums per annum and employ around 16,000 people. I arranged a meeting with Christine because of an article in which she talked about the 'Recruitment Revolution' and how the brand might be able to manage that revolution. 'There is a global shortage of talented staff. And since talent is what business needs to deliver their strategies, people become the asset of every business,' Christine explains. The brand is the technique by which to manage the Recruitment Revolution in order to win the so-called 'War for Talent'. This 'War for Talent' had resulted from a long economic boom in the Western world, including Australia. The current economic climate, with rising unemployment figures, might change the balance of power in this 'War'. That said, professional services firms continue to do well; for instance, PricewaterhouseCoopers reportedly charged £200,000 per hour for overseeing the winding up of Lehman Brothers.[16]

The brand becomes the mechanism – or as Christine says, the 'tool' – for creating and managing a unique employee experience. A globally mobile workforce of Gen Y-ers has high consumer standards – and they expect work to be an experience too. The brand becomes the mechanism for attracting and retaining them. In other words, the brand provides a conceptual framework and a practical tool for managing people and performance *inside* the organization. How does this work at IAG?

If there is a revolution going on, business wants to manage it. So does Christine:

The key thing is to manage the recruitment revolution. We try to understand who we want to attract and what the needs of those people are. The process really starts with understanding their mindsets. Then we ask, how do you have to adapt roles in your organization to attract these people? This critical question might lead to total job redesign. Most organizations design a job and then try to find staff to fit in. We do it the other way around: How can we accommodate people we want to work for us, like a mature-aged workforce or the Gen Y-ers? How can we design jobs around their needs and expectations? For instance, we have people who sign up to work for us and another company over the next four years, learning different skills and having different experiences whilst having some security.

What IAG effectively does is use the principles of branding to position itself in the recruitment market. Of course, IAG employs a diverse workforce ranging from highly skilled professionals to call centre operators. Christine's managerial view segments IAG employees into different groups with different needs. For each of those audiences, IAG develops a different value proposition, or as Christine puts it, different 'employer brands'. The

---

[16] *Accountancy Age*, 3 December 2008; see www.accountancyage. com/accountancyage/news/2231800/pwc-set-200-hour-lehmans-job (acessed 1 February 2009).

employer brands are based on understanding different mindsets. Christine elaborates:

In an inbound call centre, you need caring people who listen to callers who've had just a tree fall onto their house; in an outbound call centre, it is different – people try to sell our products and represent the company. So you need different people with different skills that are attracted to a different value proposition. The employer brand reflects these different cultures.

For Christine, it is only a matter of time until the majority of companies start to develop their internal culture along the lines of their brand. She has a simple yet compelling theory about change: 'Change correlates with the amount of pain you feel. Today, most companies don't feel enough pain – yet. But we are at the tipping point where the pain of not changing might outweigh the pain of changing.' Following this view, brands are becoming increasingly important when it comes down to managing the internal culture of an organization. For management, they offer a framework for making sense of these changes and a springboard for action.

Living brands

Recently, writers have stressed the importance of communicating the brand internally and using it as a catalyst for change. Majken Schultz, for instance, argues that 'corporate brand implementation can be best conceived as processes of organizational change'.[17] Implementing the brand strategy becomes synonymous with cultural change. What is the promise of embedding the brand in the culture? The advocates of managerialism uncritically assume that an aligned brand culture will lead to passion and commitment, and ultimately better performance: 'If the values are deeply rooted and coherently interlinked, then the relevance of the brand's values and the connections staff make with the brand enable them to deliver the brand promise in a more natural manner, with passion and commitment. This, in effect, brings the brand to life and enhances the likelihood of a better performance.'[18] Blending the brand and culture turns employee into a 'living brands', as Nicholas Ind argues: 'The relationship between employees and customers is at the heart of the brand experience. Just as in any successful relationship, the employee/customer relationship needs honesty, openness and a unity of interest. When

[17] Schultz, 2005: 181.
[18] De Chernatony, 2002: 122.

the unity of interest is intuitive, with employees and consumers sharing the same passions, it is particularly powerful.'[19] According to this functionalist perspective, the brand goes through an anthropomorphic transformation and manifests itself as passion in the heart of the employee/consumer relationship. The objective is employee identification with the brand, which is ensured 'through the employee's socialisation into the organization's values. From this perspective, the role of the employee is to represent the brand, where the content and promise of the brand is expressed through the behaviour and the attitude of the employee.'[20] But brand culture does not stop at the mere representation of values; the process might go further, implying a deep personal and emotional connection and involvement: 'We might think of the employee as being the brand ... the norms and values based perspective builds on the premise that the personal values off the employee become congruent with the brand values.'[21] In this view, people are the soul of a company and therefore they 'constitute the soul of the brand. The first step towards creating brand authenticity is therefore to ensure that its core values are clear and have been fully internalised by those who work within the company.'[22]

We know from critical research into organizational culture how organizations attempt to achieve such congruence. Brands are designed, and so are employees who internalize the brand, to a point were they *become* the brand. For Casey, the ultimate 'designer employee' is depicted in Singapore Airlines' flight attendants. Such a designer culture is characterized by individual enthusiasm, dedication, loyalty, self-sacrifice and passion. Designer cultures are the outcome of highly developed culture programmes conducted under the auspices of an integrative focus.[23] Baudrillard analysed the employee's total transformation into corporate brand values as the 'Pathos of the Smile':[24] He dissected the 'network of "personalized" communication' that becomes part of everyday consumption. As he argued, 'we are seeing the systematic reinjection of human relations – in the form of *signs* – into the social circuit, and are seeing the *consumption* of those relations and of that human warmth in *signified form*'. Baudrillard concluded that we are surrounded by that 'institutional smile' and by 'waves of fake spontaneity, "personalized" language, orchestrated emotions and personal relations'. Indeed, as with so many designed things, the smile of the designer employees might feel

---

[19] Ind, 2001: 26.
[20] Karmark, 2005: 108, with a reference to Schein, 1992.
[21] Karmark, 2005: 108 and 109.
[22] Marzano, quoted in Lury, 2004: 34.
[23] Casey, 1995; van Maanen and Kunda, 1989.
[24] Baudrillard, 1970/2003: 160–162.

plastic, too. Like the Party member in Orwell's *Oceania*, the well-socialized, self-disciplined corporate designer employee is 'expected to have no private emotions and no respite from enthusiasm ... the speculations which might possibly induce a sceptical or rebellious attitude are killed in advance by his early-acquired inner discipline'.[25]

The trouble with strong cultures

But this is not the only problem with the current take on strong, brand-mediated cultures. Chan suggests that culture should be thought of as a verb rather than a noun, as a way of accounting for what has been done in and around an organization.[26] Thought of it in this way, culture is far harder to engineer than the strong culture perspective suggests. Rather than being just a matter of replacing one set of normative assumptions with an alternative set, culture consists of loosely negotiated, tacit ways of making sense that are embedded in specific situations in the organization. Being a member doesn't necessarily mean accepting the formal rhetoric of an organization. Taking a salary does not mean a suspension of judgement or critical faculties; neither does possessing a business card mean subscribing to everything done in the organization's name. Moreover, empirical coherence need not be reflected in the views of those who hold these positions and cards, as empirical case studies of 'divided managers' have shown.[27] Every person regulates his or her own position within the cultural spaces created for and around them. Because culture is overwhelmingly situational, the culture usually will be quite fragmentary, forming around certain emergent issues and then dissolving.

Joanne Martin has argued that culture might be more differentiated and fragmented than the functional perspective *à la* Peters and Waterman suggest. In their view, strong cultures are shared cultures – and what is not shared is not part of culture. Deviations from the cultural ideal are seen as unfortunate, yet exceptional, shortcomings. Often, this approach results in culture being the reflection of an organization's elite, but it hardly comprises everyday organizational life with its mundane routines and its over time grown venacular. Martin argues that such homogeneity is problematic and

[25] Orwell, 1954: 220; see Barker, 1993.
[26] Chan, 2003.
[27] Knights and Murray, 1994.

that, in reality, organizations are more differentiated and maybe even more fragmented.

Charles Perrow's article on extrinsic and intrinsic prestige in a hospital illustrates the point.[28] He argued that different internal groups such as doctors and administrative staff have different ideas about prestige. Prestige could be sought either externally or internally. Perrow found that staff complained because resources were used for brand-building activities that would create the image of a 'good hospital' – but 'good' for whom? And 'good' by which standards? This is where conflicts become evident. For instance, the service culture as promoted by management interfered with ethics of care as advocated by doctors and nurses. Treating someone as a patient is fundamentally different from treating them as customer.[29] Second, prestige for doctors meant recognition by colleagues and the profession via write-ups in journals and magazines. For the hospital administration, prestige was linked to mentions in local newspapers and being part of a good community. Finally, management started to invest more in measures of quality that could be promoted than in quality itself: wine with meals, a beauty salon, television for patients, coffee carts for visitors and so on gave hospital visitors the impression of being in a modern and state-of-the-art medical facility. As a result, the reputation of the hospital was good and the occupancy rate was high. However, medical staff complained that these things took up resources that were needed for treatments. Since the quality of these treatments was hard for patients and their relatives to evaluate, the amenities served as a proxy for quality. Service culture indicated care, but as medical staff argued, in reality it took up resources and decreased the quality of care. Perrow's hospital can be described as a differentiated culture, or better, as a set of differentiated sub-cultures in which doctors' and administrators' values were incompatible and inconsistent.

The fragmentation argument refuses to draw a clear battle line between sub-cultures. According to the fragmentation view, culture is neither clearly consistent nor clearly contested. The picture is more likely to be one that represents contradictory and confusing cultures battling for the soul of the organization as much as for that of the individual. Individuals are more likely to exist in a state of competing cultural interpellations – where they are constantly under competing pressures to identify themselves and their organization with rival conceptions of what is an appropriate cultural identity. In such

[28]   Perrow, 1961.
[29]   See Seemann *et al.*, 2007.

a situation, 'consensus is transient and issue-specific, producing short-lived affinities among individuals that are quickly replaced by a different pattern of affinities, as a different issue draws the attention of cultural members'.[30] To make things more complicated, this does not mean that fragmented cultures replace one strong integrated culture. As Joanne Martin has argued, cultures always contain elements of integration, differentiation and fragmentation at the same time. Martin Parker has described such fluid and ambiguous states as 'fragmented unities in which members identify themselves as collective at some times, and divided at others'.[31] Culture does not make us free but fragmented; and it does not make us incarcerated but incoherent. Culture is not about a clear, sharp image of corporate and individual identity but about ambiguity. Confusion is normal, asking questions about clarity is not. This has important implications: If culture is fragmented and complex, how could it be used as a management tool? And how could culturally based brand management deliver against its promise to increase performance through 'living brands'?

Strong cultures support the status quo. This can have bad consequences. For instance, Sims and Brinkmann analysed Enron's collapse in terms of its cultural context: the strong culture that did not accept dissent set the organization on a path where critique and reflection were nothing but signs of hesitation.[32] Similarly, Stein analysed the 1995 collapse of Barings Bank, finding that 'the conditions for Leeson's fraud were set in place substantially prior to his arrival at Barings'.[33] Organizational culture played a major role in both collapses: organizational members did not so much decide to do wrong as find themselves in a context where the historically constituted practices embedded in the organization's culture prepared the field for unethical behaviour.

Literature on corporate disasters, unlawful behaviour and deviance show that starting points for disasters are often embedded in strong cultures.[34] As Vaughan argues, deviance is routine nonconformity and, as such, a predictable product of all organizations. For instance, strong cultures such as a police organization breed, in many cases, corruption.[35] Vaughan argues on Durkheimian lines that the conditions of the normal that organizations

---

[30] Martin and Frost, 1996: 609, citing the work of Kreiner and Schultz (1993) on emergent culture in R&D networks.

[31] Parker, 2000: 1.

[32] Sims and Brinkmann, 2003; Tonge et al., 2003.

[33] Stein, 2000: 1227; Drummond, 2002. The global Financial Crisis can be partly interpreted as another example for the failure of strong cultures.

[34] Turner, 1978; Beamish, 2000; Vaughan, 1981–1982, 1990, 1999.

[35] See Gordon et al., 2009.

define are the preconditions of the abnormal that they create with the norm. In Vaughan's words, 'the same characteristics of a system that produce the bright side will regularly provoke the dark side'.[36] Thus a strong culture that defines what is normal breeds its own transgression. The 'dark side' is a necessary by-product of strong cultures. That's bad news for strong brand-culture advocates, as scandals literally destroy brand value overnight, as Arthur Andersen found to their cost.

Most functional literature promises leadership, domination and control over the organization through smart management, and sometimes manipulation, of culture. The idea is that culture is the result of a top-down process. 'I believe that cultures begin with leaders who impose their own values and assumptions on a group,' says Schein.[37] The leader has to be able to step outside the culture, diagnose it and then implement the changes needed to fix it. This highly simplified image might provide cause for optimism for a manager reading about it while hanging around in an airport lounge, but as an extremely under-socialized account of culture, it is likely to fail. Imagine the CEO of Wal-Mart stepping outside his office in Bentonville, Arkansas, and deciding that the underlying assumptions and subconscious beliefs of his 1.9 million employees need to be changed. Hmmm. Unfortunately, the brand literature has adopted this functionalist and naïve view of culture: branding literature sees culture as an instrument. It is deeply functionalist. Because this view is one-dimensional and conceptualizes culture as a homogeneous 'thing', it runs theoretically and practically into trouble.

People resist colonization by brand values and do not swallow the latest brand values like pills. Designer employees are hard, if not impossible, to manufacture. Van Maanen's Disneyland analysis shows exactly that.[38] In the 'smile factory', as he calls it, a strong corporate culture makes sure that every employee behaves according to Disney's philosophy. Uniforms, specific language codes (work is a 'stage', customers are 'guests' etc.), education through the Disneyland University and employee handbooks embody this spirit. Did employees turn out to be corporate clones? Although employees were very much indoctrinated, they resisted the 'smile factory'. The stressed staff found its own way of dealing with the masses of visitors. They developed informal mechanisms for disciplining especially nasty customers. For instance, the 'seatbelt squeeze' on amusement rides is but a 'small token of appreciation given to a deviant customer consisting of the rapid clinching-up of a required

---

[36] Vaughan, 1999: 274; to the logic of the normal and abnormal, see Canguilhem, 1943/1968.
[37] Schein, 1992: 1.
[38] Van Maanen, 1991.

seatbelt such that the passenger is doubled-over at the point of departure and left gasping for the duration of the trip'.[39] Or bothersome pairs are separated into different units so that they have to enjoy a ride without each other (the so-called 'break-up-the-party' gambit). These and many other unofficial and informal rules and practices are learnt and developed on the job and form a part of the culture of Disneyland. Not quite what the Disney University's culture and brand bible had in mind.

Reframing brand culture

In early management studies, such as Taylor's *Scientific Management*, employees were seen as passive 'hands' until it dawned upon management practitioners and theorists that employees' perception and behaviour were shaped by culture. The emotion of and the interaction between employees was seen as a productive, innovative resource. Usually, it is a delusion of management that it can augment its power through controlling resources. Culture is no exception: management's vision of a strong culture simply echoed its desire for control. The literature on branding has embraced the control function that developed alongside the concept of culture. It simply repeats the mistakes that management made in the early days: understanding culture as the new wonder-weapon in its quest for domination. Based on Bernays' theory, the equation was simple and seductive: if brands can control consumers, could they not also be used to control employees?

We would like to suggest a different view. Rather than trying to create strong cultures, we suggest linking internal cultures with external brand communities.[40] Culture is a set of practices that creates links between people. Branding forms the interface through which the internal and external start communicating. The brand becomes the concept that relates externally focused brand communities and internally organized cultures. Put simply, the brand becomes the medium, the catalyst that creates a community consisting of internal and external stakeholders. The co-creation of value captures the experience and the output of the interaction between internal and external stakeholders. Just like Stendhal described the scintillating and dazzling crystallization process that he observed in the salt mines of

---

[39] Van Maanen, 1991: 71.
[40] Mary Jo Hatch and Majken Schultz's work on branding has stressed the brand's ability to manage internal culture as well as engage with external environments; see Hatch and Schultz, 2001, 2002 and 2008.

Hallein, the brand crystallizes a community that spans internal and external audiences.[41]

The concept of brand culture bridges the gap between inside and outside, engages the organization with its environments and establishing communities around brands. Those communities cut across organizational boundaries just as organizational cultures cut across functional areas. It's not about strong cultures but about weak ties embedded in brand communities that span boundaries. Brand culture becomes an open and open*ing* concept: it's not about the excellence of think-alike managers but about the diversity of internal and external brand communities.

Our argument develops in three steps. First, we have to clarify the degree to which consumers are creative. Just like Taylor thought of employees as passive hands that conduct manual labour, so think most brand theorists of consumers as passive hands that pick items off the shelves. Second, we have to discuss how they form communities around brands. And third, we have to understand how organizations and consumers collaborate and engage in the co-creation of value.

Creative consumers

In management theory, culture became an important concept once it was clear that employees are creative and have ideas. At present, marketing is having the same enlightened revelation: consumption is not just a passive undertaking but a cultural activity. Already Veblen's concept of conspicuous consumption made clear that people consume not as *homo economicus* but because they are after prestige and status. Indeed, consumption is a social practice that is interpreted, and sometimes perverted, by people.

For de Certeau, the question is: What do people do once they have bought something? What do they make of the images they consume sitting in front of the TV? For him, consumption is a creative act – in fact, a different kind of production:

[41] Stendhal, 1822/1975, 284: 'In the salt mines, nearing the end of the winter season, the miners will throw a leafless wintry bough into one of the abandoned workings. Two or three months later, through the effects of the waters saturated with salt which soak the bough and then let it dry as they recede, the miners find it covered with a shining deposit of crystals. The tiniest twigs no bigger than a tom-tit's claw are encrusted with an infinity of little crystals scintillating and dazzling. The original little bough is no longer recognizable; it has become a child's plaything very pretty to see. When the sun is shining and the air is perfectly dry the miners of Hallein seize the opportunity of offering these diamond-studded boughs to travellers preparing to go down to the mine.'

but a hidden one, because it is scattered over areas defined and occupied by systems of 'production' (television, urban development, commerce, etc.), and because the steady expansion of these systems no longer leaves 'consumers' any *place* in which they can indicate what they make or do with the products of these systems. To a rationalized, expansionist and at the same time centralized, clamorous, and spectacular production corresponds *another* production, called 'consumption'. The latter is devious, it is dispersed, but it insinuates itself everywhere, silently and almost invisibly, because it does not manifest itself through its own products, but rather through its *ways of using* the products imposed by a dominant economic order.[42]

De Certeau suggests seeing systems of production and distribution as the raw material for users who carry out their own operations. In fact, users create, alter, change, abuse etc. while they are consuming. Therefore consumption becomes a productive activity.

Take the example of text messaging. Initially, mobile phone providers did not put much faith into this function. Rather, users' creative practices shaped the service and its value. Teenagers started using text messages as a cheap way to avoid the overpriced charges of their network providers. Once the industry realized the commercial value of text messaging (with a profit margin of 90 per cent), TV shows such as Big Brother used mobile phones as tools for direct user involvement. Interestingly, Endemol, the Dutch production company that pioneered Big Brother, is owned by Telefónica de España. Today, the text messaging industry is worth a staggering US $80 billion per annum.[43]

Since de Certeau, metres of shelf space have been filled with writings about creative consumption. In his typology of consumption practices, Holt has argued that consuming is a creative and productive act that is underdetermined by the consumed object.[44] He differentiates between four main categories: (i) *consuming as experience* focuses on the subjective and emotional states of consumption; (ii) *consuming as integration* analyses how consumers make objects part of themselves or vice versa, and how they access a product's symbolic property; (iii) *consuming as classification* looks at objects that classify the consumer, which is achieved through possession and social display of an object; and (iv) *consuming as play* focuses on how people use objects to create social relations and create interaction with fellow consumers.

---

[42] De Certeau, 1980/1984: xii.
[43] See the *ITU Internet Report 2006* available at www.itu.int/publications (accessed 19 June 2009).
[44] Holt, 1995.

Far from being passive hands, consumers become the *de facto* editors of their own reality. They create *bricolages* out of the unlimited access to those endlessly floating signifiers called brands and re-combine them into meaningful (life)styles.

The last category is particularly interesting, as Holt points out: 'Spectators, when they play, adopt a meta-communicational frame that defines the content of their talk and actions as meaningless except for its role in enhancing interaction with others.'[45] Understanding consumption as a fundamentally creative activity makes consumers themselves 'unruly *bricoleurs* who engage in nonconformist producerly consumer practices'.[46] These practices are inherently political, since they are ways of connecting things, people and ideas in different ways. Again, de Certeau: 'the tactics of consumption, the ingenious ways in which the weak make use of the strong, thus lend a political dimension to everyday practices'.[47]

Consumption is also an inherently social activity. As Miller puts it in his chapter 'Making love in supermarkets', consumption is a matter of social relationships.[48] The social context determines the meaning we make, and give, to brands. Think of an expensive new mobile phone: in a meeting with business people, you might use it confidently to signal you are at the vanguard of technology and style; with your family, you might display it as a sign of success and status; with friends, you will downplay its role; at university, you will hide it because you don't want people to know that you spent so much on a phone, and so on. The point is that the same object has very different meanings in different contexts. Take the Coke can: in the former Soviet Bloc in the early 1990s, it symbolized freedom; in other spaces, it might be regarded as an iconic example of American cultural crassness or the unacceptable side of globalization. This flexible extension allows us to perform who we are and who we want to be. Through consumption, we engage in these more or less nonconformist producerly practices. Users are creative: they use, abuse and appropriate things. Brand meaning is the most valuable resource for

---

[45] Holt, 1995: 9.
[46] Holt, 2002: 94, quoted in Arvidsson, 2005: 237; as always, Wikipedia offers a simple and nice definition: a *bricoleur* is someone who creates something by using a diverse set of things that happen to be available.
[47] De Certeau, 1980/1984: xvii.
[48] Miller, 1998a. As Joanne Martin told me, in San Francico's Marina district as well as in Sydney's affluent Eastern Suburbs, many singles often do their shopping late at night, hoping to pick up someone. The items in the trolley serve as social signifiers of taste, status, preferences etc. Playing with Miller's title, they are getting ready to make love in the supermarket.

those 'unruly *bricoleurs*' because it allows them to add a political and social dimension to consumption.[49]

Brand communities

Marketing has traditionally focused on the relationship between individual and brand. It is the individual's needs and desires that have to be satisfied, and sometimes created. Whatever one thinks of the psychological achievements of Maslow, his hierarchy of needs is sociologically very naïve. Putting the focus on individual desire overlooks the social aspects of consumption. In a similar vein, most critical theories argue that consumerism destroys cultural bonds and traditions, that consumption individualizes and hence destroys community.

This view is just as problematic as the idea of passive consumers. In fact, researchers of consumer culture and behaviour have studied consumption communities and found that the 'collective identifications grounded in shared beliefs, meanings, mythologies, rituals, social practices and status systems' define consumer sub-cultures.[50] Consumption has a collective character; it is a social activity, as Wroe Alderson called it, a 'collective behaviour system' that should be analysed on the level of households or firms – not individuals.[51] Similarly, Daniel Boorstin analysed 'consumption communities' that consist of

people with a feeling of shared well-being, shared risk, common interest, and common concerns. These came from consuming the same kind of objects: from those willing to 'Walk a Mile for a Camel', those who wanted 'The Skin You Love to Touch', or who put faith in General Motors, the advertisers of nationally branded products constantly told their constituents that by buying their products they could join a selected group, and millions of Americans were eager to join.[52]

For Boorstin, the new communities formed around consumption created social identity that the US as a country of immigrants had lost through the ethnic and cultural diversity of its population. Instead, people united through consumption: 'Nearly all objects, from the hats and suits and shoes men wore to the food they ate, become symbols and instruments of novel communities. Now men were affiliated less by what they believed than by what they consumed.'[53]

[49] See Hebdige's study from 1979.
[50] Arnould and Thompson, 2005: 874.
[51] Alderson, 1965.
[52] Boorstin, 1973: 147.
[53] Boorstin, 1973: 90; de Grazia, 2005.

The notion of brand communities develops this idea further. Brand communities' 'primary bases of identification are either brands or consumption activities … whose meaningfulness is negotiated through the symbolism of the marketplace'.[54] New social and cultural forms emerge out of creative consumption practices, facilitated by brands. In their seminal 2001 paper, Albert M. Muñiz and Thomas C. O'Guinn proposed a refined definition of this mushrooming phenomenon. They define a brand community as 'a specialized, non-geographically bound community, based on a structured set of social relationships among admirers of a brand'.[55] Brand communities are non-geographical because they are not determined by a specific place or spatial boundaries like neighbourhood communities; needless to say, through modern information and communication technology, these communities spread and grow virtually. This also means that brand communities are often imaginary communities in which members relate to an abstract totality that they do not know personally – or only know partially. Brand communities are specialized because they have, as a central organizing principle, one brand. This differentiates brand communities from other forms of community, such as the local bowling club. Because they are created around a brand, brand communities have an important role in the interpretation, appropriation and actual constitution of the meaning of the brand. Brand community members don't just consume the brand but are critical players in its creation.

Brand communities are defined by three characteristics.[56] First, they have a shared consciousness. This means community members have a sense of their collective identity and, hence, their difference from other non-community members. The single source of their identity is the brand, amplified by the link to other individuals who cluster around the brand. Muñiz and O'Guinn use Apple as an example. The identity of a Macintosh community that they studied showed that identity was developed around Apple being threatened by the incarnation of US corporate power, namely Microsoft and IBM. Community members identified with each other by saying that an Apple person is creative and open-minded, would wear jeans and would not vote conservative.[57] The brand allows community members to create distinction and differentiation within a group of like-minded people. Second, brand communities have certain rituals and traditions that bind them together. People

---

[54] McAlexander *et al.*, 2002: 38.

[55] Muñiz and O'Guinn, 2001: 412.

[56] We follow Muñiz and O'Guinn, 2001; for an application and critical extension of the concept, see McAlexander *et al.*, 2002; Fueller and von Hippel (2008) offer an interesting perspective on the creation of brands through communities.

[57] Muñiz and O'Guinn, 2001: 420.

who ride Harley Davidsons have a greeting ritual (consisting of a skilful wave with one hand as the bikes pass each other) that they use every time they pass another Harley rider on the road. People who work creatively and use Apple have insider stories on shortcuts that are useful when working with Adobe programs. In fact, Adobe programmers build in special shortcuts that do funny things with your computer (if you press a certain combination of keys on your keyboard, certain icons pop up). To know one of them is to be part of the inner circle of the community.

Tradition and history are crucial too. At Apple, the aura of the founder Steve Jobs, the years of decline during the reign of the corporate John Scully, the revival, the iPod – these are all stories that the community rehearses by way of narrating their identity. Belk and Tumbat analysed 'The Cult of Macintosh' as a brand cult that is based on several myths around the brand.[58] They argue that the brand cult around Apple is equivalent to a religion that is based on the myth of the founder and leader, Steve Jobs, the initial creation of the brand (being produced in a garage), the faith of its followers, their belief in the righteousness of the brand, the identification of a satanic opponent (IBM and Microsoft, the former being depicted as Big Brother in the famous 1984 Apple ad) and that salvation can be achieved by finally transcending capitalism through bringing beauty, wisdom and function together.[59] The story gains further appeal through the myth of the revolutionary entrepreneur Steve Jobs, who is on record as saying 'it is better to be a pirate than join the Navy'. It is also no coincidence that he and Steve Wozniak founded Apple on April Fool's day, in 1976.[60] After he was forced to leave Apple, Jobs returned to bring glory and victory to the brand – first with the iMac, later with the iPod. Even the logo – the bitten Apple – reminds one of the apple from the biblical tree of knowledge. It reinforces the brand values of lust, knowledge, hope and anarchy.[61] Ads such as the *1984* ad or the 'Think Different' campaign use counter-culture to establish the image of rebellion. As Jobs said, 'Apple is built on refugees from other companies. These are the extremely bright individual contributors who were trouble-makers at other companies.'[62] Even when Apple drops a product that failed, such as the Apple Newton PDA device, its community of evangelists religiously congregate around the failure. They sustain their community and perform the

[58] Belk and Tumbat, 2005.
[59] Belk and Tumbat, 2005: 207–208.
[60] Belk and Tumbat, 2005: 209.
[61] Belk and Tumbat, 2005: 213.
[62] Belk and Tumbat, 2005: 214.

brand through tales of persecution ('The product was not a failure – people just did not get it!'), tales of miraculous recovery ('The batteries in my Newt suddenly worked again!'), and tales of resurrection ('Wait and see – Apple will reintroduce the Newton!'), among others.[63] Often rumours about the past, present and future feature in brand-community stories. Rumour, word of mouth/mouse and viral marketing can be understood as important communication channels in the marketing mix.[64] However, these new forms of peer-to-peer communication cannot be controlled. Social media develop through stories that are told and re-told by community members. As we argued above, these stories constitute the meaning of the brand. The social construction of brand meaning by community members involves 'accommodation, negotiation, text rejection, interpretation, evaluation, and use of communal symbol systems'.[65] This renders the boundaries around brand ownership blurry. Nonconformist producerly consumer practices might well interfere with marketers' ideas on what the official brand meaning ought to be. This can be problematic – especially if the brand wants to change or broaden its appeal.

Third, brand communities share a sense of moral responsibility in the form of obligations and duties towards others.[66] The community shares a sense of what is the right thing to do and what not. By helping other Apple users with retrieving information from broken hard-drives or providing advice on useful software, community members help each other. By doing so, they also communicate how a brand should be consumed.

Muñiz and O'Guinn summarize brand communities as important because they focus on the social nature of brands: brands are socially constructed through rituals, traditions, stories and history enacted by a community. In doing so, brands provide social structure between consumers and producers. While they provide meaning for the producer, they offer social cohesion and identity for the community.[67]

This implies that consumerism might not lead to an ever-more fragmented and atomized society. Theories ranging from Tönnies' *Gemeinschaft und Gesellschaft* (1887/2005; translated into English in 1957 as *Community and Society*) to Riesman's *Lonely Crowd* (1950) and Putnam's *Bowling Alone* (2000) have for more than a 100 years criticized the lack of cohesion and the

---

[63] Muñiz and Schau, 2005.
[64] Muñiz *et al.*, 2006.
[65] Muñiz and O'Guinn, 2001: 424.
[66] Muñiz and O'Guinn, 2001.
[67] Muñiz and O'Guinn, 2001: 427.

breakdown of traditional social organization within society. But their contemporary followers have overlooked that brands usher new forms of sociality into being.

Through brand communities, brands connect people from different countries and cultures, as Cayla and Eckhardt have argued.[68] They base their argument on Anderson's work on imagined communities. He had argued that newspapers and books provided people with a shared experience that allowed them to imagine themselves as part of the same community. Print media shapes a national consciousness that allows people to be part of the same social and cultural events.[69] Through telling powerful stories and embodying myths, brands play a similar role in global and fragmented communities. They are the medium through which new, imagined, yet very real communities take shape.

If one believes the advocates of brand communities, the future for organizations looks bright: brand communities lead to consumer loyalty – by embedding the brand in the consumers' social world, the brand creates high exit barriers and switching costs.[70] Moreover, brand communities turn consumers into active brand evangelists and create enormous potential for brand extension. Consumers 'who are highly integrated in the brand community are emotionally invested in the welfare of the company and desire to contribute to its success'.[71] Muñiz and his colleagues suggest that brand communities are not just good for big business. Indeed, the advantages for consumer communities are manifold: brands are functional by providing useful information, they undo the Weberian disenchantment with the world, they are democratic and they are living proof that there is a sense of community left in our consumer society.[72]

---

[68] Cayla and Eckhardt, 2008.

[69] Cayla and Eckhardt, 2008; Anderson, 1983.

[70] McAlexander *et al.*, 2002: 50.

[71] McAlexander *et al.*, 2002: 51.

[72] Muñiz and O'Guinn, 2001. For instance, Nadeau, one proponent of this new-found harmony, proclaims that collaborative branding does not have an 'us vs them' mentality any more. As he puts it, 'Let's face it, the war is over! The customer won.' (Nadeau, 2007: 55). However, this victory looks somehow odd: Nadeau talks about a democratic brand that has been voted into existence by costumers: 'These kinds of online voting booths are great for immediate "yes" or "no" determinations about specific questions: red or green for the packaging? Nicole Kidman or Charlize Theron for the movie?' (65). This seems to reflect a rather shallow understanding of democracy and voting. Another example is Nadeau's explorations into DNA marketing that reconnects us with 'our own essential human nature. We are gaining a deeper understanding of the consumer as a biological entity, allowing for true, not just topical, customisation. Call it the *DNA of desire* (which is linked directly to the real DNA of a person)' (95). For different reasons, we come to the same conclusion as Nadeau: this feels like the eastern edge of the new Wild West.

Brand tribes

According to *Google Zeitgeist*, seven out of the ten fastest-rising websites in 2007 were social networking and user-generated content sites.[73] These community-based sites are the catalyst for a new form of re-tribalization that is unfolding in front of our eyes. It seems as if we fell from an economical, under-socialized account straight into the other extreme – an over-socialized reality in which individuality is determined by tribalism. The concept of tribalism allows us to gain some critical distance to the euphoria around brand communities.

Michel Maffesoli has argued that re-tribalization means that individuals are not seen as having a function in a society but a role to play in different tribes.[74] Naturally, as individuals *play* roles, aesthetic appearances become more important including styles, expressions, tones, designs and everything else that helps to develop a script and props for the authentic enactment of the role. For Maffesoli, the tribe is the *'most final expression of the creativity of the masses'*.[75] Brands are key in this setting – they are ready-made scripts and props to express mass creativity.

The result of that play is mass spectacles. As Guy Debord anticipated in his 1967 book, we live in a society of the spectacle. Indeed, *Work Is Theatre and Every Business a Stage*.[76] If efficiency and effectiveness was the model of the early twentieth century, now it is image, experience and sensation. Each tribe performs their own show, which is characterized by their own styles. The relation between the tribes is a relation between differences in style. Hence lifestyles become the all-defining properties of brand tribes. And because tribes perform for each other, the audience is as significant as the actual players. This is normally described as the attention economy, depicting attention as a scarce resource.[77] Many viewers also mean many opinions and conflicting interpretations, which results in increased ambiguity and vagueness. Thus the atmosphere and the ambience of the event become more crucial for the evaluation of the event than the act itself.

Because tribes are more often than not informally constituted, they constantly need to reaffirm each other about their substance and truthfulness.

---

[73] They are Badoo, Facebook, Dailymotion, YouTube, Second Life, hi5 and Club Penguin – see www.google.com/intl/en/press/zeitgeist2007 (accessed 18 June 2008); see also Godin, 2008.

[74] Maffesoli, 1988/1996.

[75] Maffesoli, 1988/1996: 96.

[76] Pine and Gilmore, 1999.

[77] Davenport and Beck, 2001.

The most important currency, therefore, is authenticity: 'A revolution is start-ing that is going to mean trouble for businesspeople and marketeers alike, as their most conscious consumers suddenly launch a determined rejection of the fake, the virtual, the spun and the mass-produced'.[78] Tribes are motivated by a never-ending quest for the authentic and 'the real thing'.

Of course, the underlying notion of 'real' is in itself rather naïve: for instance, Boyle preaches that we need 'real' relationships and 'real' con-nections as opposed to the 'unreal' ones in internet chat rooms. While some weddings might be made in heaven, many more are made online, so why is the virtual less 'real' than a 'farmer's market' or a 'reading group', both of which are 'real' according to Boyle?[79] Is Second Life not a 'real' community and a 'real' economy? The argument is wrong because the question is wrong: in a tribalized community, reality consist of signs, images, symbols, icons and events. Authenticity and its thirst for the 'real thing' are mere symptoms of a tribe's ongoing quest for self-affirmation and self-assurance.

As Maffesoli reminds us, a tribe's social life is only based on the relations among members. Tribes have an in-group and an out-group, which explains why they are constantly looking for what's 'in'. Rather then being ex-tensive, the tribe is in-tensive, always searching for new stimulus. Because of that, tribes are somehow self-sufficient and apolitical: they do not differentiate through *pro* and *con* but through what's *in* and *out*.

We suggest describing brand communities as tribes.[80] Tribes turn brands into cults by blurring the boundary between the sacred and the profane.[81] Tribes can have adverse consequences. For instance, they might reject change: members of the Saab tribe publicly rejected the new models that were produced after GM had bought Saab. People who drove the new models were 'yuppie scum'[82] – at least in the eyes of the old aficionados. The same happened to the VW Beetle community: the new version from 1998 was dis-carded as nothing but a commercial cash-in version of the real thing. Tribes might reject marketing-speak and are critical towards corporations – and especially towards advertising. Tribe members develop a clear idea of what

---

[78] Boyle, 2004: 4.
[79] See the rather obscure list of real and fake experiences in Boyle, 2004: 67.
[80] Wipperfürth, 2005, 131: 'A brand tribe is a group of people who share their interest in a specific brand and create a parallel social universe ripe with its own values, rituals, vocabulary, and hierarchy.' Cova and Cova 2001, discuss the difference between a tribe and a market segment as follows: a tribe is a network of heterogeneous people who share a passion; a market segment is a group of homogeneous people that are not connected.
[81] Atkin, 2004.
[82] O'Guinn and Muñiz, 2005.

the brand is, and if the ads do not reinforce the preferred image, communities become critical. An example is GM's launch of the new Pontiac, which was not approved by the user community and was criticizsed heavily.[83]

Since consumers become active co-authors in the narration of the brand, it is understandable that if one part of the editorial team (the organization) starts to change the narrative through ads, the other party is upset. Brands such as Harley Davidson that manage to create tribes around them are often outlaw brands or underdogs.[84] Frequently they are based on a strong rivalry (Pepsi vs Coke, Apple vs PC) that demonizes the other brand. Although despised, the enemy brand needs to be kept up in order to sustain the brand tribe itself. Finally, tribes are inclusive and thus desire marginality. This means members might not want to grow or admit new members.[85] Of course, this can have adverse effects on the brand because it limits its growth beyond life as an underdog with sub-culture status.

Brand communities, just like organizational culture, are neither homogeneous phenomena nor the answer to all problems. They are ambiguous at best. But as new forms of social organization, they do provide opportunities that open up potential for change. This is what we are interested in: using the brand as a platform for the engagement between internal cultures and external communities. Brands as interface give rise to the co-creation of value.

Engaging internal cultures and external communities: the co-creation of value

The point we want to make is that organizational cultures and brand communities while different are compatible. Structurally, they are mirror images of each other, both emanating from the brand. Rather than trying to develop 'designer cultures' or 'living brands' that are the result of managerial wishful thinking, we suggest engaging internal cultures and external communities with each other. Such an engagement when done well can result in the co-creation of value.

With his book *Third Wave*, Alvin Toffler pioneered the concept of the 'prosumer'.[86] He argued that the Industrial Revolution separated the

---

[83] Muñiz and O'Guinn, 2005.
[84] Schouten and McAlexander, 1995.
[85] O'Guinn and Muñiz, 2005.
[86] Toffler, 1980.

consumer from the producer. That's Marx's point: the capitalists seize the means of production and the exploited and alienated worker is condemned to consume what its peers produce in isolation from each other. The 'prosumer' was meant to reverse this arrow and make consumers producers and vice versa. But Toffler was ahead of his time. In 2006, the cover of *Time* Magazine was a reflective silver foil announcing the Person of the Year: *You – You* because it was *You* who developed content for online applications, spent hours on end on YouTube, socialized on MySpace and created knowledge for Wikipedia. *Time*'s choice reflected the fact that consumers had become truly productive.

The marketer Venkat Ramaswamy and strategy professor C. K. Prahalad described this new phenomenon as the co-creation of value: 'Co-creation converts the market into a forum where dialogue among the consumer, the firm, consumer communities and networks or firms can take place.'[87] This dialogue shapes both experiences and expectations. The authors attribute this revolution to the changing nature of the consumer's activity, from 'isolated to connected, from unaware to informed, from passive to active'.[88] It is the interaction between consumers and producers on all levels of the value-creation process, from development to design, manufacturing, distributing and marketing, that changes the way business gets done.

More knowledgeable consumers challenge old industry boundaries and demand bundled services from hitherto unconnected industries. Think of the 'wellness space' in which insurance, medical expertise, beauty care, fitness, tourism and more esoteric products merge and form an experience that no single traditional industry is able to deliver.

In short, consumers will be involved in the creation of value that contradicts three dearly and long-held assumptions: first, that companies create value unilaterally; second, that value resides exclusively in the company's products or services; and third, that consumption is passive. Rather, consumers enact value in a network of products and services provided by diverse industries. To put it as simply as possible, the company-centred point of view that talks about a B2C relationship will be substituted by a C2B2C relationship. And this is the optimistic forecast for business: websites such as www.propser.com or www.ebay.com work on a C2C basis, cutting business out

---

[87] Prahalad and Ramaswamy, 2004: 122.
[88] Prahalad and Ramaswamy, 2004: 2.

altogether. All they offer is a strong brand that people who have never met rely on when they collaborate with each other.

According to Ramaswamy and Prahalad, the points of interaction between consumers and producers become the crucial element in the co-creation process. They argue that it is at these points that the co-creation of value occurs: 'Points of interaction provide opportunities for collaboration and negotiation, explicit or implicit, between the consumer and the company – as well as opportunities for those processes to break down.'[89] The interface for this interaction is the brand: *the co-creation experience is the brand*.[90] Linking internal culture and external community, the brand becomes the engine for the co-creation of value.

Summary

The brand as a tool for managing meaning plays an increasingly important role in organizations. Fuelled by fantasies emanating from Peters and Waterman's excellence studies, the brand promises the nirvana of a strong, aligned, homogeneous firm marching in one direction. The fantasies of the 'living brand' – a kind of new Leviathan made up of the actions of subordinates – exemplify this. However, there are some good functional, conceptual and ethical reasons why strong cultures might be weak cultures after all. While framed in a language that promises increased managerial control, the brand is not likely to deliver human puppets that move according to the brand style guidelines. While brands will be enacted locally and appropriated contextually, they represent a new discursive resource that management and employees alike can draw upon to formulate positions and legitimize claims. As such, brands influence organizational power relations and inject a new dynamic.

Rather than focusing solely on the internal environment, we have introduced a perspective that sees internal cultures reflected in external communities. Following this argument, the brand can be conceptualized as the mechanism around which their interaction crystallizes. With the theorem of the co-creation of value, this interface (the brand) becomes the pivotal hinge that allows producers and consumers to interact. The brand becomes the intermediary between internal and external environment. It is the

---

[89] Prahalad and Ramaswamy, 2004: 33.
[90] Prahalad and Ramaswamy, 2004: 134.

metaphorical shop window, the interface between inside and outside, that Baudrillard has described as follows:

The shop-window – all shop-windows – which are, with advertising, the foci of our urban consumer practice, are also the site *par excellence* of that 'consensus operation', that communication and exchange of values through which an entire society is homogenized by incessant daily acculturation to the silent and spectacular logic of fashion. That specific space which is the shop-window – neither inside nor outside, neither private or wholly public, and which is already the street while maintaining, behind the transparency of its glass, the distance, the opaque status of the commodity – is also the site of specific social relation ... [It is] a generalized communication between all individuals, not via the contemplation of the same objects but via the reading and recognition in the same objects of the same system of signs and the same hierarchical code of values. It is this acculturation, this training, which take place at every moment everywhere in the streets ... Shop-windows thus beat out the rhythm of the social process of value: they are a continual adaptability test for everyone, a test of managed projection and integration.[91]

Just as the shop window is the managed physical interface between employees and consumers, the brand becomes the intellectual, social and cultural medium connecting inside and outside. The 'consensus operation' that Baudrillard observed might still be at work in communities, and especially in their more tribal forms. The logic of seduction and desire is supplemented with the logic of co-creation that is enabled through the brand as the interface between production and consumption.

Ultimately, the question is whether inter-organizational brand communities have the potential to become change agents of society. Philosophers such as Agamben in his *The Coming Community* and Nancy in *The Inoperative Community* would agree. Communities might well be that space of becoming and transformation, driven neither by individual needs nor corporate greed or state-sponsored control.[92] Adding the powers of co-creation, brand communities might become a generator of new forms of social organization, new ideas and new experiences. But they might also result in unintended consequences. For instance, brand tribes are far from representing cosy communities in which people joyfully congregate around brands. Rather, they might hijack the brand for their own purposes, just like British hooligans hijacked Burberry

---

[91] Baudrillard, 1970/2003: 166.
[92] Agamben, 1990/1993 and Nancy, 1982/1991.

In the next chapter, we will explore how the co-creation between brand communities and internal organizational cultures affects the innovation process – and how it can result in unintended consequences. Our argument is that a particular form of innovation – open-source innovation – crystallizes its community around the brand. Following this argument, the brand becomes a pivotal mechanism to attract (and to a lesser degree, manage) open-source innovation.

6 Innovation

Playing with LEGO

In 1998, LEGO released a new product called LEGO Mindstorm. The heart of it was a yellow microchip that made all sorts of movements and behaviours possible. The product became an instant hit – within three months, 80,000 sets had changed hands. There was just one small problem: the buyers were not children but adults. And that was despite the fact that LEGO marketed the product to children, not adults. Worse, these adults did not consume the product as the LEGO Masterminds had anticipated. Within weeks, hackers from all over the world had cracked the code of the new toy and created all sorts of new applications: Mindstorm users built everything from soda machines to blackjack dealers. The new programs spread quickly over the World Wide Web and were far more sophisticated than the ones LEGO had developed. More than forty guide books advised on how to get maximum fun out of your 727-part LEGO Mindstorm set.

Yun Mi Antorini, back then Senior Director of Global Brand Strategy at the LEGO Group, recalls how that storm took LEGO by surprise. The people who bought and changed the product did not appear in LEGO's marketing plan at all. Consumers were meant to consume, not produce their own versions. They were not meant to challenge LEGO's in-house product developers. LEGO was confused. It did nothing for a year. Then it decided to listen and try to understand what those users were actually doing with the LEGO brand.

What we will be recounting over the next few pages is as much LEGO's story as Yun Mi Antorini's. She moved on from being Senior Director at LEGO to do a PhD at Copenhagen Business School on Brand Community Innovation at LEGO. So let's see what happened.

Up until 1999, communication between LEGO and its brand community consisted mainly of lawsuit threats because the communities used the LEGO logo without authorization. LEGO saw the whole movement as a 'shadow market' that distracted from its real target – children. The brand community, in turn, saw LEGO as arrogant and unresponsive.

Finally, in 1999, LEGO acted. Senior Vice President and Head of the LEGO Direct division, Brad Justus, posted the first official LEGO message on Lugnet, the international fan-created LEGO Users Group Network. Notice that he was allowed to do so by the Lugnet administrators. What did he say?: 'Here are some words that should gladden your hearts: we are listening. And more than that, we will endeavour to be very responsive to your needs and desires … We want to be the company you'd like us to be.'[1]

This marked the point at which LEGO understood that threatening legal action was not the best way to manage its brand community. It dawned on Brad Justus and his colleagues that the LEGO community was doing something interesting, and that just because the LEGO business strategy did not include it in its planning did not mean it was not important.

LEGO realized that its brand community did not passively consume but was engaging in de Certeauian consumption practices: it had started to co-create and innovate. LEGO's brand was the medium through which that co-creation experience occurred. Its brand identity had become relational, as defined in interaction with stakeholders, rather than being narcissistically focused on the self.

Users gave mixed responses to the message: 'Brad, well this is interesting but I have a hard time believing this …'. Some thought it was a hoax: 'Lego has never cared about us. Why should they now?' Brad and his team had to work hard to convince the community that they actually did care. LEGO hired people in its newly formed Community Development Group to travel the world and appear at LEGO events. Blogs and online channels where

---

[1] Quoted in Antorini, 2007: 142.

users could talk to LEGO were established. In 2002, LEGO invited the North America LEGO User Group to join the *What Will You Make, America?* roadshow. This encouraged kids to play with LEGO while giving the LEGO communities a broader audience.

How was the LEGO community organized? LEGO had a diverse community around its brand that was divided into two camps: on the one hand, there were the LEGO fans who were into outer space; and on the other hand, there were those who were into trains. The two could not be more different. The former was about fantasy, science fiction, humour and free building; the latter was about real-world models, suburban life, no nonsense and scaled modelling.[2] Despite these differences, they formed a community around LEGO. As one LEGO designer said, 'LEGO bricks define a visual language system. By a grammar of visual shapes, elements are combined into expressions (structures, models) and take up meaning. The meaning of elements depends on its context. The vocabulary of elements defines an infinite range of possibilities, but there are patterns, underlying structures, and styles.'[3] Note that this LEGO user did not happen to have a PhD in semiotics – a good reason to be even more fascinated by his description of LEGO as a language. As with any other form of cultural expression, the challenge is to say something new with a limited vocabulary and a grammar that is shared within a community. This philosophy was at the heart of the brand community.

LEGO's innovation engine

Most importantly, the LEGO community developed new products and experiences. The key argument of this chapter is: brand communities are innovative. They fundamentally change the way innovation takes place, moving organizations from a closed to an open model of innovation. But open-source innovation does not occur in a vacuum; it is organized around strong platforms that mediate between explorers and exploiters. As we will see, brands are the platforms where creative consumers meet, form communities and become productive.

But let's go back to the LEGO community. What kind of innovations did they produce? Yun Mi Antorini found four different types of innovations.[4] First, LEGO users produced physical and aesthetic add-ons such as batteries

[2] Antorini, 2007: 177.
[3] The quote is taken from Kornberger, 2005: 26.
[4] We follow Antorini, 2007: 187ff.

for cars and trains, or clothes for figures. Almost 50% of all innovations were part of this category.

Second, users developed new play themes such as LEGO Harry Potter or LEGO Life on Mars, which explored new experiences for users. When LEGO entered a licensing agreement and produced LEGO Star Wars, it was required to discontinue the more old-fashioned LEGO Space product line. This opened the door for users to develop their own play themes – such as LEGO Life on Mars.[5] Users also started to experiment with new ways of experiencing the product. For instance, the LEGO community developed what it described as a 'vignette'. A vignette is a creative action or an idea that should look like a snapshot in time and should photograph well. For example, one user developed a self-designed LEGO figure to document his travels through Venice by placing the LEGO figure at touristy spots and then taking pictures of it from unusual perspectives. The idea here is to introduce a new way of experiencing LEGO and playing with it.[6] Almost 25% of all innovations belonged to this new-experience category.

Third, new building techniques, such as new styles of buildings, models or colour effects that can be achieved through the combination of existing bricks, accounted for 13% of all innovations. For instance, on the LEGO user fan website www.fbtb.net, I found the following example of a Star Wars Fighter Plane:

This model is part of what I call my 'Episode 3 Collection', referring to 5 models I completed in a very short time for a movie theatre lobby Episode 3 display … The interior, and perhaps my favorite part of the model, the seat. I used my enlarged UCS R-2 design again too … I'll be very surprised if LEGO doesn't eventually give us a system version of this.

Finally, users developed computer-related improvements, such as software or programming. These innovations accounted for 14% of all innovations.

But community members toying around with ideas do not develop automatically marketable new products. As Antorini has analysed, 88.4% of all innovations represented minor improvement innovations. These included: accessories such as clothes or weapons to improve the aesthetics of the product; batteries for trains to increase performance; and new play themes, such as LEGO Sea Monkeys or LEGO Lord of the Rings, which recreated the LEGO experience

---

[5] A play theme is a narrative that provides the context for playing with LEGO, such as LEGO City, LEGO Star Wars, and so on.
[6] Antorini, 2007: 171.

in a new context. In the case of the latter, users could even buy user-produced Lord of the Rings equipment for their own LEGO figures.

How about the remaining eleven-point-something per cent? Antorini found that 4.5% of all innovations were major improvement innovations, and 7.1% were first-of-type innovations.[7] While the former improve processes, performance and functionality, the latter introduce radically new experiences and possibilities. What were the major first-of-type innovations that Antorini found? These included strategy games with multiplayer features and role-play elements, such as BrickWars. Or take Mosaic Building Techniques: rather than copying existing images with LEGO bricks, an image is translated into pixels (LEGO bricks) and then assembled digitally. Software called Pixelego (see www.ericharshbarger.org) has been developed and distributed for free by users to translate images into LEGO Syntax. Another example is LDraw (www.ldraw.org), an open-source software program that allows users to create virtual LEGO models and scenes. Or take www.brickfilms.com, where animators create short films using LEGO figures. You can watch *Indiana Scones and the Quest for the Platinum Waffle* ('Indy's back, and more Lego'ish than ever') by EAnimation, just like 32,000 other YouTubers have done in less than eight weeks after its launch. Finally, users developed their own customized LEGO kits with LEGO elements, building instructions and custom-designed packaging. For instance, www.mechanizedbrick.com sells LEGO kits for military model builders, including a German Panzerkampfwagen VI 'Tiger I' Heavy Tank that retails for US$215. These are all examples of first-of-type innovations that truly develop LEGO and the user experience further.

What motivated these innovators to develop complex software or design their own LEGO kits? Why did they come up with these innovations? How can we explain their behaviour? A recurring theme among creative users was that they had a need or experienced a problem and could not find the solution elsewhere. The second most-often mentioned reason was that it is simply fun to build new stuff.[8]

Looking at when innovations occurred, Antorini found a sharp rise from 1998 onwards. This is not really surprising: the advent of the internet made co-creation much easier. It also provides some possible answers for the question: Where does innovation happen? Most of it happens online. There are countless LEGO user group websites, such as www.lugnet.com, www.1000steine.de, www.brickworld.us, www.brickish.org, www.

---

[7] Antorini, 2007: 192.
[8] Antorini, 2007: 216.

debouwsteen.com, www.legofan.org, and even more personal websites, Yahoo! Groups, Facebook communities, and so on. And this list does not include renegades such as www.neutronbot.com, where LEGO enthusiasts show their latest creations, including scenes from the movie blockbuster *Kill Bill*.

Since its inception in 1998, 25 million people have visited the German LEGO user group 1000steine, and more than 150,000 unique visitors click on Lugnet per month. Other sites such as www.bricklink.com operate as a grey marketplace for LEGO products, with almost 3,000 registered sellers or stores offering some 85 million different items. There are countless specialized user groups, such as LEGO Train Clubs, LEGO Mindstorm User Group of LEGO Star Wars Experience (www.fbtb.net).[9] Annual get-togethers and country-specific community events such as Brickfest in the US provide face-to-face contact for LEGO freaks. As the Brickfest programme from 2003 explained, LEGO fans run workshops on how to build things ('Medieval Building' or 'Joys of Building in Microscale'), show their models ('Classic-Castle Show and Tell'), run competitions, show LEGO-based animations and films and discuss community activities. Other games such as Dirty Brickster (?!) are played in the German 1000Steineland event.

According to Antorini, a quarter of the LEGO community has come up with one or more new things. Who were the non-innovators compared to the innovators? The two groups did not differ in terms of engaging with the product, but on average the innovators spent twice as much time discussing and exchanging ideas and engaging in dialogue with other LEGO users. Interaction was key to the community's innovation capacity.[10]

Of course, correlation does not prove causality: innovative people might simply talk more because they have news to tell. In this case, interaction follows from innovation. On the other hand, innovation might be based on bouncing ideas through virtual chat rooms until they manifest in new products and experiences. Either way, interaction matters. But it is not only innovation that is linked to chatty LEGO users. The LEGO brand itself is a result of those conversations. The brand is the sum total of stories that people tell each other. While LEGO users spin off new ideas, they also spin the narrative of the LEGO brand.

The benefits for LEGO as a company are blindingly obvious. First, having an active and innovative user community helps the company keep on eye

---

[9] Antorini, 2007: 127 and 148.
[10] Antorini, 2007: 212.

on trends for new products. Second, and maybe more important, it helps to develop marketable product innovations. The long list of user-based innovations that have found their way onto the shelves include LEGO Studies, based on Brickflims.com; LEGO Factory, based on LDraw; LEGO Mosaic, based on Pixelego; and LEGO Vikings, based on a user-developed play theme.[11]

These new products are likely to be more successful because they are made by consumers. Remember, in the traditional qualification-requalification process, focus groups and testing should ensure a fit between new ideas and needs. User-generated innovations are likely to outperform traditional product innovations as they have this qualification process more deeply and intrinsically embedded in their DNA.[12]

Out of control?

There are some less obvious yet quite important issues that the LEGO company had (and presumably still has) to deal with. As with any tribe, the user innovators are not easy to manage or control. In fact, at various junctures the community thwarted innovation. For instance, LEGO introduced a colour change of its bricks because it felt that new colours would be more appealing to children. However, the LEGO user group sparked controversy about that: for collectors, new colours posed a challenge in regard to integration of new and old bricks. So they responded negatively to the innovation.[13] When it comes to change, LEGO community members are purists who agree that certain LEGO products are actually not 'real' LEGO products. For instance, LEGO Gladiators (a system that used action figure elements) was seen as un-LEGO because of its lack of compatibility, and hence was rejected by the community.[14] As one user said about another rejected product, LEGO Bionicle: 'Unpure! Unclean! Evil!'[15] This shows the emotional investment that the user group has made in the brand. Change or innovation that does not come from users is seen as a potential threat and might be resisted fiercely.

That poses the challenge of the integrity and consistency of the brand. How could LEGO follow that 'eternal truth' to protect its brand?[16] This is exactly

[11] Antorini, 2007: 220; although LEGO did not simply copy these ideas and market them, it is important to note that LEGO community developed them, which proves the community's ability to innovate.
[12] Von Hippel, 2005.
[13] Antorini, 2007: 148.
[14] Antorini, 2007: 182 and 239.
[15] Antorini, 2007: 228.
[16] Blackett, 2003: 23.

what LEGO did initially when it threatened to sue the community groups when they started to toy around with the brand. This was clearly a wrong assessment of the situation, but where does LEGO draw the line between legitimate use and illegitimate abuse?

Take the example of Nike and its offer to customize shoes. The idea behind this exercise in user-involvement was freedom of expression, allowing every user to print on their shoes what they wanted. Users became instant DIY-designers who could shape the look of their shoes. By extension, this would also affect Nike's brand: if you saw a particularly ugly shoe with the Nike logo on it, you would not know that it was designed by a colour-blind amateur. You might instead think that Nike had lost the plot. Or what if you wanted to have a message on your shoe that was critical of Nike? That's exactly what happened when Jonah Peretti ordered a pair of shoes with the customized print design 'Sweatshop'. Here's his email exchange with Nike:[17]

From: 'Personalize, NIKE iD'<nikeid_personalize@nike.com>
To: 'Jonah H. Peretti' <peretti@media.mit.edu>
Subject: RE: Your NIKE iD order o16468000

Your NIKE iD order was cancelled for one or more of the following reasons.

1) Your Personal iD contains another party's trademark or other intellectual property. 2) Your Personal iD contains the name of an athlete or team we do not have the legal right to use. 3) Your Personal iD was left blank. Did you not want any personalization? 4) Your Personal iD contains profanity or inappropriate slang, and besides, your mother would slap us.

If you wish to reorder your NIKE iD product with a new personalization please visit us again at www.nike.com
Thank you,
NIKE iD

From: 'Jonah H. Peretti' <peretti@media.mit.edu>
To: 'Personalize, NIKE iD' <nikeid_personalize@nike.com>
Subject: RE: Your NIKE iD order o16468000

Greetings,
My order was canceled but my personal NIKE iD does not violate any of the criteria outlined in your message. The Personal iD on my custom

---

[17] See www.shey.net/niked.html (accessed 2 June 2008).

ZOOM XC USA running shoes was the word 'sweatshop.' Sweatshop is not: 1) another's party's trademark, 2) the name of an athlete, 3) blank, or 4) profanity. I choose the iD because I wanted to remember the toil and labor of the children that made my shoes. Could you please ship them to me immediately.
Thanks and Happy New Year,
Jonah Peretti

From: 'Personalize, NIKE iD' <nikeid_personalize@nike.com>
To: 'Jonah H. Peretti' <peretti@media.mit.edu>
Subject: RE: Your NIKE iD order o16468000

Dear NIKE iD Customer,
Your NIKE iD order was cancelled because the iD you have chosen contains, as stated in the previous e-mail correspondence, 'inappropriate slang'.
    If you wish to reorder your NIKE iD product with a new personalization please visit us again at www.nike.com
Thank you,
NIKE iD

From: 'Jonah H. Peretti' <peretti@media.mit.edu>
To: 'Personalize, NIKE iD' <nikeid_personalize@nike.com>
Subject: RE: Your NIKE iD order o16468000

Dear NIKE iD,
Thank you for your quick response to my inquiry about my custom ZOOM XC USA running shoes. Although I commend you for your prompt customer service, I disagree with the claim that my personal iD was inappropriate slang. After consulting Webster's Dictionary, I discovered that 'sweatshop' is in fact part of standard English, and not slang. The word means: 'a shop or factory in which workers are employed for long hours at low wages and under unhealthy conditions' and its origin dates from 1892. So my personal iD does meet the criteria detailed in your first email.
    Your web site advertises that the NIKE iD program is 'about freedom to choose and freedom to express who you are.' I share Nike's love of freedom and personal expression. The site also says that 'If you want it done right ... build it yourself.' I was thrilled to be able to build my own shoes, and my personal iD was offered as a small token of appreciation for the sweatshop

workers poised to help me realize my vision. I hope that you will value my freedom of expression and reconsider your decision to reject my order.
Thank you,
Jonah Peretti

From: 'Personalize, NIKE iD' <nikeid_personalize@nike.com>
To: 'Jonah H. Peretti' <peretti@media.mit.edu>
Subject: RE: Your NIKE iD order o16468000

Dear NIKE iD Customer,
Regarding the rules for personalization it also states on the NIKE iD web site that 'Nike reserves the right to cancel any Personal iD up to 24 hours after it has been submitted'.
    In addition it further explains:
'While we honor most personal iDs, we cannot honor every one. Some may be (or contain) others' trademarks, or the names of certain professional sports teams, athletes or celebrities that Nike does not have the right to use. Others may contain material that we consider inappropriate or simply do not want to place on our products.
    Unfortunately, at times this obliges us to decline personal iDs that may otherwise seem unobjectionable. In any event, we will let you know if we decline your personal iD, and we will offer you the chance to submit another.'
With these rules in mind we cannot accept your order as submitted.
    If you wish to reorder your NIKE iD product with a new personalization please visit us again at www.nike.com
Thank you,
NIKE iD

From: 'Jonah H. Peretti' <peretti@media.mit.edu>
To: 'Personalize, NIKE iD' <nikeid_personalize@nike.com>
Subject: RE: Your NIKE iD order o16468000

Dear NIKE iD,
Thank you for the time and energy you have spent on my request. I have decided to order the shoes with a different iD, but I would like to make one small request. Could you please send me a color snapshot of the ten-year-old Vietnamese girl who makes my shoes?
Thanks,
Jonah Peretti
{no response}

The email went from the fingertips of Jonah Peretti around the globe, challenging the US$1-billion per year Nike brand machinery. Jonah did not agree with Nike's rhetoric of freedom and its practice of 'employing' workers in developing countries under inhumane conditions. While Jonah could have voiced his opinion over a drink with his friends, he would not have had the same kind of reach as Nike. In this unequal fight, Nike would win. But something challenged this hegemony: co-creation invites consumers to contribute. What they contribute is largely up to them. In the case of Nike, the company had become more vulnerable and people like Jonah more powerful. Co-creation invites a public to form around an issue. Once the public is assembled, outcomes are hard to determine.[18] This is the Trojan horse of open-source innovation: companies need to engage in it because it provides them with better ideas, faster. But this also means they will lose hegemonic control over their brands. Co-creation instigates mutual dependency. In such mutually constituted networks, power works relationally: no one controls the network totally, but each player's power depends on a set of complex relations to others. Simply put, engaging in co-creation and open source innovation will open up and, to some extend, democratize the corporate world.[19]

At LEGO, there were tensions between the corporate agenda and the LEGO community. The latter was by nature non-commercial and had a different interest in the brand. For instance, LEGO users liked to support LEGO – to a point. They did not like being 'sales people for LEGO', as one user put it: 'We probably help to sell a lot of LEGO product at our robotics events because there are always a lot of kids and parents that come and ask and we tell them where they can buy it. We encourage them to buy it, and tell them about it, but we do not like to be sales people.'[20]

There were also attempts to build an umbrella organization that would unite the fragmented communities. Attempts such as EuroBrick or a Global AFOL Group failed because of a lack of activity and drive.[21] Obviously, LEGO as a company would have embraced one unified global user group (preferably led by some kind of CEO), but communities work differently: they are bottom up. When LEGO tried to institutionalize them, they found it next to impossible to control the hundreds of user groups out there.

Perhaps one of the most successful attempts at tapping into users' power was the LEGO Ambassador Programme. As part of the programme, LEGO

---

[18] See Foster's article on co-creation and the public (Foster, 2007).
[19] Von Hippel, 2005.
[20] Quoted in Antorini, 2007: 145.
[21] Antorini, 2007: 146.

invited between twenty and twenty-five LEGO fans to join each year. They were asked for their input on new product development and ideas in general. However, the community reacted in a mixed way, since some Ambassadors had to sign non-disclosure agreements with LEGO. Ironically, the official Ambassador logo showed one LEGO person talking to two others who listen – obviously the Ambassador tells the other non-ambassadors what he knows. The programme introduced a sense of hierarchy and exclusion. The free sharing and revealing – the hallmark of every open-source community – was written off with the signing of the non-disclosure agreements.[22]

LEGO is not a single case study; rather, it can be seen as the blueprint for innovative brand communities in other industries. LEGO user communities share their 'love for the brick', but everything else is negotiated every day on websites, grey markets and hundreds of blogs. The brand emerges from these conversations; it is not owned by LEGO. That is an important point – the brand is not the property of the company but belongs to its customers. Unilateral action by LEGO is punished, while conversation and dialogue are key. Our argument is that these conversations can become the engine room of innovation: as we have seen, consumers are creative, non-conformist producers. What they create rivals what comes out of those big-budget corporate R&D labs. Users can compete – and often outperform – the better-resourced corporate innovation players because they can draw on an open platform for innovation. The open-source movement has been pushing this point.

What open-source theorists have neglected to date is that creative users do not congregate around just any kind of platform. Rather, they are attracted to, and contribute to, a brand that acts as the platform for interaction and innovation. In this sense, brands become drivers of open-source innovation: they are the glue that keeps communities together. Innovation occurs as result of interaction in these brand communities. But how exactly does this work?

Innovating innovation

In 1963, at the Annual Conference of the American Marketing Association, William E. Bell talked about consumers as innovators. He thought of them being innovative when they 'break their established patterns of behaviour and buying when they purchase a new product'.[23] This is how marketing

---

[22]   Antorini, 2007: 248.
[23]   Bell, 1964: 85.

imagined customer innovation. Bell introduced the notion of 'early adopters' to name avant-garde consumers who try out what business had innovated. The consumer's innovation capacity remained restricted to accepting and buying new things; the locus of real innovation was inside organizations.

This simple image provided the blueprint for most of our theories on innovation. Innovation is created inside the firm; consumers' role is being passive users. The co-creation hypothesis and the concept of brand communities challenge the idea of firm-centric value creation: consumers are creative and innovative, blurring the old dividing line between production and consumption. Co-creation describes exactly that: insiders and outsiders innovate as they gather in communities formed around brands.

Michel Callon and his colleagues suggest that the 'economy of qualities' is distinguished through an intensification of the collaboration between supply and demand.[24] Normally, we think of a good as what is being exchanged. But a good in itself is a complex operation, a consequence of many translations, as Callon reminds us. He uses the term 'product' for this invisible qualification process that results in a good. He describes the process of turning a product into a good as a process of ongoing singularization: throughout its journey, the product becomes ever-more distinctive while, at the same time, it has to remain comparable to competing goods and retain some kind of familiarity with categories well established in the consumer's mind. We've discussed this process in more detail in Chapter 3 as the qualification-requalification process, which is at the heart of the dynamic of markets.

What has changed in our co-creative environment is the number of players who are involved in this process. Callon *et al.*, give the example of a simple bottle of orange juice: the taster works with the buyer to ensure quality and consistency; the sales manager deals with bottle design, market testing, focus groups, the advertising agency, and so on.[25] Callon *et al.*, call this process one of 'progressive profiling', which ensures that the good matches demand and creates consumer desire. But their example still follows the old-fashionsed, firm-centric logic. In the LEGO example, users are much more involved in the process of profiling – up to the point where it is users themselves who develop new products and experiences.

In the case of LEGO, the process of profiling increasingly involves the consumers directly. Consumers have input not only via focus groups and market testing but they actually start to play around with things and produce their

[24] Callon *et al.*, 2002.
[25] Callon *et al.*, 2002: 204–205.

own versions. Organizations start to co-profile products and co-create what makes a good singular while simultaneously retaining its categorization. Think of this as a constant negotiation process through which the product moves until it is called a good. At this point, the production process is arrested for a moment and things are stable enough to be traded. Importantly, this co-profiling creates attachment to the good: the consumers get involved in the development of the product and once its development process is finished and it is transformed into a good, they have a positive emotional connection with it. Innovative brand community members turn into passionate brand ambassadors.

Callon *et al.* highlight two important implications: first, they argue for an intensification of collaboration 'between supply and demand, in a way that enables consumers to participate actively in the qualification of goods … Design, as an activity that crosses the entire organization, becomes central: the firm organizes itself to make the dynamic process of qualification and requalification of products possible and manageable.'[26] As we have illustrated with the case of LEGO, an open-source approach invites consumers to become producers and shape the qualification and requalification process significantly.

Second, the intensification of the relationship between producer and consumer is both rational and emotional: 'Consumption becomes both more rational (not that the consumer is more rational but because (distributed) cognitive devices become infinitely richer, more sophisticated and reflexive) and more emotional (consumers are constantly referred to the construction of their social identity since their choices and preferences become objects of deliberation: the distinction of products and social distinction are part of the same movement).'[27] This intensification is exactly what we can observe at LEGO: the brand community engages in co-creation that results in intensive rational as well as emotional connections. Through the collective intelligence of literally thousands of users, the LEGO products become increasingly sophisticated. At the same time, emotionally, the social identity of the community members is inextricably interwoven with the LEGO brand.

In the case of LEGO, the actual organization still plays a dominant role in the innovation process. Although LEGO invites consumers to interact, it is still an organization with (more or less fluid) boundaries. An extreme example of co-creation occurs when boundaries are torn down, and traditional

---

[26] Callon *et al.*, 2002: 212.
[27] Callon *et al.*, 2002: 212.

producers – organizations – get cut out of the innovation process altogether. There is a nice acronym for that: C2C, or consumer-to-consumer business.

C2C

Consumer culture research analyses the whole cycle from acquisition, consumption and possession to disposition processes.[28] We've seen that these processes are more creative than one would assume: people are actively involved in the creation of the object through consumption. Put simply, consumption is not passive; rather, consumers are actively engaged in production. This should be alarming news for management, which used to control the production process. Facilitated by technology, consumers start working with other consumers and drive big business out of the picture.

The most visible examples are new organizations with new business models that cut across traditional corporate thinking. Take Linux, the open software platform that is the only serious competitor of giant Microsoft. eBay, which breaks the uniformity of markets by bringing unique people and unique products together, at a unique price, is another example. Think of Jones Soda, which received a lot of attention for its labels – all designed by consumers. Have a look at Craig's List for anything from a new job to a new flat or a new partner. The site was started off as community newsletter in 1995 by Craig Newmark; now it has more than 10 billion page views per month and more than 40 million users. Check out Prosper at www.prosper.com with its tagline 'Let's bank on each other'. This is basically a community bank that brings private lenders and borrowers together and lets them arrange the details of their loan. You can read how much borrowers are asking for and what they propose to do with the money. Then you can decide whether the conditions suit you and bid for the deal. Does it work? So far, Prosper has funded $165 million worth of loans.

Think of Wikipedia, the forever growing online knowledge bank that is entirely written by users. It uses *The Wisdom of Crowds* to generate its more than 2,500,000 entries (and counting – we checked mid 2008).[29] In comparison, the *Encyclopaedia Britannica* offers some 80,000 articles. Is Wikipedia more accurate? According to a study by the prestigious science journal *Nature*, a typical Wikipedia article contained four errors. On average, an article in

---

[28] Arnould and Thompson, 2005.
[29] This is the title of Surowiecki's 2004 book.

Encyclopaedia Britannica contains three errors. It's main error though is not commission but omission, as Chris Anderson put it: it simply cannot keep up with the breadth and the speed of new entries and improvements of old ones that Wikipedia's open-source model allows.[30]

Compared to these developments, traditional consumer involvement with brands sounds boring and stale. For instance, Aaker and Joachimsthaler tell the story of 'groundbreaking' research into consumer insights at the coffee brand Folgers in which 'participants were asked to drift back to their childhoods and recall how coffee was involved in their life. The insight that aroma connected with feelings of home led Folgers to a successful market position around the tagline "The best part of Wakin Up … is Folgers in your cup!" '[31]

From the brand-community perspective, Aaker and Joachimsthaler's example sounds like a rather sheepish use of consumers' time and intelligence. In reality, brands are the interface, the window, the access point for a much deeper and more challenging engagement between consumers and producers. The intensification of the profiling that Callon and his colleagues have described leads to the discovery of ever-new differences that distinguish a brand. This process of co-creation is the lifeline of innovation. If we believe the advocates of an open-source model, it democratizes organizations and improves the innovation process.

Democratizing innovation

Eric von Hippel is the pioneer of open innovation. Since the 1970s, von Hippel has built a global network of researchers that explore how open innovation works in different industries and countries. His latest book, *Democratizing Innovation*, is in many ways the summary of his long journey into innovating how innovation works. By democratizing innovation, von Hippel means that users of products and services have the ability to innovate. Users, in his definition, are either end-users or organizations that use a product to build another one. The new, user-led approach has many advantages over the old producer-focused approach: 'Users that innovate can develop exactly what they want, rather than relying on manufacturers to act as their (often very imperfect) agents. Moreover, individual users do not have to develop

---

[30] Anderson, 2006.
[31] Callon *et al.*, 2002: 59.

everything they need on their own: they can benefit from innovations developed and freely shared by others.'[32]

In their traditional role, all the user could do was voice their needs, which would be satisfied by manufacturers who protected their innovations by patents, copyrights and other legal means. The key hypothesis of von Hippel's school of thought is that 'users are the first to develop many and perhaps most new industrial and consumer products. Further, the contribution of users is growing steadily larger as a result of continuing advances in computer and communications capabilities.'[33] Von Hippel uses the example of 3M, one of his case studies, to demonstrate the effectiveness of the user-driven approach:

A natural experiment conducted at 3M illustrates this possibility. Annual sales of lead user product ideas generated by the average lead user project at 3M were conservatively forecast by management to be more than 8 times the sales forecast for new products developed in the traditional manner – $146 million versus $18 million per year. In addition, lead user projects were found to generate ideas for new product lines, while traditional market-research methods were found to produce ideas for incremental improvements to existing product lines. As a consequence, 3M divisions funding lead user project ideas experienced their highest rate of major product line generation in the past 50 years.[34]

If you think that 3M is ahead of its time and von Hippel lives far in the future, you're wrong. Depending on the industry, 10 to 40% of users are already innovating products. Studies were conducted in such diverse industries as printed circuit CAD software, surgical equipment, server software, extreme sporting equipment, outdoor consumer products, and others.[35] These studies have refined the idea of user-led innovation. Von Hippel and his colleagues found that consumers are better at certain kinds of innovation than others. Which ones? Users outperform traditional manufacturing in developing new functional capabilities: 82% of user-led innovation develops such new functional capabilities as opposed to 18% of manufacturing-driven innovation. The game changes when we look for convenience or reliability improvement: in this case, manufacturers developed 87% of the innovation, whereas lead users contributed only 13%.[36] In other words, users revolutionize

---

[32] Von Hippel, 2005: 1.
[33] Von Hippel, 2005: 2.
[34] Von Hippel, 2005: 15–16.
[35] See von Hippel, 2005, with references to detailed studies. For a practical example, see http://sourceforge.
net, the world's largest open-source software development website with more than 1.8 million 'developers' working on some 175,000 projects.
[36] Von Hippel, 2005: 71.

products while manufacturers evolve and refine existing ones. Users explore new opportunities; traditional firm-centered innovation exploits them.[37]

Again, the 3M study illustrates the point: lead user-driven projects resulted in five new major product lines, whereas traditional innovation methods resulted in forty-one incremental improvements but only one new major product line. The lead user approach did not generate any incremental improvements at all. Having said that, product evolution is far less profitable than product revolution: as mentioned above, the estimated sales for the lead user-driven innovation over five years was $146 million as opposed to $18 million for the traditionally developed innovation.[38] By now, you might be asking: Who are these lead users? They are those at the cutting edge of trends. In fact, trends follow them. In marketing-speak, lead users are what comes before early adopters – they do not adapt but create. They are the unruly *bricoleurs* we met in the previous chapter. This is not mere semantics but an important conceptual difference.

Von Hippel describes them as follows: 'lead users are defined as members of a user population having two distinguishing characteristics: (1) They are at the leading edge of an important market trend(s), and so are currently experiencing needs that will later be experienced by many users in that market. (2) They anticipate relatively high benefits from obtaining a solution to their needs, and so may innovate.'[39] Lead users are in a good position to innovate because of what von Hippel calls 'information stickiness': tacit knowledge is important but hard to render explicit and transfer. If we attempt to translate this knowledge into explicit knowledge for the sake of learning or changing, we miss the most important points. You might be able to ride a bicycle, but you would be hard pressed to explain in detail how you do it. Exactly therein lies the advantage of user-led innovation: 'sticky information'. While a user-innovator knows implicitly how a new surfboard should behave when she attempts to ride even bigger waves, this knowledge is definitely maybe (to quote the Brit pop band Oasis) lost in focus group discussions where a marketing manager takes notes of what people can hardly describe. Because sticky information 'sticks' with users, it is hard for manufacturers to develop insights into their needs. This is the single most important reason why new products based on closed innovation models fail so frequently.[40]

[37]   March, 1988.
[38]   Von Hippel, 2005: 139–140; Lilien *et al.*, 2002.
[39]   Von Hippel, 2005: 22.
[40]   Von Hippel, 2005: 108.

The second reason lead users are good innovators is that they bring a combination of know-how with them that is unusual. Von Hippel gives the example of a human movement scientist who works in ergonomics and bio-mechanics. He designed new frames for mountain bikes that were suitable for conditions such as downhill and uphill. Because of his knowledge about the human body and his passion for mountain biking, he was in a perfect position to innovate. Brand communities consist of literally hundreds of such experts who have cross-functional knowledge. Since they communicate intensively, they cover a much wider field of knowledge in which innovation may occur. This is coincidental – but because of large user groups it is effective. It is like a massive lab replete with a dazzling array of expertise and, quite simply, you do not know what they will contribute to innovation. In such a case, random trial and error are rational strategies.[41] This is exactly what happens in those communities. Because of the unique combination of detailed knowledge about needs and useful knowledge from multiple areas, lead users are able to outperform organizations.[42]

Think of LEGO: you might have an architect, a product designer, a railway employee and a physics professor collectively building a new LEGO train set. They are likely to outperform the in-house LEGO team because the community group not only draws on a deep understanding of LEGO (probably as deep as the know-how of the LEGO employees) but, additionally, they bring their experiences from their day jobs with them, which might spark truly innovative breakthrough ideas.

There is also a quite rational, market-based reason that users are sometimes better innovators. Organizations only provide goods for large audiences so, naturally, not everybody's needs are satisfied. Needs might be heterogeneous, but producers prefer homogeneous products. It is this tension that gives rise to lead user-driven innovation: people start to modify, experiment, innovate and create new products to satisfy their needs. This would be not economical for the manufacturer because, initially, only a small number of people would pay for the product. But it is highly relevant because lead users may experience a need now that will become a need of many people tomorrow. Take mountain bikes that were developed by users. Professional manufacturers did not develop them, nor did they want to get involved in the production at the early stages. Mountain bikes were seen as a fringe product that would never make it into a mass market. Today, more than 60 per cent of all bikes sold in the US are mountain bikes. In other words, what starts as

[41] Serres, 1985.
[42] Von Hippel, 2005: 75.

an experiment on the fringe might end up as a mainstream innovation. After all, an error is nothing but an unexpected outcome that might well turn into a solution.[43]

A last important characteristic of user-led innovation is its social aspect. Users do not innovate in isolation; they innovate in communities. This is simply more valuable for users because of the increased speed and effectiveness of innovations. In a community, new ideas are diffused rapidly, they are tested and feedback is given instantly. The social element allows individuals to build a larger system than they could individually. Think, for example, of Linux: users share their knowledge about and passion for the open platform. They communicate regularly via chat rooms and build the cohesion of a tribal brand community.

The implications of user-led innovation could hardly be more radical: open innovation undermines the entire division of labour that has been established in the capitalist society. Organizations are meant to produce stuff that consumers are meant to buy. That's true for Adam Smith's world: if you want to produce a needle (to use his famous example), you have to organize resources into a value chain to maximize output. But in the twenty-first century, organizations are forced to include ever-more differentiated solutions for increasingly fragmented markets. In turn, mass production gave way to mass customization. And mass customization gives way to mass innovation. Von Hippel's work concentrates on this second leap. And although he and his colleagues do not focus on it, it has big implications for marketing: if users start creating new products, then marketing can no longer be about promoting a product that has its origins in the market anyway. Rather, the task of marketing is then to nurture an innovative community that crystallizes around the brand.

For organizations, von Hippel suggests the following three ways to feed into user-led innovation: '(1) Produce user-developed innovations for general commercial sale and/or offer custom manufacturing to specific users. (2) Sell kits of product design tools and/or "product platforms" to ease users' innovation-related tasks. (3) Sell products or services that are complementary to user-developed innovations.'[44] Basically, the organization's role is to either manufacture user-developed innovations or provide tools to help communities to innovate. Remember that lead users lacked the capacity to refine existing products. This is exactly where the strength of traditional organizations

---

[43] Von Hippel, 2005: 36; Lüthje *et al.*, 2002.
[44] Von Hippel, 2005: 15.

lies: in evolving products and exploiting them. For lead users, exploration is far more attractive. Prahalad and Ramaswamy have coined the rather awkward term 'evolvability' to describe the process in which there is enough embedded intelligence in a product or service for it to change and evolve according to its context.[45] This vision of 'evolvability' can only be achieved in an open-innovation model where multiple users with 'sticky information' develop ideas.

As pointed out above, open innovation relies on communities. Open innovation only works as a network of distributed intelligence where players are attracted to participating, contributing and sharing freely. The attractor that pulls the community together is the brand. While von Hippel and his colleagues assume that communities are formed somehow naturally, they overlook how the brand as an institutionalized window enables exchange. Simultaneously, what emerges and evolves out of these conversations is the brand. As in an Escher drawing, the odd couple of cause and effect give way to inter-activity.

Innovation and brand communities

Innovation occurs because of a heterogeneous mix of people interacting in an open system that allows for the serendipitous exchange of ideas. The anthropologist Ulf Hannerz developed the notion of the 'cultural swirl' to describe the social milieu in which individuals interact and innovate.[46] Brand communities organized around open-source platforms are one manifestation of such cultural swirls. These swirls provide an accurate image of the way sticky and widely distributed information flows until it manifests itself in innovation. It illustrates the qualification and requalification process that increases the speed and the variety of the search for differences that make a difference.

For organizations, innovation might become synonymous with the cultivation of brand communities that create cultural swirls. The alternative is a closed system of innovation in which you have to rely on the unlikely event that your organization has hired the next Bill Gates. But even one lone genius or a team of very smart Ivy League graduates can hardly compete with the sum total of insider knowledge of literally thousands of users.

---

[45] Prahalad and Ramaswamy, 2004: 211.
[46] Hannerz, 1992; Welz, 2003.

Clayton M. Christensen analysed the reasons successful organizations such as IBM and Xerox – which do hire those smart graduates – fail when it comes to innovation. Describing this failure as the 'Innovator's Dilemma', he puts forward the provocative thesis that not poor but *good* management is the reason: 'Precisely *because* these firms listened to their customers, invested aggressively in new technologies that would provide their customers more and better products of the sort they wanted, and because they carefully studied market trends and systematically allocated investment capital to innovations that promised the best returns, they lost their position of leadership.'[47]

Why does traditional innovation management fail? Disruptive technologies are the key to innovation, but most technologies are *sustaining technologies* – meaning they improve the performance of existing products rather than replace them. Disruptive technologies, on the other hand, result in worse product performance (at least in the short term) for existing products. Compared to established products, new disruptive technologies often perform at a lower level. For instance, top-end decks and immaculate-quality vinyl beat early CDs hands down for tonal warmth and resonance, but CDs did not scratch as easily and were easier to use, played more music and were portable. CDs had characteristics that were valued by markets: they were smaller and easier and more convenient to use. Another example of disruptive technologies was the off-road motorbike manufactured by Honda and Kawasaki. Compared to sleek BMW and Harley Davidson machines, these models were primitive, but they could go places that the big bikes, with their smooth finish, could not.

The problem for established companies is that they generally do not invest in disruptive technologies because they are simpler and cheaper and thus promise less profit. They develop in fringe markets that are not important to big players and, after the market is big enough to create serious profits, it may be too costly or too late to join. Often, the established firm's best customers do not want, and cannot use, the new disruptive technologies, and the potential customers of the new technology are unknown. Open-source innovation communities that form around brands and engage users in co-creation might be the only way to counter this dilemma.

The price an organization has to pay for open innovation is a certain loss of control and predictability. Rather than trying to influence single developments and innovations, organizations might create the context for cultural swirls to emerge. In this game, the brand takes on the role of the crucial

[47] Christensen, 1997: xii.

interface between inside and outside. As we have argued in the previous chapter, the co-creation experience is the brand. Building communities around this co-creation experience might be the only way to systematically tap into the innovation potential of users.

Interactivity or interpassivity?

Critics argue that the democratizing innovation agenda is naïve at best, with the potential to be outright dangerous. There are two main concerns. First, the innovation potential and creativity we talked about is not truly open but rather a mere illusion of openness that is in reality framed by corporate agendas and the narrow boundaries of a pre-defined system. Second, user innovation might be often counterproductive – after all, our society invests heavily in the education of experts whose knowledge cannot be replaced by the eagerness yet cluelessness of a teenager in front of a screen, equipped with enormous processing power, a high-speed broadband cable and the social conscience of a toddler.

Is it truly innovative to play with LEGO and create new models and play themes? Isn't the game invented and all you do is, quite literally, fiddle with the pieces? Wouldn't it be real innovation to create the next LEGO rather than staying within the boundaries of the old one? This question points at a more fundamental one: is innovation creation *ex nihilo*? Or is it a process of assimilation, appropriation and improvisation? Are new things written on a *tabula rasa* or are they merely cleverly edited yet previously unconnected ideas? To put it bluntly: are innovators authors of new thoughts or DJs that re-mix existing ones? Do they act or react?

Our guess is that innovation results from neither action nor reaction but rather interaction. In his book *Action and Reaction: The Life and Adventures of a Couple*, Jean Starobinski traces the history of interaction. Interaction 'suggest more agents and moments than does the elementary couple action/reaction. It recovers the notion of a complex montage of feedbacks.'[48] With interaction, one avoids assigning clear cause and effect relations. As Wittgenstein said, to identify someone as cause is like pointing the finger and blaming him. With interaction, the culprit disappears in favour of a reciprocal relationship in which cause and effect, means and ends, are mutually and simultaneously constituted.

[48] Starobinski, 1999/2003: 219.

The digital and new media sage Lev Manovich argues that interactivity is a new form of narcissism – just a more active one.[49] We don't see our picture in the water (which is passive), but we see the reaction to our initial action on screen. The new form of narcissism is a more active form of seeing how potent we are. The screen becomes a mirror for our activities; the cursor moves with us, things change when we press buttons: we are in control – or we feel like we are. And we like it. However, the truth is that people are controlled while acting under the illusion of choice: 'With the help of mass communication, the phrase "interactive games" has entered everyday speech. However, strict reciprocity is not found in such games since the user – regardless of how many options he is presented with – is always captive to the programmer who prepared the system.'[50] The critical point is that users are invited to make choices that a programmer has mapped out for them already. The decisions become pseudo-decisions. The really burning issues might have been left off the map in the first place. Bachrach and Baratz have described this form of power as 'dynamics of non-decision making': while the community faces a decision that it believes might challenge the status quo, the really challenging issues have been excluded from the discussion.[51] Developing a new play theme for LEGO, a new product for 3M or mountain bikes might be an honorable exercise, but it hardly questions the dominant logic of our *zeitgeist*. The open-source movement might be seduced by the idea of openness, but in reality the open space has been pre-defined by interests beyond the community's reach. Brand communities that innovate around certain brands, in particular, will hardly question the fundamental values and logic of that brand. The label of open innovation promotes the image of 'democracy' and 'real participation', creating a warm and fuzzy feeling, while in reality things have been put into place already.

Second, the move towards user involvement in production processes through brand communities might have unintended yet dire consequences. This has to do with the reliance of the open-source movement on modern information and communication technologies. Through these technologies, life becomes more decentralized and fragmented. By definition, a book or a newspaper creates a unified perspective on an issue. They are central communication organs. The telegraph and later the telephone and now the internet have changed this picture. These new media break the central position

[49] Manovich, 2001: 233.
[50] Starobinski, 1999/2003: 222.
[51] Bachrach and Baratz, 1962.

of the print media and allow people to make their own news, spread gossip and see things from a more potentially endless number of perspectives. One can be critical and ask: What sense does it make to create one's own weather forecast? Is it not better to listen to experts? How useful are those channels where you can choose which news you want to hear? Isn't news by definition what everyone shares as news?

The internet intensifies this problem as it constitutes a total field of possible relations where everything can be related to everything else. People become editors of their own realities. They decide what makes news and what does not. They decide what is innovative and what is not. As Deleuze and Guattari reminded us, such a decentralized, fragmented and rhizomatic reality should not be confused with freedom or absence of power. It is an ironic coincidence that the telegraph and Kierkegaard's *Concept of Dread* emerged in the same year – 1844.[52] Power shifts with increasing speed and technology, but it does not disappear.[53] Anxiety spreads with the speed of bits and bytes pumping through broadband cables.

McLuhan has anticipated that involvement will become key in these new social situations: 'As the speed of information increases, the tendency is for politics to move away from representation and delegation of constituents toward immediate involvement of the entire community in the central acts of decision.'[54]

The culture of polling gives a taste of such immediate involvement: public policy is reduced to what hockey mums, the infamous Essex Man and other constituents of the chattering classes tolerate in opinion polls and focus groups. Professional knowledge is replaced by the wisdom of crowds that is aggregated via search engines. 'If you like this book you might also want to buy that one' gives rise to the tyranny of the average. The algorithms that run the Web flatten the idiosyncrasy of human decision-making. What started off as open invitation for interactivity might end up as interpassivity: rather than acting, people hand over part of their agency and rely on a branded infrastructure to enact their remaining freedom within the constraints of a preset programme.[55]

[52] Kierkegaard's *Concept of Dread* (1844/1957) has been interpreted as one of the first texts that gave rise to the philosophical movement labelled Existentialism.
[53] Virilio, 1977.
[54] McLuhan, 1964/2006: 221.
[55] Žižek, 1997.

An open end for open innovation

The jury is out on whether brand community-driven open innovation is an answer to the complexities of innovation. Don't expect it to be back any time soon. What we do know is that there are different ways of engaging consumers in the production process: 'Having the user at one's place, being at his place or building a place to be with him: in all three cases, the economy of goods gives way to an economy of relations.'[56] The brand as interface between production and consumption is the central mechanism for managing this co-creation experience. For in an economy of qualities and relations, what are brands if not the medium *and* the message?

[56] Callon *et al.*, 2002: 213.

Part III

How brands transform lifestyle

7 Politics

Trailer II

Thus far, we have focused on how brands transform management and organizations. Our pitch was that a brand perspective would offer a new conceptual map for thinking about key organizational phenomena, including identity and change, internal and external engagement, and innovation. We're also inclined to believe that such a new map might serve well as a springboard for organizational action.

In this third and final part of the book, we shift the focus from management, organization and production to something that has become second nature to us: consuming. In a nutshell, we'll argue that brands have brought about a new way of living life: the ubiquitous, pervasive yet little analysed notion of lifestyle encapsulates brands' power to quite literally stylize life. Brands, we shall see, provide the raw material that we use to build our individual lifestyles.

The troika of politics, ethics and aesthetics offers itself as a promising analytical framework within which to dissect the notion of lifestyle. Since we will at least partly fly above the clouds, we'll need reliable conceptual instruments to guide our flight. The concept of politics (Chapter 7) directs our attention towards a (short) genealogy of lifestyle, and analyses its power effects. Chapter 8 raises the issue of the ethicality of brands, and investigates whether brands are part of the problem, or the solution, for living a good life. Finally, in Chapter 9, we focus on the aesthetic consequences of brands: the aesthetics of branding has changed fundamentally the way we experience the world around us. As such, brands represent not only a formidable conceptual challenge but also a powerful stimulus for our senses.

But we are rushing ahead of our story – let's start at the beginning, with the making of our lifestyle-driven world.

Performativity

Performativity is a complex word that hints at a surprisingly familiar phenomenon: 'The story goes that three umpires disagreed about the task of calling balls and strikes. The first one said, "I calls them as they is." The second one said, "I calls them as I sees them." The third and cleverest umpire said, "They ain't nothin" till I calls them." '[1] As the third umpire argued, balls and strikes do not exist independently of judgement; rather, they become real only when they are pronounced as such. The umpire's judgement creates the reality it is supposed to describe. This is performativity in action.

Most of the time, most of us are involved in games that are far more complicated than baseball, have far more ambiguous rules and there is no umpire. The world of branding fits this description. So how is branding 'performed'?

In his paper on the performativity of economics, Callon tackles the same issue as our three umpires: How can a discourse be outside the reality it describes and simultaneously constitute this reality?[2] Austin's book *How To Do Things With Words* provides the first clue: sometimes we say things that make these things reality because we say them.[3] A For instance, if I say 'I marry you' the sentence actually does what it says. Language does not represent reality but creates it. In this sense, talk is action: language does something; it is an activity.

Callon argues that science is performative as well. Not in the way that a scientist says what she wants and the world adjusts, of course. Callon says more carefully that the world that has been 'supposed' in a theory has become

[1] Weick, 1979.
[2] Callon, 2006.
[3] Austin, 1955/1962.

'actualized'. Let's take Maslow's theory of needs, which supposes that there are different levels of needs, the highest of them being 'self-actualization'.[4] Let's assume that marketing professionals embrace this theory and start advertising their products as a means of actualizing your inner self. Once you are exposed to products that are marketed as prostheses of your self and that offer to help you be who you are, you will consume them as such. *Et voilà* – the theory has gone full circle and starts reinforcing itself. Put simply, Maslow's theory is performative; it actually does what it supposedly describes.

Of course, not every theory will be able to actualize the world it supposes (to use the words of Callon). Its ability to do so depends on a whole range of technical, social and cognitive parameters that are highly contextual.[5]

In this chapter, we want to find out how marketing actualized the world of brands. Marketing has been defined 'as a distributed and heterogeneous set of agencies involved in the process of facilitating market exchange and constructing market institutions'.[6] In other words, marketing is a performative discipline that facilitates change and constructs markets. It 'performs' markets, consumers and their desires.[7] As Cochoy put it: 'Halfway between producers and consumers, halfway between economics and managerial practices, marketing specialists have gradually reinvented the fundamental actors and processes; they have succeeded in disciplining (mastering/codifying) the market economy.'[8]

How did this disciplining process unfold? What are the roles of brands in it? Brand managers such as Thom Braun, Vice President for Brand Development at Unilever, know what brands do: they provide 'the opportunity to manage consumer choice'.[9] As we will see, branding as a body of knowledge and as a performative theory has developed from being a simple technique of influencing to become one of the most powerful institutions in our society. The power of brands is insinuated in the notion of lifestyle: through lifestyle, brands start to manage, control and 'style' life itself.

---

[4] Maslow, 1954.

[5] Another example is Donald MacKenzie's book *An Engine, not a Camera*, where he has shown how the emergence of modern economics fundamentally shaped financial markets. He argues that economic models are better understood as engines of enquiry rather than a camera to reproduce or represent facts. Economic theories with their models make new markets possible (such as the $273 trillion derivatives market) by explaining the function and providing legitimacy. In a similar vein, Osborne and Rose (1999: 382) have shown that 'the phenomenon of [public] opinion is an artefact of the technical procedures that are designed to capture it'.

[6] Araujo, 2007: 212.

[7] See Lury, 2004: Chapter 2.

[8] Cochoy, 1998: 218.

[9] Braun, 2004: 174.

Myth of the production era

The end of the nineteenth and the beginning of the twentieth century were turbulent times. Previously, mankind had been offended by Galileo (we are not the centre of the universe), then by Darwin (we are not descended from a biblical paradise), and then Freud finished it off by claiming that we are not the masters of our own psyches but ruled by an *id*. Nietzsche declared the Death of God before he was sent to an asylum. In art, Cubism foreshadowed a new reality with no central perspective. While Van Gogh and the Impressionists blurred the object, now the subject itself fell apart. Taylor and Ford demonstrated the mechanical nature of production. Motion studies revealed the mechanical nature of nature itself. Weber complained about the ongoing rationalization of society and the resulting disenchantment. The world was looking like a gigantic machine, ready to be taken over by engineers. Finally, it seemed, the uncompromising materialism of French enlightenment, represented by Julien Offray de La Mettrie's *Man a Machine* from 1748 and Baron d'Holbach's *System of Nature* (1770), had arrived at its most brutal expression.

It was in this context that the era of production supposedly flourished, before it was surpassed by a demand-driven consumer society from the 1930s onwards. As the story goes, from the mid-nineteenth century until 1930, we lived in a production epoch. The focus of this era was on the physical production of goods and efficient management techniques such as scientific management. Marketing was not needed as demand outstripped supply. Because of limited competition and limited choice, things sold themselves. The relationship to consumers was a simple, straightforward sales relationship. The control focus of management was internal. The rise of marketing as a discipline started in the 1930s as competition and consumer spending increased. This development marks the birth of the consumer society that forms the bedrock of our lives.

There are some good reasons why this thesis of a production era that was followed by a consumption-oriented economy is questionable. The control of consumption was always a key concern of management. Neil McKendrick and his colleagues argued in the book *The Birth of a Consumer Society* that the Industrial Revolution is less a revolution of production than a revolution of demand.[10] Using the pottery entrepreneur Josiah Wedgwood as an

---

[10] McKendrick *et al.*, 1982. In his article on 'Prehistories of Commodity Branding', Wengrow (2008) argues that already the urban revolution in the fourth millenium BC used simple techniques of branding.

example, they argue that it was his ability to create demand that made him successful. By 1772, every piece of pottery that left Wedgwood's workshop had his name printed on it. He asked in a letter to his partner how much of their success could be attributed to their way of marketing the product and how much to 'real utility and beauty'.[11] For Wedgwood, the answer was simple: he realized that the real product features mean only so much – more important was the image of the product. Consequently, he set up showrooms in which 'business and amusement can be made to go hand in hand'.[12] He sent unsolicited parcels of his pottery to more than 1,000 German aristocrats along with an invoice asking them to either buy the goods or send them back. He realized that consumption is a social practice and possession an extension of the self: thus he actively looked for commissions and endorsements from aristocracy that would elevate his product and make his products a desirable brand for the aspiring middle classes.[13] He instructed his staff to scan the English peerage for additional 'lines, channels and connections', as these groups were what he called the 'legislators in taste'.[14] Wedgwood not only created demand – he actually created a brand that allowed consumers to build relationships with Wedgwood.

Consumer engineering

John Levi Martin summarized the unattainability of the consumption-economy thesis succinctly when he wrote: 'There can be no switch to a consumption-oriented economy because all capitalist economies are consumption oriented.'[15] Production and marketing worked in tandem from the very beginning. Fullerton shows that 'demand creation' was one of the fundamental business tasks in the early 1900s – way before the supposed shift to the consumer society was meant to have happened. Business writers did not leave any doubt about the importance of creating desire. Jackman and Russell wrote in 1910: 'It is one thing to make goods and another to manufacture markets for them. This is the theory of modern business.'[16] Advertising

---

[11] Quoted in Koehn, 2001: 12.
[12] Wedgwood, quoted in Koehn, 2001: 30.
[13] Arvidsson, 2006: 67: 'Wedgwood *put the aristocracy to work* in producing a certain quality to be attached to the product, by giving it a place in the shared meanings and social relations that formed their now more visible lifeworld.'
[14] Koehn, 2001: 34.
[15] Martin, 1999: 438.
[16] Quoted in Fullerton, 1988: 108.

executive Harry Tipper wrote in 1914 that mass production requires consumers to 'be taught to use more than they formerly used'.[17] In 1936, marketing theorist Eliasberg retrospectively found that the market had been totally transformed over the past 100 years 'through the stimulation, intensification, diversion and awakening of needs'.[18]

Consumption was, from the beginning, a key concern for management. Between 1875 and 1930, the total consumption of the US population tripled.[19] With this growth came an increased focus on advertising, selling and distribution techniques that managed consumption. Witness the wave of new 'convenience products' such as throwaway tissues, or precise accounts for the preparation time of ready-made meals that were advertised to the America housewife in the 1920s. In the shadow of the scientific management movement and the broad enthusiasm for automatization, the desire for convenience as a core product quality (as opposed to quality, value or durability) was created through the advertising machinery of American corporates.[20] The term 'consumer engineering' introduced by Sheldon and Arens in 1936 merely summarized the desire to manage and control the growth of consumption.[21]

This urge to manage consumption took shape before its theory was formulated by Sheldon and Arens. People had to be taught how to consume and how to become consumers. The education process started in the arcades of Paris, as described by Walter Benjamin, and found its most effective form in those temples of consumption, department stores.[22] In fact, department stores were pivotal in teaching people how to consume;[23] those that sprang up in Paris, Chicago and New York in the 1850s fundamentally transformed buying into shopping. Visiting a department store became like visiting a museum – a leisurely activity to explore what was in and what not. Department stores represented a liminal space in which women could go unaccompanied, different classes could mix and goods could be touched – all of which was facilitated by the logic of consumption. But visiting a department store was not only a leisure and pleasure activity: to be a good housewife, one had to compare prices and find bargains.[24] One of the most important shifts was in the display

[17] Quoted in Fullerton, 1988: 112.
[18] Quoted in Fullerton, 1988: 113.
[19] Martin, 1999: 446.
[20] See Gideon, 1948; Strasser, 2003.
[21] Fullerton, 1988: 120.
[22] Benjamin, 1927–1940/2002.
[23] Laermans, 1993; see also Cochoy, 2005.
[24] Laermans, 1993: 87; Jeacle, 2003.

and communication of goods. Because people wandered through the stores without the objective of satisfying a need, desires had to be created and then satisfied. Commodities had to speak for themselves, they had to seduce, they had to awaken desire. Everything else was designed to support desire – the architecture of the store, the display of merchandise and the service created a 'technocracy of the senses'.[25]

Even leisure time had to be engineered for consumption. In his 1932 book *The Challenge of Leisure*, Arthur Pack attempts to explain how to use leisure time productively – because leisure should not be confused with idleness or indulgence. Rather, it should be used constructively in such activities as learning how to play golf. Obviously, for the Great Unwashed, the concept of leisure was less self-explanatory. Leisure time was created to manage consumption as opposed to production. Real leisure time was a container that could be filled with commodities and experiences that were for sale.[26] This is how leisure time was advertised: not as in opposition to production but as its supplement.

On a theoretical level, John Kenneth Galbraith has pointed out that consumption and production mutually constitute each other. He introduced the concept of the 'dependence effect'. According to this effect, desires are created (by advertising and other means), so it is nonsense to argue that production only satisfies people's needs. Rather, production fills the void it first creates. Of course, this will not lead to happiness or satisfaction since the gap between what is supplied and what is demanded needs to remain stable. As production (and wealth) increase, our desires do too, condemning us to be less and less satisfied with more and more goods.[27]

An important consequence of Galbraith's thesis and our brief historical exploration is that the linear development from a producer to a consumer society looks over-simplified. Markets and demand have to be created. As one interviewee in Hennion and Méadel's study put it, 'there are no pre-defined needs. It is supply that creates markets, always. When you think you are getting a picture of demand, all you are doing is describing the other person's supply.'[28] Similarly, Sergio Zyman, Coca-Cola's former Head of Marketing, leaves no doubt that consumers need to be controlled: 'Leaving things up to the consumers' imagination is something you never want to do. Customers

[25] Haug, 1986.
[26] De Grazia, 1962.
[27] Galbraith, 1958.
[28] Hennion and Méadel, 1989: 197.

are dangerous, and if you let them decide how they want to be satisfied, you're going to have a terrible time living up to their dreams. It's better if you can control both the promise and the delivery.'[29] How did marketing attempt to control these 'dangerous customers'?

Discovering the 'inner Joneses'

In order to manage consumption, the complex interaction between producers and consumers and the design of interfaces (brands), marketing requires knowledge. The birth of market research gave rise to an inflationary knowledge about people's habits, user patterns, desires, needs and wants. The archives of advertising agencies and marketing firms might well form the biggest collection of anthropological data on this planet. In turn, this knowledge constituted the object for the marketing professional – the customer.

What kind of customer did marketing project? At the beginning of the last century, the approach was what has been dubbed 'tell and sell'. Claude Jopkins argued in 1922: 'Give people facts ... the more you tell, the more you sell.'[30] The creation of a more psychological and sociological knowledge about people's tastes, preferences and habits was driven by the publishing industry. Publishers needed to know about audience and demographics in order to sell advertising. J. Walter Thompson's chief researcher developed a basic ABCD typology in 1924:

A. Homes of substantial wealth above the average in culture that have at least one servant. The essential point, however, in this class is that the persons interviewed shall be people of intelligence and discrimination.
B. Comfortable middle class homes, personally directed by intelligent women.
C. Industrial homes of skilled mechanics, mill operators or petty trades people (no servants).
D. Homes of unskilled labourers or in foreign districts where it is difficult for American ways to penetrate.[31]

These simple categorizations allowed the streamlining of marketing activities and the standardization of communication. However, these categories were descriptive and did not say anything about the motivations or desires of the people they classified. The focus was on what people do and what they have but not on what they are.

[29] Quoted in Wipperfürth, 2005: 8.
[30] Quoted in Feldwicko, 2003: 130.
[31] Quoted in Arvidsson, 2006: 49.

The economist James S. Duesenberry implicitly criticized this approach. When he studied consumption in the US in the 1950s, he found that people were most worried about 'keeping up with the Joneses'. His argument was that consumption was a social activity and could not be explained with descriptive accounts of people's backgrounds. Duesenberry said,

It is well known that there are societies in which prestige is gained by the acquisition of some sort of good that is completely useless in fulfilling any need whatsoever. In spite of the complete uselessness of things in general, their acquisition may be vital to the acquisition of prestige or maintenance of self-esteem. A great deal of effort may be expended in acquiring these useless items.[32]

Consumption behaviour could not be explained by simply focusing on the needs of the individual and their buying decisions. Rather, one had to look at the social dynamics of consumption – a dynamic he called the 'demonstration effect'. In Duesenberry's terminology, consumption cannot be understood without taking into account people's need to 'keep up with the Joneses'.[33]

Put simply, Duesenberry had found – contra economic theory – that consumption is not limited to the individual sphere but is a fundamentally social phenomenon: people don't buy things because they need them but because others have them, expect not to have them or impress others by having them. Prior to Duesenberry, Veblen's concept of conspicuous consumption proposed that consumers spend large amounts on goods for the purpose of displaying status and wealth.[34] (Paradoxically, people's preference for these Veblen Goods increases as their price goes up. A good example is perfume: its true value is hard to estimate, so we use price as an indicator of quality. The more expensive it is, the better it must be.) But while Veblen focused on the relatively small elite, Duesenberry located the Joneses in the suburbs of everyday America.

Consumption was not just a social phenomenon. It became also a psychological issue. Maslow's *Motivation and Personality*, published in 1954, marked the breakthrough publication. Rarely has such a simple theory been spread so widely and used so wildly. Maslow's hierarchy of needs moves from physiological needs to safety needs, social needs, esteem needs and, finally, to the top of the pyramid: self-actualization. As we have seen in the first part of this book, self-actualization was just what marketers needed – an endless

[32] Duesenberry, 1949, 29.
[33] See Mason, 2000.
[34] Veblen, 1899.

desire to become oneself that could be satisfied with ever-new products and services.

Dr Ernest Dichter, then Head of the influential Institute for Motivational Research Inc., speculated in the *Harvard Business Review* in 1965 that ' "What will the neighbors say?" might become an obsolete phrase.'[35] In a very Maslowian way, he argued that mankind always strives for new development. In earlier stages of history, Dichter pointed out, we struggled with survival and with the Joneses from next door, 'warning them not to make the mistake of pegging us too low'.[36] But history progresses, and with it Dichter could announce the advent of a new Jones, 'the Inner Jones'. He gave an example: people ceasing to buy furniture that pleases other people and increasingly buying pieces that please them personally. People were also rediscovering the spatial beauty of the atrium: rather than having an expensive façade for the neighbours to admire, they opted for an atrium as a symptom of an inward focus. These examples heralded a new value system – a rebellion on the part of consumers in search for 'inner satisfaction'. Uniqueness and personal happiness of the Inner Joneses would triumph over competition for status with the Joneses from next door. The Joneses from next door were not any longer the authority to judge who one was by peeking over the fence and counting what one possessed. From now on, the new Joneses inside one's head would evaluate progress on the consumption-based self-actualization project. The external control mechanism had been internalized.

Dichter was quite prophetic – he forecast the i-generation and the trouble with mass marketing. He predicted that sales displays would be less driven by technology and more by psychology, enabling 'insightful advertising' based on symbolism and mindsets. The main goal of this new communication technology would be to produce a feeling of ' "Yes, they're talking about me – they've read my mind." We might even develop the courage to revive and use the word *soul*.'[37]

Dichter realized that 'real value' for the consumer lay in 'self-development', 'realization of self-potential' and adding 'new dimensions to his consciousness', not phony materialistic possessions. A new era of mass culture was about to start, in which people satisfied psychological desires through products that were linked to cultural experiences. The 'Inner Jones' became the judge and

[35] Dichter, 1965: 6.
[36] Dichter, 1965: 6.
[37] Dichter, 1965: 7.

critic of life: as Dichter prophetically put it, 'who more truly becomes himself will be the one admired by the new "Joneses"'.[38]

Market research descended on the newly discovered 'Inner Joneses' in order to study their personalities. Information that was especially sought after related to 'the unconscious or hidden ideas, associations or attitudes of the consumer in connection with … [a] particular product'.[39] It was this research that promised to hook the ad to the *id*, as McLuhan put it.[40] But it did much more than this: as it surveyed those 'Inner Joneses', it discovered that it was not just their personalities but social and cultural patterns – in short, lifestyles – that influenced their purchasing decisions.

While all those Joneses from next door defined a standard of living that one had to achieve or surpass, the Inner Joneses defined a new micro-politics of consumption. Standards of living are relatively rough macro-categorizations; lifestyles are a much more intimate and integrated set of practices that incorporate associations, emotions, behaviour, preferences, tastes and other socio-cognitive functions. A standard of living is a formula for what's acceptable and expectable in a given society; lifestyle, on the other hand, is a pervasive rhythm that forms the narrative of the individual's identity. The invention of lifestyle through marketing, and its somnambulistic acceptance by society, represents one of the most mysterious yet consequential events.

Inventing lifestyle

One of the key insights of early studies was that the *relationship* between consumer and product was more important than either of the two. Brands would act as the interface through which these objects and subjects could relate to each other and work their magic. This juncture where the individual relates to objects and uses this relationship to make sense of and give meaning to life is the birthplace of lifestyle. It marks the moment when life could be given form and styled through consuming brands. The Inner and the Outer Joneses were the intellectual parents of the lifestyle idea. Given their emphasis on the social and the psychological realities of consumption, individuals could shape their psycho-social environment through buying into a certain lifestyle. In order to understand this seismic shift, we have to go back to its origins.

---

[38] Dichter, 1965: 9.
[39] Weiss and Green, 1951: 36, quoted in Tadajewski, 2006: 433.
[40] McLuhan, 1964/2006: 240.

In 1959, Lee Rainwater, Richard P. Coleman and Gerald Handel published a ground-breaking study on the *Workingman's Wife: Her Personality, World and Life Style*.[41] It was the first study that used the concept of lifestyle to understand consumption. The study was the most detailed empirical analysis of working class women that had ever been undertaken. It interviewed 420 working class housewives from Chicago, Louisville, Tacoma and Trenton, and an additional 120 middle-class women to cross-reference their data.

Generally, suburbia was seen as the new ecology of the Joneses. The *Interurbia Report* – sponsored by Yale University, JWT and *Fortune* magazine – from the 1950s paved the way for the rise of the suburbs in the consciousness of the powerful.[42] A summary in the *Journal of Marketing* from 1957 reiterated that suburbia was home to half of the population and accounted for half of the sales of all goods. The prognosis was that it would account for 60% of the American population and 70% of retail sales by 1975. The report diagnosed a strong 'upgrading urge' in suburbanites who were motivated to 'work for the "extras" of a modern society'. Suburbia represented a 'total sales opportunity' – both profits and the habits of people would be made in the suburbs. The growth of consumer markets in cars, perfumes and household articles was forecast to happen not in the metropolis but in those areas between city and country where the masses lived, trying to re-create their dream of a good live.

Rainwater and his colleagues were interested in the average, mundane and normal Joneses – or better, their wives. They surveyed them; they interviewed them; they let them tell their stories; they showed them pictures and let them interpret them (through a test called the Thematic Apperception Test, which is not unlike a commodity-version of the Rorschach Test) – with the underlying hope that '[w]hen a woman tells about a *thing*, she also tells quite a bit about *herself*'.[43] They would gather data on their subjects' socioeconomic status, their daily routines and how they changed from weekdays to weekends, from summer to winter, and so forth. They collected material on a woman's relation to her husband, including what she wanted from him how she dealt with him, and her hopes about how he related to her. They scrutinized her relationship to her children; her attitudes towards the church and social clubs; her behaviour towards her community, the government, politics

---

[41] Rainwater *et al.*, 1959.
[42] Arvidsson, 2006: 25; *Journal of Marketing*, 1957.
[43] Rainwater *et al.*, 1959: 23.

and other institutions; her future aspirations; and her patterns of taste and aesthetics.[44]

Rainwater *et al.* justified their curiosity as follows: 'we need to know some of the basic facts about the working class housewife's personality and life style, about the pressures which bear on her, and the satisfaction she seeks, before we can understand her or predict her behaviour or influence it through counselling or education, or persuasion, or advertising'.[45] What Rainwater and his colleagues were interested in was their subject's 'consuming style' – the way she bought and used products in her everyday life-world. The explicit focus of the study was the personality and the lifestyle of the working class woman. This was important because working class women made everyday decisions in regard to household purchases, and influenced bigger decisions such as purchasing a house or car. And since the purchasing power of the working class was growing rapidly, Rainwater and his colleagues were convinced that no product could succeed unless it was consumed by the masses – the working class.

They focused on working class housewives who had children and were still of child-bearing age – because, for them, this was

the period of greatest significance to the woman. Before she becomes a wife, and then a mother, she regards herself as getting ready for that role decreed by society and nature; as her children grow up, the working class woman is inclined to feel that her life is 'over'. It is in the child-bearing and mothering years, then, that we find the working class woman most fully engaged with life.[46]

Here we encounter again the performative function of theory in action: indeed, marketing did what it supposedly only described.

So what did their study find? More than anything else, it reflected the power relations of the times. For instance, one of the findings was that the central characteristic of the working class wife was '*her underlying conviction that most significant action originates from the world external to herself rather than from within herself*'.[47] Of course, in a patriarchal society, women had little power. As was the practice of so many social 'scientists', Rainwater and his colleagues made the mistake of naturalizing social relations: they turned a social phenomenon into a natural fact. While the former could be challenged, the latter had to be accepted. It might be true that women felt that most action originates outside their sphere of influence. However, what

---

[44] Rainwater *et al.*, 1959: 22–23.
[45] Rainwater *et al.*, 1959: 20.
[46] Rainwater *et al.*, 1959: 19.
[47] Rainwater *et al.*, 1959: 44.

Rainwater *et al.* did was to naturalize these power relations and take them for granted.

Workingman's Wife: Her Personality, World and Life Style is full of examples that illustrate this fallacy. Women rely on the outer world being presented to them in a very clear and orderly manner: 'they require, indeed crave, explicit guidance' when they relate to the outer world that they neither understand nor control in any way.[48] The working class wife is also psychologically passive: she accepts things as given because she '*has little interest, energy or skill to explore, to probe into things for herself* ... She is very much open to suggestion and amenable to guidance that is presented in terms that fit in with her needs and with her view of the world.'[49] This lack of reflection results in the working class wife's

negative view of thinking. Mental activity is arduous for her ... she tends to experience discomfort and confusion when faced with ambiguity or too many alternatives. She does not know how to estimate long-range consequences of situations. By and large, the working class woman is a person who wants to have things she can believe in with certainty rather than have things she has to think about. Thinking is associated in her mind with discomfort, and hence preferably avoided.[50]

Rainwater *et al.* go on to argue that the lack of rationality described is coupled with the working class woman's unstable and hard-to-control emotional life. Strong feelings can arise from minor causes – which strongly differentiates them from middle-class women, who can control themselves. The working class woman '*seems to feel somewhat more vulnerable to sexual temptation than does the middle class woman*'.[51] This is a vicious circle: '*The volatility of the working class woman's emotions contributes to her sense of the world being chaotic.*'[52]

Of course, this lack of rationality also opened the doors to manipulation through 'education' and advertising. Rainwater *et al.*'s conclusion is that the working class wife needs to be educated about the use of products: 'the *ability to consume* is as important as the desire to consume ... the woman who has never had a coffee table, and has not grown up in a home with a coffee table, needs as much to learn how it is used and how one behaves with a coffee table, as she needs to be encouraged to want it'.[53] Put simply, since women

[48] Rainwater *et al.*, 1959: 45.
[49] Rainwater *et al.*, 1959: 59.
[50] Rainwater *et al.*, 1959: 59.
[51] Rainwater *et al.*, 1959: 62.
[52] Rainwater *et al.*, 1959: 62.
[53] Rainwater *et al.*, 1959: 211.

are 'quite uncertain of their own competence as participants in the core culture, they need a good deal of reassurance from advertising that the object is within their reach socially and psychologically, as well as economically'.[54] The lifestyle brand Martha Stewart is performing exactly this function: it demonstrates to a predominately white, female, middle class audience how every aspect of life, no matter how small and trivial it might seem, can and should be designed. We shall return to Martha Stewart later in the book.

Back in the 1950s, Rainwater *et al.*'s study was an implicit critique of the *homo economicus* assumption. The black box of the consumer had been opened and the tools of the researcher started to operate. Specifically, the emotional and irrational behaviour of *The Spenders* was of interest.[55] The researcher worked as 'psycho detective' to uncover motivations: in a form of 'mini-psychoanalysis', 'every phrase, every gesture, and every intonation of the respondent' was noted.[56] An article in the trade magazine *Printer's Ink* from 1950 described the mechanics of decision-making as follows:

When a new experience … enters the conscious, it is assimilated and passed on to the subconscious, where it is stored away for future use and reference. That use or reference is seldom conscious. But once the correct stimulus has been presented or exposed to the brain or mind, the subconscious immediately reacts to it. Within these experiences lies the key to inducing the consumer to buy your brand.[57]

At no point was the individual characterized as a rational decision-maker. Rather, the individual was a melting pot of irrationality and outer-directedness. For this individual to be turned into a consumer, her life would have to be reorganized more fundamentally. What she felt as her 'needs' was related back to a certain way of conducting life. Traditionally, class, religion, gender and other social stratification mechanisms would determine these life patterns. Implicitly, these patterns represented barriers for marketing. Rather than developing products to fit into lives that were based on these more traditional patterns, lifestyle would become the powerful context from which individual needs would emerge in the first place. Lifestyle melted all social categories into air and promoted consumption practices as building blocks for individual identity. Brands set out to be the alphabet of that new-found language.

---

[54] Rainwater *et al.*, 1959: 211.
[55] Britt, 1960.
[56] Dichter, quoted in Tadajewski, 2006: 444.
[57] Yoell, 1950, quoted in Tadajewski, 2006: 455.

Losing the privacy of our minds?

This new lifestyle focus was soon critiqued as blunt manipulation. Vance Packard's *The Hidden Persuaders* sold more than a million copies when it came out in the late 1950s. Packard was an outspoken critic of the new approaches to consumer research as practised by Dichter and others. According to Packard, the old technique of 'nose counting' that divided the population into large demographic segments did not work anymore.[58] These large segments did not reveal enough information about the individual. In fact, the individual was a poor source of information for the marketer for three reasons. First, individuals do not know what they want – people say they don't like the shape of a ketchup bottle and when you change it, they complain that the old one is gone. Second, even if people know what they want, they might not tell you the truth – for example, if you ask what magazine people like they will say something with culture, arts and politics, but what they really buy are trash magazines full of gossip. Third, people cannot be trusted to behave in a rational way. If you give housewives three differently designed washing powder boxes that contain the same powder, they will say that the yellow box ruins their clothing, the blue one is not strong enough and the blue-and-yellow one is just wonderful. Facing these inconsistent, capricious and irrational consumers, what to do?

This is where Packard's critique came in. He criticized the 'depth approach' to motivation research that used mass psychoanalysis and other methods to manipulate the masses and, as Bernays had promised, to engineer consent. The depth approach capitalized on the idea that people did not buy a functional commodity but an emotional, cultural and social brand with meaning: as one of the depth-approach advocates put it, people do not buy a car but prestige; they do not buy oranges but vitality; and they don't buy cosmetics but hope.[59] Strong evidence for this thesis came from an experiment with smokers: in a blind test, more than 98 per cent of 300 brand-loyal smokers proved to be incapable of identifying their favourite brand. The conclusion was obvious: people smoke an image, not a cigarette.[60] Thus the focus would be on building an image, a personality around the product that would appeal emotionally, not rationally, to the masses. For Packard, these manipulations

[58] Packard, 1957: 17–19.
[59] Packard, 1957: 15.
[60] Packard, 1957: 45.

were regressive steps and not progress 'for man's long struggle to become a rational and self-guiding being'.[61] What Packard ultimately tried to protect was the 'privacy of our minds'[62] and with it the idea that consumers are rational human beings, capable of making rational decisions.

Branding life, governing people

Despite the critique of people such as Packard, the notion of lifestyle became one of the master concepts in marketing. Its attraction was simple: lifestyle would describe – or better, prescribe – a set of practices that give meaning and identity. The building blocks for lifestyles would be individual brands that, consumed *en masse*, would form a stylish assemblage. Rather than persuading people that certain brands fit into their lives, the concept of lifestyle turns this reactive logic around: from now on, branding would be about defining lifestyles and then, proactively, selling products into the newly stylized context.

Sidney Levy delivered the theoretical base for the rapid expansion of the lifestyle concept. According to Levy, symbolizing is natural to humans, just like breathing is. Although most of the time we are not conscious of it, we constantly use symbols to express who we are. Lifestyle is 'a large complex symbol in motion' and '*to explore this large, complex symbol in motion that is man's grand life style is to seek to define his self-concept*, to describe the central set of beliefs about himself and what he aspires to, that provide consistency (or unpredictability) to what he does'.[63] Once we understand this self-concept, we can understand the desires, decisions and seemingly irrational behaviours that are all related back to the self-concept. Levy sees products as what he calls 'sub-symbols' 'that are used to play out this general symbolic meaning and to embody it'.[64] Products possess 'potentialities', symbolic resources that people use to build their lifestyle. People put together their lifestyles, and by extension their lives, through sub-symbolic products. Hence a '*consumer's personality can be seen as the peculiar total of the products he consumes*'.[65]

This sounded like a marketer's wildest fantasy come true: from now on they would not '*sell isolated items that can be interpreted as symbols*' but '*sell

---

[61] Packard, 1957: 13.
[62] Packard, 1957: 216.
[63] Levy, 1964: 141 and 144.
[64] Levy, 1964: 145.
[65] Levy, 1964: 149.

pieces of a larger symbol – the consumer's lifestyle.[66] Marketing thus becomes an aid that helps consumers to put together their own individual life-styles: consumers become *'artists of their own life style'*.[67] Marketing would no longer try to sell products by creating an image around them. Here was a much better, much subtler framework consisting of two ideas. First, a person was reduced to the sum total of all she or he consumes. Second, those pieces, when put together, form a pattern of life, called 'lifestyle'. Products and services that were seen as a more or less welcome addition to life are now the very form in which life can be experienced. Marketing had prevailed and showed business how to write itself into society.

In the past, social structure and status was established through one's position in the production of things; you are what you produce. Lifestyles, on the other hand, are based on people's consumption patterns. They cut across older sociological concepts such as class or religion.[68] Lifestyle defines people by what they consume, and this increasingly covers every aspect of life, including leisure, health, politics, work, education, and so on.

Today, in the privileged parts of our world, we are driven by lifestyle more than anything else. The question we ask is whether one or the other lifestyle would be better, healthier or more comfortable. We can hardly imagine a life without the kind of lifestyle experience that brands provide. Lifestyle is our grammar, brands our alphabet: Club Med would tell us how to spend our holidays, IKEA how to live, McDonald's what it means to have a family meal and Nike how to turn hobbies into high-performance activities. Brands are not about a product and its features anymore but about a form of living. The welcome side effect of this shift was a change in the pricing model for goods. While commodities that were marketed on functionality were priced on cost, goods that were branded as lifestyle choices were priced on perceived value. In other words, price was not a function of costs but of the value that consumers saw in the product. Linking the product to lifestyle meant that the potential value of products was enormous: they provided consumers with a sense of who they are through what they consumed.

Historically, Pepsi Cola was one of the first to embrace the lifestyle concept.[69] From 1933 onwards, its positioning was purely based on price. This caused several problems. Consumers were not loyal to the product. When the price of raw materials went up during the war, Pepsi could no longer promote the

---

[66] Levy, 1964: 150.
[67] Levy, 1964: 150.
[68] Zablocki and Moss, 1976; Bogenhold, 2001.
[69] Tedlow, 1991.

image of the cheap drink. And most importantly, Pepsi had an image problem: it was the cheap cola that was bought for children. People even went so far as to put Pepsi into Coke bottles before serving it to their guests. It was, in the words of Tedlow, a drink for the kitchen, not the living room.[70]

Pepsi changed its fortunes by positioning itself as a lifestyle drink for a certain audience. Whereas Coke promoted itself for everybody, always, Pepsi invented the Pepsi Generation. Pepsi become a drink for the young at heart and the youthful; it was the drink for the 'sociables'. In this sense, Pepsi 'not only recognize[d] the existence of a demographic segment (i.e., the youthful population) but also in essence manufactured a segment of those who wanted to feel youthful'.[71] As Tedlow put it, segmentation worked performatively as verb, not descriptively as noun: with the Pepsi Generation, Pepsi constructed a desirable identity, a subjectivity around 'youthfulness' that people from different age groups would find attractive and could use to remodel their personal identity around a certain lifestyle. Although marketers would insist that they simply discover segments, the Pepsi Generation is a fine example of the performative powers of marketing. It created what it supposedly described.

Following the lifestyle revolution, marketers had to change the way they studied consumers. The new world of lifestyles 'laughs at the grossness of personality inventories or the stodginess of questionnaires that fail to take account of the ludicrous, shy, quicksilver, or perverse elements of life style, the felt absurdity of caring about invisible differences in unessential products'.[72] Research became a matter of identifying minute differences that people deployed in order to create what Bourdieu would describe later as 'distinction'.[73]

Today, anthropologists research consumers using ever-more detailed methodologies. The dominant psychographic approach 'assumes, at the heart, that a set of personality traits guides consumer motivation, decisions and behaviour'.[74] The ethnographer's video camera is the new gaze that does not miss anything. It presents the consumer nicely packaged as an object for influencing. It is a form of voyeurism that allows the collection of data and the exercise of power at the same time. By observing people in their natural setting, researchers 'can get past rational barriers to consumption and learn more about people's "true" emotional motives. This idea of the emotional motive

---

[70] Tedlow, 1991: 100.
[71] Hollander and Germain, 1993: 109.
[72] Levy, 1964: 150.
[73] Bourdieu, 1979/2007.
[74] Sunderland and Denny, 2003: 190.

they then tie into the equity of the brand.'[75] As Ian Ryder, formerly a Director of Global Brand Management for Hewlett-Packard, put it enthusiastically, 'powerful subconscious drivers that force us into action may seem like a brand manager's heaven, and, if we understand these anthropological blueprints, they certainly are'.[76] The brand managers' heaven comes through detailed ethnographic research: 'The success of the knowledge gained in this [ethnographic research] exercise tightens the grip of the capitalistic machine ... The anthropological boom in advertising is related to business' discovery that ethnography extracts knowledge.'[77] The knowledge it extracts is the conduit for power to conceive of new ways of influencing and shaping lifestyles. The researchers' job is 'making culture visible'.[78] They understand themselves 'not just as custodians of brands but as social architects'.[79]

Brand-driven companies such as Procter & Gamble invest heavily in making culture visible. In 2006 alone, the company and its brands, including Gillette, Tide, and Pringles, spent US$200 million on consumer research through some 10,000 different research projects. That's five times more than the company had spent in 2000.[80]

The well-funded brand managers / social architects expand their domain with the concept of lifestyle. Branding is now concerned with life itself – with how it is lived, how it is represented and made sense of. Branding guru Aaker explains:

A brand cannot develop deep relationships without a rich and insightful understanding of the customer. The need is to find the customer's sweet spot, that part of his or her life that represents significant involvement and commitment and/or expresses who they are – their self-concept ... The key is to learn from customers as individuals rather than about customers as a group. How is the brand linked to the customer's self-concept and living patterns?[81]

From now on, branding will invest in the quest for the self-concept and lifestyle that reveals the 'truth' of the individual. Branding becomes a mechanism for understanding life, and then, as a result, governing it. Take, for example, the loyalty programmes that have mushroomed recently. They not only consolidate consumer spending but have a much more subtle and important function, as a Senior Data Analyst for the supermarket chain Tesco says: 'You

---

[75] Malefyt and Moeran, 2003: 24.
[76] Ryder, 2004, 353.
[77] Baba, 2003: 205.
[78] Sunderland and Denny, 2003: 194.
[79] Sherry, 2003: xi.
[80] The numbers are taken from Walker, 2008: 231.
[81] Aaker, 1996: 264.

can find people interested in cooking from scratch, or people who shop with distinct flavours in mind, or where convenience is key. We are trying to track lifestyles in terms of what is in the basket.'[82] The real purpose of loyalty cards is to collect information that can be used to refine brands' targeting strategies and develop new lifestyles.

Take the example of Continental. Our case does not refer to Conitental, the US airline that serves ready-made meals of varying quality, but rather to the Australian-based business named Continental that manufactures ready-made meals and other foods. As DDB's Vice Chairman and Creative Director Matt Eastwood, explains:

We work for Continental, who produce ready-made meals for the home. They're all about making life easier for families. I have been doing a lot of reading about the destruction of the family, so we decided that our next campaign should be all about the value of family time. Of course it is about selling their product, but what we do is to make it about the importance of family. About the importance of sharing stories and talking about problems. There is a lot of research that shows that kids who have regular mealtimes with their family are less likely to do drugs, they are better at school, all these kinds of things. So Continental is all about 'family time matters'.[83]

Life itself becomes branded: 'family time matters' is a message that asks us to conduct our lives in a certain way. By doing so, Continental starts to pre-scribe how life should be lived. The brand becomes performative.

The virtual world accelerates this process. Google currently makes money by selling advertising, but this is not the main point of the Google brand. What it ultimately does through its many different applications is measure consumer preferences and track lifestyles. The euphemism is 'personalized search', whereby Google develops a detailed profile of users that is based on cash, clicks and the customs of browsers. As Google CEO Eric Schmidt described the company's mission, 'The goal is to enable Google users to ask questions such as "What shall I do tomorrow?" and "What job should I take?" This is the most important aspect of Google's expansion.'[84] One could not be more blunt than the CEO: Google wants to know enough about your lifestyle patterns to be able to safely advise you what to do next. If you bought this book, you might also like this one. If you like this brand, you might also want to join this community.

---

[82] Quoted in Lury, 2004: 134.
[83] Interview conducted on 11 June 2008.
[84] Eric Schmidt, quoted in the story 'Big Friendly Giant ... or Big Brother?' by David Smith, in *The Sydney Morning Herald Good Weekend*, 13 September 2008, page 43.

From Hobbes to Foucault, philosophers have argued that power and knowledge are inextricably intertwined. As you read, Google creates the largest knowledge database in the world. But don't worry: it's just about tracking and measuring to optimize your choices and provide you with more opportunities. After all, Google's company philosophy is 'don't be evil'.

Google's move into the Chinese market posed a serious challenge to its ethics: the Chinese authorities coupled access to a billion people and dollar market with censoring sensitive words such as freedom and democracy on the Google search engine. On the Chinese Google site, the search for freedom ended abruptly at the new Great Firewall with something along the lines of 'Your search did not match any documents.'[85] When asked about the censorship of its Chinese services, Google CEO answered: 'We actually did an evil scale and decided not to serve at all was worse evil.'[86] Tempted by its own powers and its appetite for more, Google's moral compass is starting to swivel. It is only a small step from collecting data on consumer preferences to using this data to *influence* consumer preferences. A tempting step, which is, by the way, worth billions of dollars.

Power brands

Brands were always tempted by their own power. At the beginning of our story, brands were the weapon of choice for persuading and influencing. Propaganda tried to control passive consumers that needed to be seduced into doing the 'right' thing. But people are stubborn. They do things to please the 'Joneses' on the other side of the fence and the 'Joneses' inside their own mind. This gives birth to the idea of lifestyle in which the individual is nothing but the sum total of what it consumes. Analytically, what kind of power do brands exercise?

Brands are the medium through which power operates – a medium between production and consumption, an interface that controls both. We have already seen how brands influence organizational culture and communities. This is but one of their effects.

---

[85] See BBC's News Channel report from 25 January 2006 entitled 'Google move "black day" for China' at http://news.bbc.co.uk/1/hi/technology/4647398.stm (accessed 30 January 2009).

[86] The quote is taken from the story 'Google CEO on Censoring: "We Did an Evil Scale"' by Stacy Cowley on January 2007 in InfoWorld (see www.infoworld.com/article/ 06/01/27/74874_ HNgoogleceocensoring_1.html (accessed 24 June 2009)). The whole quote is worth reading: 'We concluded that although we weren't wild about the restrictions, it was even worse to not try to serve those users at all,' Schmidt said. 'We actually did an evil scale and decided not to serve at all was worse evil,' he said, referring to the company's famous 'don't be evil' creed.

The power of branding consists of its power to structure the field for possible actions. Power does not determine behaviour but structures potential responses and actions. Foucault's notion of governmentality describes this form of power: it 'conducts' as it leads and drives others to make certain choices. To govern means 'to structure the possible field of action of others'.[87] This includes governing things, events, words, images and people alike – a heterogeneous assemblage of things that creates forces within a given field.

From this, it follows that power is dispersed throughout society. Power is Budweiser telling you how to be cool; it's Maybelline telling you how to look good; it's IBM telling you how to manage risk; and it's mobile communications provider Verizon 'teaching' American Hispanic women 'another important skill: life' by helping them 'navigate the difficult road back to independence' after domestic violence incidents.[88] There is nothing wrong with corporates trying to help – as long as we keep in mind that their objective is to make money. It's dangerous when a mobile network provider starts teaching 'life' and how to be independent – one could question whether Verizon has the legitimacy or the expert knowledge to 'teach people about life'.[89] But that critique misses the point: for brands, life itself becomes the playground. It is about dominating context, content and communication. In short, it is about styling life through brands.

Branding produces certain knowledge, and it needs knowledge to function. Knowledge and power work with and through each other: nothing can be knowledge unless it goes through a process of testing and exposes itself to rules and rituals of verification. Every piece of information, every story, has to go through a rite of passage before it turns into something we can legitimately call knowledge or truth. In turn, this is what power depends upon: power needs knowledge to know how to operate; it needs knowledge to develop and refine its techniques and practices. Every power – except maybe the worst tyrannical power – needs a discourse within which it legitimizes itself. It needs to create knowledge around itself to ensure its acceptability.[90]

The knowledge branding produces is manifold: it creates a discourse of freedom and desire, of expression and development. At the same time, it is building an archive of behaviours, attitudes and mentalities of people through researching the population in ever-greater detail. It segments, classifies and orders the social world so it can act on it. In order to exercise power,

[87] Foucault, 1982/2003: 138; 1978a/2003.
[88] See the Verizon ad in *The New Yorker*, 21 July, 2008.
[89] For detailed discussion of this argument, see Reich, 2008.
[90] Foucault, 1976/2003; 1978b/2003.

knowledge presents itself as truth: self-actualization, the pinnacle in Maslow's hierarchy, is the *telos* of our existence, and consuming brands will help us to actualize these selves. Importantly, this is not simply an insight from a marketing report or knowledge from branding textbooks. Rather, it is believed to be true, and it functions as the truth.

The truth does not exist outside media, practices and technologies: newspapers talk about the self; practices as displayed on Big Brother promote a certain relation between oneself and others; and technology frees us by creating 24/7 availability. Above all, governmentality needs the truth to be able to legitimately exercise its power – as Nikolas Rose put it, to govern 'is to be condemned to seek an authority for one's authority'.[91] In our regime of power, legitimacy comes from the truth. The discourse of a free market where people are free to choose how to satisfy their needs legitimizes branding. Branding does not try to manipulate aspects of life. Rather, through the regime of lifestyle, brands become ready-made narratives about oneself, society and culture. As Giddens put it:

A lifestyle can be defined as a more or less integrated set of practices which an individual embraces, not only because such practices fulfil utilitarian needs, but because they give material form to a particular narrative of self-identity … Lifestyles are routined practices, the routines incorporated into habits of dress, eating, modes of acting and favoured milieux for encountering others; but the routines followed are reflexively open to change in the light of the mobile nature of self-identity.[92]

In doing so, lifestyle is one of those paradoxical forces that individualize and at the same time have a totalizing effect. Let us explain. Branding divides the masses into psychological units – the *individuum* – and locates desire in them. It produces a discourse around each one, which focuses on its individual needs and its uniqueness. Simultaneously, it creates trends and fashions that homogenize the individual and strip it of its possibilities for expressing itself. Think of all those people who express their freedom, their uniqueness, even their resistance vis-à-vis society by listening to Eminem and wearing Tommy Hilfiger. Or think of those managers who all come up with a unique solution to a problem – as long as it is part of the repertoire of the McKinsey brand. The sociologist Simmel has analysed this paradox as fashion: it allows us to express our individuality and, at the same time, reassures us that we remain within what others expect of us.[93]

[91] Rose, 1999: 27.
[92] Giddens, 1991: 81.
[93] See the last chapter of this book, where we use Simmel's approach.

Finally, it is worthwhile to analyse brands by looking at what seems to resist their power. Take Greenpeace or the Red Cross or Amnesty International: what do they have in common with the corporate world that they are critical of? They are well aware that they compete for a share of people's minds: what is more important, refugees in Africa, victims of a natural disaster in Asia or breast cancer? Tough call, tough competition. Hence, Greenpeace and all those others use the tools of branding to communicate who they are and tell their story. Share of market follows share of mind.

Our point is that branding as a mechanism for governing people is not restricted to corporations. Rather, public organizations and NGOs are among the most subversive influencers. In his book *Endless Propaganda*, Paul Rutherford analyses the advertising of public goods.[94] Civic advocacy, the domestic name for propaganda, is concerned with the selling or unselling of public goods and social risks such as human rights, the environment, cancer, animal rights, torture, obesity, homelessness, AIDS, and so on. What makes it so powerful is that it is focused on the public sphere itself. Often, there are 'campaigns of truth' that engender themselves as a fight for the good, just and right.[95] The members of an elite that can afford media space, including public bodies, NGOs and to a lesser extent corporates, divide the world into problems and solutions and engage in what Kotler and Zaltman have dubbed 'social marketing'.[96] Marketing becomes the all-absorbing discourse in this regime of power, and branding is the weapon of choice. Things turn into goods, citizens turn into consumers, the public sphere turns into a marketplace of risks and participation becomes a choice between (safe) alternatives.

Greenpeace and Gucci are both lifestyle brands: they are ways of modelling life and relating to life itself. Branding has established true hegemony over our society. It is a way of thinking about the world, about our organizations and even about those who criticize them. Branding structures how we behave as consumers, and how we engage with society as citizens. It is a discursive regime, a body of knowledge, a set of techniques that structure our field of possible action. It enacts what Foucault has called the 'politics of truth'.[97] Its regime tells us to focus on attention, not intelligence; intensity, not duration; images, not words; values, not rules; and freedom, not liberty. Power focuses on life itself – it cares about it, it nurtures it and it manages it.

[94] Rutherford, 2000.
[95] Rutherford, 2000: 93.
[96] Kotler and Zaltman, 1971.
[97] Foucault, 1976/2003.

Branding has an insatiable appetite for new lifestyles. It creates desires and values that we think reflect our innermost selves. Its objective is to manage desire, to control consumption, to structure satisfaction and link all of these back into the production of goods, services and experiences that are for sale. It sets free a world of distinctions, a social dynamic of symbols and relations that define what it means to be 'human'. Every year, these life-styling efforts are backed by a US$450 billion global spend on advertising.[98] This is more than twenty times the entire budget of the United Nations. It's almost as much as Russia, China and Europe's combined 2008 defence budget. And it is still more than 60 per cent of the US expenditure on weapons in 2008.[99]

Maybe most importantly, branding has set up a system in which any attempt to change or revolutionize it will be absorbed immediately. As Holt has argued, 'since the market feeds off the constant production of difference, the most creative, unorthodox, singularizing consumer sovereignty practices are the most productive for the system'.[100] In fact, engineering consent would be a system failure. Holt continues that consumers therefore produce ever-new markets and players within these markets with new products. A system based on the exploitation of difference produces new brands. But at no point does this system threaten the market system in itself: consumer resistance 'is actually a form of market-sanctioned cultural experimentation through which the market rejuvenates itself'.[101] Every form of resistance is absorbed into the system that sees that 'for every cultural movement, there is an opposing cultural opportunity'.[102]

Where to from here?

Habermas lamented the transformation of the public sphere into commercial space in his book the *Structural Transformation of the Public Sphere*.[103] On the other side of the Atlantic, it was his German colleague Herbert Marcuse who amplified the anxieties and anger of a generation. *The One-Dimensional Man* was an assault on those forces that started to govern life, especially mass

[98] Estimate by ZenithOptimedia; they forecast that advertising expenditure will reach US$540 billion by 2010. See www.zenithoptimedia.com (accessed 23 June 2007).
[99] See www.globalissues.org/article/75/world-military-spending (accessed 15 September 2008).
[100] Holt, 2002: 88.
[101] Holt, 2002: 89.
[102] Nadeau, 2007: 44.
[103] Habermas, 1962 – see especially the chapters on 'The Public Sphere as Platform for Advertising' and 'The Practices of Public Relations and Political Marketing'.

media. Marcuse asks rhetorically: 'Can one really distinguish between the mass media as instrument of information and entertainment, and as agents of manipulation and indoctrination?'[104]

This critical thinking is aligned with Horkheimer and Adorno's dark analysis of our consumer culture: the culture industry becomes a commodity resulting in conformity and a one-dimensional person in a one-dimensional society, as Marcuse had it. This results in an atomized society of other-directed individuals: *The Lonely Crowd*, as Riesman put it in his famous 1950 publication.[105] The latest advocate of this thinking is George Ritzer and his thesis of *The McDonaldization of Society*.[106] According to these accounts, branding is nothing but manipulative propaganda. Wally Olins, one of the gurus of design and branding confesses bluntly that branding is about 'persuading, seducing and attempting to manipulate people into buying products and services'.[107] Propaganda and its more civil sibling, civic advocacy, is a particularly powerful way to manage and control the behaviour and attitude of a population: 'Propaganda can set the agenda (determine what issues are of importance), prime discussion (determine what criteria are used to assess a person or issue), excite controversy (where news outlets take different stands), or generate support (where the media elaborate its message). Whatever its impact, the result is productive – of comment, argument, and discourse.'[108] In a Foucauldian sense, propaganda is about the 'politics of truth' – the establishment of a discourse that makes a statement false or true. But is consent really engineered? Are lifestyles propaganda? Are we living in Orwell's *1984*? Is this Huxley's *Brave New World*?

In 1920, Sergei Eisenstein hypothesized that film could control thinking. Using this new technology, he pondered a screen adaptation of Marx' *Das Kapital*. His idea was to show viewers thesis and anti-thesis so that they would arrive at the right conclusion, guided by history's invisible hand and Eisenstein's programming.[109] Of course, it did not work. Fears of manipulation through media are as old as media itself. We might laugh about

---

[104] Marcuse, 1964/2002: 10.
[105] Riesman, 1950.
[106] Ritzer, 1995/2008.
[107] Olins, 2003: 7; for a more general criticism, see Chomsky, 1997.
[108] Rutherford, 2000: 268.
[109] The story is reported in Manovich, 2001: 58; another example is Vance Packard, who, in his *The Hidden Persuaders*, thought that by the year 2000, 'depth persuasion' (the use of psychological methods to control the individual) would be perfected, and through the new science of bio-control, mental processes and emotional reactions would be controlled (Packard, 1957: 195–196).

Eisenstein, but the core of his argument has been repeated a million times, including by critical social theorists.

Maybe we have taken marketers' claims too literally. Marketers and advertisers were trying to legitimize themselves in the eyes of corporations. They promised a lot as they tried to gain more influence and bigger budgets. Watson is a good example – he did not work in the labs of JWT but travelled the country talking about what he would do. No doubt, corporations listened, increased budgets and made marketing a powerful function. For their own professionalization, marketers needed to exaggerate the effects of their art. They were chasing corporate budgets, and in their quest for jurisdictional power, promised what would get them closer to the prize.

Consumers and critics listened to these exaggerations, too – and took the marketing-sales talk quite literally. Consumers used marketing-speak to undermine and resist consumer culture as it was dished up by business in the 1950s and 1960s. A big push-back in the 1960s changed the landscape, as Holt has argued: 'Branding could no longer prescribe tastes in a way that was perceived as domineering. People had to be able to experience consumption as a volatile site of personal development, achievement, and self-creation. Increasingly, they could not tolerate the idea that they were to live in a company-generated template.'[110]

Brands had to change. They did not present themselves as company-generated templates but as cultural resources with which to build one's own identity – a 'useful ingredient to produce the self as one chooses'.[111] As Holt notes, brands became authentic cultural resources. During the creative revolution, brands turned ironic and more reflexive – think of the Volkswagen Beetle ads 'Think Small' or 'Lemon'.

Brands embedded themselves in cultural epicentres such as the American ghetto and its black and Hispanic populations, which became one of the most valuable cultural mines for modern brands. Brands also developed an appetite for ironic reflexivity, as in the example of the 1998 re-launch of the VW Beetle.[112] In short, brands became increasingly embedded in culture, and that changed them fundamentally. Culture, on the other hand, changed too, and became more branded: rock stars or movie stars turned into brands

---

[110] Holt, 2002: 82.
[111] Holt, 2002: 83.
[112] See the interesting essay by Brown *et al.*, 2003; building on Walter Benjamin, they analyse the relation between community, aura and authenticity in brand-meaning management.

themselves, while brands are as famous as individual pop stars used to be. What we are witnessing is a Deleuzian becoming, where both sides change as they engage with each other.

This also means that the power of brands to govern lifestyles is never absolute. Power needs a discourse to exercise its authority, to justify itself, to universalize its values and to legitimize its doings. Rather than being on one side or the other, in the regime of governmentality, power needs to set the agenda and divide the world into pros and cons. Power needs to talk, more than anything else. It is productive by its nature. And it refrains from suppressing, burdening and wearing down; rather, it frees individuals and invites them to actualize themselves and choose their lifestyle.

If one analyses power though the lens of the consumer, one ends up quickly with a story of manipulation and repression. The basic assumption here is that there is a human nature that has been covered up and distorted by branding. If we could liberate mankind from brands, we would find the essence of women and men. That resonates with the 1968 refrain 'underneath the pavement, the beach': we are not convinced that there is a human essence that we could reveal if we peeled away brands. Rather, people's desire for objects as psychological, cultural and social phenomena is constituted by, and constitutes, a complex web of interactions. We might well be a consequence of these interactions. More to the point, we argue that we are inextricably tangled up with brands for they are what we desire. To peel them off would mean to peel away what we call our self. But that also means that brands need us – like parasites, they need us as hosts to live off. Which means that brands don't determine our actions. There is always resistance, struggle and a way out.[113]

Power, as its very condition, assumes freedom. One can always develop what Foucault called a critical attitude and find ways of escaping from, displacing or fighting existing power relations. But one mustn't think of this struggle as liberation: it will be a struggle to be governed differently, not quite so much in that way or at that cost.[114] Power is not evil *per se*, as Foucault put it, but it is dangerous.[115] We have to figure out what is most dangerous at this point in time. Which power/knowledge regime produces realities we do not want to accept? If Deleuze was right when he said that we live in a society in

---

[113] In fact, Foucault has insisted that in every power relation, 'the other' over whom power is exercised has to be 'recognized and maintained to the very end as a subject who acts'. (Foucault, 1982/2003: 138).

[114] Foucault, 1978b/2003.

[115] Foucault, 1983a/2003.

which the control of communication becomes the most important struggle, then branding and its lifestyle regime are propelled to the top of the list.[116] Hence the exploration of the ethics of brands and lifestyle become pivotal. We will attend to these important issues in the next chapter.

---

[116] Deleuze, 1990; he contrasts the control society with the disciplinary society; while the latter is based on incarceration, the former takes shape through constant control in an open milieu.

8 Ethics

Two schools of thought

Most ethical debates are framed around two opposing schools of thought. On the one hand, there is liberal philosophy with its focus on freedom, the private and the individual; on the other there is a more loosely connected set of ideas that advocate society, the common good and justice.[1] In the world of business, the liberal tradition, with its ideology of free markets leading to all other freedoms, including democracy and personal freedom, dominates the debate. The brand plays an important role in the defence of free-market principles: brands create accountability, loyalty and wealth for everybody. In other words, brands liberate. The more critical tradition sees brands as part of the problem, not the solution. Brands are the lubricants of free-markets in which the consumer mentality bulldozes all other forms of life. Brands are the avant-garde of the capitalist quest for world domination, spearheading the invasion of culture and privacy (or what's left of it).

The two schools are implacably opposed. When people talk about ethics, they normally join one or the other camp. Their arguments miss each other, like ships passing in the night. The problem is that if you judge each

[1] Rorty, 1989.

tradition by its own criteria, both are right. They both present fairly cohesive, closed logical systems that make sense from the inside. But trying to compare them feels like going in circles, because both systems have had smart people developing clever arguments for their respective positions and they have waterproofed their points of view. The scripts have been developed almost to perfection. But like two opposing magnets, the respective positions remain separate and logically incommensurable. Let's rehearse what these two schools have to say about the ethics of branding.

Why brands liberate

The traditional neoliberal view of ethics can be easily summarized: ethics is a consequence of efficient markets. Adam Smith's famous invisible hand brings into and keeps markets in perfect equilibrium. Maximizing one's self-interest will automatically lead to the best outcome for all. Business does not have to worry about ethics since the invisible hand takes care of ethics too. Ethics are a by-product of free markets, as the Nobel Prize winner Milton Friedman argued: 'There is one and only one social responsibility of business – to use its resources and engage in activities designed to increase its profits so long as it stays within the rules of the game, which is to say, engages in open and free competition without deception or fraud.'[2]

In the neoliberal view, ethics fall outside market relations. Because maximizing one's own self-interest includes being concerned about reputation, following profits leads automatically to fine principles: 'When firms, acting within the law with a view to their reputation, pursue profits, the result is to advance social good, almost by accident.'[3]

The neoliberal view advocates a philosophy based on freedom. The idea is that free markets allow individuals to choose freely what they want to consume or where they want to work. This choice equals freedom: 'Our free enterprise system, which emphasises individual rights, is based on the philosophy that we shall not have a dictator telling us what to do – but there are still some who would substitute a commissar for the free consumer.'[4] The neoliberal view argues for a 'consumer democracy', which is 'harmonized with political democracy'. The link between free markets and free democracy has been at the core of neoliberal rhetoric. In this view, brand managers and

---

[2] Friedman, 1970.
[3] Ahmad, 2003: 175.
[4] Sandage, 1972/1990: 5.

advertisers turn into 'consumer advocates' because they facilitate the process of free choice.[5] Brands help consumers make decisions and 'provide a route map through the bewildering variety of choices'.[6] In a world where 'rational choice has become almost impossible, brands represent clarity, reassurance, consistency, status, membership – everything that enables human beings to help define themselves. Brands represent identity.'[7]

Brands are the catalyst for the neoliberal free-market society. As Sameena Ahmad wrote in her 'Pro Logo' story for *The Economist*:

Brands began as a form not of exploitation, but of consumer protection. A brand provided a guarantee of reliability and quality ... The flip side of the power and importance of a brand is its growing vulnerability. Because it is so valuable to a company, a brand must be cosseted, sustained and protected. A failed advertising campaign, a drop-off in quality or a hint of scandal can all quickly send customers fleeing. The more companies promote the value of their brands, the more they will need to seem ethically robust and environmentally pure. Hence, brands are levers for lifting standards.[8]

In other words, brands are the market mechanisms that ensure the ethicality of business. With brands, commerce and creativity, ethics and efficiency finally become synonymous. There are no more ethical dilemmas because consumers enforce ethicality through participating in the market economy and buying brands. In an economy of qualities, heralded by brands, values are the most important asset of an organization. The co-creation of value opens up even further opportunities for exchange. Until now, you had two options: either do well or do good. Now, 'You have the never-before-possible ability to actually achieve both [do well and do good], and you will have the support of a brand-new invincible force: the consumer and the culture he or she – and you – share.'[9]

As a consequence of this intensified collaboration, there is more and more scrutiny not only on 'what' a company is doing but on 'how' it is doing business. Ask Nike or Shell or McDonald's – they can tell you how external parties try to change their internal process. In fact, internal processes are no longer internal affairs. Companies are accountable not only for the end product but also for the processes that are deployed to get there: 'The truth is that brands don't control anyone – and consumers control everything. Brands are

---

[5] Sandage, 1972/1990: 8.
[6] Blackett, 2003: 18.
[7] Olins, 2003: 27.
[8] Ahmad, 2001. The story was written in response to Naomi Klein's bestseller *No Logo* (Klein, 2000).
[9] Nadeau, 2007: 281.

the ultimate guarantee, making companies accountable. In the West, if our Gap jeans fray or our Mercedes car breaks down, we know exactly where to go to complain.'[10] This accountability created through brands makes organizations very vulnerable: just think of the Nike customization email that went around the world (see Chapter 6).

The pedestrian version of the neoliberal marriage of morals and money is that, basically, consuming is voting. Every dollar that a consumer spends is a vote for or against an organization. If people are unhappy with the way Nike produces shoes, they will stop buying them and punish Nike. A competitor will seize the opportunity, will act more morally and will swiftly attract the dollar votes and prosper while making the world a better place. It's that simple: your local shopping centre is actually a voting booth and you can spend your way into a better world. The consumer is sovereign in supermarket politics, her most powerful weapon being the buy-cott.[11]

One of the most advanced forms of the 'shopping as voting' theory is the Fair Trade movement, a form of collective action that is focused on social and ethical change through market mechanisms. Fair Trade is based on three principles. First, alternative trade networks are organized as social networks of independent producers, sellers and buyers. Second, Fair Trade products are marketed through licensed channels with certificates that guarantee the goodness of the product. Third, campaign-based promotions are launched to change the traditional buying behaviour of consumers.[12] As such, Fair Trade politicizes consumption while remaining within the logic of market capitalism. It is one of the fastest growing markets: in 2006, in Europe alone it was worth €600 million.[13] The main vehicle for growing market share is the aggressive branding of Fair Trade organizations (remember, share of market follows share of mind). This leads to the ironic situation that both the Fair Trade café Cafédirect and Starbucks are using the same methods for different ends: both use branding as strategic growth formula.

The challenge for most Fair Trade organizations is managing their own success – initially there were more radical groupings that fought for social inclusion. With a growing appeal to new markets, the brand Fair Trade is being remodelled and new values that attract new customers, such as environmental sustainability, healthiness of the product and safety, are being included. Also, in its early days, Fair Trade goods were consumed as a political act; taste was a

[10] Ahmad, 2003: 174.
[11] Stolle *et al.*, 2005; Shah *et al.*, 2007.
[12] Wilkinson, 2007: 219.
[13] Wilkinson, 2007: 225.

secondary consideration. When facing a mass-market taste, aesthetics and the nutritional values of the products must be consistent and competitive.[14]

What works for Fair Trade also works for Wall Street. For Zwick and his colleagues, markets make morals. In their study of investors and stock traders (not a species normally known for its ethical concerns), they argue that the increased connectivity brought about by ICT and globalization created heightened awareness of the consequences of individual action, even on stockmarkets: 'The market becomes a lens through which global events are linked to personal desires and hopes.'[15] Because of this lens, the moral consequences of behaviour come into sharper focus, resulting in an increased sense of responsibility. Free markets become the actual source of, rather than the barrier to, politically progressive consumerism. Take the example of the Norwegian Finance Minister who announced that the Norwegian Pension Fund (worth some US$360 billion) will sell its US$1-billion stake in the global mining giant Rio Tinto. As the news reported:

Finance Minister Kristin Halvorsen said that the mining operation was causing 'severe environmental damage' and that the fund's Council on Ethics had determined that Rio Tinto was directly involved through its participation in the mine. 'There are no indications to the effect that the company's practices will be changed in future,' Halvorsen said. 'The Fund cannot hold ownership interests in such a company.'[16]

The announcement sent Rio Tinto's share price down by 3 per cent overnight. Maybe, after all, there are ethical principles embedded in the profits of the free markets? Of course, since the financial crisis, proponents of this view have been a bit more quiet than usual.

Brands also create wealth and are 'a great ally of social progress' as Hilton points out in a book on branding published by *The Economist*.[17] Since all of the top brands in the world are domiciled either in the US, Japan or the EU, Hilton concludes that brands are not attracted to rich countries but that rich countries are rich because of their brands: 'Without brands, modern capitalism falls apart. No brand: no way to create mass customer loyalty; no customer loyalty: no guarantee of reliable earnings; no reliable earnings: less investment and employment; less investment and employment: less wealth created; less wealth: lower government receipts to spend on social goods.'[18] Of course, just because the wealth of countries and the number of valuable

[14] Wilkinson, 2007.
[15] Zwick *et al.*, 2007: 187.
[16] Reported in the Melbourne-based newspaper *The Age*, 10 September 2008.
[17] Hilton, 2003: 48.
[18] Hilton, 2003: 49.

brands correlate does not prove that one causes the other. Also, one could argue that without loyalty, consumer spending is spread over more firms rather than concentrated on a few big brands. This would give rise to an entrepreneurial economy that might be more innovative. To the contrary, free-market economists describe brands as engines of innovation: 'Brands create customer value because they reduce both the effort and the risk of buying things, and therefore give suppliers an incentive to invest in quality and innovation.'[19]

Finally, brands build bridges between people and nations. They cross borders and introduce different cultures to each other. Brands promote social cohesion 'by enabling shared participation in aspirational and democratic narratives ... The greatest brands in the world seek to be social unifiers: Coca-Cola sought to teach the world to sing; Nike celebrates human endeavour; Nokia connects people; Lux soap gives women confidence; Budweiser made heroes of the blue-collar workers who built the land of the free.'[20] Social unification has its boundaries though, as Ahmad reminds us. In fact, it can actually be dangerous to bring Western values to countries that are economically less developed. For instance, Nike was forced out of Pakistan in the 1980s as it was made public that it employed children to stitch footballs. Nike left because of the criticism of the West. The ultimate consequence of not letting Nike do its job but insisting on bringing our value system to Pakistan resulted in the fact 'that children were forced into more dangerous, more poorly paid employment and [it] did nothing to change the fact that over 200m [*sic!*] children in Pakistan work and probably will until the country becomes rich enough to afford to develop a moral conscience about the practice.'[21]

Even when brands like Nike seem to exploit poor countries such as Pakistan, it is argued by some that they actually do good by offering less dangerous and better-paid child labour. You can see the (cynical) logic of the argument: the free market has not produced schools yet, so the best we can do is employ those children until the society is wealthy enough to build schools for its children. This trickle-down effect has not reached anybody – yet, as the neoliberals would add.

In summary, brands are the catalysts that make the market economy freer, more just and more ethical: 'The search for new values will become a

---

[19] Barwise, 2003: xv.
[20] Hilton, 2003: 48 and 64.
[21] Ahmad, 2003: 179; please note that, according to Unicef statistics, Pakistan's population under the age of 18 was just over 70 million in 2006. The total population was just above 160 million. See www.unicef.org/infobycountry/pakistan_pakistan_statistics.html#47 (accessed 30 January 2009).

necessity in branding – if only because *current* values are limited as a basis for new brand positionings ... brands and branding will therefore lead us towards a morality that is a more accurate reflection of our real beliefs and aspirations.'[22] Because branding is concerned with values, it will listen to consumers and be careful to give them what they want. After all, they are free to vote brands off the shelf if they do not agree with their morality.

Why brands incarcerate

One hundred years ago, things were still in balance. In 1910, the *Encyclopaedia Britannica* explained consumption as 'wasting away', or in a more technical and economic sense, as the 'destruction of utilities'.[23] Today, life is caught up in non-stop consumption. Brands are the face of this consumer society, and, if one believes the critics, they are ugly, wasteful and downright danger-ous.[24] The baseline is that the consumer society demonstrates the shift from a society that satisfied desire to one that produces desire. While the former was dominated by a Protestant ethic that was future-focused, the consumer society strives on an infantilist ethos in which satisfaction and instant grati-fication are most important. For Barber, this is a serious threat for capital-ism.[25] Rather than investing in the future, it is about consuming the present. It is only logical that in the face of the 9/11 attacks, George W. Bush told his fellow Americans to be good citizens and go back to the mall to consume. Business as usual actually means shopping as usual.

Indeed, all that people have in common in a consumer society is their capacity to consume. Social inclusion and exclusion is not organized along bloodlines, gender, religion or class, but through consumption. One's iden-tity used to be linked to what one did: farming, bookkeeping, writing; now, you are what you consume. Esteem and its opposite – stigma – are earned through consumption practices. Social outcasts are not the unemployed – those who are not productive – but those who do not or cannot consume. Poor is someone who cannot afford brands and has to settle for no-name home brands. A good citizen is someone who frames her rights and responsibilities

[22] Braun, 2004: 133.
[23] Bauman, 2007: 54.
[24] Ironically, it is virtually impossible to consume all books on the consumer society – although they put forward similar arguments, there are lots. Beside classics such as Baudrillard and Featherstone, we use mainly Bauman, 2007 and Barber, 2007.
[25] Barber, 2007.

as consumables. With the shift from income tax towards value added tax, taxes are increasingly based on consumption, not production.[26]

In a consumer society, the individual is impoverished. Heidegger's *Man* and Marcuse's *One Dimensional Man* were early warning signals. As Bauman observed, consumers turn themselves into commodities, becoming simultaneously *'promoters of commodities* and the *commodities they promote'*.[27] The social space they inhabit is the market, and the language they use to make sense of their environment is marketing. Consumers become commodities themselves: they consume things, and as they do so, they become consumed themselves. They become what they buy. People's subjectivity is made up of the consumption choices they make. Identity becomes a matter of shopping. Barber has criticized this trend as the 'commercialisation of identity', where brands replace religion or tradition and become substitutes for identity.[28]

People turn themselves into 'brands', offering unique value to their employer, occupying niches and constantly developing themselves through lifelong learning. They start to describe themselves in marketing language, seeing themselves competing with others in a market space. As Tom Peters puts it, you perform 'The Brand Called You' and your real job is being 'CEO of Me Inc.'.[29] Individual identity becomes a project of the self, and the self turns into a succession of career steps.[30] Not only do we self-manage our work life but we have careers as consumers too. We travel to ever-more exotic locations and spend our leisure time in ever-more sophisticated ways, which must be learned and practised. The art of lifestyle requires the organization of consumption patterns into a coherent image, reflecting one's identity.

Consumerism creates a Pointillist version of time: like those paintings by Seurat, time is broken into little unconnected dots, pulverized into eternal moments following on but not from each other.[31] Like Impressionist paintings, identities and reality are fragmented and their boundaries are dissolved. Things bleed into people, people bleed into things. Simulacrum and reality become indistinguishable. The actors in this plot step from one dot onto the next, without experiencing the safety of a stable set design that could frame their crumbling narratives. The blueprint for such a Pointillist life is the famous Pepsi ad from 1968, with its jingle 'you've got a lot to live, you've got

---

[26] To be sure, income tax is still in most countries the major form of taxation.
[27] Bauman, 2007: 6.
[28] Barber, 2007.
[29] Peters, 1997.
[30] See Giddens, 1991 and Grey's 1994 article on career as a project of the self.
[31] Bauman, 2007: 32.

a lot to give'.[32] In one of the TV ads, fifty-nine different images bombard the viewer in just sixty seconds, showing random shots of young people enjoying all sorts of leisure activities. The ad depicted the kind of lifestyle Pepsi wanted you to live – with Pepsi being the fuel for all that fun, which did not make sense except as a collection of Pointillist moments without underlying coherence.

The consumer society understands itself as being dedicated to the pursuit of happiness of the masses. It gives people what they want, instantly and perpetually. Critics argue that we might be materially better off, but the amount of consumables we have does not correlate with personal happiness. The consumer society does not satisfy needs but produces desire: the whole capitalist machine would fall apart if people's needs were ever satisfied. So every need that is supposedly satisfied has to create new desire. As Bauman put it, a '*satisfied* consumer is neither motive nor purpose – but the most terrifying menace … Satisfaction must be only a momentary experience.'[33] Economic growth is based on the idea that demand (desire) grows faster than supply (satisfaction). Hence a consumer society cannot produce happiness. Galbraith has described this as the 'dependence effect': production fills the void it first creates through manufacturing desire. *Status anxiety* becomes the status quo when freedom is experienced as free market-style insecurity, uncertainty and unpredictability.[34] As Žižek put it, liberal ideology 'endeavours to sell us the insecurity caused by the dismantling of the Welfare State as the opportunity for new freedoms'.[35]

If the consumer society and its brands do not make us happy, do they at least bring freedom? Remember the neoliberal promise about the free market and free democracies harbouring free people. Doubtless, freedom is one of the highest values in our Western society. We fight for free speech, free individuals, a free world – you name it. Freedom legitimizes actions, including wars. As Henry Kissinger, former Foreign Minister in the Nixon and Ford government and winner of the Nobel Peace Prize who also wanted to bomb Cambodia back into the Stone Age, argues, since creating its constitution, the US has been on an ideological crusade in the name of freedom and democracy: 'Whether fighting world wars or local conflicts, American leaders always claimed to be struggling in the name of principle, not interest.'[36] George W. Bush's debacle in Iraq is but the latest manifestation of this hypothesis.

[32] See Frank, 1997: 180.
[33] Bauman, 2007: 98.
[34] De Botton, 2004.
[35] Žižek, 2001: 116.
[36] Kissinger, 1994: 810.

Freedom is not just a political force but also a private burden. As Nikolas Rose has put it,

the problem of freedom now comes to be understood in terms of the capacity of an autonomous individual to establish an identity through shaping a meaningful everyday life. Freedom is seen as autonomy, the capacity to realize one's desires in one's secular life, to fulfil one's potential through one's own endeavours, to determine the course of one's own existence through acts of choice.[37]

Rose suspects that freedom is not an innocent concept at all. If we have to be free in order to be ourselves, then how much does the concept of freedom, paradoxically, govern us? What kind of freedom is it that makes us wage wars and go on crusades? Rose argues that freeing up zones of the individual, the family, the social and the public introduced a whole set of new management and control devices in the name of freedom. In order to make up our free society, we need complex laws; we need layers of government; we need public opinion polls reporting about trends; and we need media to amplify them. In order to make up the free market, we need regulations, taxes, organization and, above all, marketing. Rose's argument is that the process of freeing society is attempted with means that are not more or less 'free' than other forms of government.

Consumption is one arena in which this 'freedom' manifests itself. What are the practices that make freedom free? Research has to identify needs; advertising has to fuel desire; and brands are positioned as lifestyle choices that will allow us to be who we want to be. But lifestyle might well be the single most tyrannical concept of our age: we work to maintain a certain lifestyle, we stay with or change partners for lifestyle reasons and we consume to experience, build and express our lifestyle. Ironically, lifestyle choices reflect back on the person whose life is made up of the style she can afford.[38] In other words, your life is designed by someone else, who turns your decisions into pseudo-decisions and sells you what you need to retain the style that is supposedly yours.

Lifestyle shapes life itself. And lifestyle is shaped by brands. The freedom to express ourselves is tightly linked to the production machinery of capitalism. In this context, freedom is an illusion: you can choose between different lifestyles, but you are not free to be not governed through lifestyle. Bauman argues that it is a tragic and dangerous mistake to confuse the choice between alternatives with freedom. Michel Serres made the same

[37] Rose, 1999: 84.
[38] See Rose, 1999: 85–89; see also Rose, 1990.

argument by saying that the system precedes decision – or that the structure put in place is more important than the strategy.[39] Before we decide which road to take, we should question the people who planned the roads. They had freedom – we have choice.

The same is true in our consumer society: what we see on a menu or in a supermarket or in a shop window is choice among things but not freedom. Barber gives the example of a car: we can choose which one we want, but we cannot choose proper public transport so we would not need a car in the first place. This fundamental decision has been made without us, and to camouflage it we have been given a choice between pseudo-alternatives.[40] For Žižek, 'formal freedom' is constrained to choice within the coordinates of a system; 'actual freedom', on the other hand, 'designates the site of an intervention which undermines these very conditions'.[41] The freedom of the free market is formal freedom that deprives us of the possibility of experiencing actual freedom because it masquerades as actual freedom.

For Barber, the theory of liberal rights and its notion of freedom are useful in the context of tyranny. It is defined as a freedom *from* someone else's power and control. The notion of liberty, or better liberties, is pivotal to European history from the fifteenth century onwards. But liberties are always defined vis-à-vis another group that either suppresses or is suppressed, as French historian Braudel reminds us: 'Liberties … were the privileges protecting this or that group of people or interests, which used such protection to exploit others, often without shame.'[42] The concept of 'individual liberty' makes no sense to him if we mean the freedom of the individual, because we are only aware of individual liberties if authoritarian or technocratic states threaten them.

In the free market, there is no such threat, and therefore government is not needed to defend our liberties. This is why neoliberalism results in the paradoxical situation whereby politicians such as Ronald Reagan or Margaret Thatcher saw their own governments as part of the problem, not the solution. As an ultimate consequence, government outsources itself and is run like a contracting agency.[43] Soon, marketing is better positioned to satisfy taxpayers through constant polling and surveys than bureaucratic governments are; after all, these instruments are more appropriate for gauging the needs and

---

[39] Serres, 1974.
[40] Barber, 2007: 139.
[41] Žižek, 2001: 122.
[42] Braudel, 1987/1995: 316.
[43] See Friedman's famous essay *Why Government is the Problem* (1993); for a recent critique, see Klein, 2007.

desires of the citizen-consumer than are old-fashioned elections. This is what John A. Quelch and Katherine E. Jocz, both from Harvard Business School, suggest in their book *Greater Good: How Good Marketing Makes for Better Democracy* (2008). In their view, marketing principles should govern democracy. To critical minds, it may seem as if our political system got into trouble because of an over-reliance on marketing. Diane Ravitch analysed the content of presidential election debates and found that, during the Bush-Gore debate, Bush spoke at sixth-grade level and Gore at high seventh-grade level. Going back to the Lincoln-Douglas debate in 1858, the level was 11.2 and 12 respectively.[44] Ruling by spin might lead to intellectually impoverished, populist governments. It turns politicians into brands: image campaigns replace political controversy.

In liberalism, personal choices count as autonomous and *ultima ratio*. Barber, and to some extend Reich's book *Supercapitalism*, argue that this belief is not only wrong but actually dangerous for democracy, leading to what Barber calls 'civic schizophrenia'. As we have seen above, the liberal notion of choice is misleading, since it has little to do with actual freedom. Moreover, the aggregation of private wants does not equal public goods. Rather, the public has to be created as public – the *res publica* is what cannot be reduced to private choices. Thus a consumer democracy is an oxymoron: while the market can address the question 'What do I want?', it fails when it tries to answer the question 'What do we as a community need?': 'Private choices do inevitably have social consequences and public outcomes. When these derive from purely personal preferences, the results are often socially irrational and unintended.'[45] This is where civic schizophrenia sets in: as an individual, I want a big four-wheel drive; as citizens, we should use public transport to avoid pollution and reduce our dependency on oil. If the 'I' starts to dominate the 'we', the public domain disappears. If health insurance, education, security, transportation and other public goods become a matter of private choice, it leads to disastrous results: it is impossible to live safely and in an environment free of pollution unless the whole community commits to the same values.

Products that deny their negative consequences are the symptoms of civic schizophrenia. As Žižek put it:

On today's market, we find a whole series of products deprived of their malignant property: coffee without caffeine, cream without fat, beer without alcohol … And

---

[44] Quoted in Furedi, 2004: 73.
[45] Barber, 2007: 128.

the list goes on: what about virtual sex as sex without sex, the Colin Powell doctrine of warfare with no casualties (on our side, of course) as warfare without warfare, the contemporary redefinition of politics as the art of expert administration as politics without politics, up to today's tolerant liberal multiculturalism as an experience of Other deprived of its Otherness.[46]

Brands become the pills that fight the symptoms of civic schizophrenia, without touching its cause. In summary, critics of the consumer society argue that brands are inextricably linked to the ideology of free markets. Because they are embedded in society and because they feed off values, brands become one of the most powerful tools of the free-market avant-garde. But the freedom they afford is framed by the interests of corporations. The choice they offer is deceptive and superficial. Identity is reduced to lifestyles that can be sold profitably. At best, brands are ethically problematic and remain a dangerous because potentially manipulative symptom of the uncurable ills of free-market capitalism.

Who's right?

In both the liberal and the critical world view, brands play an eminent role – but on different sides of the equation: for liberals, brands are part of the solution, while critics see brands as part of the problem. The dilemma results from the fact that both have valid arguments that are rationally and logically derived from their individual sets of assumptions. They are incommensurable and divided by what Lyotard called the *différend*:

A differend would be a case of conflict, between (at least) two parties, that cannot be equitably resolved for lack of a rule of judgement applicable to both arguments. One side's legitimacy does not imply the other's lack of legitimacy. However, applying a single rule of judgement to both in order to settle their différend as though it was merely a litigation would wrong (at least) one of them ... A wrong results from the fact that the rules of the genre of discourse which one judges are not those of the judged genre or genres of discourse.[47]

Both sides present a set of coherent and logical arguments, but unfortunately there is no third discourse that would allow us to judge which side is wrong. What the proponents of each side normally do in this case is repeat their position until, usually, the louder one prevails. If we agree that volume has never

[46] Žižek, 2002: 10.
[47] Lyotard, 1983/1988: xi.

been a good indicator of truth, how can we come to a conclusion that does not wrong one of the two sides? Let's have a look at a couple of examples.

Take the Green Marketing movement. In his *Green Marketing Manifesto*, John Grant argues that green marketing campaigns are good for the planet and for business. Green marketing is both 'commercial and environmental – a win-win'.[48] Marketing's role is to make people willing and able to go green by educating them about green products and offering them a green life-style that is more sophisticated than living in a commune and eating berries: 'Green marketing is mostly about making (breakthrough) green stuff seem normal – and not about making normal stuff seem green.'[49] Green marketing relies heavily on branding to communicate the benefits of its products and legitimize the higher costs. In this scenario, we need more and better branding to fight for a better planet. Branding becomes the ethicist's weapon of choice.

The crux is that, starting with the same premises, you can end up in the opposite corner: green marketing does not question the logic of consumption. After all, consuming more green stuff is still consuming more. The problematic assumption is that we can consume our way out of the mess we are in, after we consumed ourselves into it.[50] For example, the washing powder brand Ariel won several awards for its 'Ariel Turn To 30' campaign, which promoted lower energy consumption and, of course, its washing power. Is such green marketing ethical or not? Does it solve the problem or deepen the crisis?

Another example is McDonald's. Grant has suggested that 'the more you look at McDonald's, the better it gets'.[51] The magazine *Ethisphere* went so far as to vote McDonald's as one of the most ethical businesses of 2007.[52] Did they lose their minds? The answer is no, if you believe Matt Eastwood, Vice Chairman and Creative Director of Advertising Giant DDB, which holds the global McDonald's advertising account:

Ethics have to be driven by people like me – you need some kind of moral compass. I want to deliver a positive message into the world – and if you can do this with your client, all the better. We all work with companies where you find something that they have done wrong if you dig hard enough. It's like with individuals – we all did something wrong at one point in our lives. We all have things that we could

---

[48] Grant, 2007: 11.
[49] Grant, 2007: 56.
[50] Grant, 2007: 189.
[51] Grant, 2007: 38.
[52] See http://ethisphere.com/2007-worlds-most-ethical-companies (accessed 25 June 2009).

do better. To use McDonald's as an example, we developed a campaign for them about the food value of the product. They wanted to tell people about the quality of the food and the produce that goes into the food. So we generated the campaign for them called 'Make up your own mind'. It was about confronting the myths and being very honest. People said that there was pig fat in the milkshakes. People said that the nuggets are not made of real chicken. We showed that this was not true. We invited people to ask questions and got McDonald's to answer. And McDonald's openly answered them.

McDonald's and other brands such as Wal-Mart, BP or Nike are under enormous scrutiny. They collaborate with NGOs around the world to ensure that they stay out of the headlines. Does this represent just the latest marketing spin or true commitment to their responsibility as corporate citizens?

Let's take Benetton's *Colours* Magazine as our last example. It reports on social issues such as the life of prisoners or the independence struggle of Tibet.[53] Of course, its overall objective is to reinforce the Benetton brand as a socially conscious and aware company. Is it great news that Benetton has realized its ethical obligations and engages in the fight for a more just world? Or are we witnessing the worst excesses of profit-seeking greed, a willingness to use even prisoners and beaten-up minorities to build brand value? The list of examples is endless, but the problem is the same: depending on whether you buy into the liberal ideology or its critics' premises, you will end up on one side of the fence or the other. The crux is that both lines of thought are divided by what Lyotard has called a *differend*. And without doing wrong to one or the other side, we will not be able to come to a conclusion.

A solution could only be derived from a kind of Archimedean point that rests above the two conflicting camps. The trouble is that there is no such Archimedean point. That's the problem that Nietzsche summarized with those famous three words: 'God Is Dead'.[54] We simply don't know with certainty what is good or evil because we have no single point from which to judge. It might be absurd to try to find that Archimedean point from which

---

[53] See www.colorsmagazine.com (accessed 25 June 2009).

[54] It is interesting that Nietzsche describes how the news of God's death will affect us in spatial metaphors – it is quite literally about losing a central point from where to judge things: 'What were we doing when we unchained this earth from its sun? Whither is it moving now? Whither are we moving? Away from all suns? Are we not plunging continually? And backward, sideward, forward, in all directions? Is there still any up or down? Are we not straying as through an infinite nothing? Do we not feel the breath of empty space?' (Nietzsche, 1882/2002: 119–120). The flipside of this is that everything is a matter of perspective and that there is no possible absolute truth.

to establish ethics. In fact, Voltaire's *Candide* is a more humorous attempt to show the absurdity of such a position.[55] This brings us dangerously close to nihilism: anything goes while at the same time *rien ne va plus*.

Where to from here? If we do not allow ourselves to join one of the camps, we might have to follow Foucault's advice to 'approach politics from behind and cut across societies on the diagonal'.[56] What Foucault meant was that we should refrain from totalizing accounts that would look for abstract explanations. Instead, he opted for an approach that would be as concrete as possible and focus on problems 'that are at once constituents of our history and constituted by that history'.[57] For us, this translates into an analysis of brands and following possible lines of resistance and engagement with the phenomenon. It is about suspending one's own judgement and thinking instead about new problematizations in which ethics are at stake. Judging something as ethical or unethical will be always contested: one person's freedom fighter is another person's terrorist. Suspending judgement, we can delineate the space where this contest takes place and ethics are at stake.

Travelling on the diagonal

One can think of several layers that describe ways of engaging with problems. The first and most direct form is to make a decision about a particular issue. Whether you manage an organization or organize your daughter's birthday party, it is likely you will make decisions. The German sociologist Niklas Luhmann went so far to equate organizing with decision-making.[58] The second layer is slightly more reflexive: it pauses to discuss options and deliberate their pros and cons. Let's call this approach problem-solving: you try to find a solution to a given challenge. If you have ever sat a multiple-choice exam, you will know what I am thinking of. The third layer steps further back: rather than discussing the pros and cons of an issue at hand, it tries to think in alternatives. It effectively widens the scope

---

[55] Voltaire, 1759/1993. If you look for an Archimedean point, you resemble Dr Pangloss, that literary *persona* invented by Voltaire to show the absurdity of developing a philosophical system to justify the *status quo*. Dr Pangloss teaches Candide that the world we live in is the best possible system – otherwise it would not be the way it is. Candide's life increasingly disproves Dr Pangloss' hypothesis – he gets kidnapped, tortured and experiences all evils. For Dr Pangloss, not seeing the positivity in that is not being able to see the bigger system in which everything is arranged in the best possible way. Voltire's satire shows the absurdity of this position.

[56] Foucault, 1983b/2003: 376.

[57] Foucault, 1983b/2003: 376.

[58] Luhmann, 1984.

of the decision-making space to include new, as yet unconsidered, options. Thinking in alternatives focuses on as yet unexplored solutions to a given problem, such as Free Trade. The fourth layer represents what Foucault has called problematization: it is the space in which the problem itself is questioned. Rather than looking for alternatives, it means scrutinizing the question itself to find out whether another question, another problem, is more important. Put simply, rather than trying to answer an impossible question, we might have to change the question itself and re-frame the problem.[59]

The discussions between neoliberals and their critics fall somewhere between the second and the third mode. Which is the appropriate level of enquiry for ethics? Ethics is not about decision-making or problem-solving, as they are always framed by a specific context and their very own rhythm. We argue that ethics are at stake in the various problematizations of ourselves and society. Borrowing one of Nikolas Rose's formulations, an ethics of problematizations 'would help us to calculate the cost of being what we have become; hence it might allow us to invent ways of becoming other than that what we are'.[60] Problematizations are about spaces that open up and allow transformations to emerge. Critics of the consumer society depict branding as a quite simple process of colonization. Take Bauman's argument about the 'invasion, conquest and colonialization of the web of human relations' through consumption, which is a common complaint amongst critics.[61] The idea here is that the force of consumerism lands at some kind of *terra nullius* and conquers it. In this case, the ethical debate is about the pros and cons of the new civilization. If we choose Foucault's problematization as our point of departure, the ethical issue is in how far the clash of the two opposing systems allow a third, more hybrid form to develop, and what possibilities this hybrid form affords.

Deleuze has proposed a different model of change that he refers to as 'becoming'. The basic idea is that when two forces meet, they both form a third space, an in-between in which something new emerges. This space in-between is the zone of becoming. Both sides that form the space in between change as they start to interfere with each other. Colonialization thinks of change as the adaptation of one to the other. Change as becoming focuses on the space between where both sides melt into an unpredictable new mixture: '*Between* things does not designate a localizable relation going

---

[59] See Foucault, 1983b/2003, who discusses the differences between alternatives and *problématiques*.
[60] Rose, 1999: 97.
[61] Bauman, 2007: 24.

from one thing to the other and back again, but a perpendicular direction, a transversal movement that sweeps one *and* the other away, a stream without beginning or end that undermines its banks and picks up speed in the middle.'[62] In between is the zone where two or more things meet and start to change each other. One side rarely only imitates the other, nor does one side dominate fully. Rather, they co-evolve and co-shape each other. For Deleuze, becoming is at work everywhere – even when we learn to swim or speak another language:

Learning to swim or learning a foreign language means composing the singular points of *one's own body or one's own language with those of another shape or element*, which tears us apart but also propels us into a *hitherto unknown and unheard-of world of problems*. To what are we dedicated *if not to those problems which demand the very transformation of our body and our language*?[63]

Following Deleuze, the kind of problems where our identities are transformed represents true ethical challenges. It means we have to focus on the space in between, where things melt into each other, where they de- and re-territorialize each other. How does this work? Let's look at an example – the public sphere and private space. Both the private and the public changed as they started to infiltrate each other. The private and the public, the secret and the spectacular, the interior and the exterior have morphed into a strange, hybrid new zone. Think of all the reality TV shows in which intimate and mundane activities become the most publicized and public of acts. In this new space, it is not the private that needs to be defended from the prying eyes of the public; nor is it the public that is threatened by the intrusive intimacy of the private. Rather, both lose their privileged positions as the axis of organizing society and ethics.

Brands are new problematizations in which things collide, forming a space for becoming. Ethics are at stake in these spaces: in them we have the opportunity to develop something new and, in the words of Nikolas Rose, invent ways of becoming other than that which we are.

---

[62] Deleuze and Guattari, 1980/1987: 25; see also page 11: 'Each of these becomings brings about the deterritorialization of one term and the reterritorialization of the other; the two becomings interlink and form relays in a circulation of intensities pushing the deterritorialization ever further. There is neither imitation nor resemblance, only an exploding of two heterogeneous series on the line of flight composed by a common rhizome that can no longer be attributed to or subjugated by anything signifying.' And page 305: 'Becoming is always double, that which one becomes becomes no less than the one that becomes – a block is formed, essentially mobile, never in equilibrium.'

[63] Deleuze, 1968/1994: 192.

Subjectivities

What are we? For Nietzsche, man is the 'not yet determined animal' – the animal that can choose and act to determine its fate.[64] This also means we are not pre-determined by nature: since it is our 'nature' to have no pre-given nature, it is an oxymoron to speak of human nature. How do we form our subjectivities? How do we create identity and ideas about a good life?

Traditionally, society and its institutions have been powerful agents in the constitution of subjectivity. We will argue that brands have replaced some of these institutions and form a new, powerful and ambiguous ethics of subjectivity.

Of course, we have always believed that we are what we possess: as the Roman rhetoric teacher Quintilian taught, *vestis virum reddit* – the clothing makes the man. In 1866, Gottfried Keller's novella *Clothes Make People* picked up on this idea, telling the story of a poor tailor who was mistaken for a count because of his looks.

While possession has an impact on status, brands build identity. More precisely, they enable identity creation. They are symbolic resources for identity construction. They are the grammar that allow the subject to express itself. In a Goffmanian sense, people perform their selves – and brands are the scripts and the props that allow them to do so. The actual performance constitutes the roles and the actors in the play. Brands are *the* catalyst that makes the 'labour of identity' possible.[65]

There is no lack of studies that analyse the relation between identity, consumption and brands. In his paper on plastic surgery, Schouten stressed the importance of symbolic consumption for the process of self-reconstruction. Especially during times of transition, Schouten found, consumption provides people with the opportunity to reintegrate their selves through exercising control and engaging in 'identity play'. The actualization of the new self 'may occur via the consumption of instrumental goods and services as the individual accumulates the appropriate symbols of the new self'.[66] The crucial word here is 'appropriate' – which happens through brands and lifestyles.

Belk has argued that *we are what we have* is the 'most basic and powerful fact of consumer behaviour'.[67] It is the incorporation of objects into our extended selves that allows us to be who we are. Holt differentiates between

---

[64] Nietzsche, 1886/2002.
[65] Elliott and Wattanasuwan, 1998; Atkins and Lury, 1999; Walker, 2008.
[66] Schouten, 1991: 422.
[67] Belk, 1988: 139.

two ways of creating identity through consumption.[68] First, consumption practices can integrate objects into the sphere of one's identity. Second, practices can allow people to realign their identity with socially desirable external identities. In other words, people make objects their own and use them as extensions of themselves. Sometimes, it might be the other way round and objects make people their own, transforming them into living extensions of what they are. Objects become a resource for constructing identity as consumers enact and personalize 'cultural scripts that align their identities with the structural imperatives of a consumer driven global economy'.[69]

Even advertisements become a source of identity construction. For instance, a study of the consumption of advertising by school kids shows how the youngsters bend the ad messages to fit their lifestyles rather than bending their lifestyles to fit the pressure from the ad. Put simply, it is the ad that is consumed, not what the ad hints at.[70]

Identity-creating consumption is not to be seen as a 'crutch to shore up weak personalities'; rather, possessions are 'personal museums' that allow us to reflect on our history and change. They provide a sense of community for those with whom we share them.[71]

Even 'the homeless employ unique adaptation strategies in their search for, and consumption of, goods and services. These alternative consumer behaviours allow them to survive, serve to restore meaning to their lives, and bolster their sense of self.'[72] The point is that homeless people consume too as they collect food, occupy shelters and care about clothing and other goods. Clearly, their sense of self is tied up to what they have, ironically illustrated by the shopping trolleys in which they often carry around their belongings (fearing they may be stolen otherwise). In a famous phrase, Lukács lamented the 'transcendental homelessness' of mankind.[73] Regardless of whether we are transcendentally or actually physically homeless, we all engage in consumption practices to build our identities.

Identity is accomplished not only through individual consumption: you are what you consume and what you consume is who *else* consumes it. Schau and Muñiz have studied the ways in which personal identity and brand communities are linked.[74] Practices range from people subsuming their identity

[68] Holt, 1995: 6.
[69] Arnould and Thompson, 2005: 871.
[70] Ritson and Elliott, 1999.
[71] Belk, 1988: 159.
[72] Hill and Stamey, 1990: 319–320.
[73] Lukács, 1920.
[74] Schau and Muñiz, 2002.

to one single brand community to consumers with multiple memberships who create a unique identity out of many brands.

The brand-driven self extends even further in the digital age. In the purely semantic space of the internet, consumers can put forward any kind of representation of themselves (avatars), which may be totally detached from their real selves. With a potentially massive audience, feedback on this avatar locks the consumer into a certain identity that is then constructed narratively. In their study of web users, Schau and Gily found that 'consumers use multiple self-presentation strategies to construct digital collages that represent the self'.[75] These strategies range from digital associations including references to brands, objects, places, links to other sites etc. to the reorganization of linear narrative structures where telling one's own life story does not have to follow conventional genres or structures.

Virtual users can develop relationships between and with brands that are only limited by their computer skills. Such digital association starts to blur the differences between the real and the possible. Keeping up with the Joneses becomes an easy thing because 'we are what we post'.[76]

The individual's capacity to construct its own identity can result in extreme scenarios when paired with neoliberal optimism. Nadeau quotes a report by the trend agency Genius Insight that predicts salvation in 'extreme self-determination': 'Extreme self-determination is the idea that everything about ourselves – how we look and even how we feel – is within our power to change ... The individual becomes a product of his or her own deliberate (and ever-changing) choices. It's basically a form of wish fulfilment.'[77] So-called transformative tools empower us to be who and what we want to be – free of anxiety, depression and sexual dysfunction and, above all, attractive. Cosmetic surgery and other techniques allow people to experiment and live out fantasies. Nadeau uses the concept of 'individual performances' to describe this future: '[I]t provides a means for "everyday" people to live fantastic adventures, attain dreams, and explore, test, and develop themselves in every way imaginable.' He sees an enormous potential for improved 'self-actualization' and 'self-creation' that is modelled on the idea of celebrities who 'provide a heightened vision for an ultimate level of empowerment, self-creation, and unbridled personal expression'.[78]

---

[75] Schau and Gily, 2003: 390.
[76] Schau and Gily, 2003: 402.
[77] Quoted in Nadeau, 2007: 23.
[78] Nadeau, 2007: 26.

We have mentioned the zones of becoming between which things melt into each other and disclose new spaces. These zones, we have argued, constitute the space in which ethics are at stake. With brands, a new zone of subjectivity is opening up that allows us to become different from what we are now.

For Bourdieu to exist within a social space as an individual means to differ and to be different.[79] Brands offer a ready-made system of differences, a grammar if you want, that enables people to put together their identities. An existence designed by brand consumption turns into a lifestyle. Such lifestyle identities do not function based on *who you are* (and all the facets this question takes in – e.g. class, religion, race, nationality, and so on). To be sure, these identity markers have dominated society for centuries and produce and reproduce enormous inequalities. Lifestyle identity is based on *what you do*. This can be more freely chosen than class or gender. Identity becomes a function of brands, appearances and playfulness as opposed to pedigree, substance and tradition.[80]

The question of whether this is good or evil might be the wrong question: what brands allow is enhanced cultural mobility. Brands are the trajectories along which people can develop preferences, passions and pleasures. It blows the top off Maslow's hierarchy of needs as it de-naturalizes what it means to be human. Rather than satisfying needs, brands provide lifestyles: a thick texture of symbols and meanings that shape one's lifeworld. Rob Walker has described 'the secret dialogue between what we buy and who we are' as 'murketing' (a mix of murky and marketing): the dividing line between brands and life becomes increasingly blurry as we actively and creatively engage with brands, using them to style our lives and identities.[81]

Does branding obscure and maybe even destroy a more 'natural' way of living? Baudrillard is wrong when he laments that we move from the principle of autonomy, character and the inherent value of the self to something less important when we 'enter the cycle of consumption and fashion [which] is not simply to surround oneself with objects and services as one pleases; it is to change one's being and directedness'.[82] Baudrillard implicitly argues that there is an essence, a deep truth about humans that we are losing or that is obscured through branding. But what are we losing here? What being and directness are we giving up for the new one that is brought to us through

[79] Bourdieu, 1979/2007.
[80] Machin and van Leeuwen, 2008; Chaney, 1996.
[81] Walker, 2008.
[82] Baudrillard, 1970/2003: 170.

lifestyles? What is contested is a more traditional identity that has been defined by the nation states, values, religion, family, profession, and so on.

For Nietzsche, the *individuum* with an essential human nature is a fiction. The subject is much more political: it is constructed, deconstructed and reconstructed in the midst of power struggles. Today, brands are key players in this struggle as we make up our identities through them: 'Brands provide an answer to our identity crisis by giving us meaning. They help us construct our social world.'[83] As such, the ethics of branding is about experimentation with new subjectivities in these hybrid spaces. Valéry said towards the end of his life: 'I am a reaction to what I am.'[84] We are complicated – we act and react; we use things we find, like Robinson Crusoe on the beach, and build them into who we are. Brands will give rise to new subjectivities – not better, and hopefully not worse, than the previous ones.

Cultures

Empire incorporates, it differentiates, and it manages.[85] Brands are the soul of empire. As engines of difference, brands launch into a conquest of culture itself. Branding does not know boundaries – it is a semiotic engine that integrates everything. Brands infiltrate sub- and counter-cultures. But cultures also change the way brands work. In the zone of becoming that this clash creates, both are being transformed.

The notion of cool is one of the most illuminating examples.[86] It has become key in youth culture and in advertising alike. Cool has its roots in the black urban culture of North America. It described an attitude that black Americans developed when facing prejudices and resistance. Cool was a form of detachment. It dates from before World War II and quickly became associated with drugs and jazz music. Cool was about being in the know, outside society's norms, slightly in the illegal. In the 1960s and 1970s, it became mainstream and spread cross the world to end up as a dominant counter-culture attitude that included narcissism, ironic detachment and hedonism. Cool was a reaction against the mass-manufactured, standardized and soulless consumer society of the 1950s. Efficiency had been the

---

[83] Wipperfürth, 2005: 119.
[84] Quoted in Starobinski, 1999/2003: 370.
[85] Hardt and Negri, 2000: 201.
[86] Frank, 1997; Pountain and Robins, 2000; Nancarrow *et al.*, 2001. We use the latter for our excursion into cool.

mantra since Taylor, conformism the social imperative and hierarchy the predominant organizational form of estranged, all-powerful corporations. Whyte's incredibly successful *Organization Man* (1956) was a direct attack on the grey and soulless bureaucrat oiling of the cogs and pulling the levers of the corporate machinery. McGregor's Theory X described the old image of the employee, while Theory Y heralded the new, self-directed, open and creative employee.[87] What these books did for the theory of business was what Norman Mailer's provocative essay 'The White Negro: Superficial Reflections on the Hipster', originally published in 1957, did for culture. The remedy for Theory X and *Organization Man* was the 'hipster' – a jazz-, drugs- and pleasure-loving nomadic existentialist.[88] Fitting in with the crowd and buying what was on TV was out; consumer culture was debunked as a big fraud. Salvation came in the form of counter-culture, which enabled resistance to conformity and rebellion against conventions.

With this movement, brands turned hip too; they started to associate with the counter-culture and become, paradoxically, the main critics of consumer society. Frank's *The Conquest of Cool* tells the story of the corporate rebellion that led to 'hip' consumerism. In 1968, 7-Up framed itself as 'The Uncola' in a clear reference to the critique of the establishment, as one JWT executive explained: 'We were still struggling to try to get out of Vietnam, and there was this whole anti-establishment everything … The timing was brilliant, because it allowed the younger people to, in effect, say, "this is my soft drink", and it allowed us to violate taboos that were very much part of the generation that was there.'[89] The campaign was about dissent, about transgression, about rejection of the status quo. In fact, what corporate America was asking for was rebellion – as long as it was expressed through consumption of the brands being promoted. In fact, brands become the vocabulary of rebellion against the status quo.

The rise of notion of 'hip' illustrates the point. In his book *Hip: The History*, John Leland writes its biography from its origins in the African Wolof verb *hepi*, 'to see', or *hipi*, 'to open one's eyes'.[90] African slaves started using the word in the 1700s as code for their critical distancing from and subversion of authority. They used it to describe their desire for autonomy and freedom as outsiders, creating a world that insiders did not understand. From there, in the 1900s it moved with African Americans into the urban settings of Greenwich and Harlem, before it was taken up by the Beat generation after

87   McGregor, 1960.
88   Mailer, 1957; see Frank, 1997: 12.
89   Quoted in Frank, 1997: 166.
90   Leland, 2004.

World War II to express their disdain towards the mainstream. Via bebop, hip had become the signifier of counter-culture – and as such, it accelerated in the 1970s punk movement and on to the beginning of hip hop. *Wired* magazine and *Fastcompany* imported hip into Silicon Valley as an insignia of the new information engineers. And now here we are – in the midst of a society where hip is the currency for all things considered cool. It's an 'under-current of enlightenment, organized around contradictions and anxieties', an 'alternate status system' as Leland puts it: 'In a society run on information, hip is all there is.'[91]

How do 'hip' and 'cool' operate? As Nancarrow and his colleagues found, mainly as mechanisms to exclude others and perform the self as part of an elite in-group.[92] They found that authenticity was the key ingredient of cool. Whereas this attitude was important, the knowledge about what would be considered cool brands and hip consumption practices was equally important. This cultural capital created distinction and, importantly, excluded the mainstream. Cool is a commodified concept that is defined through know-ledge about the 'right' kind of bars, films, fashion, and so on. Marketers try to define what's cool and try to align their products with it. 'Coolhunters' are a new breed of consultancy that tries to identify the next hot thing.

Coolhunters, or 'the legal stalkers of Youth Culture' as Naomi Klein calls them, turn counter-culture into mainstream, with an enormous and increasing appetite for everything that is different.[93] The fashion designer Franco Moschino used fashion to demonstrate against the vanity of the fashion industry with sweaters saying 'This sweater costs £180' or a jacket with 'a waist of money' printed along the waistband.[94] Because of branding's appetite for differences, this form of resistance against fashion became very fashionable in itself. The pattern repeats itself wherever you look.

Ambivalence and flirting with the anti exerts a strange attraction over brand managers and equips brands with a certain auto-eroticism. Think of the Sprite 'Image Is Nothing' campaign, the anti-retail stores of Comme des Garçons or Kesselskramer's Nike campaign that turned a 78-year-old German marathon runner into a hero. As Stephen Brown puts it, these brand campaigns are soft, subtle and subversive – but they still (try to) sell.[95] This might well be a viable strategy – an ambiguous world rewards brands that

[91] Leland, 2004: 15.
[92] Nancarrow *et al.*, 2001: 314.
[93] Klein, 2000.
[94] Ger and Belk, 1996:89.
[95] Brown, 2006: 52.

mirror the ambiguity of their context – rather than trying to simplify things and unavoidably miss the mark.[96]

The collective around the magazine *Adbusters* represents a truly paradoxical ambi-brand. The self-appointed culture-jammers became world-famous for trashing ads through the production of counter-ads. *Adbusters* 'subvertized' even its own brands, Blackspot Shoes, t-shirts, and so on, which are – of course – on sale on its website's 'Culture Shop'. Its *Media Manifesto* reads as follows:

> We will take on the archetypal mind polluters and beat them at their own game. We will uncool their billion-dollar brands with uncommercials on TV, subvertisements in magazines and anti-ads right next to theirs in the urban landscape. We will seize control of the roles and functions that corporations play in our lives and set new agendas in their industries. We will jam the pop-culture marketeers and bring their image factory to a sudden, shuddering halt. On the rubble of the old culture, we will build a new one with a non-commercial heart and soul.[97]

Culture-jamming and sub-vertising were always part of the mainstream advertising business. For some strange reason, the profession felt always out of sync with its own deeds and wanted to undo at night what it had fabricated during the day. David Ogilvy, one of the big figures in advertising, famously stated in his *Confessions of an Advertising Man* written in 1963:

> As a private person, I have a passion for landscape, and I have never seen one improved by a billboard. Where every prospect pleases, man is at his vilest when he erects a billboard. When I retire from Madison Avenue, I am going to start a secret society of masked vigilantes who will travel around the world on silent motor bicycles, chopping down posters at the dark of the moon.

It has not been reported how many billboards Ogilvy jammed; what we do know, though, is that he built one of the biggest advertising empires in the world.

Brands are cultural forms: they are a way of relating to and interpreting the world. As Arnould and Thompson put it, brands are symbolic devices

---

96 Another example are tattoos, which have long been symbol of deviance for outcasts and outsiders. Consumerism has changed that: people have brands tattooed on to their skin (Apple, Nike and Harley Davidson are the most frequent), while tattooed models are used in commercials (David Beckham). Anders Bengtsson *et al.* (2005) have analysed the consequences of branded tattoos penetrating a sub-culture that was opposed to the market. Initially an artful expression of individuality and personality, tattoos of brands pervert the very meaning of using the body as a canvas. It is a cultural form that capitalism integrates into its system, transforming it fundamentally. Tattoo culture, once the sign of resistance to the system, becomes both a product and an expression of the system it denied.

97 Lasn, 1999: 128; see www.adbusters.org (accessed 25 June 2009).

framing 'horizons of conceivable action, feeling and thought'.[98] With their insatiable appetite for the new, brands create an array of new cultural forms. They become what John Grant has dubbed clusters of cultural ideas.[99] (Popular) culture becomes a resource, or a database, as the marketing writers Bernd Schmitt and Alex Simonson put it.[100] For better or worse, brands re-define what it means to be a cool teenager, a good mother, a beautiful woman or an attractive man. They change what it means to have fun, sex or a good time. Brands change culture, including counter-culture. *Adbusters* follows the logic of branding and, if it wants to be heard, it needs to turn itself into a brand too. And so does Greenpeace, Eminem, The Red Cross and The Simpson's. The power brands exercise lies in the fact that it is virtually impossible to locate oneself outside its sphere. Brands are not simply one possible expression within our culture, but they come to represent the very form of our culture. In Kantian terms, they become the condition of the possibility (the *a priori*) of being visible in our society.

Critically speaking, one could argue that brands are mass entertainment, not cultural forms. As Hannah Arendt put it, in an age of 'mass entertainment', we need to feed on the 'cultural objects of the world' – and by doing so we destroy them.[101] As with our argument about subjectivity, we hesitate to call branding a less authentic contribution than other cultural forms. Brands *do* structure people's actions, feelings and thoughts like no other medium. As such, they *are* cultural forms. They give rise to new forms of expression. An ethics of branding would suspend judgement and try to understand the possibilities that emerge in this new hybrid space.

Worlds

Critics have insisted that global brands crush local providers and homogenize the world. Ritzer's McDonaldization thesis or Klein's *No Logo* are among the chief critiques. We experience globalization through brands: without brands, globalization would be a meaningless notion. Under the communist regimes of the Soviet Bloc, brands such as Coke or Levi's were seen as symbols of resistance against the establishment; when the Iron Curtain finally fell, the people of Moscow experienced the new global realities by queuing outside

[98] Arnould and Thompson, 2005: 869.
[99] Grant, 2006.
[100] Schmitt and Simonson, 1997.
[101] Arendt, 1961/1993: 211.

McDonald's. I assume this was not for the taste of the burgers; rather, it was the brand McDonald's that made it an attractive site and consumption a symbolic form.

How do we experience the global and the local in brands? David Machin and Joanna Thornborrow looked at different national versions of the magazine *Cosmopolitan* in order to understand what remains consistent across the globe. They looked at all forty-four issues of the November 2001 issue and analysed three stories in detail. What *Cosmo* sells to readers is not just a magazine but a lifestyle based on independence, power and fun. The audience for this imaginary *Cosmo*-land is the fun and fearless female. This recipe remains the same across countries: the core values of independence, power and fun are promoted, and, based on them, how a fun and fearless female engages in work, relationships, sexual practices, health, beauty and fashion. But it is not only what is said that is stable; the style of the magazine – images, colours, layout etc. – creates a consistent brand appearance. Pictures are generally abstracted, sensual and stylized, evoking an image of a fantasy world of harmony and beauty that empowers women; and they communicate agency through motion and energy. Studying articles about sex, Machin and Thornborrow found that readers are often addressed using the personal 'you', making them feel naïve and immature. Articles also feature transgressive practices (e.g. sex with a stranger; dominating in bed etc.) in which women take control through seduction and using their bodies. Despite taking control, though, in most articles the 'main goal of sex for the fun, fearless female remains pleasing men'.[102]

What is the global *Cosmo* brand? The image of a woman as someone who advances through pleasing or manipulating (seducing) others through the power of her sexuality. This image is presented as 'playful fantasy' against a background of abstracted and stylized images that contrast with everyday reality. Undoubtedly, *Cosmo* homogenizes the image of what a woman should be. The question is: How is this image read in the context of different local cultures? While it might simply reinforce and echo other cultural stereotypes in Australia, how do Afghani women make sense of the fun and fearless female? She might be a cliché in New York, but in Nairobi the *Cosmo* woman might be the only counterweight to a tradition that is not exactly liberating either.

The *Cosmo* example hints at a more fundamental problem: Are brands hegemonic? Do they homogenize the world? Brands change and translate into local contexts. Take the example of Deloitte: it is the same all over the

---

[102] Machin and Thornborrow, 2003: 464.

world – but not quite. Similarly, *Cosmo* is the same all over the world, but countries do produce their own variations. Brand identity is not based on sameness but on difference; brands are engines for exploiting differences; they absorb differences – and the local is an inexhaustible source of idio-syncrasies. As Askegaard put it, brands are hegemonic vehicles of diversity and difference.[103] Brands to not dominate the world by unifying it: they rule through diversity and difference. To homogenize would represent a system failure. This has important ethical implications.

Brands are enacted by people: brands do not belong to organizations but are made up of the ongoing meaning-making activities of users. This means that people are partners in crime with brand managers: brands do not have total control over the destiny of their brand as they emerge out of a conver-sation between consumer and producer. This idea makes the claim of brand hegemony difficult to sustain, because different people interpret brands dif-ferently – and since interpretations are indistinguishable from 'facts', brands become different things for different people.

This means that local consumers appropriate brands, enact them in their own weird and wonderful ways, add new meanings and translate the global into the local.[104] For instance, migrant and ethnic groups in Israel 'watched' the TV series *Dallas* in a very different way, understanding it as critique of Western values and lifestyles.[105] Ger and Belk report on Turkish people who used old washing machines to make butter, ovens to dry clothes and dish-washers to wash spinach.[106] Milk crates in Australia are variously used as street furniture, storage devices and transportation units.

Hannerz coined the rather awkward term 'creolization' for the mix of meanings from different sources.[107] This practice includes the mixing of Western products such as fashion items or design with traditional clothing or furniture. Although to observers, while this often looks like postmodern absurdity, it makes sense and creates a coherent experience for locals. New cultural forms become hybrids of the old and the new – they are created through mixing. The editor replaces the author as cultural producer.

Global brands don't homogenize the world. Since brands are engines that produce differences, homogeneity would actually equal a system fail-ure. The role of brands is far more complex. Thompson and Arsel argue

[103] Askegaard, 2006: 97.
[104] For example, Miller, 1998b; Ger and Belk, 1996.
[105] Liebes and Katz, 1990.
[106] Ger and Belk, 1996: 289.
[107] Hannerz, 1992.

that, first, although the homogenization thesis might be, academically speaking, wrong, it could be a useful framework that consumers apply in order to make sense of their local experience. In short, it is a folk theory. Second, while global brands do not homogenize every market, they exercise a hegemonic influence that shapes the local market, consumer tastes, consumption practices and 'brandscapes'. A brandscape refers to 'consumers' active construction of personal meanings and lifestyle orientations from the symbolic resources provided by an array of brands'.[108] Global brands change the brandscapes of consumers and other industry players (competitors) through new meanings and experiences. Thompson and Arsel argue that even if you're opposed to Starbucks, you will position yourself in relation to Starbucks. Similarly, consumers' potential identities are shaped by their relation to Starbucks. Smaller, local competitors of Starbucks can do very well by building their brand on the anti-corporate sentiment of the folk theories of McDonalidization. Values such as authenticity thrive on the back of Starbucks and Co.

There is a new space, framed by brands, between the local and the global, in which ideas about who we are and ought to be start to emerge. Just as newspapers made a national perspective possible, brands make a global perspective possible.[109] It is less a matter of who is right and who is wrong – an answer that will always depend on political context, and is inherently undecidable because of the underlying *différend*. Our argument is more complex than that of the neoliberals and their critics. Brands transform subjectivity, culture and our world. As such, brands open up new hybrid spaces that are neither doomed to be prisons nor destined to be paradise. Brands give rise to new forms of sociality and new spaces that we have analysed as 'imagined communities' and open communities (see Chapter 6). These new communities and spaces are contested and constituted by brands. In them, ethics are at stake. Brands blur not only the line between production and consumption but also between subject and object. As such, they make new ways of being possible. Whether these new possibilities will be better or worse than what we have experienced in the past is for us to contest. How we sensually experience these new possibilities is the topic of the final chapter.

---

[108] Thompson and Arsel, 2004, with reference to Sherry.
[109] See Cayla and Eckhardt, 2008, with reference to Anderson's 1983 publication.

From ethics to action

'We still don't know whether branding is good or bad', you might say. 'These circumlocutions avoid drawing a line in the sand and answer the question: How should we act? What principles can we use to adjust our moral compass?' It's true we have argued that ethics might start with suspending one's judgement, but we have not given any guidance on what to do when the pressure to act does not afford the luxury of suspension.

Our answer has two parts: thinking about and discussing ethics might be done most fruitfully on the level of problematizing. Once you have to choose between two alternatives, it is likely that a fundamentally important decision has been made without being exposed to the scrutiny of an ethical debate. Hence a simple principle to ensure the ethicality of a discussion would be that neither solutions nor alternatives are accepted but that the very problem that is presented is questioned.

Which brings me to the second point: how should we act? There can be no simple guide as to how to act ethically. Every decision is inextricably entangled in its political, social and cultural context. Reflecting on these contextual factors through problematizing will bring ethical issues to the fore. Reflection is no substitute for action, however. Existentialists from Kierkegaard to Sartre and Camus have stressed that we have a certain element of freedom in our actions and decisions. This freedom comes with a 'nothingness' that surrounds our existence: we are free, and hence there are no truths that could guide us. This lack of eternal principles is what Nietzsche described as the 'Death of God'.

If we accept this freedom, and accept that we are free to construct and deconstruct our own problematizations, we also accept the responsibility for our decisions and actions, which is a long-winded way of saying that ethics is the way we experience our freedom. As such, ethics cannot be summarized in handy rules or codes of conduct; it can only be practised as the critical faculty that uncompromisingly problematizes our decisions.

9 | Aesthetics

Large Glass

Marshall McLuhan proposed to understand art as 'exact information of how to rearrange one's psyche in order to anticipate the next blow from our own extended faculties'.[1] Indeed, art did prepare us for what was about to come. At the beginning of the twentieth century, artists in Paris and New York were exposed to the golden days of the machine age. While impressionists had deconstructed the world, and expressionists decentered the subject, Picasso was about to break up both in favour of assemblages. But nobody else would come close to one artist's diagrammatic yet precise anticipation of the brand society as Marcel Duchamp. Duchamp was obsessed with machines. His early works such as *Coffee Mill* (1911) or *Chocolate Grinder* (1914) resemble product descriptions of machines: they do not show (however distorted or abstracted) objects or forms but describe a mechanism.[2] These paintings show how things work: they explore machines that produce; they are diagrams of production.

---

[1] McLuhan, 1964/2006: 72.
[2] Others such as Francis Picabia had similar focus – see his *Daughter born without Mother* (1916–1917) or his *Paroxysm of Suffering* (1915). For an excellent introduction to Duchamp's Oeuvre, see Demos' book *The Exiles of Marcel Duchamp* (2007).

This approach reflected (quite literally) the daily grind of a society that had turned itself into industrial mass-production mode.

Duchamp's *Nude Descending a Staircase* (1912) was born out of the same *zeitgeist* as the motion studies of Étienne-Jules Marey's photographic analysis of movement of people, birds or a galloping horse. Marey quite literally shot his 'animated zoo' with a photographic gun that would inspire the motion studies of Frank B. and Lillian Gilbreth and, later, Frederic W. Taylor's *Scientific Management*. For Duchamp, this was only half of the truth. He understood that consumption driven by desire would be equal to, if not more important than, mechanized production.

Duchamp's early enquiries into consumerism are his ready-mades, everyday objects that he found interesting enough to be seen as artwork. It was not the act of creation but the act of choosing (by artists) and consuming (by critics) that turned mundane objects into art. Creation equals choice, as is explained in reference to the ready-made urinal (*Fountain*) in the magazine *The Blind Man*, which was edited by Duchamp and others: 'Whether Mr Mutt with his own hands made the Fountain or not has no importance. He CHOSE it.'[3] For Duchamp, choice had taken the place of creation.

In the 1920s, Duchamp went further and reinvented himself, assuming a new identity – Rrose Sélavy. He signed artworks as Rrose, and Man Ray took images of him dressed up as woman. Rrose's artwork included *Belle Haleine, Eau de Violette*, a perfume bottle in the original box that resembled other ready-mades (1921). Duchamp used branded goods to communicate Rrose's (or his new) identity. Duchamp knew that if he wanted to reincarnate himself, he would have to use brands to do so. This was the easiest and quickest way to a ready-made identity. With Rrose Sélavy he showed of what little importance authorship and the subject behind it really was. More importantly, he explored how subjectivity was constructed in the burgeoning brand society.

In order to bring his vision alive, Duchamp had to square the circle: bringing together a system of mechanistic production, and a second system of consumption and emotional desire. No artist had ever brought the two together before. The efforts resulted in his *chef-d'oeuvre*, his most famous work, *The Bride Stripped Bare by Her Bachelors, Even* (1915–1923), also sometimes called *Large Glass*. In it he combines the mechanism of production with the anatomy of desire. *Large Glass* is the blueprint for the brand society, where the machinery of production is linked to endless desire – through the medium of a gigantic shopping window.

---

[3] Quoted in Mink, 2004: 67.

Large Glass is an almost 11×70-inch large-framed window in which Duchamp inserted wires, foil and other materials (including dust that would settle quite naturally on the artwork). In the top half there is the bride who is stripping. In the bottom half are the bachelors (represented by empty jackets and uniforms) grinding away. While the bachelors are doomed to repeat their machine-production, the bride is the desire-engine that keeps the system going. Duchamp left a set of notes to go with the artwork: the *Large Glass* is powered by 'Love Gasoline' – a mystical fuel that runs the 'desire motor'. It is a diagram that shows, in its most abstract form, how consumption and production work with each other on a plane of immanence. *Large Glass* is a 'free machine' – an endlessly self-perpetuating desire-producing engine.[4] The glass itself is like a massive shopping window – in fact, Duchamp referred to it as a shopping window, neither inside nor outside the processes that take place through it. The glass hides nothing but reveals whatever is behind it, which becomes instantly part of it. It absorbs everything. It is a time- and space-less frame onto, and a window into, the world.

Duchamp said about *Large Glass* that there is nothing spontaneous about it; the subconscious that spoke to so many artists before, guiding their hand, falls silent. *Large Glass* is the opposite of all that. It is the ultimate aesthetic transformation from the machine age to the age of desire. The logic of production and the logic of consumption are combined and expressed in one piece of art. It gives us the complete picture of the brand society as endless desire and production, organized and framed by the medium of the shop window. After *Large Glass*, Duchamp retired from being an artist and focused on playing chess instead.[5] He said that 'I like living, breathing better than working.' And right he was: what could he have created after the blueprint was exposed, the diagram drawn?

The next generation of artists would pick up where Duchamp left off and turn into a critique or celebration, or sometimes both, of consumerism. Its most famous exponent, Andy Warhol, came not from a highbrow art background but from advertising. In many ways, his work was the logical extension of Duchamp's: art as choice that momentarily stops the circle of production and consumption to hold up a mirror in which we see our branded identities.

[4] Hughes, 1980/2005: 56; see also Eco, 2004: 399.
[5] This is not entirely correct – see his posthumus work *Given*. The most ironic piece Duchamp produced in his later years was his *From or by Marcel Duchamp or Rose Sélavy* (probably from around 1943). It is a kind of best-of miniaturized collection box of his early artworks. The box works like a portable museum and was produced in a limited edition of twenty only.

Pop art

Stuart Davis' 1924 painting *Odol* can be seen as the first true pop art painting. 'I like popular art,' Davis said. For him, and later pop artists, pop is not about the representation of values or symbols but simply about descriptions of what people do. Clement Greenberg, a prominent art critic, criticized this approach as *ersatz culture* and *kitsch*. In response, the English critic Laurence Alloway coined the term *'mass popular art'*, arguing that mass communication, new technology and new consumption patterns would change art. With pop art, art was not a renaissance activity by the enlightened few for the chosen few; rather, art became a seismograph of what happened in society. Pop art is not an alternative project to consumerism but its black twin.[6]

In Richard Hamilton's *Just What Is It That Makes Today's Homes So Different, So Appealing?* (1956), the notion of 'pop' pops up for the first time. What makes the home so different and so appealing for the indulgent supersexed couple in the picture are brands – Ford, Rosenquist ham, TV and radio (the evangelists of brands), the vacuum cleaner, the cinema and its star-machinery all form part of Hamilton's pop world. Accordingly, for Hamilton, pop art should be:

Popular (designed for a mass-audience)
Transient (a short-term solution)
Expendable (easily forgotten)
Low-cost
Mass-produced
Young (aimed at youth)
Witty
Sexy
Gimmicky
Glamorous
Big business ...[7]

The most famous pop art exponent, Andy Warhol, was just capitalizing on that movement, which was well established prior to his arrival on the art scene. While he was not an early mover, he had a decisive advantage over his fellow pop artist friends: he was trained in advertising and worked as New York's most famous commercial illustrator. There could have been no better

[6] See Alloway, 1958.
[7] Quoted in Hughes, 1980/2005: 344.

training for a young aspiring artist than advertising: 'I didn't really change,' Warhol stated. 'All that happened was I moved my work from a department store window ... to a gallery. I didn't change my style.'[8] He was well aware of the rapidly changing nature of his profession: 'Business Art is the step that comes after art. I started as a commercial artist, and I want to finish as a business artist.'[9] His real art was, according to Hughes, in advertising, just without the gloss: 'he inverted the process on which successful advertising depends, becoming a famous artist who loved nothing but banality and sameness'.[10] Warhol loved everything machine-like, to the point were he proclaimed 'I want to be a machine'. His paintings are repetitions of something that did not have a point of origin in the first place. Marilyn Monroe was a media-hype, a simulacrum, a fantasy that he simply reproduced. His famous studio on 231 East Forty-Seventh Street in Manhattan was appropriately called *The Factory*, where everyone got their fifteen minutes of fame.

If we admire pop art, it is not for its mastery but its originality. Pop artists were the first to use brand names, logos, designs and products as raw materials for art production. As Baudrillard put it: 'This is neither play nor "realism": it is recognizing the obvious truth of the consumer society which is that the truth of objects and products is their *brand name*.'[11] Warhol perfected what Duchamp had started: the brand itself had become meaning and represented the narratives people organized their lives by. Brands were the style people adopted. Art, as reflection of what people do, had no choice but to follow.

Duchamp's *Large Glass* is a diagram of the coming consumer society; Warhol's art is a sociological critique of the brand society – in fact, he might be more of a sociologist than an artist after all. Since Duchamp and Warhol, art is framed by branding and branding is utilizing art to construct itself. They share the same ambiguity and fate.

Two extreme examples may suffice to make our point. Damien Hirst is probably the wealthiest living artist and certainly a brand himself. He holds the auction record for a living artist with his *Lullaby Spring*, sold for £19.2 million in 2007. Two months later, he sold *For the Love of God* for £50 million. While the financial markets were in free fall in September 2008, Hirst held a two-day auction where he sold the record amount of more than £111-million's worth of work. As Hirst said, 'I'm totally amazed that my art is selling while banks are falling.' The amounts of money paid and made in the

---

[8] Warhol, 2006: 150; see also Jonathan Schroeder's 2005 article 'The Artist and the Brand'.
[9] Warhol, 2006: 62.
[10] Hughes, 1980/2005: 348.
[11] Baudrillard, 1970/2003: 116.

Hirst world calls for serious investors. A high-profile collector described it as a market: 'The Damien Hirst industry is a skilfully managed market. It would be in a lot of people's interest to make sure this sale worked.'[12] It seems as if Hirst is one of the best ways to finish off what Warhol described as 'business art'.

At the other end of the spectrum is Banksy, the anonymous graffiti artist. He calls his work 'Brandalism', which follows a simple logic: 'Any advertising in public space that gives you no choice whether you see it or not is yours. It's yours to take, re-arrange and re-use. Asking for permission is like asking to keep a rock someone just threw at your head.'[13] Banksy is the antipode of the art industry that Hirst manages so effectively: 'The Art we look at is made by only a selected few. A small group create, promote, purchase, exhibit and decide the success of Art. Only a few hundred people in the world have any real say. When you go to an Art gallery you are simply a tourist looking at the trophy cabinet of a few millionaires.'[14] That's why graffiti is the only viable alternative:

There is no elitism of hype, it exhibits on the best walls a town has to offer and nobody is put off by the price of admission. A wall has always been the best place to publish your work. The people who run our cities don't understand graffiti because they think nothing has the right to exist unless it makes profit, which makes their opinion worthless … The people who truly deface your neighbourhoods are the companies that scrawl giant slogans across buildings and buses trying to make us feel inadequate unless we buy their stuff. They expect to be able to shout their message in your face from every available surface but you're never allowed to answer back. Well, they started the fight and the wall is the weapon of choice to hit them back.[15]

The most famous artists of the nineteenth century – Van Gogh, Cézanne and Gauguin – were not celebrated artists while they were alive. They were outsiders and non-conformists who became famous posthumously.[16] There was simply no frame or convention that would allow the individual to position himself as artist. Society was too fragmented to agree on what was valuable and what not. By the end of the twentieth century, we have re-established a frame: this frame is the world of branding. An artist's originality is a function of her ability to engage with our consumer society – including, ironically, being able to offer new ways of consuming art itself.

[12] *The Times*; see www.timesonline.co.uk/tol/news/uk/article4795010.ece (accessed 22 September 2008).
[13] Banksy, 2006: 196.
[14] Banksy, 2006: 170.
[15] Banksy, 2006: 8.
[16] Gombrich, 1950: 384.

Real aesthetics: objects as art

While the art world became ever more entangled with brands, brands themselves absorbed and changed aesthetics. Branding itself is an engine that relentlessly creates differences: it is cultural production on a large scale with an immense budget. It changes the way we perceive the world. As art becomes the seismograph of these shifts, brands turn into art. Brands as cultural forms transform objects into pieces of art in their own right. Roland Barthes' description of 'The New Citroën' from 1957 is a brilliant example:

I think that cars today are almost the exact equivalent of the great Gothic cathedrals: I mean the supreme creation of an era, conceived with passion by unknown artists, and consumed in image if not in usage by a whole population which appropriates them as a purely magical object. It is obvious that the new Citroën has fallen from the sky inasmuch as it appears at first sight as a superlative *object*.[17]

An extreme love for details turns the object into a fetish: 'one keenly fingers the edges of the windows, one feels along the wide rubber grooves which link the back window to its metal surround'.[18] The public consumes the car accordingly – not as if it was a car but more as if it was a prostitute:

The public, it seems, has admirably divined the novelty of the themes which are suggested to it … The bodywork, the lines of union are touched, the upholstery palpated, the seats tried, the doors caressed, the cushions fondled; before the wheel, one pretends to drive with one's whole body. The object here is totally prostituted, appropriated: originating from the heaven of Metropolis, the Goddess is in a quarter of an hour mediatized, actualizing through this exorcism the very essence of petit-bourgeois advancement.[19]

Barthes' Citroën is, as he put it succinctly, 'humanized art'.[20] Just like Warhol turned art into consumer objects without any pretence at originality or authenticity, brands transform objects into art. Their aesthetic can be analysed as realistic and objective.

Take Absolut Vodka. It leveraged its aesthetics to build a brand around its name and the iconic shape of the Absolut bottle. The design is simple, stylish and sophisticated. The play with the shape of the bottle made it an impressive aesthetic mark: the shape of the bottle is embedded in everyday contexts with the copy reading Absolut-plus-a-descriptor that puts a twist on the ad.

[17] Barthes, 1957/2000: 88.
[18] Barthes, 1957/2000: 89.
[19] Barthes, 1957/2000: 90.
[20] Barthes, 1957/2000: 89.

The imprint of a bottle on Manhattan with the title Absolut Manhattan or a bottle-shaped swimming pool reading Absolut LA are but two of the many well-known examples. Absolut has used artists such as Andy Warhol, Keith Haring and Iggy Pop to create their own ads. And fashion designers such as Donna Karan were invited to design a pair of gloves for the 'Absolut Warmth' campaign. This branded creativity made commercial sense, too: within ten years of the campaign's start, Absolut became the best-selling imported vodka in the US, growing from 5,000 cases imported per year to 2.5 million by the late 1980s.[21]

When Absolut launched its latest mixer drinks, it went one step further and asked people to submit images of their own Absolut experiences. The best entries were collected and published in a booklet. The brand launch itself was done with almost no advertising; rather, Absolut hired venues in inner city areas and turned them into Absolut Bars for a couple of weeks. Cool DJs, hip Absolut drinks and a fun crowd were supposed to create an Absolut experience that triggered word of mouth. What Absolut did was create more than an object as art: it created an aesthetic experience that would touch all senses. Absolut created a kind of *Gesamtkunstwerk* – a total 'work of art' in which people's relation to the brand, to each other, to their lifeworld and to themselves was designed around the brand. It is no longer about the fetishization of a product but about the aestheticization of the world.

The objective behind creating such brand experiences is increased influence over people's behaviour and decisions, as McLuhan argued: 'Everybody experiences far more than he understands. Yet it is experience, rather than understanding, that influences behaviour.'[22] The aesthetics of brands shift dramatically from the realist, object-driven beauty of the Absolut bottle or Barthes' Citroën to a sublime, interactive world where products turn into events and brands into experiences.

Actual aesthetics: brand experience as Gesamtkunstwerk[23]

ING Direct is the consumer arm of the Dutch banking giant ING. From the begining, ING Direct faced the challenge that it is an online bank that does

---

[21] Schmitt and Simonson, 1997: 4–7; for more examples, see the collection on http://absolutad.com (accessed 26 June 2009).

[22] McLuhan, 1964/2006: 347.

[23] According to Wikipedia, the term *Gesamtkunstwerk* means 'total', 'integrated', or 'complete artwork' and is attributed to the German opera composer Richard Wagner. He used it to refer to an operatic performance encompassing music, theater, and the visual arts.

not have any branches. Nonetheless, since it started up in Canada in 1997, it now operates in more than seven countries, serving some 25 million customers that have more than £300 billion parked at ING Direct. Because of the lack of the usual touch points (e.g. branches), ING Direct had to think creatively about how consumers could experience the brand.

Ruud Polet, Global Head of Brand Marketing at ING, explains: 'We opened cafés where you can have a coffee, go online, eat something and have an "Orange Experience". Of course, the staff of the café tell people about the bank, about products and so on. It's a bit like Starbuck's, just focused on the ING brand.'

The café concept was born in Canada, where ING Direct first saw the light of the market. Ruud explains how it all began:

We started by building the system, the IT infrastructure, the call centre and so on. When we opened the first day for business, the phones rang off the hooks – but also a lot of people came in to see whether we were real and whether real people were working for us. They wanted to know whether we existed! A couple of hundred people stood outside our call centre and came up to the 10th floor to see us! So our CEO decided to have a café at the ground floor where people could meet us, and if they want they can come to level 10 – but not in the hundreds!

What started as a reaction to consumers' curiosity and need to be reassured turned into the brand philosophy. Every touch point with the brand is designed to create an aesthetic experience that re-enforces the ING Direct identity. As Ruud tells, 'our success is based on a strong brand experience – when you call us you will speak to a person in ten seconds; when you go online, it's fast and simple; when you go to a café, it is always fun. Every touch point is exciting. This is key to winning 25 million customers in ten years.'

Rather than creating beautiful objects, ING Direct sees all consumer touch points as 'points of truth' where consumers make up their minds. Points of truth are break points: you either win the consumer or your lose her. The key to brand-experience management is constant auditing of the consumer experience and careful control of those 'moments of truth' that can make or break the brand.

ING Direct is no exception: experience branding becomes the core of corporate marketing plans. This is a response to the problems of the traditional way of advertising. The traditional techniques are summarized as above-the-line communication methods. They use mass media such as TV, radio and print advertising to communicate the brand. The problem is three-fold. First, viewers of TV ads are passive. They sit in front of a TV and cannot react, which limits the aesthetic brand-building capacity of ads enormously. Second, ads aired on TV lack authenticity: the medium only allows for very indirect, pre-programmed mass communication that cannot be personalized. TV ads are designed for an anonymous mass. Unfortunately, no one wants to identify with this mass any longer. Third, it is impossible to control the context in which individuals consume the ad. Think of a TV ad after the news: the news might be about a horrible war story or a mass murderer – and your ad is aired only three minutes afterwards! Even if the news is picture perfect, the couple in front of the television might have an argument about who's neglecting the relationship as the ad rushes over the screen. Because of this lack of control of context, above-the-line brand communication has limited powers.

Experiences control the context in which communication happens – something other communication channels such as TV cannot do. Therein lies their power. Think of the ING Direct café where (potential) consumers are in an absolutely controlled environment: such a branded context is more likely to influence behaviour than a shallow print ad. Experiences are all-encompassing, using symbols and meaning to communicate the brand. They engage all senses and build on total aesthetics.[24]

The 'moment of truth' is an aesthetic experience that is all-encompassing, just like Richard Wagner's idea of the *Gesamtkunstwerk*. The direct engagement of all senses creates the sensation of authenticity: the ING Direct café is authentic as it features 'real' people, 'real' coffee and 'real' communication in a 'real' environment. Because the brand is experienced directly, (that is, psychologically, socially, culturally and physically), it gains a level of authenticity a TV ad can never provide. Brand experiences offer a controlled, immersive, aesthetic experience that touches all five senses and leaves a far stronger impression. Rather than broadcasting a 30-second ad to as many people as possible, experiences zoom in and narrowcast a given brand message to a precisely targeted audience.

Addis and Holbrook argue that the 'explosion of subjectivity' delineates a move from passive, uniform consumer to active, unruly *bricoleur*.[25] With this shift, consumption becomes a subjective expression of fantasies, feeling and fun. Pine and Gilmore have used the label of 'The experience economy' to describe this shift. Experiential branding explicitly acknowledges this shift and embraces emotion, theatre and experience as its core principles. Brands

[24] Lindstrom, 2005; Schmitt, 1999.
[25] Addis and Holbrook, 2001: 50; Holbrook and Hirschman, 1982.

create an inter-textuality that links people, places and products into one over-arching experience. The product or the service on sale becomes just one of the props in the overall brand-experience script. As David Polinchock, CEO of Brand Experience Lab, explains, 'a product or a service is nothing more than an artefact or an act around which customers have experiences'.[26]

Renzo Rosso, founder of fashion brand Diesel, put it this way: 'We don't sell a product, we sell a style of life. I think we have created a movement … The Diesel concept is everything. It's the way to live, it's the way to wear, it's the way to do something.'[27]

The experience transforms the passive receiver of an ad into an interactive co-creator who actively designs her own lifestyle in concert with the brand. In the ING Direct café, you have to do things and act on the actions of others. This path produces your very own personal experience of ING Direct. The brand is the lived experience – and the lived experience emerges from the interaction between people, place and product. The brand takes on the character of an event: 'Events constitute key moments in the life of a brand's story. By selecting key events and portraying them in an ad, a firm provides the framework for the story that it wants consumers to create about the brand.'[28]

The objective of the event is not to convince the viewer but to create an all-immersive brandscape and identification of the consumer with the brand: 'The primary objective [of brandscaping] is not to sell the product but to generate a fascination with the brand; to get the customer to identify with the world of the brand, creating a brand awareness and providing it with a deep-set emotional core.'[29] Clearly, the actual selling of a product is not the main objective; rather, brand experiences aim at the control of the medium and the message, creating a brandscape onto which the consumer projects her identity that flourishes through interaction with the brand. It is an aesthetics that is actualized through the interaction between consumer and brand.

Take, again, the example of Bacardi Breezer: as former Bacardi Marketing Director Paul Hugh-Jones tells, the product was launched through a brand-experience campaign. Bacardi Parties with artificial beaches in clubs promoted the new mixer drinks and the Bacardi brand values of sun, sea and

---

[26] Polinchock, quoted in Nadeau, 2007: 123; see also Bond and Kirschenbaum, 1998, about the challenges of reaching consumers.

[27] Rosso, quoted in Klein, 2000: 23–24.

[28] Zaltman, 2003: 233; Baudrillard, 1970/2003: 126, already argued that in a consumer society products tend to turn into events.

[29] Riewoldt, quoted in Barber, 2007: 166.

sand (and the unofficial fourth one – sex). In this 'perfect ambience, with perfect drinks, we wanted our consumers to have the best night out ever. They will remember for the rest of their life that this was a Barcardi night,' Paul explains.

Toyota's Scion, Volkswagen's Fox, Axe, Red Bull and even the low-budget horror movie *Blair Witch Project* have been launched through carefully designed experiential campaigns. To launch its Fox, Volkswagen opened a lifestyle hotel in Copenhagen (called, appropriately, Hotel Fox) that was designed by up and coming artists. Hotel Fox hosted parties, events and talks. The whole experience was not about the car but about the ambience that create the desired meaning around the newly launched car. According to a senior partner of the market research firm Yankelovich, such an experience promotes what people want: a non-passive media experience that offers authenticity, authorship and autonomy.[30]

Brand experiences such as the ING Direct café or the Bacardi Party offer a new aesthetics. Everything can turn into a medium for experience-based communication: themeparks, sport events, airports, flagship stores, conventions, malls, showrooms, festivals, cultural events, shopping centres and all sorts of captive environments including taxis, buses, trains, planes etc. Take shopping centres, which turn rapidly into brandscapes that are seen as three-dimensional magazines offering three-dimensional ad-space for sale. Based on detailed information about who spends how much time and money where, and detailed audience profiles, shopping centres sell space to willing marketers.

But experiences do not have to be big to be powerful. One campaign for headache and hangover pills simply 'bought' space on the stamps that trendy nightclubs use to put on the hand of their guests. The next day, when you wake up with a slight headache, the stamp not only reminds you where you were but also what you need to switch off that jackhammer inside your head.

Both examples show how brands start weaving themselves into the everyday life of people. Brand experiences are powerful because they control the context of communication and influence behaviour in a much more subtle way. They provide a total aesthetic experience inasmuch as they engage all senses. Niketown, Prada's Epicenters, Disneyland – they are all set up to create fascination with the brand and blur the line between the brand and life itself.

[30] The quote is taken from Walker, 2008: 75; for more examples, see Walker (2008) and also Wipperfürth, 2005; for Hotel Fox, see www.hotelfox.dk (accessed 26 June 2009).

As Arvidsson has argued, the brand 'refers not primarily to the product, but to the *context of consumption*'.[31] Brand experiences are vehicles to create this context as a way of life. Once embedded in lifestyles, brands do not try to manipulate consumers into buying a product. Rather, 'brand management works by enabling or empowering the freedom of consumers *so that it is likely to evolve in particular directions*'.[32] In order to be successful, brands have to respect (at least to a certain degree) the autonomy of consumers. For instance, the ING Direct café does not ask you directly to open up a bank account but invites you to think about your future plans and the financial needs that you might have. Arvidsson's point is that the brand entices consumers to create meanings and social relationships around the brand. These meanings and social relationships create the immaterial brand value in the first place. The brand value is not produced by companies or ad agencies but by consumers who create relations, emotions and communities around brands.

In this sense, brands could not be real unless we actualized them: in fact, without our *doing*, brand experiences would not be possible. As Dewey has noted in his *Art as Experience*, experience is the reward and the sign of an interaction between an organism and an environment, which has the potential to transform interaction into participation.[33] We become actively involved as we participate in creating brands. To turn an event into an experience, one has to bracket the flow of events in space and time, unify its many components and give them one direction. Brands are the organizing force that arranges this new aesthetic. The brand meaning emerges as a result of aligned action and perception. This means that we become more powerful as brands rely on our active participation to actualize their potential; but it also means we become less powerful as brands start to control not only messages but the media in which experiences present themselves as meaningful. With the advent of new information and communication technology, these conditions shift radically.

Virtual aesthetics: digital worlds

To say that new media is a revolution is somewhat conservative. Normally, revolutions revolt against the establishment. However, the new media revolution is promoted by the establishment. This should make us suspicious. The

---

[31] Arvidsson, 2005: 244.
[32] Arvidsson, 2005: 244.
[33] Dewey, 1934/2005: 22.

medium of the digital revolution is the screen. The screen is aggressive as it frames reality, and in doing so it, quite literally, screens out certain elements and deems non-existent whatever does not fit into the frame.[34] Lev Manovich argues that the digital revolution is linked to the previous two: the print press was a revolution concerning the distribution of ideas; photography revolutionized the production of ideas and images; now, the digital or information revolution integrates the two and adds a new dimension – the consumption of ideas.[35]

The information revolution brings a new aesthetic with it – one that Manovich calls 'info-aesthetics': 'Information access has become a key activity of the computer age. Therefore, we need something that can be called info-aesthetics – a theoretical analysis of the aesthetics of information access as well as the creation of new media objects that "aestheticize" information processing.'[36] In our information society, the notion of the interface becomes central as all content is accessed through some kind of interface. Manovich's theory of info-aesthetics revolves around interfaces and databases that replace the old duo of form and content.

The new info-aesthetics has several key characteristics. First, every digital experience (such as a website visit) invites the user to create her own path through the site. This makes the total number of unique experiences endless. Every user can create her own version of the experience. In front of our computers, we are all unique. This turns Walter Benjamin on his head: rather than claiming that the artwork has lost its aura through being reproducible, its endless reproducibility becomes the condition for its aesthetic value.[37]

Second, the problem of the digital world is no longer a problem of creation of content but one of finding and editing already existing information. As Manovich put it, 'by the end of the twentieth century, the problem was no longer how to create a new media object such as an image; the new problem was how to find an object that already exists somewhere'.[38] Search engines replace the creative drive of the producer.

Third, consumers can seamlessly and effortlessly become producers in the digital sphere. Quite often, producers only develop basic codes and leave it to consumers to build their own applications. In gaming, this is called 'game

---

[34] Manovich, 2001: 94–96.
[35] Manovich, 2001: 19.
[36] Manovich, 2001: 217.
[37] See Benjamin, 1936/1990.
[38] Manovich, 2001: 35.

patching' – people create their own rules, characters, sounds, architectures, and so on.[39]

Fourth, and following from that, creativity is not about originating something new but about editing something pre-existing: as Manovich argues, authentic creation has been replaced by individual selection. You don't start from scratch like a painter or a photographer but you modify an already existing signal: 'the modern subject proceeds through life by selecting from numerous menus and catalogs of items … now anybody can become a creator by simply providing a new menu, that is by making a new selection from the total corpus available'.[40] Authorship equals editorship: it is not about the creation of unique expressions, once the driving force of art (be unique and new!); rather, creation becomes the skill of editing your very own reality.

From the end of the nineteenth through to the twentieth century, art was about being innovative and original. This was a new demand – for centuries before, it did not matter whether art did something new. The quest for newness (with shock potential) became the driver in the twentieth century, with absurd consequences, such as a gallery opening with no artwork (Yves Klein) or 30 grams of the artist's shit offered for sale in a can (Piero Manzoni). For Manovich, the DJ expresses the new logic that supersedes the old one: her art is selecting and combining already existing materials. She is a Certeauian unruly *bricoleur* whose act of creation mirrors Duchamp's art of selection.

Finally, the old divide between epistemology and ontology collapses. In the virtual world, the map is the territory and clicking is performative: you are what you click.[41] In fact, the click is the missing link between acting and thinking: in one single moment, clicking combines choice and execution. The old divide between thinking and being, between body and mind, is dissolving online. Take the virtual world Second Life where 15 million registered users run a $20-million US economy buying and selling property, designs and services online.[42] After more than thirty-five years, Umberto Eco's essay 'Social Life as a Sign System' has materialized itself in Second Life: social life = sign system.[43]

Aesthetics become virtual: the seductive object and the total experience of content/context or medium/message have been substituted by the digital

[39] Manovich, 2001: 120.
[40] Manovich, 2001: 126–127.
[41] Manovich, 2001: 82.
[42] See information provided by Second Life at http://secondlife.com/whatis/economy_stats.php (accessed 26 June 2009).
[43] Eco, 1973.

world where info-aesthetics enable the endless re-creation and experience of realities.

The brand plays an even bigger role online than offline. All there is in the virtual world are brands: signs that engender trust and meaning with no signifier to refer to at all. In a traditional market system, the seller has an information advantage, which he will use to his benefit. Online markets are 'reverse markets', where this advantage disappears. Consumers can learn about anything, at any time. Given that there are literally zero switching costs, the only thing that might keep people coming back to one particular site is an attractive brand.[44]

This new info-aesthetics has important consequences. The digital basically dissolves all kinds of hierarchy and creates a flat world. The world is a rhizome, not a tree anymore. That comes at a price. In a hierarchical world, everything has its place and order. There is logic that structures the narrative that leads from inside out or outside in. In the virtual world, the opposite is true: every object is treated the same. As Manovich put it, the database and the narrative 'are natural enemies'.[45] The structure is flat, consisting of a series of mini-events co-located on the same plane. The Web is like a database that provides neither origin nor end point, and no narrative that would structure the information. Manovich explains:

Contrary to the popular images of computer media as collapsing all human culture into a single giant library (which implies the existence of some ordering system), or a single giant book (which implies a narrative progression), it is perhaps more accurate to think of the new media culture as an infinite flat surface where individual texts are placed in no particular order … If there is a new rhetoric or aesthetic possible here, it may have less to do with the ordering of time by a writer or an orator, and more with spatial wandering. The hypertext reader is like Robinson Crusoe, walking across the sand, picking up a navigation journal, a rotten fruit, an instrument whose purpose he does not know; leaving imprints that, like computer hyperlinks, follow from one found object to another.[46]

The language of the digital is spatial: we surf the Web, we browse, we send links … The digital tolerates things next to each other, without forcing them into a taxonomy. This might empower (and fragment) the user since there is no grand narrative to follow but a myriad of possible stories that can be constructed and deconstructed.

---

[44] See Arvidsson, 2006.
[45] Manovich, 2001: 225.
[46] Manovich, 2001: 77 and 78.

This also implies that, through digital databases, the world becomes less coherent, more fragmented and more inconsistent. Action is more localized: it can evolve from any point in the Web, not only from the top or the bottom, the beginning or the end of a story. This has important consequences. First, communities become more important because they help individuals to focus and make sense of databases. They provide frames of reference and allow meaningful enactment. Second, search engines become obligatory points of passage: rather than having legislators or interpreters making sense of the world, as Bauman suggested, the logic of search engines creates an alternative order of things that is based on statistics. The algorithms of statistics have replaced the judgement of the expert; the credo of the programmer at Google and elsewhere is simple: more data is better data.[47] Take a newspaper journalist who comments on recent developments – she reduces complexity and interprets things following a certain logic. This is a typical intermediary. But their influence is dwindling. With a mouse click, taxonomies are established and dissolve again. User-driven search engines such as Amazon or eBay are becoming standards, and organize the world according to past preferences and locate individual user's preference among others. The anonymous *man* that Heidegger described has replaced the professional opinion-former.

What then is a new media object? According to Manovich, it is not a narrative and it is not a meaningless database. It is an interface that organizes access to a database. The old pairing of form and content gives way to the new one – interface and database.[48] Form does not follow function but meaning follows interface. There are new narratives possible in this new regime – not old grand narratives but the kind of narratives that brands offer us. They are stories in sequence – stories that repeat each other, and in each repetition they introduce difference. Just as Menardes' Don Quixote is different from Cervantes', every user leaves her own unique trace.

Virtual aesthetics enable users to play endlessly with the driftwood they find on the shores of the World Wide Web. Like Alice in Wonderland, users go down a rabbit hole in order to come out in a different world. While this new aesthetic is virtual, it has very real effects on the way we perceive the world. Manovich explains that computer-produced images do not look 'real': this is not because they lack realism but because they are too real. Film, for instance, has a certain graininess, whereas computer-generated images are sharp, clean and geometrical. The movie *Terminator II* looked realistic

---

[47] See Vise and Malseed, 2006.
[48] Manovich, 2001: 227 and 66.

because the final battle is staged in a dark environment with lots of smoke, which softens the sharpness of the digital images and makes them greyer, as in the 'real' world: 'The synthetic image is the result of a different, more perfect than human vision. Whose vision is it? It is the vision of a computer, a cyborg, an automatic missile.'[49]

Brand aesthetics

Famous brand and design guru Wally Olins argued that 'brands and the idea of branding are the most significant gifts that commerce has ever made to popular culture'.[50] We'd agree. But branding has not only transformed popular culture; it has also changed what we define as beautiful.

For example, ads in newspapers, magazines or online are a testimony to, as well as a symptom of, our collective desires. They are very well-researched images of what we want to have and who we want to be: they are our Narcissus mirror. As McLuhan put it, no sociology department can keep up with the funding that corporate consumer researchers have at their disposal: 'The ads are by far the best part of any magazine or newspaper. More pain and thought, more wit and art go into the making of an ad than into any prose feature of press or magazine. Ads *are* news. What is wrong with them is that they are always *good* news.'[51] Ads are the only positive messages in between all that news about corruption, war, murder, horror and terror. They have a monopoly on utopia and beauty. As Bill Bernbach, founder of advertising agency DDB, stated: 'so the most important thing as far as I am concerned is to be fresh, to be original – to be able to compete with all the shocking news events in the world today, with all the violence'.[52]

In contrast, the imagery in the news features belong to the realm of the pictorial. Compared to the iconic imagery of the ad world, the features look boring and pale. Whereas a picture represents something, an icon refers to itself only. It is a sign that has become a thing. In this *icon*omy, a lot of resources are invested to create new aesthetics.

So what kind of beauty do brands bring with them? Let's start, but not end, with the useful distinction drawn by the philosopher Edmund Burke in

[49] Manovich, 2001: 202.
[50] Olins, 2003: 15.
[51] McLuhan, 1964/2006: 227; see also page 252 where he states: 'The historians and archaeologists will one day discover that the ads of our time are the richest and most faithful daily reflections that any society ever made of its entire range of activities.'
[52] Quoted in Arvidsson, 2006: 52.

his book *A Philosophical Enquiry into the Origin of Our Ideas of the Sublime and Beautiful* (1757/1998). Immanuel Kant picked up Burke's concepts and used them in his *Critique of Judgment*, first published in 1790 as the third of his three critiques. For Kant and Burke, the beautiful is what pleases. It follows the old Roman definition '*pulchra sunt quae visa placent*': beautiful is what pleases to look at. The viewer contemplates the object as she has no direct interest in the object itself. Kant insists that beauty can only be experienced if we view something without interest: desire clouds our judgement and destroys the contemplative distance between the viewer and the object.

The description of the Citroën by Roland Barthes is a good example of this beauty: the object is presented and the viewer, without interest, is taken by its beauty. Or take European advertising posters from the early days up until the 1930s. Often, the product is shown as an oversized, real object, as in Osram's big light bulb. This aesthetic reflected a beauty of consumption that worked through seduction.

The sublime is a very different form of aesthetic. For Kant, the sublime is a much stronger and more powerful sensation that arises between the viewer and something that opposes her interests. For example, a mighty storm with lightning might be a sublime spectacle – but not beautiful because we cannot contemplate it without interest.

Rilke has described the beauty of the sublime in an unsurpassed line: 'For beauty is nothing but the beginning of terror, which we are still just able to endure, and we are so awed because it serenely disdains to annihilate us.'[53] For Kant, the sublime causes an 'outrage on the imagination' as it creates 'mental movement' in the viewer. Hence the sublime is not a characteristic of the object but 'the disposition of the soul' of the subject. The sublime creates both pleasure and displeasure simultaneously:

The feeling of the sublime is, therefore, at once a feeling of displeasure, arising from the inadequacy of imagination in the aesthetic estimation of magnitude to attain to its estimation by reason, and a simultaneously awakened pleasure, arising from this very judgement of the inadequacy of the greatest faculty of sense being in accord with ideas of reason, so far as the effort to attain to these is for us a law.[54]

And Kant continues:

The mind feels itself set in motion in the representation of the sublime in nature; whereas in the aesthetic judgement upon what is beautiful therein it is in restful contemplation. This movement, especially in its inception, may be compared with

53 Rilke, 1922/1977.
54 Kant, 1790/2004 : 77.

vibration, i.e., with a rapidly alternating repulsion and attraction produced by one and the same object. The point of excess for the imagination (towards which it is driven in the apprehension of the intuition) is like an abyss in which it fears to lose itself.

Quoting Burke, Kant describes the sublime as a 'sort of delightful horror, a sort of tranquillity tinged with terror'. Every brand experience ultimately aims at creating a sublime aesthetic. Brand experiences want to create a dynamic (or to use the more modern word, interaction) between the subject and the brand. Experiences strive to create an interaction between the brand and the subject, instilling the 'vibration' Kant has described. It is not a beauty of passive seduction but a beauty of provocation.[55]

The digital offers a fundamentally different aesthetic experience. The virtual experience is neither beautiful nor sublime. It not only relates the subject to objects but centres everything around the subject as possible identity-building devices. It is a beauty that is transformative, manipulative and powerful. The beauty of the virtual can be described as performative aesthetics. Because of its audio-visual stimulation (as in a cinema), its interactivity (as in a game) and its sociality (as on dating websites and chat rooms), the digital experience has the capacity to absorb the subject totally. Of course, the three layers of the beautiful, the sublime and the performative do not exist separately from each other. While the beautiful may reside in objects, the sublime in brand experiences and the performative aspect of aesthetics in the virtual world, all three dimensions overlap and coincide. They form the basis of the aestheticization of life.

Aestheticization of life

We argued in the previous chapter that man is the 'not yet determined animal' – the animal that can choose and act to determine its fate. Of course, this freedom brings a certain responsibility, as existentialists have noted. Theoretically, this makes human existence a dark matter that is framed by nothingness. Practically, however, the tragedy of life tends to be lived as comedy. More often than we feel free, we will feel bored – this is Kierkegaard's ironic diagnosis of the *condition humaine*. For him, nothing more mundane than boredom is the source of evil:

---

[55] Eco, 2004; Kant described war as a potentially sublime event.

Since boredom advances and boredom is the root of all evil, no wonder, then, that the world goes backwards, that evil spreads. This can be traced back to the very beginning of the world. The gods were bored; therefore they created human beings. Adam was bored because he was alone; therefore Eve was created. Since that moment, boredom entered the world and grew in quantity in exact proportion to the growth of population. Adam was bored alone; then Adam and Eve were bored *en famille*. After that, the population of the world increased and the nations were bored *en masse*. To amuse themselves, they hit upon the notion of building a tower so high that it would reach the sky. This notion is just as boring as the tower was high and is a terrible demonstration of how boredom had gained the upper hand. Then they were dispersed around the world, just as people now travel abroad, but they continued to be bored. And what consequences this boredom had: humankind stood tall and fell far, first through Eve, then from the Babylonian tower.[56]

The real art of life is to escape boredom – and this is only possible if one practices the art of remembering and forgetting. The truly happy person has perfected this to an art that allows her 'to play shuttlecock with all existence': 'Thus *nil admirari* [marvel at nothing] is the proper wisdom of life. No part of life ought to have so much meaning for a person that he cannot forget it any moment he wants to; on the other hand, every single part of life ought to have so much meaning for a person that he can remember it at any moment.'[57] The only way of being able to 'play shuttlecock with all existence' is through making sense of life as aesthetic phenomenon. Like a piece of art, life should be designed such that harmonies and contrasts delight our senses and capture our attention. Nothing should be so important that it could not be excluded from that piece of art called life. In fact, life has no meaning or higher purpose beyond being a play. The only criteria to analyse and judge that play is beauty.

Philosophically, Nietzsche has suggested this view: life can only be justified as an aesthetic phenomenon. The more pedestrian version of this saying goes something like this. Question: Why is there evil in the world? Answer: To thicken the plot. Indeed, a plot with good people doing good things only would make a terrible book, play or movie. Why would that not hold true for life itself?

Art is the only salvation from boredom and the often-destructive will to knowledge that leads to the disenchantment of the world. In an aphorism entitled 'Our ultimate gratitude to art' from *The Gay Science*, Nietzsche elaborates this thought:

---

[56] Kierkegaard, 1843/1987: 286.
[57] Kierkegaard, 1843/1987: 293–294.

If we had not welcomed the arts and invented this kind of cult of the untrue, then the realization of general untruth and mendaciousness that now comes to us through science – the realization that delusion and error are conditions of human knowledge and sensation – would be utterly unbearable. Honesty would lead to nausea and suicide. But now there is a counterforce against our honesty that helps us to avoid such consequences: art as the good will to appearance. We do not always keep our eyes from rounding off something and, as it were, finishing the poem; and then it is no longer eternal imperfection that we carry across the river of becoming – then we have the sense of carrying a goddess, and feel proud and childlike as we perform this service. As an artistic phenomenon existence is still bearable for us, and art furnishes us with eyes and hands and above all the good conscience to be able to turn ourselves into such a phenomenon.[58]

For Nietzsche, honesty and knowledge lead to despair and misery. At the bottom of things, the world is dark, irrational and dangerous. If science succeeded and got to the bottom of things, all we would be confronted with is that bleak reality. Only art can bring a sense of fulfilment and happiness to our lives as it allows us to understand our existence as artistic phenomenon. An ethics that strives for honesty leads to agony; an aesthetics that transforms life into art results in ecstasy.

The idea that the only ethical position towards life is an aesthetic one has also been suggested by Foucault, who asked: 'But couldn't everyone's life become a work of art? Why should the lamp or the house be an art object, but not our life?'[59] While morality might be the stuff that angels are made of, ours is the world of beauty. Rather than searching for the truth, we should be content with what is beautiful.

This brings us back to the aesthetics of brands. The aestheticization of everyday life is by and large accomplished through consumption, as Featherstone reminds us: 'Rather than unreflexively adopting a lifestyle, through tradition or habit, the new heroes of consumer culture make lifestyle a life project and display their individuality and sense of style in the particularity of the assemblage of goods, clothes, practices, experiences, appearance and bodily disposition they design together into a lifestyle.'[60] Brands are enablers of lifestyle: they are the bits and pieces that form life as art in the everyday context. Brands are the props for the stage we call life. They allow us to perform our roles, or better: they enable us to perform our identities. Brands facilitate identity creation. Through brands, we re-create ourselves as aesthetic

---

[58] Nietzsche, 1882/2002: 104.
[59] Foucault, 1983/2003: 109.
[60] Featherstone, 1991: 86.

phenomena. Brands are symbolic resources for identity construction: they are the grammar that allows us to narrate our story.

Nil admirari: brands provide enough meaning so we can build our lives on them; but they allow for a level of playfulness that does not put chains around our ankles. *Nil admirari* is in fact a brand's ironic value proposition. It allows us to turn our lives into an aesthetic phenomenon.

Style

Brands are stylized images. As Bernd Schmitt and Alex Simonson put it, 'cutting edge corporations' focus on aesthetics: 'The consumer today makes choices based on whether or not a product fits into his or her lifestyle or whether it represents an exciting new concept – a desirable experience.'[61] In order to do so, products have to become a holistic sensory experience: all aspects of aesthetics become part of brand experience. Touch, smell, sound, sight and taste are put together to express lifestyles. In fact, it becomes 'one of the foremost tasks of identity management through aesthetics ... to associate the organization and its brands with a certain style'.[62] In order to create life-style, brands need to express style.

Style is something active, something we do and exercise. As the design guru Bruce Mau writes, 'life does not simply happen to us, we produce it. That's what style is. It's producing life ... style is a decision about how we will live.'[63] Think of a style of music or a style of playing tennis or a style of swimming: in each case, style is a way on being in the world, 'an invention that then re-disposes that world according to entirely new rhythmic values ... When we give style to our character, we do nothing else than to claim and renounce freedoms.'[64] In short, style is the aestheticization that we give our own individual lives. The notion of lifestyle captures this meaning perfectly well.

Martha Stewart claimed to have pioneered lifestyle as a new media category.[65] *Martha Stewart Living* shows how life should be lived – from cooking to gardening, being a good housewife, decorating your home beautifully, having your hair done or getting into craft and designing your own picture frames.

---

[61] Schmitt and Simonson, 1997: 16.
[62] Schmitt and Simonson, 1997: 85.
[63] Mau, 2000: 27.
[64] Kwinter, 2000: 35.
[65] Mau, 2000: 70; see Goldstein, 2005.

Even when she was sent to prison for fraud, Martha applied her lifestyle to the Big House. She collected flowers in the prison yard, cooked new dishes in microwaves and kept her cell neat and tidy. The implication is clear: *Martha Stewart Living* works everywhere – even in prison!

Lifestyles consist of patterns of action that differentiate people from each other. For Levine, lifestyle 'emerges from the mutual adaptation of parts of experiences felt so intensely that their contrasts and organization produce an emotionally gratifying whole'.[66]

Lifestyle represents some kind of pattern or whole. For instance, people can crudely be classified into security seekers or explorers. Both lifestyles pattern their followers' choices, from buying a car to choosing a restaurant or going on holidays. Lifestyle organizes the endless possibilities that a consumer society offers and provides a basic rhythm for life. Lifestyle enables people to differentiate themselves from each other. Think of lifestyle as an individual's story, with the vocabulary made up of a combination of brands. Like language, lifestyle only makes sense as a system of differences that create relations between each other. Lifestyles are ready-made narratives for identity, culture and society. Lifestyles create patterns that describe what is a good and appropriate form of life. Brands are the building blocks, the symbolic resources of the new *icon*omy – the combination of the beautiful, the sublime and the performative offer an aesthetic that stylizes life.

The paradox of style

Simmel has identified the paradox – or tragedy, as he put it – of style at the heart of culture.[67] According to Simmel, culture has an objective and a subjective element. The objective element is the style of a particular school of painting or music. It is what artists share and what makes them part of a larger movement or *zeitgeist*. The subjective part represents the individual's expression, her ability and willingness to create something new. This 'something' is unique and individual as we relate it to a particular creator and her *oeuvre*.

For Simmel, culture comes into being if these two spheres collide without coinciding with each other – the subject is objectified and the object

---

[66] Levine, 1968, quoted in Zablocki and Moss, 1976: 271; Chaney, 1996; see also the interesting collection of essays in Bell and Hollows, 2005.
[67] Simmel, 1911–1912/2000.

is subjectified. If we only deal with subjectivity, we have expression without structures; if we only have objectification, we call it formalism without originality. Take Adolf Wölfli, who spent most of his time in a psychiatric hospital in Switzerland producing the most amazing drawings, a unique numerical system, his own musical notation scale and an imaginary autobiography including an explanation of the world system in more than 8,000 pages. This subjective expression only becomes art once it is framed within a tradition – in Wölfli's case, 'Art Brut' and subsequent exhibitions from the 1970s, forty years after his death, onwards. On the other hand, if someone copies Duchamp's ready-mades and puts them into a gallery, he will not be seen as an artist because the structure of art and the convention of our times are different.

The spontaneity of 'art worlds' is in fact organized around myriad players, resources, tools and discourses that turn creative expression into art.[68] This system ensures that the expectations of the audience are met – even when these expectations include surprise and the unexpected.

It is in the clash of the objective and the subjective where Simmel sees the tragedy of culture unfolding: the objective structure annihilates the individual, forcing conventions upon her, while the individual attempts to break free from conventions. Only in this tragic struggle emerges what he calls culture.

The crux of the story is, according to Simmel, that the relation between the subjective and the objective is changing in modernity: the objective part of culture becomes more and more dominant. It becomes increasingly difficult for the individual to challenge conventions and subjectify the objective, resulting in the paradoxical state in which 'things become more and more cultivated but people are capable only to a lesser degree of deriving from the improvement of objects and improvement of their subjective lives'.[69] People quite literally buy into objectified forms of expression, leaving them with an empty formalism.

The problem is resolved through what Simmel calls fashion or style. Style prescribes clear conventions and objective structures; at the same time, it allows the individual to satisfy his need for distinction and difference. Style allows an individual to identify with a certain group or movement and be part of an objectified culture. While it connects with others, style simultaneously

---

[68] Becker, 1982/2008.
[69] Simmel, 1908a/2000: 45; 1905/2000.

allows one to differentiate oneself from others. Style elevates *and* equalizes; it creates envy *and* approval.

The aesthetization of life in the brand society follows this path. The stylization of life is the logical consequence. From behaviour to homeware, style provides ready-made templates or conventions for individuals to buy into and show creative expression without putting the subjective to work or at risk. You can express your individuality and uniqueness by buying into and choosing among different styles that you can wear like masks.[70]

Hence lifestyle starts to govern individuals: the choice of brands provides the 'substance' we are made of. The subjective part of culture, according to Duchamp, is reduced to the act of choosing.

Cultures are split up into myriad sub-cultures that act as conventions for a smaller group of people. These conventions are more easily accessible and more open to change, hence they allow the individual to enter into the play between individual expression and objective convention. The proliferation of brand communities and tribes are a vivid testimony of this transformation. They form sub-cultures that choose their own styles of life, which allow them to turn their existences individually and collectively into an aesthetic phenomenon.

To buy a brand is to set ourselves in relation to culture. To buy a brand is a cultural expression: brands are ready-made objects for us to express who we are and aspire to be. What we think of as our innermost desire to express our individuality is, in fact, nothing but the selection of prefabricated styles. Of course, this shift can hardly be seen as liberating revolution. As Manovich has pointed out, the 'non-transparency of the code' that structures brand aesthetics is problematic.[71] The new axis of interface and database pre-structures the possible choices the individual faces. Choice between pre-given alternatives replaces a more fundamental freedom: 'Paradoxically, by following an interactive path, one does not construct a unique self but instead adopts already pre-established identities.'[72]

Does branding lead to an aesthetization of life that turns us into works of art? I guess the answer depends on how you define a work of art: thanks to brands, you might be able to turn yourself into pop art, but I am not sure

---

[70] Simmel, 1908b/2000.

[71] Manovich, 2001: 64. On page 61, he elaborates: 'Interactive media asks us to identify with someone else's mental structure. If the cinema viewer, male or female, lusted after and tried to emulate the body of the movie star, the computer user is asked to follow the mental trajectory of the new media designer.'

[72] Manovich, 2001: 129. On the same page, he describes his solution to the problem as follows: 'I would prefer using Microsoft Windows exactly the way it was installed at the factory instead of customizing it in the hope of expressing my "unique identity".'

what the odds are if you try to become something slightly more classical or choose a different style. The brand-driven aestheticization of life might result in tragic and unreflexive consumerism that gives rise to comical and unleashed subjectivities living out their dreams with a shopping bag full of brands in the one hand and their credit card in the other.

At least, such a life might not be boring.

Conclusion

'The conclusion, in which nothing is concluded'

Thus did Samuel Johnson head the final chapter of his novel *Rasselas*. Will we be able to offer you much more? At the end of our odyssey through several disciplines and traditions, can we draw up some take-away implications, packaged up conveniently in bullet-point form?

As Jean-Luc Godard famously said, a story should have a beginning, a middle and an end – but not necessarily in that order. You will have drawn some conclusions from the introduction of this book and formed an opinion after the first couple of pages. Love letters and good books share this uncontrollable, viral and contagious flow of meaning. So while you hopefully have used this book as a ladder to get somewhere where the book cannot get to, and climbed beyond it (to use Wittgenstein's famous metaphor from his *Tractatus*), we'd like to step back to the three main concepts of this book – brands, management and lifestyle – and offer some speculations about their future evolution. Please note that this narrative has not been derived from staring into a crystal ball; rather than clairvoyance, the following represents only one of many possible conjectures.

Lifestyle

At the beginning of our journey, we argued that brands form a mountain range of evidence in search of a theory. Brands are pervasive and ubiquitous.

263

We take them for granted – from pop art to McDonald's, from Starbucks to Greenpeace, brands are the mechanism that connects organizations and people.

As phenomena, brands enjoyed a meteoric rise. The love affair that John B. Watson, Vice President at J. Walter Thompson and founder of behaviouralism, and Andy Warhol had with brands illustrates their exceptional reach. While Watson went from psychology into advertising, Warhol moved from advertising into the world of art. These two reverse movements are good proxies for advertising's transformations in the last century: Watson legitimized advertising as social engineering, while Warhol turned it into an art form. Today, brands not only seduce us into perpetuating the consumer society's vices, but they are also the cultural forms that allow us to express who we are.

Brands are the soul of corporations, organizations and movements. For Deleuze, the idea that corporations have souls is 'the most terrifying news in the world'.[1] On the other hand, for the first part of the twentieth century, the concept of organizations as soulless machines and faceless bureaucracies was equally terrifying. For Max Weber, bureaucracy creates an iron cage whose bars are made up of rationality replacing traditional forms of authority. Long-dominant social signifiers such as religion, family, class, nationality and so on become less important. In other words, capitalism did its best to melt not all but at least some of what was solid into air.

With the notion of brands, capitalism reintroduces social signifiers into the market economy. Brands supplement the cold logic of transaction with their chatty logic of interaction. Brands re-enchant the world, after capitalism has done its best to dis-enchant it. Brands substitute the cold bars of the iron cage with seductive images that form the invisible walls around our lifestyles. Brands ignore the traditional lines of segregation (class, nationality, religion, and so on); and they do not attribute status according to one's role in the production process. Rather, brands enable an individual to construct one's identity on the basis of one's consumption patterns. Brands become the resource for identity formation. They are the ready-made elements for styling our lives.

Douglas Holt put it more colloquially when he argued that '[c]onsumers want to author their lives, but they increasingly are looking for ghost-writers to help them out'.[2] In fact, consumers are looking for ghost-scripts

[1] Deleuze, 1990.
[2] Holt, 2002: 87.

and ghost-props that allow them to put on convincing identity performances. That's exactly what brands deliver: they provide the narratives we live by.

Brands represent values, not functionality. They turn products into social signifiers and consumption into a social phenomenon. Brands are the means by which you actualize your inner self and satisfy (albeit temporarily) this desire to become yourself. Brands are ready-made identities. They link our *id* to the ad, offering space for identification, representation and differentiation. Above all, in a world in which confusion is the norm, they offer certainty, clarity and stability.

For a good part of the twentieth century, capitalism was accepted because it increased the 'standard of living'. The standard of living showcased the purchasing power of a nation and was an indicator of progress. Of course, the standard of living did not take into account a whole range of important yet hard to measure indicators, including what could not be bought because it was offered by government; whether what people really wanted what was on offer; what changed hands in the grey markets of non-monetary exchange; and the human, social and environmental costs of increased productivity.[3]

The standard of living was a simple measure that placed people either below or above a certain line. One could argue that the concept of lifestyle has replaced the standard of living. Lifestyle is about shaping life through the consumption of brands. It does not provide a benchmark for judging who is below and who is above. Rather, lifestyle shapes life in a capillary way: lifestyle cares about how you cut your hair, where you shop, what you eat, to which music you move through the city, where you go on holidays, what films you like and what books you read. Lifestyle is that pattern of activities and practices that give meaning to the world and, by extension, identity to the individual.

For Sidney Levy, the problem with brands was that they could not realize their value in isolation. A consumer personality was the sum total of what she consumed. But how to link those different consumer brands? How to make sense of the myriad possible choices? Consumption was in need of a grammar, a context, that would allow those different brands to be related to each other. Lifestyle provides this grammar, this context: people consume brands as sub-symbols of a larger symbol system that Sidney Levy called so tellingly 'lifestyle'.

At present, we are sleepwalking into the brand society: we are lifestyle-driven but do not see the fundamental shift that this ostensibly innocent concept

---

[3] See de Garzia, 2005: 102, and especially page 354 for a critique.

brings with it. Lifestyle is our grammar, brands our alphabet: McDonald's makes your family happy, IKEA shows you how to live, Club Med gives you the holiday you deserve, L'Oréal teaches you what beauty is, Apple shows you what's cool … The list is endless, the logic behind it simple: brands position themselves as pieces of the mosaic that constitutes a lifestyle.

Lifestyle resolves the old metaphysical conflict between individual and society by combining the two: like fashion, style homogenizes as it forms patterns that the individual has to accept as given. At the same time, style (and fashion) allow us to be who we are as they offer a repertoire for self-expression. According to Simmel, style paradoxically performs both functions: it makes us increasingly the same while simultaneously allowing us to be ever more different. The relentless drive for difference makes brands the major ally in this paradoxical endeavour: they are, in the words of Søren Askegaard, the hegemonic engines of diversity.

Brands also have important consequences for society and the state. They become even more significant as we move from the nation state idea(l) into market states: in market states, it is not the wellbeing of the people as a whole but the satisfaction of individual needs that is pivotal. In order to deliver on this agenda, governments will redefine themselves as brands, and democratic practices (such as voting) will be overshadowed by marketing techniques such as focus groups and the constant polling of so-called 'public opinion'. Institutions, for so long the source of meaning and trust, are being replaced by brands that generate meaning and trust as part of market relations. While institutions are failing, brands are on the rise.

Despite their pervasiveness, however, brands do not turn us into puppets. Rather, they exercise a positive form of power: they seduce, convince and stimulate. As Bauman put it, 'coercion has by and large been replaced by stimulation, the once obligatory patterns of conduct by seduction, the policing of behaviour by PR and advertising, and normative regulation by the arousal of new needs and desires'.[4] Brands therefore structure a field of possible action. They do not discipline us but encourage our freedom – after all, in consumer democracies, people have 'free' choice to vote with their dollars, spending their way into a better and brighter future. Whether we can spend our way out of the mess we're in is a different question. And whether the choice we have in a supermarket represents freedom is equally questionable: choice between alternatives does not equal freedom. Lifestyle promises

[4] Bauman, 2007: 89–90, with reference to Bourdieu.

freedom (think Harley Davidson), but what brands actually offer is choice between limited alternatives.

The form of power that brands exercise might be described as hegemonic: even phenomena such as Naomi Klein's *No Logo* movement, *Adbusters'* sub-vertising or Banksy's brandalism use the tools of branding to fight branding. Remember, there is no better indicator of the hegemonic form of power than the degree to which resistance to that very power has to rely on it and its means. Brands explore and exploit difference: be it hip, cool or hop, brands absorb what's different and integrate it into their machinery. Sameness and homogeneity would indicate system failure in the brand society, where lifestyle places a premium on difference. This relentless quest for difference turns brands into potential Trojan Horses. We should not confuse what they prefigure with hope for a better world; nonetheless, the phenomenon of brands can be seen as the twilight on the horizon that illuminates the potential to challenge and change the order of things.

Management

Brands transform the way we manage organizations. Deloitte and ING both demonstrate the transformation of management through brands. Through the brand lens, organizations see themselves from the outside in. The brand becomes the vantage point for restructuring the organization, the catalyst that transforms internal processes. In order to become 'easier', ING has to change its IT system; it has to challenge the way people respond to consumers; it has to develop better products, faster, and so on. In this scenario, brand management equals change management – especially in knowledge-intensive organizations that are driven by people whose behaviour is the brand. In short, the brand becomes the organizing principle that transforms management practice.

The brand provides a new way of thinking about, and managing, organizational identity. Branding becomes the practice of managing one's identity as seen from the outsider's perspective. When managers think about their organization's identity, they frame their thoughts in the language of brands. Brands provide the discursive frame in which identity is constructed and contested. In fact, the brand becomes the medium for identity construction. Brands move identity from something that is ostensibly essential, distinctive and enduring to something that is constructed out of language. Think of logos, symbols, words, buildings, packaging, uniforms, websites, behaviour, and so on – they all constitute the discursive universe of a brand, and by extension, an organization's identity.

Brands also constitute the boundary around the arena in which identity is contested. Defining a brand means defining a set of values, a way of behaving, right down to minute details such as the tone of voice of an email. From management's perspective, brands are scripts that promise to direct the organization in two ways. First, the brand should guide employees' internal sense-making processes by providing readily available meanings and interpretations of events. Second, the brand should ensure the smooth production of consumable experiences for an organization's consumers or clients. As such, the brand imposes its logic across the boundaries between internal organization and external environment.

The brand as discursive device for framing and managing identity exercises power both in and beyond organizations. If we understand brands as Wittgensteinian language games, they resemble rule-based systems that allow certain moves whilst sanctioning others. Brands are a grammar for reducing complexity (through limiting legitimate interpretations and meanings, e.g., defining organizational values); at the same time they create a new form of complexity (by enabling new and yet unexplored connections, e.g. between inside and outside). Wittgenstein argued that to imagine a language game means to imagine a form of life – a lifestyle. Insofar as they need to be socially legitimized, language games are social activities. A private language is an oxymoron. As language games, brands shape a certain form of life and style life in a particular way. Like grammar, brands are a mechanism used to produce and consume meaning. While the concept of language games is not new, management's appetite to explore and exploit brands as corporate meaning-makers certainly is.

As a framework for managing identity, brands provide the arena in which the paradox of identity is enacted. While every organization strives for a unique identity, it has to remain similar to its competitors in order to be seen as a viable alternative to them. As such, a stable identity represents a paradox: rather than searching for an enduring essence, an organization has to continuously oscillate between imitation and innovation. The brand provides the space for this movement: it enables an organization to focus narcissistically on its uniqueness and, at the same time, it forces it to keep an eye on its external environment. Organizations do not simply mimic other organizations, as institutional theory suggests; rather, like brands, organizations are organized heresy: the search for differences becomes the core of their identity.

The brand manifests itself as the interface where those different, competing and contradicting narratives clash and are, temporarily, reconciled.

Of course, to recognize that there is a paradoxical dynamic between imitation and differentiation does not imply that it can be managed (as so many books on branding promise). Think of the Edinburgh City brand. Edinburgh is a unique city with unique characteristics and history. The brand of Edinburgh reduces these differences to a single dimension ('Inspiring Capital') and then, based on this newly forged identity, tries to claim uniqueness. Of course, dozens of other cities would claim to be inspiring too. Ironically, once Edinburgh has subscribed to the logic of branding, it becomes increasingly difficult to develop a truly distinct identity. Rather, one could argue that the polyphonic Edinburgh of DI Rebus and *Trainspotting* provides a narrative that is deeply entrenched in the city's history and culture, and as such, is in competition with the smooth narrative of the 'Inspiring Capital'.

While a brand manager might create a certain identity, the brand inevitably escapes management's control. Like beauty, a brand exists in the eye of the beholder. And there it is hard to control: the sense-making processes of the reader (consumer, employee) co-constitutes, and sometimes overrides, the text of the author (brand manager). This poses a fundamental challenge to management.

Management's instinct is to use brands as mechanisms of control. The equation is simple: since brands can influence consumer behaviour, they should also be able to direct employee's conduct. A new breed of brand culture prophecy sees employees turning into living brands, expressing and reinforcing corporate values with every move they make. While the idea of branded employee-clones satisfies managerial control fantasies, it is doomed to failure. Just as the concept of organizational culture was sold to management as the solution to the problem of control, now (employer or internal) branding is pitched as the latest cure.

We'd like to think of brands as more than a new solution to an old problem. In fact, we argue that the problem has changed: rather than controlling the internal production process, the challenge might be to interact with one's environment and engage innovatively in co-creation activities. In fact, the control problem might look like a mild form of anxiety disorder once co-creation is analysed in all its consequences.

Cultures extend beyond the boundaries of the organization. Consumers form brand communities that engage in creative, unruly and co-producing practices. Empowered by new information and communication technology, users become actively engaged in previously internal organizational production processes. Creative consumption does not occur in a vacuum, though; rather, user communities crystallize around brands. These brand communities describe a new form of social organization mediated by brands.

Following more than a 100 years of mourning the decline of social organization, in everything from Tönnies' *Community and Society* to Riesman's *Lonely Crowd* and Putnam's *Bowling Alone*, brand communities provide a new form of social cohesion. Just as, according to Anderson's argument, media such as newspapers were a pivotal mechanism in manufacturing the imagined community of a nation, brands give rise to imagined communities around the globe. The brand of LEGO or Apple is used by literally tens of thousands of people to express who they are and to relate to other like-minded individuals.

This new form of social organization is far from leading towards a harmonious new society; rather, the communities that form on- and offline are testimony to the tribalization of society. The defining characteristic of a tribe is its unique lifestyle; its defining currency is not formed from the pros and cons of rational discourse but what's 'in' and what's 'out'. Being part of a tribe, individuals play roles and use brands as plots and props to stage convincing performances. But while the cohesion within a tribe is high, its tolerance to change is low. In fact, those tribes organized around brands might turn out to be particularly conservative and reactionary when the brand changes.

But as spaces of co-creation, brand communities do have the potential to innovate. Brand communities perform markets as conversations, where interaction is more pertinent than transaction. Out of the polyphony of those conversations, new ideas are born. Think of Linux or Wikipedia, where tens of thousands of people form a notional identity around a brand and routinely innovate in an open-source environment. The brand is the only interface for co-creation. Especially in the non-mediated media of the internet, brands are the only anchor point that provides stability and recognition. The control that organizations had over production and distribution vanishes as users short-cut these circuits of power and relate to each other more directly.

Finally, we see the brand emerging as a new interface between consumption and production. The brand becomes a medium that relates the two most fundamental spheres of our society. By doing so, it also changes both spheres: the concepts of the co-creation of value and the underlying notion of an economy of qualities are testimony to this profound shift.

Fundamentally, our economy has been organized around the ability to quantify qualities. Money was – and still is – the measure of all things. Only what can be counted counts. Brands start to change the picture by reintroducing values into the circle of production and consumption. Explicitly, they bring meaning back into the exchange of things. After most parts of the production process have been outsourced to globally connected value chains, all that is left to manage in-house is meaning. Nike's trainers are made in the same factories, from the same raw materials, as Adidas' sneakers.

The sole difference is the meaning of the brand. The process of the production and consumption of meaning is impossible to disentangle. While the production of shoes can be outsourced, brands have to be built locally. The cultural economy, in which cultural products were commodified, gives way to the brand society, in which meaning is managed and objectified in lifestyles.

Disclaimer

We unhesitatingly admit that this book has been sketched out on a large canvas. Rather than a sharp pencil, we used a broad brush – or better, a spray-can – to get our message across, so what we want to say should be visible from afar. The downside of this approach is that, not unlike an Impressionist painting, things start to blur when you get too close. There are several questions that this book raises but leaves unanswered.

How much, for example, does the talk about brands in different organizations signify a change in the rhetoric of management practice but not necessarily in its reality? How does the poetry of brands relate to the prose of everyday organizational life in different industries? And to what extent do brand-driven lifestyles provide the new rhythm of life for Gen Y-ers, Baby Boomers and all those in between?

There can be no *a priori* answer to these questions. We attempted to delineate a sketch and express some suspicions about brands and their consequences. The sketches are not photographic and the suspicions are not meant to be read as conspiracy theories. Only detailed empirical research can explore how brands are enacted, played out and appropriated in different local contexts.

Nonetheless, we think that there is value in Impressionism, big canvases and broad brushstrokes. They help stir up the order of things and make us see them differently. This is an important ability, since we tend to turn the world upside down rather than dispose of old ideas. Most of the time we entertain our ideas to explain away anomalies, differences, black swans and other unexpected things. Our brain processes data from the past in order to control, predict and forecast. As long as the future is nothing but a linear extrapolation of the past, this method works just fine. When we go through more radical change, however, the method proves fatal. All it does is provide a false sense of certainty, making us believe we know how to manage step change. Our actions will be decisive (as they are based on knowledge) – but wrong.

Only extensive empirical research can illuminate how far the rise of brands and the ensuing transformation of management and lifestyle represents such a step change. We're lucky because we might be able to conduct such emprircal research and collect evidence in comfort: brands are ubiquitous, they are loud and they want to be observed. In 1971, the American poet and musician Gil Scott-Heron sang 'The revolution will not be televised.' It was one of the first hip-hop songs and marked the formation of a new cultural territory. Chances are that the brand society *will* be televised: you can study the aesthetics of brands on YouTube, read about the ethics of brands (or the lack thereof) on blogs and analyse the politics of brands while reading lifestyle magazines. You can research the changes in management practice and everyday organizational life by starting with the sensory clues and working your way into observing organizational behaviour and absorbing culture. Most excitingly, you could follow the brand trajectory from the outside in and, by doing so, develop a narrative that dissolves some of our conventional ways of thinking about consumption and production.

Does this make for a happy end to our story? I have often asked myself the question: If this book was made into a film, would it feature the brand as hero, creating new unity and bridging old divisions? Or would it be a morality tale in which the branded, rich and powerful fight the authentic, natural and good guys? Or a thriller based around a conspiracy theory that blames brands for the state we are in? Or perhaps it would be a comedy depicting brands as nothing but the next chapter in the farce we call civilisation?

I have never come up with an answer that I believed in for longer than five minutes. Rather, I'd like to think of this book as a brand in itself, as a medium, as an interface, as something that creates a blackout by short-circuiting the cycles of production and consumption. Then, in line with our argument, I would like to see the next episode co-created, co-written and co-produced by you.

References

Aaker, D. A. and Carman, J. M. 1980. 'Are You Overadvertising?', *Journal of Advertising Research* **22**(4): 57–70

Aaker, D. A. and Joachimsthaler, E. 2002. *Brand Leadership*, London: Simon & Schuster

Addis, M. and Holbrook, M. B. 2001. 'On the Conceptual Link between Mass Customisation and Experiential Consumption: An Explosion of Subjectivity', *Journal of Consumer Behaviour: An International Research Review* **1**(1): 50–66

Agamben, G. 1990/1993. *The Coming Community*, Minneapolis, MN: University of Minnesota Press

Ahmad, S. 2001. 'Pro Logo', *The Economist,* 8 September.

   2003. 'Globalisation and Brands', in R. Clifton and J. Simmons (eds.), *Brands and Branding*, London: Profile Books, 171–184

Albert, S. and Whetten, D. A. 1985. 'Organizational Identity', in L. L. Cummings and B. M. Staw (eds.), *Research in Organizational Behaviour 7*, Greenwich, CT: JAI Press, 263–295

Alderson, W. 1965. *Dynamic Marketing Behavior: A Functionalist Theory of Marketing*, Homewood, IL: R. D. Irwin

Allen, T. and Simmons, J. 2003. 'Visual and Verbal identity', in R. Clifton and J. Simmons (eds.), *Brands andy / Branding*, London: Profile Books, 112–126

Alloway, L. 1958. 'The Arts and the Mass Media', *Architectural Design;* see www.warholstars.org/warhol/warhol1/andy/warhol/articles/popart/popart.html (acccessed 12 September 2008)

Alvesson, M. 1990. 'Organizations: From Substance to Image?', *Organization Studies* **11**(3): 273–294

   1993. 'Organizations as Rhetoric: Knowledge Intensive Firms and the Struggle with Ambiguity', *Journal of Management Studies* **30**(6): 997–1019

Anders, G. 1956. *Die Antiquiertheit des Menschen. Über die Seele im Zeitalter der zweiten industriellen Revolution*, Munich: Verlag C. H. Beck

Anderson, B. 1983. *Imagined Communities: Reflections on the Origin and Spread of Nationalism*, London and New York, NY: Verso

Anderson, C. 2006. *The Long Tail: How Endless Choice is Creating Unlimited Demand*, London: Random House Business Books

Anholt City Brands Index 2006. *How the World Views Its Cities*, Second Edition; see www.gfkamerica.com/practice_areas/roper_pam/placebranding/cbi/index.en.html (accessed 16 July 2009)

Antorini, Y. M. 2007. 'Brand Community Innovation: An Intrinsic Case Study of the Adult Fans of LEGO Community', Unpublished PhD, Copenhagen: Copenhagen Business School

Antorini, Y. M. and Schultz, M. 2005. 'Principles for the Second Wave of Corporate Branding', in M. Schultz, Y. M. Antorini and F. F. Csaba (eds.), *Corporate Branding: Purpose/People/Process*, Copenhagen Business School Press, 219–232

Appadurai, A. (ed.) 1986. *The Social Life of Things: Commodities in Cultural Perspective*, New York, NY: Cambridge University Press

Araujo, L. 2007. 'Markets, Market-making and Marketing', *Marketing Theory* 7(3): 211–226

Arendt, H. 1961/1993. 'The Crisis in Culture: Its Social and its Political Significance', in H. Arendt (ed.), *Between Past and Future*, London: Penguin Books, 197–226

Arnould E. J. and Thompson, C. J. 2005. 'Consumer Culture Theory (CCT): Twenty Years of Research', *Journal of Consumer Research* 31 (March): 868–882

Arvidsson, A. 2005. 'Brands: "A Critical Perspective"', *Journal of Consumer Culture* 5(2): 235–258

2006. *Brands: Meaning and Value in Media Culture*, London and New York, NY: Routledge

Askegaard, S. 2006. 'Brands as Global Ideoscapes', in J. P. Schroeder and M. Salzer-Mörling (eds.), *Brand Culture*, London and New York, NY: Routledge, 91–102

Asker, D. A. 1996. *Building Strong Brands*, London: Simon & Schuster

Atkin, D. 2004. *The Culting of Brands: When Customers Become True Believers*, New York, NY: Portfolio

Atkins, L. and Lury, C. 1999. 'The Labour of Identity: Performing Identity, Performing Economies', *Economy and Society* 28(4): 598–614

Austin, J. L. 1955/1962. *How To Do things with Words*, Oxford: Clarendon Press

Baba, M. L. 2003. 'Afterword: Looking Forward, Looking Back', in. T. D. Malefyt and B. Moeran (eds.), *Advertising Cultures*, Oxford and New York, Berg, NY: 203–206

Bachrach, P. and Baratz, M. S. 1962. 'Two Faces of Power', *The American Political Science Review* 56: 947–952

Bagwell, K. (ed.) 2001. *The Economics of Advertising*, Cheltenham: Edward Elgar

Balzac, H. 1834/1962. *Pere Goriot*, New York, NY: New American Library

Banksy 2006. *Wall and Piece*, London: Century

Barber, B. R. 2007. *Consumed: How Markets Corrupt Children, Infantilize Adults, and Swallow Citizens Whole*, London and New York, NY: W. W. Norton & Company

Barker, J. 1993. 'Tightening the Iron Cage: Concertive Control in Self-managing Teams', *Administrative Science Quarterly* 38: 408–437

Barthes, R. 1957/2000. *Mythologies*, London: Vintage

1967. 'Death of the Author', *Aspen* 5+6 (Winter/Fall), available at www.ubu.com/aspen/aspen5and6/index.html (accessed 30 June 2009)

Barwise, P. 2003. Preface in R. Clifton and J. Simmons (eds.), *Brands and Branding*, London: Profile Books, xii–xv

Baudrillard, J. 1970/2003. *The Consumer Society: Myths and Structures*, London, Thousand Oaks, CA and New Delhi: Sage

Bauman, Z. 2007. *Consuming Life*, Cambridge and Malden, MA: Polity Press

Beamish, T. 2000. 'Accumulating Trouble: Complex Organizations, a Culture of Silence, and a Secret Spill', *Social Problems* **47**(4): 473–498

Beck, U. 1986/2007. *Risk Society: Towards a New Modernity*, London: Sage

Becker, H. S. 1982/2008. *Art Worlds*, Berkeley, Los Angeles, CA and London: University of California Press

Beigbeder, F. 2000. *99 Francs*, Paris: Bernard Grasset

Belk, R. W. 1988. 'Possessions and the Extended Self', *Journal of Consumer Research* **15** (September): 139–168

Belk, R. W. and Tumbat, G. 2005. 'The Cult of Macintosh, Consumption', *Markets & Culture* **8**(3): 205–217

Bell, D. and Hollows, J. (eds.) 2005. *Ordinary Lifestyles: Popular Media, Consumption and Taste*, Maidenhead: Open University Press

Bell, W. E. 1964. 'Consumer Innovators: A Unique Market for Newness', in S. A. Greyser (ed.), *Toward Scientific Marketing*, Chicago, IL: American Marketing Association, 85–95

Bengtsson, A., Ostberg, J. and Kjeldgaard, D. 2005. 'Prisoners in Paradise: Subcultural Resistance to the Marketization of Tattooing', *Consumption, Markets and Culture* **8**(3): 261–274

Beniger, J. R. 1986. *The Control Revolution, Technological and Economic Origins of the Information Society*, Cambridge, MA: Harvard University Press

Benjamin, W. 1927–1940/2002. *The Arcades Project*, New York, NY: Belknap Press
    1936/1990. *The Work of Art in the Age of its Technological Reproducibility, and Other Writings on Media*, Boston, MA: Harvard University Press

Blackett, T. 2003. 'What is Brand?', in R. Clifton and J. Simmons (eds.), *Brands and Branding*, London: Profile Books, 13–26

Bobbitt, P. 2008. *Terror and Consent: The Wars for the Twenty-First Century*, London: Allen Lane

Bogenhold, D. 2001. 'Social Inequality and the Plurality of Life-Styles: Material and Cultural Aspects of Social Stratification', *The American Journal of Economics and Sociology* **60**: 829–847

Bond, J. and Kirshenbaum, R. 1998. *Under the Radar: Talking to Today's Cynical Customers*, New York, NY: John Wiley and Sons

Boorstin, D. J. 1973. *The Americans: The Democratic Experience*, New York, NY: Random House

Borgerson, J. L., Magnusson, M. E. and Magnusson F. 2006. 'Branding Ethics: Negotiating Benetton's Identity and Image', in J. Schroeder and M. Salzer-Mörling (eds.), *Brand Culture*, London and New York, NY: Routledge, 171–185

Borges, J. L. 1939/1982. *Labyrinths: Selected Stories and Other Writings*, London: Penguin Books

Bourdieu, P. 1979/2007. *Distinction: A Social Critique of the Judgement of Taste*, New York, NY and London: Routledge

Boyle, D. 2004. *Authenticity: Brands, Fakes, Spin and the Lust for Real Life*, London: Harper Perennial

Braudel, F. 1987/1995. *A History of Civilizations*, London: Penguin Books

Braun, T. 2004. *The Philosophy of Branding*, London and Philadelphia, PA: Kogan Page

Britt, S. 1960. *The Spenders*, New York, NY: McGraw-Hill

Brown, A.D. 1997. 'Narcissism, Identity and Legitimacy', *Academy of Management Review*, **22**(3): 643–686

Brown, A.D. and Starkey, K. 2000. 'Organizational Identity and Organizational Learning: A Psychodynamic Perspective', *Academy of Management Review* **25**(1): 102–120

Brown, S. 2006. 'Ambi-brand Culture: On a Wing and a Swear with Ryanair', in Schroeder and Salzer-Mörling (eds.), *Brand Culture*, London and New York, NY: Routledge, 50–66

Brown, S., Kozinets, R.V. and Sherry, J.F., Jr., 2003. 'Teaching Old Brands New Tricks: Retro Branding and the Revival of Brand Meaning', *Journal of Marketing* **67** (July): 19–33

Burke, E. 1757/1998. *A Philosophical Enquiry into the Origin of Our Ideas of the Sublime and Beautiful*, Oxford: Oxford University Press

Caldwell, N. and Freire, J. 2004. 'The Differences between Branding a Country, a Region and a City: Applying the Brand Box Model', *Brand Management* **12**(1): 50–61

Callon, M. (ed.) 1998. *The Laws of the Markets*, London: Blackwell
    2006. 'What Does It Mean to Say that Economics is Performative?', CSI Working Papers Series Number 5, Ecoles des Mines de Paris

Callon, M., Méadel, C. and Rabeharisoa, V. 2002. 'The Economy of Qualities', *Economy and Society* **31**(2): 194–217

Canguilhem, G. 1943/1968. *The Normal and the Pathological*, Cambridge, MA: MIT Press

Carter, C., Clegg, S. and Kornberger, M. 2008. *A Very Short, Fairly Interesting and Reasonably Cheap Book about Strategy*, London, Thousand Oaks, CA and New Delhi: Sage

Casey, C. 1995. *Work, Self and Society: After Industrialism*, London: Routledge

Castedello, M. and Schmusch, M. 2008. 'Markenbewertung nach IDWS5', *Die Wirtschaftsprüfung* **8**: 350–356

Cayla, J. and Eckhardt, G.M. 2008. 'Asian Brands and the Shaping of a Transnational Imagined Community', *Journal of Consumer Research* **35**(2): 216–230

Chan, A. 2003. 'Instantiative versus Entitative Culture: The Case for Culture as Process', in B. Westwood and S. Clegg (eds.), *Debating Organizations: Point-Counterpoint in Organization Studies*, Oxford: Blackwell, 311–320

Chaney, D. 1996. *Lifestyles*, London: Routledge

Chomsky, N. 1997. *Media Control: The Spectacular Achievements of Propaganda*, New York, NY: Seven Stories Press

Christensen, C.M. 1997. *The Innovator's Dilemma: When New Technologies Cause Great Firms to Fail*, Boston, MA: Harvard Business School Press

Christensen, L.T. and Cheney, G. 2002. 'Self-absorption and Self-seduction in the Corporate Identity Game', in M. Schultz, M. J. Hatch and M. H. Larsen (eds.), *The Expressive Organization: Linking Identity, Reputation, and the Corporate Brand*, Oxford: Oxford University Press, 246–270.

City of Edinburgh 2007. *Inspiring Success Progress Report May 2005–October 2007*, Edinburgh: City of Edinburgh

Clegg, S., Rhodes C. and Kornberger, M. 2007. 'Organizational Identity in an Emerging Industry: The Case of Business Coaching in Australia', *Organization Studies* **28**(4): 495–513

Clifton, R. 2003. 'Introduction', in R. Clifton and J. Simmons (eds.), *Brands and Branding*, London: Profile Books, 1–10

Clifton, R. and Simmons, J. 2003. *Brands and Branding*, London: Profile Books

Cochoy, F. 1998. 'Another Discipline for the Market Economy: Marketing as Performative Knowledge and Know-how for Capitalism', in M. Callon (ed.), *The Laws of the Market*, Oxford: Blackwell, 194–221

   2005. 'A Brief History of "Customers", or the Gradual Standardization of Markets and Organizations', *Sociologie du travail* **47**: 36–56

Cocteau, J. 1958/1988. *Die Schwierigkeit zu Sein*, Frankfurt: Fischer

Cohen, M. D., March, J. G. and Olsen J. P. 1972. 'A Garbage Can Model of Organizational Choice', *Administrative Science Quarterly* **17**(1): 1–25

Cooper, D. and Ezzamel, M. 2008. 'A Social Analysis of the Balanced Scorecard: Towards a Dialogic Strategic Performance Measurement System', Working Paper, Alberta: University of Alberta

Corley, K. G., Harquail, C. V., Pratt, M. G., Glynn, M., Fiol, C. M. and Hatch, M. J. 2006. 'Guiding Organizational Identity through Aged Adolescence', *Journal of Management Inquiry* **15**(2): 85–99

Costa, J. A. 1995. 'The Social Organization of Consumer Behaviour', in Sherry, J. F., Jr. (ed.), *Contemporary Marketing and Consumer Behavior: An Anthropological Sourcebook*, Thousand Oaks, CA, London and New Delhi: Sage, 213–244

Coutu, D. 2000. 'Creating the Most Frightening Company on Earth: An Interview with Andy Law of St. Luke's', *Harvard Business Review* (September–October): 143–150

Cova, B. and Cova, V. 2001. 'Tribal Aspects of Postmodern Consumption Research: The Case of French In-line Roller Skates', *Journal of Consumer Behaviour* **1**(1): 67–76

Csaba, F. F. and Bengtsson, A. 2006. 'Rethinking Identity in Brand Management', in J. Schroeder and M. Salzer-Mörling (eds.), *Brand Culture*, London and New York, NY: Routledge, 118–135

Csikszentmihalyi, M. and Rochberg-Halton, E. 1981. *The Meaning of Things: Domestic Symbols and the Self*, Cambridge: Cambridge University Press.

Czarniawska, B. 1997. *Narrating the Organization: Dramas of Institutional Identity*, Chicago, IL: University of Chicago Press.

Danesi, M. 2006. *Brands*, New York, NY and London: Routledge

Danser, S. 2005. *The Myths of Reality*, Wymeswold: Alternative Albion

Davenport, T. H. and Beck, J. C. 2001. *The Attention Economy: Understanding the New Currency of Business*, Cambridge, MA: Harvard Business School Press

De Botton, A. 2004. *Status Anxiety*, London: Penguin Books

De Certeau, M. 1980/1984. *The Practice of Everyday Life*, Berkeley, CA: University of California Press

de Chernatony, L. (2002). 'Would a Brand Smell Any Sweeter By a Corporate Name?', *Corporate Reputation Review* **5**(2/3): 114–132

De Grazia, S. 1962. *Of Time Work and Leisure*, New York, NY: Twentieth Century Fund

De Grazia, V. 2005. *Irresistible Empire: America's Advance through 20th-Century Europe*, Cambridge and London, MA: The Belknap Press of Harvard University Press

Deal T. E and. Kennedy A. A. 1982. *Corporate Cultures: The Rites and Rituals of Corporate Life*, Reading, MA: Addison-Wesley

Debord, G. 1967/2006. *The Society of the Spectacle*, New York, NY: Zone Books

Deleuze, G. 1968/1994. *Difference and Repetition*, New York, NY: Columbia University Press

1990. *Pourparlers 1972–1990*, Paris: Les Éditions de Minuit

Deleuze, G. and Guattari, F. 1980/1987. *A Thousand Plateaus: Capitalism and Schizophrenia*, Minneapolis, MN: University of Minnesota Press

Demos, T. J. 2007. *The Exiles of Marcel Duchamp*, Cambridge, MA and London: MIT Press

Devlin, J. F. and Azhar, S. 2004. '"Life Would Be A Lot Easier If We Were a Kit Kat": Practitioners' Views on the Challenges of Branding Financial Services Successfully', *Brand Management* 12(1): 12–30

Dewey, J. 1934/2005. *Art as Experience*, New York, NY: Penguin

Dichter, E. 1965. 'Discovering the "Inner Jones"', *Harvard Business Review* (May/June) (3): 6–10

DiMaggio, P. and Powell, W. 1983. 'The Iron Cage Revisited: Institutional Isomorphism and Collective Rationality in Organizational Fields', *American Journal of Sociology* 48(2): 147–160

Douglas, M. and Isherwood, B. 1979/2005. *The World of Goods: Towards an Anthropology of Consumption*, London and New York, NY: Routledge

Drucker, P. 1993. *Post-Capitalist Society*, London: Butterworth

1995. *Managing in a Time of Great Change*, New York, NY: Truman Talley Books

Drummond, H. 2002. 'Living in a Fool's Paradise: The Collapse of Barings Bank', *Management Decision* 40: 232–238

Duesenberry, J. S. 1949. *Income, Saving, and the Theory of Consumer Behavior*, Cambridge, MA: Harvard University Press

Dutton, J. E. and Dukerich, J. M. 1991. 'Keeping an Eye on the Mirror: Image and Identity in Organizational Adaptation', *Academy of Management Journal* 24(3): 517–554

Eco, U. 1973. 'Social Life as a Sign System', in D. Robey (ed.), *Structuralism: An Introduction*, Oxford: Clarendon Press, 57–72

1979. *The Role of the Reader: Explorations in the Semiotics of Texts*, Bloomington, IN: Indiana University Press

2004. *On Beauty: A History of a Western Idea*, London: Secker and Warburg

Elliott, R. and Wattanasuwan, K. 1998. 'Brands as Symbolic Resources for the Construction of Identity', *International Journal of Advertising* 17: 131–144

Elsbach, K. D. and Kramer, R. M. 1996. 'Members' Responses to Organizational Identity Threats: Encountering and Countering the Business Week Rankings', *Administrative Science Quarterly* 41: 442–476

Erdem, T. and Swait, J. 1998. 'Brand Equity as a Signaling Phenomenon', *Journal of Consumer Psychology* 7(2): 131–157

Featherstone, M. 1991. *Consumer Culture and Postmodernism*, London: Sage

Feldwick, P. 2003. 'Brand Communications', in R. Clifton and J. Simmons (eds.), *Brands and Branding*, London: Profile Books, 127–142

Fombrun, C. and van Riel, C. 1997. 'The Reputational Landscape', *Corporate Reputation Review* 1(1/2): 5–13

Foster, R. J. 2007. 'The Work of the New Economy: Consumers, Brands, and Value Creation', *Cultural Anthropology* 22(4): 707–731

Foucault, M. 1970/1981. 'The Order of Discourse', in R. Young (ed.), *Untying the Text: A Post-Structuralist Reader*, London and Boston, MA: Routledge and Kegan Paul, 48–78

    1976/2003. 'Truth and Power', in P. Rabinow and N. Rose (eds.), *The Essential Foucault: Selections from Essential Works of Foucault, 1954–1984*, New York, NY and London: The New Press, 300–318

    1978a/2003. 'Governmentality', in P. Rabinow and N. Rose (eds.), *The Essential Foucault: Selections from Essential Works of Foucault: 1954–1984*, New York, NY and London: The New Press, 229–245

    1978b/2003. 'What is Critique?', in P. Rabinow and N. Rose (eds.), *The Essential Foucault: Selections from Essential Works of Foucault, 1954–1984*, New York, NY and London: The New Press, 263–278

    1982/2003. 'The Subject and Power', in P. Rabinow and N. Rose (eds.), *The Essential Foucault: Selections from Essential Works of Foucault, 1954–1984*, New York, NY and London: The New Press, 126–144

    1983a/2003. 'On the Genealogy of Ethics: An Overview of Work in Progress, in P. Rabinow and N. Rose (eds.), *The Essential Foucault: Selections from Essential Works of Foucault, 1954–1984*, New York, NY and London: The New Press, 102–125

    1983b/2003. 'Politics and Ethics: An Interview', in P. Rabinow (ed.), *The Foucault Reader*, London: Geguin

Fox, S. 1984. *The Mirror Makers: A History of American Advertising and Its Creator*, New York, NY: William Morrow & Co.

Frank, T. 1997. *The Conquest of Cool: Business Culture, Counterculture, and the Rise of Hip Consumerism*, Chicago, IL: University of Chicago Press

Friedman, M. 1970. 'The Social Responsibility of Business is to Increase Its Profits', *The New York Times Magazine*, 13 September

    1993. *Why Government is the Problem*, Stanford, CA: Hoover Institution Press Publication

Fueller, J. and von Hippel, E. 2008. 'Costless Creation of Strong Brands by User Communities: Implications for Producer-Owned Brands', MIT Sloan School of Management Working Paper Number 4718–08

Fullerton, R. A. 1988. 'How Modern is Modern Marketing? Marketing's Evolution and the Myth of the "Production Era"', *Journal of Marketing* **52** (January): 108–125

Furedi, F. 2004. *Where Have All The Intellectuals Gone?*, London and New York, NY: Continuum

Galbraith, J. K. 1958. *The Affluent Society*, Boston, MA: Houghton Mifflin Company

Gardner, B. B. and Levy, S. J. 1955. 'The Product and the Brand', *Harvard Business Review* **33**(2): 33–39

Ger, G. and Belk, R. W. 1996. 'I'd Like to Buy the World a Coke: Consumptionscapes of the "Less Affluent World"', *Journal of Consumer Policy* **23**: 271–304

Giddens, A. 1991. *Modernity and Self-identity: Self and Society in the Late Modern Age*, Cambridge: Polity Press

Gideon, S. 1948. *Mechanization Takes Command: A Contribution to Anonymous History*, New York, NY: Oxford University Press

Ginzburg, C. 1976/1992. *The Cheese and the Worms: The Cosmos of a Sixteenth-Century Miller*, Baltimore, MD: Johns Hopkins University Press

Gioia, D. A. and Thomas, J. B. 1996. 'Identity, Image, and Issue Interpretation: Sensemaking during Strategic Change in Academia', *Administrative Science Quarterly* **41**(3): 370–403

Gioia, D. A., Schultz, M. and Corley, K. G. 2000. 'Organizational Identity, Image, and Adaptive Instability', *Academy of Management Review* **25**(1): 63–81

Godin, S. 2008. *Tribes: We Need You to Lead Us*, London: Penguin

Goffman, E. 1959. *The Presentation of Self in Everyday Life*, New York, NY: Anchor Books

Goldstein, D. B. 2005. 'Recipes for Living: Martha Stewart and the New American Subject', in D. Bell and J. Hollows (eds.), *Ordinary Lifestyles: Popular Media, Consumption and Taste*, Maidenhead: Open University Press, 47–62

Gombrich, E. H. 1950. *The Story of Art*, London: Phaidon Press

Gordon, R., Kornberger, M. and Clegg, S. 2009. 'Embedded Ethics: Discourse and Power in the New South Wales Police Service', *Organization Studies* **30**(1): 73–99

Granovetter, M. 1985. 'Economic Action and Social Structure: The Problem of Embeddedness', *America Journal of Sociology* **91**(3): 481–510

Grant, J. 2006. *Brand Innovation Manifesto: How to Build Brands, Redefine Markets and Defy Conventions*, Chichester: John Wiley and Sons Ltd

   2007. *The Green Marketing Manifesto*, Chichester: John Wiley and Sons Ltd

Greenberg, M. 2008. *Branding New York: How a City in Crisis was Sold to the World*, New York, NY: Routledge

Grey, C. 1994. 'Career as a Project of the Self and Labour Process Discipline', *Sociology* **28**(2): 479–497

Habermas, J. 1962. *Strukturwandel der Öffentlichkeit. Untersuchungen zu einer Kategorie der bürgerlichen Gesellschaft*, Neuwied/Berlin: Luchterhand

Hackley, C. 2002. 'The Panoptic Role of Advertising Agencies in the Production of Consumer Culture', *Consumption, Markets and Culture* **5**(3): 211–229

Hannerz, U. 1992. *Cultural Complexity: Studies in the Social Organization of Meaning*, New York, NY: Columbia University Press

Hardt, M. and Negri, A. 2000. *Empire*, Cambridge and London, MA: Harvard University Press

Hatch, M. J. and Schultz, M. 2001. 'Are the Strategic Stars Aligned for Your Corporate Brand?', *Harvard Business Review* (February): 128–134

   2002. 'The Dynamics of Organizational Identity', *Human Relations* **55**: 989–1018

   2008. *Taking Brand Initiative: How Companies can Align Strategy, Culture, and Identity through Corporate Branding*, San Francisco, CA: Jossey-Bass

Haug, W. F. 1986. *Critique of Commodity Aesthetics*, Minneapolis, MN: University of Minnesota Press

Hebdige, D. 1979. *Subculture: The Meaning of Style*, London and New York, NY: Routledge

Hegel, G. W. F. 1808/1966. 'Who Thinks Abstractly?', in Walter Kaufmann, *Hegel: Texts and Commentary*, Garden City, NY: Anchor Books, 113–118

Heidegger, M. 1927/1993. *Sein und Zeit*, Tübingen: Max Niemeyer Verlag

Heilbrunn, B. 2006. 'Brave New Brands: Cultural Branding between Utopia and A-topia', in J. Schroeder and M. Salzer-Mörling (eds.), *Brand Culture*, London and New York, NY: Routledge, 103–117

Hennion, A. and Méadel, C. 1989. 'The Artisans of Desire: The Mediation of Advertising between Product and Consumer', *Sociological Theory* 7(2): 191–208

Hill, R.P. and Stamey, M. 1990. 'The Homeless in America: An Examination of Possessions and Consumption Behavior', *Journal of Consumer Research* 17 (December): 303–321

Hilton, S. 2003. 'The Social Value of Brands', in R. Clifton and J. Simmons (eds.), *Brands and Branding*, London: Profile Books, 47–64

Hobbes, T. 1651/1962. *Leviathan*, Oxford: Oxford University Press

Holbrook, M.B. and Hirschman, E.C. 1982. 'The Experiential Aspects of Consumption: Consumer Fantasies, Feelings, and Fun', *Journal of Consumer Research* 9(2): 132–140

Hollander, S.C. and Germain, R. 1993. *Was There a Pepsi Generation before Pepsi Discovered It? Youth-Based Segmentation in Marketing*, Lincolnwood, IL: NTC Business Books

Holt, D.B. 1995. 'How Consumers Consume: A Typology of Consumption Practices', *Journal of Consumer Research* 22: 1–16

　　2002. 'Why Do Brands Cause Trouble? A Dialectical Theory of Consumer Culture and Branding', *Journal of Consumer Research* 29: 70–88

　　2003. 'What Becomes an Icon Most?', *Harvard Business Review* 80 (March): 43–49

　　2004. *How Brands Become Icons: The Principles of Cultural Branding*, Boston, MA: Harvard Business School Press

Hughes, R. 1980/2005. *The Shock of the New: Art and the Century of Change*, London: Thames and Hudson

Ind, N. (2001). *Living the Brand*, London: Kogan Page

Interbrand 2007. *All Brands Are Not Created Equal: Best Global Brands 2007*, available at www.interbrand.com (accessed 30 June 2009)

Jeacle, I. 2003. 'The Taming of the Buyer: The Retail Inventory Method and the Early 20th Century Department Store', *Accounting, Organizations and Society* 28(7/8): 773–791

Journal of Marketing 1957. 'From These City Areas Come Tomorrow's Vast Markets', *Journal of Marketing*, October: 188; citing *Printers Int.* 26 April 1957: 36–41; citing *Interurbia: The Changing Face of America*, J. Walter Thompson Company, Yale University and *Fortune* Magazine

Kafka, F. 1922/1998. *The Castle*, New York, NY: Schocken Books

Kant, I. 1790/2004. *The Critique of Judgement*, White Fish, MT: Kessinger Publishing

Kanter, R.M. 1984. *The Change Masters: Corporate Entrepreneurs at Work*, Sydney: Allen & Unwin

Kapferer, J.N. 1997. *Strategic Brand Management*, London: Kogan Page

Karmark, E. 2005. 'Living the Brand', in M. Schultz, Y.M. Antorini and F.F. Csaba (eds.), *Corporate Branding: Purpose/People/Process*, Copenhagen: Copenhagen Business School Press, 103–125

Kärreman, D. and Rylander, A. 2008. 'Managing Meaning through Branding: The Case of a Consulting Firm', *Organization Studies* 29(1): 103–125

Kemper, S. 2003. 'How Advertising Makes Its Object', in T.D. Malefyt and B. Moeran (eds.), *Advertising Cultures*, Oxford and New York, NY: Berg, 35–54

Kierkegaard, S. 1843/1983. *Repetition: A Venture in Experimenting Psychology by Constantin Constantius*, Princeton, NJ: Princeton Univerity Press

1843/1987. *Either/Or (Part 1)*, Princeton, NJ: Princeton University Press

1844/1957, *The Concept of Dread*, Princeton, NJ: Princeton University Press

Kissinger, H. 1994. *Diplomacy*, New York, NY, London, Toronto, Sydney: Simon & Schuster

Klein, N. 2000. *No Logo*, Toronto: Knopf

2007. *The Shock Doctrine: The Rise of Disaster Capitalism*, London: Allen Lane

Knights, D. and Murray, F. 1994. *Managers Divided: Organization Politics and Information Technology Management*, Chichester: John Wiley and Sons Ltd

Koehn, N. F. 2001. *Brand New: How Entrepreneurs Earned Consumers' Trust from Wedgwood to Dell*, Boston, MA: Harvard Business School Press

Koolhaas, R. 1978/1994. *Delirious*, New York, NY: Monacelli Press

Kornberger, M. 2005. 'Modelling the Future', *(inside) Australian Design Review* **38**: 26

Kotler, P. and Levy, S. 1969. 'Broadening the Concept of Marketing', *Journal of Marketing* **33** (January): 10–15

Kotler, P. and Zaltman, G. 1971. 'Social Marketing: An Approach to Planned Social Change', *Journal of Marketing* **35**: 3–12

Kreiner, K. 2008. 'Constructing the Client in Architectural Competition: An Ethnographic Study of Revealed Strategies', Copenhagen Business School, Working Paper

Kreiner, K. and Schultz, M. 1993. 'Informal Collaboration in R&D: The Formation of Networks Across Organizations', *Organization Studies* **14**: 189–209

Kreshel, P. J., 1990a, 'Jon B. Watson at J. Walter Thompson: The Legitimation of "Science" in Advertising', *Journal of Advertising* **19**(2): 49–59

1990b. 'The "Culture" of J. Walter Thompson, 1915–1925', *Public Relations Review* **16**(3): 80–93

Kwinter, S. 2000. 'The Gay Science (What is Life?)', in B. Mau, *Life Style*, London: Phaidon Press, 35–37

Laermans, R. 1993. 'Learning to Consume: Early Department Stores and the Shaping of the Modern Consumer Culture 1860–1914', *Theory, Culture, and Society* **10**(4): 79–102

Larsen, M. H. (2000), 'Managing the Corporate Story', in M. Schultz, M. J. Hatch and M. H. Larsen (eds.), *The Expressive Organization: Linking Identity, Reputation, and the Corporate Brand*, Oxford: Oxford University Press, 196–207

Lasn, K. 1999. *Culture Jam*, New York, NY: Harper Collins

Lears, J. 1994. *Fables of Abundance: A Cultural History of Advertising in America*, New York, NY: Basic Books

Leland, J. 2004. *Hip: The History*, New York, NY: Harper Collins

Levine, D. 1968. 'Cultural Integration', in D. Sills (ed.), *International Encyclopaedia of the Social Sciences*, New York, NY: Macmillan and Free Press, 372–380

Levine, R., Locke, C., Searls, D. and Weinberger, D. 2000. *The Cluetrain Manifesto: The End of Business as Usual*, Cambridge, MA: Perseus Books

Levi-Strauss, C. 1958/1963. *Structural Anthropology*, New York, NY: Basic Books

Levitt, T. 1960. 'Marketing Myopia', *Harvard Business Review* (July–August): 45–56

Levy, S. J. 1964. 'Symbolism and Life Style', in S. A. Greyser (ed.), *Toward Scientific Marketing*, Chicago, IL: America Marketing Association, 140–150

Liebes, T. and Katz, E. 1990. *The Export of Meaning: Cross-Cultural Readings of 'Dallas'*, New York, NY: Oxford University Press

Lilien, G. L., Morrison, P. D. Searls, K., Sonnack, M. and von Hippel, E. 2002. 'Performance Assessment of the Lead User Idea-generation Process for New Product Development', *Management Science* **48**(8): 1042–1059

Lindblom, C. 1959. 'The Science of Muddling Through', *Public Administration Review* **19**: 79–88

Lindemann, J. 2003. 'The Financial Value of Brands', in R. Clifton and J. Simmons (eds.), *Brands and Branding*, London: Profile Books, 27–46

Lindstrom, M. 2005. *Brand Sense: Build Powerful Brands through Touch, Taste, Smell, Sight, and Sound*, New York, NY: Simon & Schuster

Luhmann, N. 1984. *Soziale Systeme: Grundriß einer allgemeinen Theorie*, Frankfurt: Suhrkamp

Lukács, G. 1920. *Die Theorie des Romans*, Berlin: Paul Cassirer

Lury, C. 2004. *Brands: The Logo of the Global Economy*, New York, NY and London: Routledge

Lüthje, C., Herstatt, C. and von Hippel, E. 2002. 'The Dominant Role of Local Information in User Innovation: The Case of Mountain Biking', MIT Sloan School of Management Working Paper

Lyotard, J.-F. 1983/1988, *The Differend: Phrases in Dispute*, Manchester: Manchester University Press

Machin, D. and Thornborrow, J. 2003. 'Branding and Discourse: The Case of Cosmopolitan', *Discourse and Society* **14**(4): 453–506

Machin, D. and van Leeuwen, T. 2008. 'Branding the Self', in C. R. Caldas-Coulthard and R. Iedema (eds.), *Identity Trouble: Critical Discourse and Contested Identities*, Basingstoke: Palgrave, 43–58

MacKenzie, D. 2007. *An Engine, Not a Camera: How Financial Models Shape Markets*, Cambridge, MA: MIT Press

Maffesoli, M. 1988/1996. *The Time of the Tribes: The Decline of Individualism in Mass Society*, London, Thousand Oaks, CA and New Delhi: Sage

Mailer, N. 1957. 'The White Negro: Superficial Reflections on the Hipster', *Dissent* (Fall)

Malefyt, T. D. 2003. 'Models, Metaphors and Client Relations: The Negotiated Meanings of Advertising', in T. D. Malefyt and B. Moeran (eds.), *Advertising Cultures*, Oxford and New York, NY: Berg, 139–164

Malefyt, T. D. and Moeran, B. 2003. 'Introduction: Advertising Cultures – Advertising, Ethnography and Anthropology', in T. D. Malefyt and B. Moeran (eds.), *Advertising Cultures*, Oxford and New York, NY: Berg, 1–34

Malinowski, B. 1954. *Magic, Science and Religion and other Essays*, New York, NY: Anchor Press

Manovich, L. 2001. *The Language of New Media*, Cambridge and London, MA: MIT Press

March, J. 1988. 'The Technology of Foolishness', in J. March (ed.), *Decisions and Organizations*, Oxford: Blackwell, 253–65

Marchand, R. 1985. *Advertising the American Dream: Making Way for Modernity, 1920–1940*. Berkeley, CA and London: University of California Press

1998. *Creating the Corporate Soul: The Rise of Public Relations and Corporate Imagery in American Big Business*, Los Angeles, CA: University of California Press

Marcuse, H. 1964/2002. *The One-Dimensional Man: Studies in the Ideology of Advanced Industrial Society*, London and New York, NY: Routledge

Marshall, P. D. 2002. 'The New Intertextual Commodity', in D. Harries (ed.), *The New Media Book*, London: BFI Publishing, 69–92

Martin, J. 2002. *Organizational Culture: Mapping the Terrain*, Thousand Oaks, CA, London and New Delhi: Sage

Martin, J. and Frost, P. 1996. 'The Organizational Culture War Games: A Struggle for Intellectual Dominance', in S. Clegg, C. Hardy and W. Nord (eds.), *Handbook of Organization Studies*, London: Sage, 599–621

Martin, J. and Feldman, M. S., Hatch, M. J. and Sitkin, S. B. 1983. 'The Uniqueness Paradox in Organizational Stories', *Administrative Science Quarterly* **28**: 438–453

Martin, J. L. 1999. 'The Myth of the Consumption Oriented Economy and the Rise of the Desiring Subject', *Theory and Society* **28**: 425–453

Marx, K. 1867/1976. *Capital*, London: Verso

Maslow, A. 1954. *Motivation and Personality*. New York, NY: Harper

Mason, R. 2000. 'The Social Significance of Consumption: James Duesenberry's Contribution to Consumer Theory', *Journal of Economic Issues* **34**(3): 553–572

Mastercard 2007. *Worldwide Centers of Commerce Index™*; see www.mastercard.com/us/company/en/wcoc/pdf/index_2007_us.pdf (accessed 1 May 2008)

Mau, B. 2000. *Life Style*, London: Phaidon Press

Mauss, M. 1902/2001. *A General Theory of Magic*, London and New York, NY: Routledge

Mayo, E. 1933. *The Human Problems of an Industrial Civilization*, Manchester: N. H. Ayer

McAlexander, J. H., Schouten, J. W. and Koenig, H. F. 2002. 'Building Brand Community', *Journal of Marketing* **66** (January): 38–54

McCracken, G. 1986. 'Culture and Consumption: A Theoretical Account of the Structure and Movement of the Cultural Meaning of Consumer Goods', *Journal of Consumer Research* **13**(1): 71–84

McCreery, J. 1995. 'Malinowksi, Magic, and Advertising: On Choosing Metaphors', in J. F. Sherry (ed.), *Contemporary Marketing and Consumer Behavior: An Anthropological Sourcebook*, Thousand Oaks, CA, London and New Delhi: Sage, 309–329

McGregor, D. 1960. *The Human Side of Enterprise*, Ann Arbor, MI: University of Michigan

McKendrick, N., Brewer, J. and Plumb, J. H. (eds.) 1982. *The Birth of a Consumer Society*, Bloomington, IN: Indiana University Press

McLuhan, M. 1964/2006. *Understanding Media*, London and New York, NY: Routledge

Meyer, J. W. and Rowan, B. 1977. 'Institutionalised Organizations: Formal Strctures as Myth and Ceremony', *American Journal of Sociology* **83**(1): 340–363

Miller, D. 1998a. *A Theory of Shopping*, Cambridge: Polity Press
    1998b. 'Coca-Cola: A Black Sweet Drink from Trinidad', in D. Miller (ed.), *Material Cultures: Why Some Things Matter*, Chicago, IL: University of Chicago Press, 168–187

Miller, J. and Muir, D. 2004. *The Business of Brands*, Chichester: John Wiley and Sons Ltd

Miller, P. and O'Leary, T. 1987. 'Accounting and the Construction of the Governable Person', *Accounting, Organizations and Society* **12**(3): 235–265

Mink, J. 2004. *Duchamp*, Cologne, London, Los Angeles, CA, Madrid, Paris and Tokyo: Taschen

Moeran, B. 2003. 'Imagining and Imaging the Other: Japanese Advertising International', in T. D. Malefyt and B. Moeran (eds.), *Advertising Cultures*, Oxford and New York, NY: Berg, 91–112

Morgan, B. and Trentmann, F. 2006. 'Introduction: The Politics of Necessity', *Journal of Consumer Policy* **29**(4): 345–353

Muñiz, A. M., Jr. and O'Guinn, T. C. 2001. 'Brand Community', *Journal of Consumer Research* **27**: 412–432

  2005. 'Marketing Communications in a World of Consumption and Brand Communities', in A. J. Kimmel (ed.), *Marketing Communication: New Approaches, Technologies and Styles*, Oxford: Oxford University Press, 63–85

Muñiz, A. M., Jr. and Schau, H. J. 2005. 'Religiosity in the Abandoned Apple Newton Brand Community', *Journal of Consumer Research* **31** (March): 737–747

Muñiz, A. M.. Jr., O'Guinn, T. C. and Fine, G. A. 2006. 'Rumor in Brand Community', in D. A. Hantula (ed.), *Advances in Theory and Methodology in Social and Organizational Psychology: A Tribute to Ralph Rosnow*, Mahwah, NJ: Lawrence Erlbaum Associates, 227–247

Nadeau, R. A. 2007. *Living Brands: Collaboration + Innovation = Customer Fascination*. New York, NY: McGraw-Hill

Nancarrow, C., Nancarrow, P. and Page, J. 2001. 'An Analysis of the Concept of Cool and Its Marketing Implications', *Journal of Consumer Behaviour* **1**(4): 311–322

Nancy, J. 1982/1991. *The Inoperative Community*, Minneapolis, MN: University of Minnesota Press

Neumeier, M. 2005. *The Brand Gap: How to Bridge the Distance between Business Strategy and Design: A Whiteboard Overview*, Berkeley, CA: Peachpit Press

Nietzsche, F. 1873/1990. *Philosophy and Truth: Selections from Nietzsche's Notebooks of the Early 1870s*, Atlantic Highlands, NJ: Humanities Press

  1882/2002. *The Gay Science*, Cambridge: Cambridge University Press

  1886/2002. *Beyond Good and Evil: Prelude to a Philosophy of the Future*, Cambridge: Cambridge University Press

Nixon, S. 2003. *Advertising Cultures: Gender, Commerce, Creativity*, London: Sage

O'Guinn T. C. and Muñiz A. M., Jr. 2005. 'Communal Consumption and the Brand', in S. Ratneshwar and D. G. Mick (eds.), *Inside Consumption: Frontiers of Research on Consumer Motives*, London: Routledge, 252–272

Olins, W. 2002. 'How Brands are Taking Over the Corporation', in M. Schultz, M. J. Hatch and M. M. Larsen (eds.), *The Expressive Organization: Linking Identity, Reputation, and the Corporate Brand*, Oxford: Oxford University Press, 51–65

  2003. *On Brand*, London: Thames & Hudson

Olsen, B. 2003. 'The Revolution in Marketing Intimate Apparel: A Narrative Ethnography', in T. D. Malefyt and B. Moeran (eds.), *Advertising Cultures*, Oxford and New York, NY: Berg, 113–138

Ortmann, G. 2003a. *Als Ob. Fiktionen des Organisierens*, Verlag für Sozialwissenschaften: Wiesbaden

  2003b. *Organisation und Welterschließung*, Opladen: Dekonstruktionen

Orwell, G. 1954. *Nineteen Eighty-Four: A Novel*, Harmondsworth: Penguin

Osborne, T. and Rose, N. 1999. 'Do the Social Sciences Create Phenomena?: The Example of Public Opinion Research', *British Journal of Sociology* **50**(3): 367–396

Ouchi, W.G. 1981. *Theory Z*, Reading, MA: Addison-Wesley

Packard, V. 1957. *The Hidden Persuaders*, New York, NY: Washington Square Press

Parker, M. 2000. *Organizational Culture and Identity: Unity and Division at Work*. London, Thousand Oaks, CA and New Delhi: Sage

Pascale, R. and Athos, A. 1981. *The Art of Japanese Management*, New York, NY: Warner

Patteeuw, V. (ed.) 2002. *City Branding: Image Building and Building Images*, Rotterdam: NAi Publishers

Perrow, C. 1961. 'Organizational Prestige: Some Functions and Dysfunctions', *The American Journal of Sociology* **66**(4): 335–341

    1991. 'A Society of Organization', *Theory and Society* **20**(6): 725–762

Peters, T. 1997. 'The Brand Called You', *Fast Company* **10** (August): 83

Peters, T. and Waterman, R. 1982. *In Search of Excellence: Lessons from America's Best-run Companies*, Sydney: Harper & Row

Pettinger, L. 2000. 'Brand Culture and Branded Workers: Service Work and Aesthetic Labour in Fashion Retail', *Consumption Markets & Culture* **7**(2): 165–184

Pfeffer, J. and Salancik, G.R. 1978. *The External Control of Organizations: A Resource Dependence Perspective*, New York, NY: Harper and Row

Pine II, B.J. and Gilmore, J.H. 1999. *The Experience Economy: Work Is Theatre and Every Business a Stage*, Boston, MA: Harvard Business School Press

Pondy, L. 1978. 'Leadership as a Language Game', in M. W. McCall and M. M. Lombardo (eds.), *Leadership: Where Else Can We Go?*, Durham, NC: Duke University Press, 87–99

Pountain D. and Robins, D. 2000. *Cool Rules: Anatomy of an Attitude*, London: Reaktion Books

Power, M. 1992, 'The Politics of Brand Accounting in the United Kingdom', *European Accounting Review* **1**(1): 39–68

    1997, *The Audit Society: Rituals of Verification*, Oxford: Oxford University Press

    2007. *Organized Uncertainty: Designing a World of Risk Management*, Oxford: Oxford University Press

Prahalad, C.K. and Ramaswamy, V. 2004. *The Future of Competition: Co-Creating Unique Value with Customers*, Boston, MA: Harvard Business School Press

Putnam, R. 2000. *Bowling Alone: The Collapse and Revival of American Community*, New York. NY: Simon & Schuster

Quelch, J.A. and Jocz, K.E. 2008. *Greater Good: How Good Marketing Makes for Better Democracy*, Boston, MA: Harvard Business School Press

Rainwater, L.C., Coleman, R.P. and Handel, G. 1959. *Workingman's Wife: Her Personality, World and Life Style*, New York, NY: Oceana Publications

Reich, R. 2008. *Supercapitalism: The Transformation of Business, Democracy, and Everyday Life*, Melbourne: Scribe Publications

Ries, A. and Trout, J. 1972/2001. *Positioning: The Battle for Your Mind*, New York, NY: McGraw-Hill

Riesman, D. 1950. *The Lonely Crowd: A Study of the Changing American Character*, New Haven, CT: Yale University Press

Riley, D. F. and de Chernatony, L. 2000. 'The Service Brand as Relationship Builder', *British Journal of Management* 11(2): 137–150

Rilke, R. M. 1922/1977. *Duino Elegies and The Sonnets to Orpheus*, Boston, MA: Houghton Mifflin Company

Ritson, M. and Elliott, R. 1999. 'The Social Uses of Advertising: An Ethnographic Study of Adolescent Advertising Audiences', *Journal of Consumer Research* 26(3): 260–277

Ritzer, G. 1995/2008. *The McDonaldization of Society*, Los Angeles, CA: Pine Forge Press

Rorty, R. 1989. *Contingency, Irony, and Solidarity*, Cambridge: Cambridge University Press

Rose, N. 1990. *Governing the Soul*, New York, NY and London: Routledge
  1999. *Powers of Freedom: Reframing Political Thought*, Cambridge: Cambridge University Press

Rotzoll, K., Haefner, J. E. and Sandage, C. H. 1986/1990. 'Advertising and the Classical Liberal World View', in R. Hovland and G. B. Wilcox (eds.), *Advertising in Society: Classical and Contemporary Readings on Advertising's Role in Society*, Lincolnwood, IL: NTC Business Books, 27–41

Rutherford, P. 2000. *Endless Propaganda: The Advertising of Public Goods*, Toronto, ON: University of Toronto Press

Ryder, I. 2004. 'Anthropology and the Brand', *Brand Management* 11(5), 346–356

Said, E. W. 1978/2003. *Orientalism*, London: Penguin Books

Sandage, C. W. 1972/1990. 'Some Institutional Aspects of Advertising', in R. Hovland and G. B Wilcox (eds.), *Advertising in Society: Classical and Contemporary Readings on Advertising's Role in Society*, Lincolnwood, IL: NTC Business Books, 3–10

Sassen, S. 1991. *The Global City*, London, New York, NY, Tokyo, Princeton, NJ: Princeton University Press

Scanlon, J. 2005. 'American Brandstand's Hit Parade', *BusinessWeek*, 23 August; see www.businessweek.com/innovate/content/aug2005/id20050823_083548.htm?chan=db (accessed 15 June 2009)

Schau, H. J. and Gily, M. C. 2003. 'We Are What We Post? Self-Presentation in Personal Web Space', *Journal of Consumer Research* 30(3), 385–404

Schau, H. J. and Muñiz, A. M., Jr. 2002. 'Brand Communities and Personal Identities: Negotiations in Cyberspace', *Advances in Consumer Research* 29(1): 344–349

Schein, E. 1985. *Organizational Culture and Leadership*, First Edition, San Francisco, CA: Jossey-Bass
  1992. *Organizational Culture and Leadership*, Second Edition, San Francisco, CA: Jossey-Bass

Schmitt, B. H. 1999. *Experiential Marketing: How to Get Customers to SENSE, FEEL, THINK, ACT, and RELATE to Your Company and Brands*, New York, NY: Free Press

Schmitt, B. H. and Simonson, A. 1997. *Marketing Aesthetics: The Strategic Management of Brands, Identity, and Image*, New York, NY: Free Press

Schouten, J. W. 1991. 'Selves in Transition: Symbolic Consumption in Personal Rites of Passage and Identity Reconstruction', *Journal of Consumer Research* 17 (March): 412–425

Schouten, J. W. and McAlexander, J. H. 1995. 'Subcultures of Consumption: An Ethnography of the New Bikers', *Journal of Consumer Research* 22 (June): 43–61

Schroeder, J. E. 2005. 'The Artists and the Brand', *European Journal of Marketing* 39(11/12): 1291–1305

Schroeder, J. E. and Salzer-Mörling, M. 2006. 'Introduction: The Cultural Codes of Branding', in J. E. Schroeder and M. Salzer-Mörling (eds.), *Brand Culture*, London and New York, NY: Routledge, 1–12

Schultz, M., 2005. 'Corporate Branding as Organizational Change', in M. Schultz, Y. M. Antorini and F. F. Csaba (eds.), *Corporate Branding: Purpose/People/Process*, Copenhagen: Copenhagen Business School Press, 181–217

Schultz, M., Antorini, Y. M. and Csaba, F. F. 2005. 'Corporate Branding: An Evolving Concept', in M. Schultz, Y. M. Antorini and F. F. Csaba (eds.), *Corporate Branding: Purpose/People/Process*, Copenhagen: Copenhagen Business School Press, 2–22

Seemann, S., Laske S. and Kornberger, M. 2007. 'The Constitution of Ethics: Discourse, Practice and Conflict in a Health-care Center', in C. Carter, S. Clegg, M. Kornberger, M. Messner and S. Laske (eds.), *Business Ethics as Practice: Representation, Reflexivity and Performance*, Cheltenham: Edward Elgar, 190–207

Serres, M. 1974. *Hermès III: La traduction*, Paris: Minuit
  1982. *The Parasite*, Baltimore, MD: Johns Hopkins University Press
  1985. *Les Cinq Sens*, Paris: Grasset

Shah, D. V., Mcleod, D. M., Friedland, L. and Nelson, M. 2007. 'The Politics of Consumption/ The Consumption of Politics', *The ANNALS of the American Academy of Political and Social Science* **611** (May): 6–15

Sherry, J. F., Jr. (ed.) 1995. *Contemporary Marketing and Consumer Behavior: An Anthropological Sourcebook*, Thousand Oaks, CA, London and New Delhi: Sage
  2003. 'Foreword: A Word From Our Sponsor – Anthropology', in Malefyt and Moeran (eds.), *Advertising Cultures*, Oxford and New York, NY: Berg, xi–xiii

Simmel, G. 1902/1950. 'The Metropolis and Mental Life', in K. H. Wolff (ed.), *The Sociology of Georg Simmel*, New York, NY: Free Press, 409–424
  1905/2000. 'The Philosophy of Fashion', in D. Frisby and M. Featherstone (eds.), *Simmel on Culture: Selected Writings*, London, Thousand Oaks, CA and New Delhi: Sage, 187–205
  1907/1978. *The Philosophy of Money*, London: Routledge
  1908a/2000. 'On the Essence of Culture', in D. Frisby and M. Featherstone (eds.), *Simmel on Culture: Selected Writings*, London, Thousand Oaks, CA and New Delhi: Sage, 40–46
  1908b/2000. 'The Problem of Style', in D. Frisby and M. Featherstone (eds.), *Simmel on Culture: Selected Writings*, London, Thousand Oaks, CA and New Delhi: Sage, 211–217
  1911–1912/2000. 'The Concept and Tragedy of Culture', in D. Frisby and M. Featherstone (eds.), *Simmel on Culture: Selected Writings*, London, Thousand Oaks, CA and New Delhi: Sage, 55–74

Sims, R. and Brinkmann, J. 2003. 'Enron Ethics (or: Culture Matters More than Codes)', *Journal of Business Ethics* **45**: 243–256

Slater, D. 1997. 'Consumer Culture and the Politics of Need', in A. Blake, I. MacRury, M. Nava, and B. Richards (eds.), *Buy This Book: Studies in Advertising and Consumption*, London: Routledge, 51–64

Smircich, L. and. Morgan, G. 1982. 'Leadership: The Management of Meaning', *Journal of Applied Behavioural Studies* **18**: 257–273

Starobinski, J. 1999/2003. *Action and Reaction: The Life and Adventure of a Couple*, New York, NY: Zone Books

Stein, M. 2000. 'The Risk Taker as Shadow: A Psychoanalytic View of the Collapse of Barings Bank', *Journal of Management Studies* **37**(8): 1215–1230

Stendhal. 1822/1975. *On Love*, New York, NY: Penguin Books

Stewart, S. 1993. *On Longing: Narratives of the Miniature, the Gigantic, the Souvenir, the Collection*, Durham, NC: Durham University Press

Stolle, D., Hooghe, M. and Micheletti, M. 2005. 'Politics in the Supermarket: Political Consumerism as a Form of Political Participation', *International Political Science Review* **26**(3): 245–269

Strasser, S. 2003. 'The Alien Past: Consumer Culture in Historical Perspective', *Journal of Consumer Policy* **26**(4): 375–393

Sunderland, P. L. and Denny, R. M. 2003. 'Psychology vs Anthropology: Where is Culture in Marketplace Ethnography?', in T. D. Malefyt and B. Moeran (eds.), *Advertising Cultures*, Oxford and New York, NY: Berg, 187–202

Surowiecki, J. 2004. *The Wisdom of Crowds: Why the Many Are Smarter Than the Few and How Collective Wisdom Shapes Business, Economies, Societies and Nations*, New York, NY: Doubleday

Tadajewski, M. 2006. 'Remembering Motivation Research: Toward an Alternative Genealogy of Interpretive Consumer Research', *Marketing Theory Volume* **6**(4): 429–466

Taleb, N. N. 2007. *The Black Swan: The Impact of the Highly Improbable*, London: Penguin Books

Tedlow, R. S. 1991. *New and Improved: The Story of Mass Marketing in America*, Portsmouth, NH: Heinemann Professional Publishing

Thompson, C. J. and Arsel, Z. 2004. 'The Starbucks Brandscape and Consumers' (Anticorporate) Experiences of Globalization', *Journal of Consumer Research* **31**: 631–642

Toffler, A. 1980. *The Third Wave*, London: William Collins & Sons and Pan Books

Tonge A., Greer L. and Lawton A. 2003. 'The Enron Story: You Can Fool Some of the People Some of the Time … ', *Business Ethics, A European Review* **12**: 4–22.

Tonglet, M. 2002. 'Consumer Misbehaviour: An Exploratory Study of Shoplifting', *Journal of Consumer Behaviour* **1**(4): 336–354

Tönnies, F. 1887/2005. *Gemeinschaft und Gesellschaft*, Darmstadt: Wissenschaftliche Buchgesellschaft

Trueman, M., Klemm, M. and Giroud, A. 2004. 'Can a City Communicate? Bradford as a Corporate Brand', *Corporate Communications: An International Journal* **9**(4): 317–330

Tungate, M. 2007. *Adland: A Global History of Advertising*, London and Philadelphia, PA: Kogan Page

Turner, B. A. 1978. *Man-Made Disasters*, London: Wykeham

Uggla, H. 2006. 'Managing Leader and Partner Brands: The Brand Association Base', in Schroeder and Salzer-Mörling (eds.), *Brand Culture*, London and New York, NY: Routledge, 77–88

Van Ham, P. 2001. 'The Rise of the Brand State: The Postmodern Politics of Image and Reputation', *Foreign Affairs* **80**(5): 2–6

Van Maanen, J. 1991. 'The Smile Factory: Work at Disneyland', in P. Frost, L. Moore, M. Louis, C. Lundberg and J. Martin (eds.), *Reframing Organizational Culture*, Newbury Park, CA; Sage

Van Maanen, J. and Kunda, G. 1989. ' "Real Feelings": Emotional Expression and Organizational Culture', in L.L. Cummings and B.M. Staw (eds.), *Research in Organizational Behaviour, Vol. XI,* Greenwich, CT: JAI Press, 43–103

Van Riel, C.B.M. 2000. 'Corporate Communication Orchestrated by a Sustainable Corporate Story', in M. Schultz, M.J. Hatch and M.H. Larsen (eds.), *The Expressive Organization: Linking Identity, Reputation, and the Corporate Brand,* Oxford: Oxford University Press, 157–181

Vaughan, D. 1981–1982. 'Toward Understanding Unlawful Organizational Behavior', *Michigan Law Review* **80**(7): 1377–1402

1990. 'Autonomy, Interdependence, and Social Control: NASA and the Space Shuttle Challenger', *Administrative Science Quarterly* **35**, 225–257

1999. 'The Dark Side of Organizations: Mistake, Misconduct, and Disaster', *Annual Review of Sociology* **25**: 271–305

Veblen, T. 1899. *The Theory of the Leisure Class: An Economic Study of Institutions,* London: Macmillan Publishers

Virilio, P. 1977. *Speed and Politics: An Essay on Dromology.* New York, NY: Semiotext(e)

Vise, D. and Malseed, M. 2006. *The Google Story: Inside the Hottest Business, Media, and Technology Success of Our Time,* New York, NY: Bantam

Voltaire. 1759/1993. *Candide,* New York, NY: Dover Publications

Von Hippel, E. 2005. *Democratizing Innovation,* Cambridge and London, MA: The MIT Press

Walker, R. 2008. *Buying In: The Secret Dialogue between What We Buy and Who We Are,* New York, NY: Random House

Warhol, A. 2006. *'Giant' Size,* London and New York, NY: Phaidon Press

Weick, K.E. 1979. *The Social Psychology of Organizing,* Second Edition, Reading, MA: Addison-Wesley

Weiss, E.H. and Green, H.E. 1951. 'Unique Human Motivation Library is Centre of Thought in This Agency', *Printers' Ink* **6** (February): 36–37

Welz, G. 2003. 'The Cultural Swirl: Anthropological Perspectives on Innovation', *Global Networks* **3**(3): 255–270

Wengrow, D. 2008. 'Prehistories of Community Branding', *Current Anthropology* **49**(1): 7–34

Whetten, D.A. 2006. 'Albert and Whetten Revisited: Strengthening the Concept of Organizational Identity', *Journal of Management Inquiry* **15**(3): 219–234

Whyte, W.H. 1956. *The Organization Man,* New York, NY: Doubleday

Wilkinson, J. 2007. 'Fair Trade: Dynamic and Dilemmas of a Market Oriented Global Social Movement', *Journal of Consumer Policy* **30**(3): 219–239

Williams, R. 1980/2008. 'Advertising: The Magic System', in G. Cook (ed.), *The Language of Advertising, Vol. I,* London and New York, NY: Routledge, 36–57

Wipperfürth, A. 2005. *Brand Hijack: Marketing Without Marketing,* New York, NY: Portfolio

Wittgenstein, L. 1953/1972. *Philosophical Investigations,* Oxford: Blackwell

Yoell, W. A. 1950. 'Base Your Advertising on the True Buying Motive', *Printers' Ink* **8** (September): 38–39

Zablocki, B. D. and Moss, K. R. 1976. 'The Differentiation of Life-Styles', *Annual Review of Sociology* **2**: 269–297

Zaltman, G. 2003. *How Customers Think: Essential Insights into the Mind of the Market*, Boston, MA: Harvard Business School Press

Žižek, S. 1997. *The Plague of Fantasies*, London and New York, NY: Verso

   2001. *On Belief*, London and New York, NY: Routledge

   2002. *Welcome to the Desert of the Real!: Five Essays on September 11 and Related Dates*, London and New York, NY: Verso

Zwick, D., Denegri-Knott, J. and Schroeder, J. 2007. 'The Social Pedagogy of Wall Street: Stock Trading as Political Activism?', *Journal of Consumer Policy* **30**(3): 177–199

Index

Lightning Source UK Ltd.
Milton Keynes UK
UKOW041808291011

181136UK00001B/10/P